# Fodor's

# PHILADELPHIA

T0049336

# Welcome to Philadelphia

The first World Heritage City in the United States celebrates its past at sites such as Independence Hall and revels in its present as a funky, modern metropolis on a cultural upswing. The city buzzes with lively neighborhoods, excellent restaurants, fun nightlife, die-hard sports fans, and avid art lovers. No matter why you visit, one thing is certain: there is much to love in the City of Brotherly Love. As you plan your upcoming travels, please confirm that places are still open and let us know when we need to make updates at editors@fodors.com.

## TOP REASONS TO GO

★ **Local Cuisine:** Cozy BYOBs, cheesesteaks, Reading Terminal Market.

★ **Iconic Landmarks:** The Rocky Steps, the *LOVE* Statue, Boathouse Row.

★ **Eclectic Neighborhoods:** Historic Society Hill, funky Fishtown, chic Rittenhouse Square.

★ **Revolutionary History:** Liberty Bell, Independence Hall, Museum of the American Revolution.

★ **Art:** World-class museums, street murals, high-end galleries, and everything in between.

★ **Bar Scene:** From lively beer gardens to chic cocktail lounges, nightlife flourishes.

# Contents

## MAPS

Chapter 1

# EXPERIENCE
# PHILADELPHIA

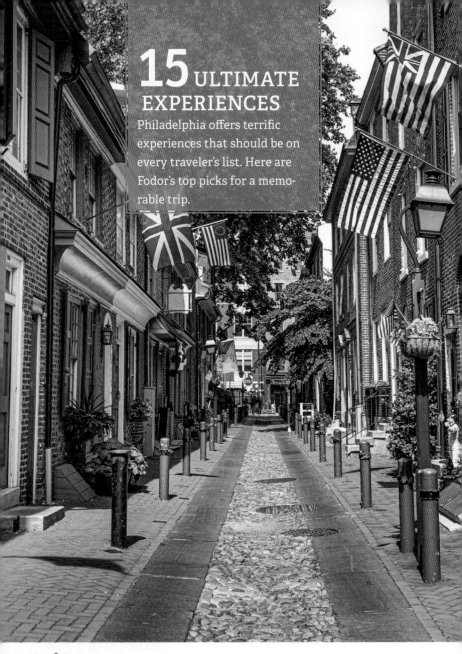

# 15 ULTIMATE EXPERIENCES

Philadelphia offers terrific experiences that should be on every traveler's list. Here are Fodor's top picks for a memorable trip.

## 1 Explore Old City

Known for its cobblestone streets and historic sites, the city's oldest neighborhood is a mix of 18th-century charm and lively nightlife spots, galleries, and restaurants. *(Ch. 3)*

## 2 Cheesesteaks. Enough Said.

Complete a trip to Philly by sampling the city's most legendary sandwich from Pat's or Geno's. Or try local spots like John's Roast Pork or Jim's. *(Ch. 8)*

## 3 A City of Murals

The city's wonderful Mural Arts program, begun in 1984, views every blank wall as a canvas. You can see the work of local artists showcased all around town. *(Ch. 9)*

## 4 Schuylkill River Bike Rides

For a fresh look at the city, rent wheels through the Indego bike share program. One place to explore is the Schuylkill Banks Boardwalk with its spectacular city views. *(Ch. 7, 11)*

## 5 Independence National Historical Park

The early history of the United States is recalled here, including the Liberty Bell, Congress Hall, and Independence Hall, where the Declaration of Independence was signed in 1776. *(Ch. 3)*

## 6 Reading Terminal Market

This historic public market is a must-visit for any food lover. Head to longtime favorite DiNic's for a famous pork sandwich, and then try some delicious ice cream from Bassetts. *(Ch. 5)*

## 7 Sports

This city is famous for its sports teams—and for its die-hard fans. Tickets to an Eagles game are almost impossible to get, but check out the Phillies, Flyers, or Sixers. *(Ch. 1, 8)*

# 8 Ritzy Rittenhouse Square

One of city founder William Penn's five original squares, Rittenhouse is known for its elegance and charm. Restaurants, shops, and apartments line this green refuge. *(Ch. 6)*

# 9 Fabulous Fairmount Park

One of the world's largest city parks, Fairmount boasts trails, bike paths, and historic mansions—as well as stunning views of Boathouse Row on the Schuylkill River. *(Ch. 7)*

## 10 Museum of the American Revolution

History comes alive through interactive displays at this museum. Step back and consider the stakes in the Revolutionary War for groups like Native Americans, enslaved Africans, and women. *(Ch. 3)*

## 11 Eastern State Penitentiary

A visit to the empty cellblocks of this semi-ruined jail is an eerie, entertaining excursion to sites like Al Capone's cell, as well as a thought-provoking look at criminal justice past and present. *(Ch. 7)*

## 12 Parkway Museums

Home to some of the city's most famous museums, the Parkway includes the Franklin Institute (pictured), Barnes Foundation, Rodin Museum, and Philadelphia Museum of Art. *(Ch. 7)*

## 13 South Street

With an unapologetically edgy vibe, this famous street combines ethnically diverse restaurants, shops, and bars into one lively area that always buzzes with activity. *(Ch. 8)*

# 14 Dining in Passyunk

A foodie favorite, the stretch of East Passyunk Avenue between Broad and 9th Streets lets you dine around the world on cuisine from Italy to Mexico to Asia. *(Ch. 8)*

# 15 Brewery Scene

Beer lovers can sip great suds at many craft breweries or brew pubs; new spots continue to pop up in funky neighborhoods like Fishtown and Northern Liberties. *(Ch. 10)*

# WHAT'S WHERE

**1** **Old City and Historic Downtown.** Given its historical importance, *everything* in Old City is a highlight including Independence National Historical Park, home to the Liberty Bell and Independence Hall.

**2** **Society Hill and Penn's Landing.** Well-preserved Society Hill is filled with cobble-stone streets and hidden courtyards. Penn's Landing features a network of parks and pop-ups.

**3** **Center City East and Chinatown.** This area encompasses every-thing east of City Hall including great restau-rants and bars, the vibrant and diverse Chinatown, and landmarks like Reading Terminal.

**4** **Center City West and Rittenhouse Square.** From City Hall to the Schuylkill River, this part of the city has great restaurants and bars. You'll also find Rittenhouse Square, the heart of upper-crust Philadelphia.

**5** **Parkway Museum District and Fairmount Park.** From City Hall, the Benjamin Franklin Parkway stretches northwest to the Phila-delphia Museum of Art.

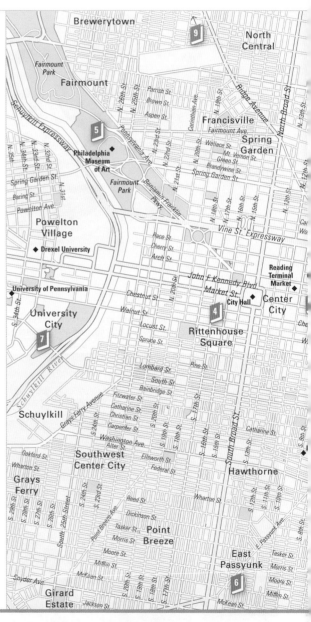

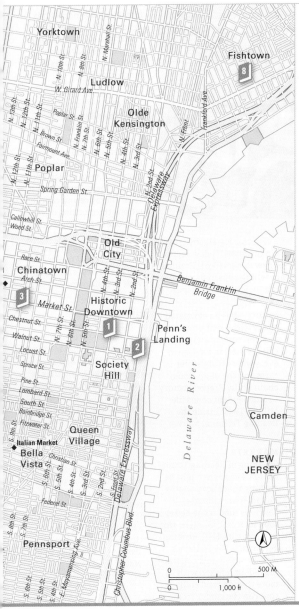

Fairmount is home to solid dining, drinking, and shopping, while 8,500-acre Fairmount Park is the world's largest landscaped city park.

**6 South Philadelphia and East Passyunk.** South Philadelphia gave the world Rocky Balboa and 9th Street's Italian Market. Bella Vista is home to a number of bars and restaurants, as is trendy East Passyunk.

**7 University City and West Philadelphia.** The University of Pennsylvania and Drexel University are the anchors of University City, the easternmost portion of West Philadelphia. Beyond is a high concentration of bars, restaurants, and cafés.

**8 Northern Liberties and Fishtown.** This area of North Philadelphia has come into its own in recent years and is one the city's best places for eating and drinking.

**9 Manayunk, Chestnut Hill, and Germantown.** Manayunk, wedged between the Schuylkill River and some steep hills, is full of restaurants and boutiques. Chestnut Hill and Mount Airy are charming residential areas, while Germantown features beautifully preserved historic homes.

# What to Eat and Drink

## WATER ICE

Known as Italian ice everywhere else, this icy, slushy treat was first created in Philadelphia in the 1930s. Today, some of the same South Philly shops—or newcomers like D'Emilio's Old World Ice Treats (above)—are selling cups in flavors like lemon, cherry, and chocolate, using their original recipes.

## CHEESESTEAKS

Other places try to replicate Philly's most quintessential food, but few get it right. Made with chopped steak, cheese—American, provolone, or Whiz—and often fried onions, all on a fresh Italian roll. A side-by-side taste test of the original Pat's King of Steaks and Geno's is a fun rite of passage, but locals love John's Roast Pork, as well as Dalessandro's, Jim's, Angelo's, Woodrow's, Tony Luke's, and Max's.

## SOFT PRETZELS

These aren't your typical mall or movie-theater snacks. The Philly version—with roots in the city's Pennsylvania Dutch culture—has an elongated shape with a soft interior and perfectly browned, salted exterior. Find them everywhere from street carts and the ubiquitous chain Philly Pretzel Factory to independent shops like Miller's Twist inside the Reading Terminal Market.

## MARKETS

Speaking of Reading Terminal Market, there might be nothing that encapsulates Philadelphia's diverse, delicious food scene better than its iconic markets. Not far from City Hall, Reading Terminal is the country's oldest continuously operating indoor market, with more than 75 food stalls that run the gamut from cheesesteaks and pretzels to Amish goodies. Philly's other famous market, the outdoor Italian Market, can be found on a lively stretch of 9th Street in South Philly. Around since the late 1800s, the market has vendors selling everything from fresh pasta and spices to meats and dry goods. There are even places to get lunch or coffee.

## ZAHAV

The James Beard Association named Zahav America's best restaurant in 2019. Reservations are tough to land, and it's not uncommon for diners to plan trips around them. Try calling to see if there are any cancellations the morning of, or visit one of the other excellent Philly eateries Michael Solomonov runs, including K'Far, Merkaz, Abe Fisher, and the newest star, Laser Wolf in Fishtown.

## HOAGIES

Don't call them subs, grinders, or heroes. In Philly, sandwiches made on long Italian rolls are called hoagies, and they're pretty outstanding—head to Carvers in Center City for a taste. Find varieties made with turkey, ham, tuna salad, veggie, and the classic Italian version—with thinly sliced meats and cheeses, shredded lettuce, tomatoes, oil, and vinegar—in delis and restaurants all over town. If you really want to eat like a local, try one of the many tiny neighborhood shops around town or stop by a Wawa.

The Philly cheesesteak—pictured as "Whiz, witout" (no onions).

### THE SCHMITTER

Speaking of the city's love of sandwiches, head to McNally's Tavern in Chestnut Hill for what many locals consider to be one of the greatest bar sandwiches of all time. The Schmitter has steak, cheese, and fried onions topped with fried salami and a special sauce, all on a kaiser roll—it's as delicious as it sounds.

### ROAST PORK SANDWICH

By now you may have picked up on the fact that Philadephians are serious about sandwiches. Also created in Italian-American kitchens, the roast pork sandwich is made with thinly sliced hot roasted pork, sharp (or mild) provolone cheese, and garlicky sautéed spinach or broccoli rabe. Most locals will tell you John's Roast Pork makes the best version in town—the no-frills spot won a James Beard Award for culinary excellence in 2006—and they're correct. Another deserving contender is DiNic's in the Reading Terminal Market.

### ITALIAN CUISINE

The city embraces Italian food in all forms, from South Philly's simple, perfect red gravy (also known as marinara or tomato sauce) joints to restaurants that showcase handmade pasta and regional cuisine, like Dante & Luigi's or Via Locusta. We can't talk about the city's great Italian food without mentioning Termini Brothers Bakery in East Passyunk. They've been churning out Italian pastries since 1921. Stop by for their filled-to-order cannoli, as well as pizzelles, biscotti, cakes, and another traditional Italian sweet treats.

### SCRAPPLE

The distinctive regional specialty—made with pork scraps, spices, flour, and cornmeal—is a Pennsylvania Dutch tradition. You can always find simple, classic versions of the breakfast specialty at diners around the city, including Dutch Eating Place in Reading Terminal Market and Sulimay's in Fishtown.

### CRAFT BOOZE

Before Prohibition, Philadelphia was home to a high concentration of breweries and distilleries, and in the past few decades booze has been making a big comeback. Yards, in Northern Liberties, is the oldest continuously operating craft brewer in the city, while Fishtown's Philadelphia Distilling is Pennsylvania's first craft distillery since Prohibition.

# Philadelphia's Best Historic Sights

**INDEPENDENCE HALL**

This redbrick building looks surprisingly low-key for a national icon, but if these walls could talk, they would tell tales of how the building that began life as the Pennsylvania State House became the site of monumental decisions and events for a new nation. *(Ch. 3)*

**MOTHER BETHEL AFRICAN METHODIST EPISCOPAL CHURCH**

Former slave Richard Allen founded this church and purchased the land it still occupies in 1787; it's the country's oldest real estate continuously owned by African Americans. He and his wife, Sarah Allen, ran a station on the Underground Railroad. In the crypt, you can see their tombs, pews from the original church, and a museum. *(Ch. 4)*

**CLIVEDEN**

The stately fieldstone house is quiet now, but back in the revolutionary days of 1777, Cliveden played an important role in the bloody Battle of Germantown. You can take a tour (by appointment only) of the house, or check out exhibits in the Carriage House visitor center that examine the historical legacy of slavery and how it can be used to understand what the house—and freedom—mean. *(Ch. 11)*

**EASTERN STATE PENITENTIARY**

This massive prison in the Fairmount neighborhood takes you through the history of criminal justice reform. Peek into cells that held Al Capone, Willie Sutton, and others. Take a guided tour or the excellent audio tour narrated by Steve Buscemi to appreciate the crumbling spaces. After the tour, see exhibits and displays on current issues in criminal justice. *(Ch. 7)*

## RITTENHOUSE SQUARE

A sculpture-filled, leafy retreat beloved by locals, the square and neighborhood remain chic and expensive, though apartments, restaurants, and fancy shops have replaced the original houses right around the square. To channel the neighborhood vibe, relax on a bench or people-watch while dining alfresco. *(Ch. 6)*

## THE BENJAMIN FRANKLIN MUSEUM

Benjamin Franklin played many critical roles in Philadelphia and in the nation's founding, and all get their due in lively exhibits at this museum in Franklin Court. Interactive displays reflect on his key qualities, and videos bring an icon to life, even for children. *(Ch. 3)*

## MUSEUM OF THE AMERICAN REVOLUTION

Opened in 2017, the Museum of the American Revolution isn't historic in itself, but it's well worth a visit to explore engaging interactive displays and intriguing artifacts that make the struggle for independence feel far fresher than the account in your high-school history textbook. *(Ch. 3)*

Elfreth's Alley

## PRESIDENT'S HOUSE

Just north of the Liberty Bell Center, an open-air site with partial brick walls and window frames marks the footprint of the President's House, home of Presidents George Washington and John Adams from 1790 to 1800. *(Ch. 3)*

## ELFRETH'S ALLEY

Built from the early 1700s to 1830, the 32 modest Federal- and Georgian-style houses on the country's oldest continuously occupied residential street were not the grand mansions of Society Hill. Craftspeople lived here, and in season you can stop by the Elfreth's Alley Museum at Nos. 124–126 to explore the quaint former homes of a Colonial dressmaker and chair maker. *(Ch. 3)*

## LIBERTY BELL CENTER

The cracked bronze bell has long inspired lovers of freedom. Learn its history at the Liberty Bell Center, a glass-enclosed complex with the bell, interpretive displays, and a video. Activist groups for women's suffrage and civil rights have embraced the bell as a powerful emblem. *(Ch. 3)*

# Best Museums in Philadelphia

The Mütter Museum is filled with unusual objects.

**BARNES FOUNDATION**
Boasting one of the most impressive collections of art in the country (81 Renoirs, 69 Cézannes, 59 Matisses, 46 Picassos, 7 van Goghs, 6 Seurats), the Barnes moved from its longtime home in the Main Line suburbs to a higher-profile Parkway plot in 2012. The unusual layout of its mixed-media galleries, a hallmark of Albert Barnes's style, remains. *(Ch. 7)*

**PHILADELPHIA MUSEUM OF ART**
A street-level entrance off Kelly Drive lets you bypass the famous Rocky Steps (or run 'em, if you'd like) and go directly into Philly's hallowed temple of art. Inside, you'll find paintings, furniture, textiles, and more from names like Diego Rivera, Georgia O'Keeffe, Charles Eames, and Frank Gehry. *(Ch. 7)*

**MUSEUM OF THE AMERICAN REVOLUTION**
Opened in 2017, the AmRev Museum (as locals have nicknamed it) emphasizes an immersive, interactive format in its retelling of the Revolutionary War from the Boston Tea Party to the Battle of Yorktown. Fans of *Hamilton* won't want to miss the gallery of 30 artifacts related to the former treasury secretary. *(Ch. 3)*

African Americans from pre-colonial times to the current day.

### RODIN MUSEUM
The only museum dedicated to Auguste Rodin outside France, Philly's beaux arts tribute features nearly 150 bronzes, marbles, and plasters. The lovely garden is the perfect place to contemplate alongside *The Thinker*. *(Ch. 7)*

### PENNSYLVANIA ACADEMY OF THE FINE ARTS
Located just north of City Hall, the country's oldest art museum and school regularly augments its diverse mixed-media collection with compelling exhibits throughout the year. *(Ch. 7)*

### THE MÜTTER MUSEUM
Lovers of the medical and the macabre should not miss this fascinating and unusual collection, which is filled with skulls, organs, skeletons, and other oddities; an expansion scheduled for 2023 will double its footprint. *(Ch. 6)*

### FRANKLIN INSTITUTE
Science is the thread stitching the various family-friendly galleries together (the giant walk-through heart is a favorite), with nationally touring exhibits often setting up shop. There's also a planetarium and Center City's only IMAX theater. *(Ch. 7)*

### MUMMERS MUSEUM
The Mummers have been part of Philly tradition for centuries, and this museum in Pennsport, the heart of Mummers culture, charts its history from its 17th-century origins to the modern New Year's Day parade, when thousands of elaborately costumed musical brigades march down Market Street. *(Ch. 8)*

### WEITZMAN NATIONAL MUSEUM OF AMERICAN JEWISH HISTORY
Founded in 1976 and relocated in 2010, this museum shares the experience of Jewish people in America through interactive exhibits, photographs, artifacts, and film. A Smithsonian affiliate, general admission (not including special exhibits) is free. *(Ch. 3)*

### AFRICAN AMERICAN MUSEUM IN PHILADELPHIA
Philly's African American museum documents the experience of the people of the African diaspora in Philadelphia and beyond. The interactive projections of important 18th-century figures in the permanent *Audacious Freedom* exhibit are especially well done. *(Ch. 3)*

# Philadelphia Today

There might not be a United States of America without Philadelphia. The Declaration of Independence was signed here, kick-starting the American Revolution, and the city went on to become the first capital of the young USA. History is everywhere. Concentrated in the Old City, where spotting costumed reenactors (Ben Franklin, Betsy Ross) is a regular occurrence, the main historical sites like Independence Hall, Liberty Bell, and the Betsy Ross House are magnets for domestic and international visitors. Newer on the scene is the Museum of the American Revolution, which chronicles the war through state-of-the-art exhibits, and the President's House, the site and partial re-creation of George Washington's presidential mansion. During the archaeological excavation, slave quarters were discovered, resulting in a frank discussion about the role of slavery in the lives of America's forefathers, one this open-air museum (refreshingly) does not shy away from exploring.

There's history outside the city, too. Less than an hour's drive brings you to Valley Forge National Historic Park, the Battlefield of the Brandywine, and the Bucks County town of Washington's Crossing, where General Washington crossed the Delaware River on Christmas Day, 1776.

But listen up: history is far from the only reason to visit Philadelphia. The city today looks forward—to tech, to newcomers, to cutting-edge design and cuisine, to climate advocacy, to social justice—as much as it looks back. Philly is a longtime Democratic stronghold. Big ideas about the future of politics, justice, and reform are percolating here and influencing the country, including Mayor Jim Kenney's soda tax, a tariff on sugary beverages that, while controversial, succeeded in funding universal pre-K. Kenney served the final year of his second term as mayor in 2023. Philadelphians are not shy about sharing their opinions, political and otherwise, especially about their award-winning sports teams, the Eagles (football) and the Phillies (baseball). But by and large, Philly is a socially open and tolerant city. Unless you are a Dallas Cowboys fan. Then no one can help you. (Just kidding. Kinda.)

## A SMALL TOWN IN DISGUISE

Philly is the sixth-largest American city by population, but it operates very much like a small town. Even as the infusion of new residents from other cities, states, and countries has hit a fever pitch in the last decade, it's not uncommon to meet third- and fourth-generation Philadelphians who have lived here all their lives. "Lived here" doesn't just mean the city, though. It might mean the same neighborhood, if not the same block. Philadelphians complain about their hometown (parking, trash, wage tax) but that doesn't mean they don't love it fiercely—and it doesn't mean outsiders should participate in the griping. Unless it's about the PPA (Philadelphia Parking Authority), which is always a safe target. It can feel like everyone knows everyone in neighborhoods, and Philadelphians are generally a welcoming bunch. Experiencing that tight knitted-ness, in the context of a big city with all the amenities you'd expect from one, is what makes Philly so special and unusual.

## SETTING THE TABLE

From Ethiopian *injera* joints to luxe Italian pasta palaces, whatever kind of restaurant you're looking for in Philly, you'll find it. The city has so evolved past its cheesesteak stereotype that even the "Philly is more than just cheesesteaks" talking point has become a cliché. You can get fantastic versions of the famous sandwich, along with its cousin, the roast pork (with broccoli rabe and sharp provolone), at places like John's Roast Pork and Angelo's Pizza, both in South Philly, but to go to Philly and only eat sandwiches would mean you're missing out on a diverse and world-class dining destination. A metaphorical buffet of modern Philadelphia might include internationally renowned lamb tacos (South Philly Barbacoa), homemade ravioli (Via Locusta), aromatic Indonesian beef *rendang* (Hardena), and jewel-like Lebanese baklava (Manakeesh). And that's just on the inexpensive end. A trip to Philly means you can easily balance the low with the high, and no restaurants do high better than Zahav, Laurel, Royal Izakaya, and Vernick Food & Drink, all must-make reservations that have earned accolades from well-respected Philly food writers and critics.

## OUTSIDE LANDS

There's no getting around it: as a dense, gridded, East Coast city, Philly can feel like a concrete jungle. Fortunately there are plenty of opportunities close by and further afield where you can alleviate the urban crush, from William Penn's four main "Squares" (aka parks) to the botanical curiosities of Bartram's Garden in West Philly and the mystical John Heinz National Wildlife Refuge out by the airport. Fairmount Park, which reaches out from the edge of the Art Museum and crosses the Schuylkill River to encompass more than 2,000 acres, is one of the largest city parks in the country. Fairmount Park is home to hiking trails, a Japanese teahouse and garden, the zoo, and Belmont Plateau, a wide grassy savanna with a killer view of the skyline. Apple orchards and sheep farms stretch out north of the city, and beyond, the Pocono Mountains lure skiers, sledders, and holidaymakers. Cross the

Delaware River and you'll soon find yourself in New Jersey's historic small towns, like Haddonfield; and major shopping destinations (Cherry Hill and Deptford). Further out, you'll find Pine Barrens, a land of cranberry bogs, woods and trails, and quirky characters. Keep going and you'll eventually reach the Atlantic Ocean, as hordes of Philadelphians do every summer. Going "down the Shore" is one Philly tradition almost everyone can agree on.

## THE AFTERMATH OF COVID-19

In the spring of 2020, the United States (including Philadelphia) was gravely impacted by the COVID-19 virus. Restaurants, hotels, shops, bars, and even cultural institutions were forced to close temporarily. At the time of press, Philadelphia is, for the most part, back to its "pre-pandemic state." Masks are not required (except in medical facilities). You may notice some restaurants with temporary outdoor areas but those are slowly being removed in 2023.

## RACISM AND UNREST

As in many places around the U.S., Philadelphia erupted in protests in early June 2020 following the senseless death of George Floyd in Minneapolis. Citizens had had enough, and protestors filled the streets from the Center City West neighborhood along the retail corridor to Rittenhouse Square. While some businesses were looted and damaged, business owners on the whole pledged to rebuild. The City of Brotherly love is no stranger to social injustice, unfortunately, as the city experienced some of its darkest days under the hands of former police commissioner and mayor Frank Rizzo. A statue and mural of the controversial figure were finally removed following the protests.

# Free in Philadelphia

Many of Philadelphia's most historic and best-known attractions are free—or suggest a small donation for admission—every day. This lengthy list includes **Independence Hall,** the **Liberty Bell, Carpenter's Hall, Franklin Court,** and the other buildings and sites of **Independence National Historic Park** including the **President's House,** an open-air space that marks the site of the nation's first executive mansion.

## MUSIC AND THEATER

Check the calendar of the **Curtis Institute of Music** (⊕ www.curtis.edu) to catch one of the frequent free student recitals. **The Philadelphia Orchestra** (⊕ www.philorch. org) also gives free neighborhood concerts. Visit **Macy's** across from City Hall; the former Wanamaker's boasts the largest pipe organ in the world, and there are daily free concerts. The Christmas show around the holidays is a definite favorite with shoppers. Check out a dress rehearsal or pay-what-you-can performance at the **Arden Theater**—they accept donations for admission for certain shows. Local independent radio station **WXPN** offers free concerts Fridays at noon at its home base, **World Café Live** (⊕ worldcafelive.com).

## OUTDOOR FUN AND FESTIVALS

Take your pick of activities in **Fairmount Park**: hike the trails of the Wissahickon (⊕ www.montcopa.org/924/wissahick-on-trail), bring a picnic to Belmont Plateau and enjoy the view; or meander around the Horticultural Center, look for the scattered pieces of public art, or take the kids to **Smith Memorial Playground,** one of the country's oldest playgrounds. All summer long, multicultural festivals at **Penn's Landing** feature live music and dance instruction. Open spring through fall, **Spruce Street Harbor Park** overlooks the Delaware River creating a great (free) spot to rest, complete with hammock-lounging.

## ARCHITECTURE, ART, AND LITERATURE

Take a free weekday afternoon tour of **City Hall** and visit the lobby of the **Curtis Center** to gawk at the giant *Dream Garden* by Maxfield Parrish. Visit the **Galleries at the Moore College of Art & Design,** the first and only women's visual arts college in the United States.

It's always fun to stroll the galleries in Old City, but it's especially fun on **"First Fridays":** the first Friday of every month is celebrated with wine receptions, and galleries keeping later hours. The first Sunday of each month and every Wednesday night (5–8:45 pm) is "pay what you wish" at the **Philadelphia Museum of Art.** The **Institute of Contemporary Art** at the University of Pennsylvania is free all the time. You can check out contemporary art at any time by taking a free tour of the city's many vibrant **murals** (⊕ www.muralarts.org).

## HISTORY TOURS

Take yourself on a walk by downloading and printing the self-guided **Constitutional Walking Tour** of more than 30 sites around historic Philadelphia. **Elfreth's Alley,** the nation's oldest continuously inhabited street, is free to stroll through; two houses, now a museum, are open for a small fee. Go solo with a call-in cell-phone tour of **Valley Forge National Historical Park** (☎ 484/396–1018). In the summer, look for the elaborately costumed storytellers with **Once Upon a Nation,** who set up at 13 benches throughout Philadelphia's historic area. Hop from bench to bench for a free, interactive tour, during which actors in character relay stories of Philadelphia in Colonial times.

# Philadelphia with Kids

Philadelphia has fantastic activities and sights for tots. Best of all, these stops appeal to adults as well.

## HISTORIC AREA

The **National Constitution Center**'s interactive exhibits are way better than learning from a textbook. Nearby **Franklin Square,** however, is the perfect place to take a break from all the history. There's a carousel, miniature-golf course (with Philadelphia landmarks), and an excellent burger stand that also serves up Cake Shakes (milkshakes made with Butterscotch Krimpet Tastykakes). Located in a restored 1902 firehouse near **Elfreth's Alley,** the **Fireman's Hall Museum** is home to some of the nation's earliest firefighting equipment. Kids can try on fire coats and boots, and it's free. For something spookier, check out one of the **Ghost Tours** offered around the Historic Area. If you're in need of a pick-me-up, head to **the Franklin Fountain,** a 1900s-style ice-cream and soda fountain, for handmade ice-cream treats.

## FAIRMOUNT PARK

The **Please Touch Museum** is essentially a giant playground for kids. In its location in Fairmount Park's majestic Memorial Hall—one of the few remnants from the 1876 Centennial Exhibition—the museum is bigger (38,000 square feet of exhibits) and better than ever before. The nearby **Philadelphia Zoo** is another great spot, with a petting zoo, tree house, and "Big Cat Crossing," a series of overhead passageways that allows lions, tigers, pumas, and other large cats to roam. The sprawling indoor–outdoor **Smith Memorial Playground and Playhouse** nearby has a giant wooden slide and a mansionlike playhouse; check the website when the family summer concert series, Kidchella, occurs.

## BENJAMIN FRANKLIN PARKWAY

At the **Franklin Institute,** kids can't resist walking through the giant heart and seeing their hair stand up in the static-electricity exhibit. The nearby **Academy of Natural Sciences** has great, kid-friendly exhibits about dinosaurs and architectural digs.

## PENN'S LANDING

At **Penn's Landing,** kids can climb in the bunks used in steerage or hop in a scull and row along the Schuylkill at the **Independence Seaport Museum.** Next take the **RiverLink Ferry** across the river (during summer only) to the Camden Waterfront to explore the **Adventure Aquarium.** The Shark Realm, an enormous tank filled with sharks, stingrays, and sawfish, is the central attraction here. The **Camden Children's Garden** is an interactive horticultural garden with exhibits that allow you to taste, smell, and touch different elements.

## AROUND TOWN

There are plenty of great snacks to pick up for days on the go at the **Reading Terminal Market.** Kids will like watching the workers at **Miller's Twist** wind the dough into pretzel shapes. They can also feed pennies to Philbert, the bronze pig at the market's center (the money goes to local charities). If you're in the mood for a ball game, **Citizens Bank Park,** home to Major League Baseball's Phillies, is one of the most kid-friendly major-league ballparks, with features like the Phanatic Phun Zone play area.

## OUTSIDE OF TOWN

About 40 minutes northwest of the city, **LEGOLAND Discovery Center Philadelphia** is a great place to take LEGO fans young and old. About 25 miles northeast of Philadelphia, **Sesame Place** will delight fans of Elmo, Big Bird, and crew. And, for the ultimate sugar rush, **Hershey** is about 100 miles northwest of the city center.

# What to Read and Watch

### ABBOTT ELEMENTARY
Created and starring the Emmy-award-winning, Philadelphia native Quinta Brunson, this comedic TV show offers plenty of authentic and fun Philly references. Set in a Philadelphia public grammar school, the heartwarming sitcom features a small group of dedicated teachers who overcome an array of challenges in the world of public education.

### PHILADELPHIA FIRE
Written by John Edgar Wideman, *Philadelphia Fire* explores the day in 1985 when the police firebombed a row home in West Philadelphia that was owned and occupied by an Afrocentric group known as MOVE. Tensions had long been high between MOVE and the Philadelphia police. The bombing took place at 6221 Osage Avenue and demolished 61 homes in the area.

### SUCH A FUN AGE
Set in Philadelphia, this novel by Kiley Reid explores themes of race and privilege in an empathetic and funny-at-times story about a black babysitter and the white family she babysits for. The story opens in a high-end grocery store, where what should be an easy evening turns into so much more.

### ROCKY (1976)
Philadelphia is perhaps best known for the classic film *Rocky,* which, even after decades, still has fans running up the Art Museum steps like the titular boxer every day. (The famed Rocky Statue is adjacent to the steps). Starring Sylvester Stallone, the now-franchise features eight films that showcase Philadelphia's grit.

### CREED (2015)
Included in the Rocky franchise is *Creed,* and the subsequent *Creed II,* both starring Michael B. Jordan and Sylvester Stallone; Jordan directed *Creed III* (2023). In the films, Adonis Creed moves to Philly to train with Rocky, and while he's here he falls in love with a Philly native who shows him spots like Johnny Brenda's and Max's Steaks. The iconic Rocky steps at the Art Museum also are seen on screen, and South Philadelphia's Victor Café plays a major role, too.

### THE SIXTH SENSE (1999)
Director M. Night Shyamalan calls Philadelphia home, which is why he sets many of his films here. During one of his biggest films, *The Sixth Sense,* locations like St. Augustine Roman Catholic Church, St. Alban's Street in the Graduate Hospital neighborhood, and 20th and Delancey Streets are featured.

### SILVER LININGS PLAYBOOK (2012)
This moving and endearing film explores mental illness, unexpected connections, and Philadelphia's intense love for its Philadelphia Eagles football team. Philadelphia Eagles's games and their home stadium, Lincoln Financial Field in South Philadelphia, are frequently seen on-screen, along with views of Jewelers' Row, the Benjamin Franklin House, and a number of homes and restaurants right outside the city in Delaware County.

### IT'S ALWAYS SUNNY IN PHILADELPHIA
The comedic television show about a group of quirky characters owning a bar in South Philadelphia shows off Philadelphia sights and South Philly attitudes throughout its 10-plus-year run. Much of the filming is done in Los Angeles, but a number of local spots are visible throughout the show, including Boathouse Row, the Benjamin Franklin Bridge, Penn's Landing, and Lincoln Financial Field during the opening credits, and the Italian Market and Rittenhouse Square during select episodes.

# Chapter 2

# TRAVEL SMART

Updated by
Joshua McIlvain

**👫 POPULATION**
1,577,000

**💬 LANGUAGE**
English

**$ CURRENCY**
U.S. Dollar

**☎ AREA CODES**
215, 267, and 445

**⚠ EMERGENCIES**
911

**🚗 DRIVING**
On the Right

**⚡ ELECTRICITY**
120–240 v/60 cycles; plugs
have two or three rectangu-
lar prongs

**🕓 TIME**
Eastern Time (same as New
York)

**🌐 WEB RESOURCES**
www.visitphilly.com

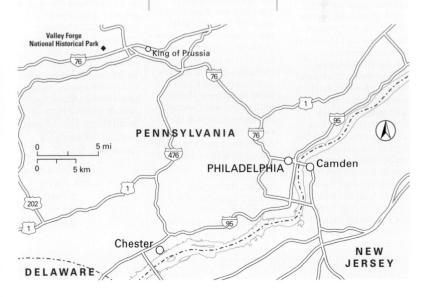

# Know Before You Go

When should I go to Philadelphia? How do I order a cheesesteak? Philly sports—are they really that important? Where can I buy booze and when? We've got answers and a few tips to help you make the most of your visit.

## WHEN TO GO

Any time is right to enjoy the area's attractions, and a variety of popular annual events take place throughout the year. Spring and fall are the prettiest times of year thanks to an abundance of flowering trees—including April's bountiful cherry blossoms in West Fairmount Park—and colorful autumnal foliage, not to mention pleasant weather. Summer can feel hot and swampy, though it is also the season of pop-up beer gardens and many festivities. If you don't mind waiting in longer lines to see popular attractions, visit around July 4, when the city comes alive with fireworks, parades, and festivals. The top draw is the Wawa Welcome America Festival, which often includes a performance by blockbuster musicians. There are special activities in the Historic Downtown area all summer long. Concert and theater seasons run from October through the beginning of June. You may find some better lodging deals—and a beautiful snowfall—in winter, if you don't mind bundling up.

## WHERE AM I?

If you ever feel lost, you can orient yourself by gauging where you stand in relation to the two main thoroughfares that intersect at the city's center: Broad (or 14th) Street, which runs north–south; and Market Street, which runs east–west. Where Broad and Market meet, neatly dividing the city center into four quadrants, you'll find massive City Hall, Philadelphia's center of gravity.

Within Center City up through West Philadelphia, the numbered streets start on the eastern side, from the Delaware River, beginning with Front Street (consider it "1st Street") and west to 25th Street on the banks of the Schuylkill (pronounced *skoo*-kull) River. In between Market to the north and Lombard to the south, most of the east–west streets have tree names (from north to south: Chestnut, Walnut, Locust, Spruce, Pine).

Center City has four roughly equal-size city squares, one in each quadrangle. In the northwest quadrangle there's Logan Square; in the southwest is Rittenhouse; in the northeast there's Franklin Square; and in the southeast is Washington Square. Running along the banks of the Delaware River is Columbus Boulevard/Delaware Avenue.

## ORDERING CHEESESTEAKS

Eating a cheesesteak is a must-do experience in Philly, but there is some lingo that you must know before you step up to the window—you don't want to get yelled at. And don't worry about temp. Cheesesteaks are well-done.

**Step 1:** Pick your cheese—Cheez Whiz, American, or provolone (never Swiss).

**Step 2:** Decide if you want onions or not.

**Step 3:** Order. If you want Cheez Whiz and onions, order "Whiz, wit." Don't like onions? Order "Whiz, witout."

So where should you get your cheesesteak? Everyone has a favorite, and loyalty is fierce. The most well-known spots are Pat's, Geno's, Jim's, and Tony Luke's, but if you want to dine like a local, head to South Philly's John's Roast Pork, or Angelo's Pizzeria South Philly. ■TIP➔ **Never, ever call this sandwich "steak and cheese."**

## SPORTS

Among the country's most high-profile sporting cities, Philly has a long and storied athletic heritage that translates to a deep passion for the local teams. That passion sometimes manifests itself in blunt and at times inelegant ways, but when the going gets good, the passion is intoxicating and joyful. Should you find yourself in a game-time environment, expect good-natured heckling if you're with the opposing team. If you're there supporting the Eagles, Phillies, Flyers, or Sixers, prepare to be welcomed with open arms.

The four major sports teams play in a sports complex in deep South Philly near the corner of Broad and Patterson, accessible by the Broad Street Line subway. The Philadelphia Phillies (baseball) play at Citizens Bank Park from April to October. The Philadelphia Eagles, the 2018 Super Bowl champs (important to know), play at Lincoln Financial Field (aka the Linc) from September through January. The Philadelphia Flyers (hockey) hit the ice at the Wells Fargo Center from October to April. Philadelphia 76ers (basketball) play at the Wells Fargo Center from November to April. College basketball fans may want to check out the Philly Six (the traditional Big 5 teams of La Salle, Penn, Temple, Saint Joe's, and Villanova, plus Drexel); the season runs from December to March. Women's college basketball is the best way to see high-level playing at an affordable price. Soccer fans need to head to Chester, a 30-minute drive south of Center City, for the Philadelphia Union.

## SAFETY

Philadelphia has had a high crime rate in recent years, exasperated by the pandemic. Typically, much of this crime is concentrated in several off-the-beaten path neighborhoods. As in any major city, visitors should always exercise caution, travel in pairs at night, and be aware of their surroundings.

## SHOP 'TIL YOU DROP

Pennsylvania has a statewide law that shoes and clothes are tax-free. Good news for those seeking two of the country's busiest outlets—Philadelphia Mills and Philadelphia Premium Outlets—plus King of Prussia in the suburbs, the biggest mall on the East Coast. They are accessible by SEPTA bus from Center City, though having a car is a better option if you plan to buy anything. Most luxury designers and big brand names operate stores on Walnut or Chestnut Streets, near Rittenhouse Square, while independents fill in the surrounding small streets and pop up in neighborhoods like East Passyunk, Fishtown, and Old City.

## LIQUOR LAWS

Philadelphia has notoriously complicated rules surrounding the purchase and consumption of alcohol, though the rules have been loosening up. You can buy wine and liquor (no beer) at Fine Wine & Good Spirits, state-run stores (locals call them "state stores") that are spread around the city; these stores don't open until 11 am on Sundays. Beer distributors sell six-packs and cases and you can buy wine and beer at many large supermarkets and at independently owned bottle shops. Bars sometimes sell six-packs and breweries can sell their own beer through growlers and cans. Liquor is also available from a number of independent distilleries such as Philadelphia Distilling in Fishtown.

Bars and restaurants with liquor licenses can serve alcohol until 2 am. Ones with special social club licenses can go until 3 am—you need to be a member (or the guest of a member) to get into these spots. Due to the prohibitive cost of obtaining a liquor license in Philly, many restaurants opt to let diners bring their own bottle (BYOB). Always check in advance so you don't show up empty-handed.

# Getting Here and Around

##  Air

Flying time from Boston is 1 hour, 20 minutes; from Chicago, roughly 2 hours; from Miami, 2 hours, 40 minutes; from Los Angeles, 5 hours, 40 minutes.

### AIRPORTS

Philadelphia International Airport (PHL) is a seven-terminal airport located roughly 7 miles southwest from downtown. Elaborate renovations over the past decade-plus have brought PHL into modern times with some decent retail and dining options. All terminals connect to each other except Terminal F. The airport has a typically slow baggage claim, but it does boast a great safety record.

An alternative is Newark Liberty International Airport (EWR), about 85 miles northeast of Philadelphia in New Jersey. From EWR, a United Airlines hub, you can take an AirTrain shuttle to the Newark Airport station, then take an Amtrak train to 30th Street in Philadelphia, about an hour ride. Book in advance as rates vary from $27 to $85 per ticket.

### GROUND TRANSPORTATION

For $8 (credit or cash on train), you can take SEPTA's Airport rail line directly into Center City directly from any of the airport terminals. It leaves the airport every 30 minutes from 5:09 am to 12:13 am. The trip to Center City takes about 20 minutes. Trains serve University City and 30th Street Station (both in West Philly near University of Pennsylvania and Drexel), Suburban and Jefferson (the Center City stations), and Temple University in North Philadelphia.

By car from the airport, the city is accessible via I–95 north or I–76 east. Allow at least a half hour, more during rush hour, for the 8-mile trip. Taxis at PHL are plentiful; follow signs in the airport and wait in line to catch one. Destinations that fall within the zone demarcated by Fairmount Avenue to the north, South Street to the south, the Delaware River to the east, and 38th Street to the west are eligible for a $28.50 flat rate, not including tip. Uber and Lyft are also good options from the airport.

Limousines and shuttles are also available from PHL. Shuttle buses cost $10 and up per person and will make most requested stops downtown as well as in the suburbs. You can make shuttle arrangements at the centralized ground transportation counter in the baggage claim areas.

### FLIGHTS

Most major U.S. airlines offer service to and from Philadelphia (PHL), which is a hub for American Airlines.

##  Bicycle

The real draw for bicyclists are the mountain bike trails in Wissahickon Park and the Schuylkill River Trail that follows the river from the Philadelphia Art Museum all the way through Valley Forge and past Royersford (32 miles!)—to do the entire trail you should have a hybrid bike as there are some non-paved areas. Within the city streets, Philadelphia has made strides to becoming a bicycle-friendly town, but you will not mistake it for Amsterdam—motorists are not the most deferential. Major streets, like Pine and Spruce Streets through Center City, feature bike-only lanes adjacent to traffic lanes, and other highly trafficked drags, like Broad Street and Spring Garden Street, are equipped with bike lanes as well. Many of Philly's older, narrower, single-lane streets are frequented by cyclists, though they might prove trickier to navigate for inexperienced riders or visitors. Out in Mount Airy and Chestnut

Hill the pace is slower and streets are easy to bike on. Though its streets are very narrow, Manayunk, with its famous "Wall" (Levering Street and Lyceum Avenue) which cyclists had to bike up 10 times in the yearly but currently moribund city bike race, is a hangout for cyclists, with several bike stores, and as a meetup point (or drinking destination).

Riders can legally use a lane in the same manner as a motor vehicle, but it's best to move to one side of the street to let auto traffic pass. Like many cities, there is intermittent friction between cyclists and motorists when it comes to issues of road sharing, traffic laws, and safety. It's wise to obey all signs and directives as if one were in a car when riding a bike in Philly.

The most difficult part of biking in the city may be finding a safe place to stash your bike while you run into a restaurant for lunch or a historic site for a visit. The installation of street racks designed for bicycle lock-ups hasn't increased to meet the amount of active riders just yet, though more permanent racks and corrals seem to be popping up regularly. Invest in a quality, heavy-duty lock, whether you're locking up your bike at a rack or on a fence or street sign.

Visitors rent bikes in the short term via Indego, Philadelphia's bike-sharing program. Dozens of bike-stocked Indego kiosks are scattered throughout the city, offering instant rentals via a high-tech kiosk system. You can pick up a bike in one area and drop it off at the kiosk closest to your destination. Rentals are also available at several bike stores.

##  Bus

A bus is generally the cheapest option to reach Philadelphia, particularly when you are coming from New York City. New Jersey Transit stops at the Greyhound terminal and offers service between Philadelphia and Atlantic City and other New Jersey destinations.

Megabus has a stop adjacent to 30th Street Station, offering service to and from midtown Manhattan in New York City. FlixBus travels between Manhattan and Philly with stops in Cherry Hill, New Jersey and Malvern, Pennsylvania; its city stop is near the corner of Market and 6th Streets, near Independence Hall. Tickets are best purchased online prior to your trip.

##  Car

Getting around Philadelphia by car can sometimes be difficult—and parking in downtown areas a headache. The main east–west freeway through the city, the Schuylkill Expressway (I–76), gets backed up during rush hour. The main north–south highway through Philadelphia is the Delaware Expressway (I–95). To reach Center City heading southbound on I–95, take the Vine Street exit.

From the west the Pennsylvania Turnpike begins at the Ohio border and intersects the Schuylkill Expressway (I–76) at Valley Forge. The Schuylkill Expressway has several exits in Center City. The Northeast Extension of the turnpike, renamed I–476 and often called "the Blue Route" by locals, runs from Scranton to Plymouth Meeting, north of Philadelphia. From the east the New Jersey Turnpike and I–295 access U.S. 30, which enters the city via the Benjamin Franklin Bridge,

# Getting Here and Around

or New Jersey Route 42 and the Walt Whitman Bridge into South Philadelphia.

With the exception of a few thoroughfares (e.g., the Benjamin Franklin Parkway, Broad Street, Vine Street, Spring Garden Street, parts of Market Street), streets in Center City are narrow and one-way. Philadelphia's compact 5-square-mile downtown is laid out in a grid. The navigational heart of the city is Broad and Market Streets, where City Hall stands. Market Street divides the city north and south; 130 South 15th Street, for example, is in the second block south of Market Street. The diagonal Benjamin Franklin Parkway breaks the grid pattern by leading from City Hall out of Center City into Fairmount Park.

## CAR RENTALS

If you plan on spending the majority of your time within the immediate city confines, especially in Center City, you don't need to rent a car, but you may want to if you plan to do a lot of day trips. For rental cars, rates in Philadelphia begin at around $60 a day.

Generally, you must be at least 21 years old to rent a car in Philadelphia and the surrounding areas, though a handful of areas hold to a 25-and-over rule. (Rates may be higher if you're under 25.) Non–U.S. residents need a reservation voucher (for prepaid reservations that were made in the traveler's home country), a passport, a driver's license, and a travel policy that covers each driver, when picking up a car.

## GASOLINE

Gas stations are sprinkled randomly throughout Center City, but there's always one not too far away. A majority are 24-hour operations, except in outlying neighborhoods.

## PARKING

In most cases, a spot at a Philadelphia parking meter will cost $5 an hour. The MeterUp app makes the process less annoying, Parking garages are plentiful, especially around Independence Hall, City Hall, and the Pennsylvania Convention Center, and rates vary. Philadelphia Parking Authority (PPA) employees are famously vigilant about ticketing for expired meters and overstaying your time limit in free spots. Fortunately, Center City is compact, and you can easily get around downtown on foot after you park, or take Uber rides to your heart's content. If you plan to stay in a hotel in Center City, check ahead of time to see if it has its own parking facility or if the hotel will direct you to a nearby parking garage for a reduced rate.

## ROAD CONDITIONS

Traffic flows relatively freely through the main thoroughfares of the city. Just pay attention: you will often see Philly natives employing the "rolling stop"—aka "Philly roll"—at stop signs and the "red light jump" when drivers sitting at a red light will drive through it just as (or just before) it turns green. Road and house construction is a way of life for residents, particularly in South Philly and Kensington neighborhoods (where many new restaurants also open), and the arbitrariness of one-way streets—and narrow two-way streets that should be one-way—are confusing. Drivers on the Philadelphia stretch of the Schuylkill Expressway (I–76) routinely drive well over the speed limit. If you're a slower motorist, consider gentler, more scenic routes such as Kelly Drive or Martin Luther King Jr. Drive, which follow the opposite sides of the Schuylkill River.

## RULES OF THE ROAD

Pennsylvania law requires all children under age four to be strapped into approved child-safety seats, and children from ages four to eight to ride in booster seats. All passengers must wear seat belts. In Pennsylvania, unless otherwise indicated, you may—after stopping—turn right at a red light if there's no oncoming traffic. Speed limits in Philadelphia are generally 25–40 mph on side streets, 55 mph on the surrounding highways.

## ⊙ Ferry

The RiverLink Ferry, a seasonal (May–September) passenger ferry, offers service between Philadelphia and Camden, site of the Adventure Aquarium, the BB&T Pavilion, the battleship *New Jersey,* and Campbell's Field. Ferries depart every hour from Penn's Landing daily between 10 and 6 Monday through Thursday, and 10 and 7 Friday through Sunday, and from Camden's waterfront on the half hour, daily from 9:30 to 5:30 Monday through Thursday, and 9:30 to 6:30 Friday through Sunday, with extended hours and continuous service for Penn's Landing and BB&T Pavilion concerts, and Camden Riversharks baseball games. The cost is $9 round-trip ($7 for children and seniors, under age two is free), the ride takes 12 minutes, and the ferry is wheelchair accessible.

■ TIP➜ **Tickets can be bought via mobile app, online, or at the ticket booth.**

## ⊙ Public Transit

Buses make up the bulk of the SEPTA system, with more than 120 routes extending throughout the city and into the suburbs. Although the buses are generally reliable, use them only when you're not in a hurry, as traffic on the city's major thoroughfares can add time to your trip. The distinctive purple minibuses you see around Center City are SEPTA's convenience line for visitors, the PHLASH. The 22 stops run from the Philadelphia Museum of Art through Center City to Penn's Landing, stopping near high-profile destinations such as the Barnes Foundation, Eastern State Penitentiary, the Philadelphia Zoo, and Reading Terminal Market. Since a ride on the PHLASH costs $2 for a one-way ticket (seniors, SEPTA pass holders, and children four and under ride free), consider the all-day, unlimited-ride pass available for $5 per passenger. These buses typically run daily in season from 10 am to 6 pm. There's service every 15 minutes.

The base cash fare for subways, trolleys, and buses is $2.50, paid with exact change or with a Key Card, which you can purchase at a kiosk and refill online (and each fare is then $2). Transfers cost $1. Senior citizens with proof of age are permitted to ride free. Up to two children, four or younger, may ride free with each paying adult.

If you plan to travel extensively within Center City, consider a SEPTA pass. A one-day Convenience Pass costs $9 and is good for a total of eight rides on any SEPTA bus, trolley, or subway train, excluding regional rail. A one-day

# Getting Here and Around

Independence Pass costs $13 and is good for 24 hours of unlimited use on all SEPTA vehicles within the city, including regional rail, the purple PHLASH bus, and the Airport Express train. Passes can be purchased both online and in the SEPTA sales offices, in the concourse below 15th and Market Streets; in the Jefferson Station (10th and Market Streets); and in 30th Street Station.

Philadelphia's subway system runs regular trains throughout the day. Their geographic reach is somewhat limited to a basic east–west line and north–south line, but they do take you close to major spots quickly. The orange-colored Broad Street Line (BSL) runs from Fern Rock Station in the northern part of the city to Pattison Avenue, aka NRG Station, in South Philadelphia, home of Citizens Bank Park, the Wells Fargo Center, Lincoln Financial Field, and XFINITY Live! The blue-colored Market-Frankford Line (MFL) runs across the city, from the 69th Street Transportation Center in the western suburb of Upper Darby to Frankford in Northeast Philadelphia. A number of "Subway Surface" lines run from Center City to a greater variety of stops in West Philly.

Sunday through Thursday, most trains on the BSL and MFL begin suspending service for the evening between midnight and 1 am, resuming around 5 am. During these times, "Night Owl" buses operate along the same routes. On Friday and Saturday nights, both lines run continuously throughout the night.

##  Ride-Sharing

Smartphone-powered ride-sourcing services, like Uber and Lyft, have a strong presence in Philadelphia.

##  Taxi

Taxis are plentiful in Center City, especially along Broad, Market, Walnut, and Chestnut Streets and near major hotels and travel hubs. They're hailed street-side; smartphone users can also download 215GetACab, a free Android/iOS app that allows you to schedule pickups instantly. At night, during prime-time hours, try your luck on a busy street corner or ask a hotel doorman to hail a taxi for you.

Fares rise according to distance: $2.70, plus 25¢ for each one-tenth of a mile and 25¢ for every 38 seconds of wait time. A standard tip for cabdrivers is 20% of the fare. All Philadelphia cabs accept credit cards, though most drivers prefer cash transactions.

##  Train

Philadelphia's beautifully restored 30th Street Station, at 30th and Market Streets, is a major stop on Amtrak's Northeast Corridor line. The 70- to 90-minute Philadelphia–to–New York trip can cost anywhere from $50 to $200 each way, depending on the type of train, class, and when tickets are purchased. Amtrak's Northeast Regional trains and its high-speed Acela line cater to business travelers, and are equipped with conference tables and electrical outlets. A cheaper train option between Philadelphia and New York City is had by taking the SEPTA's Trenton rail line to Trenton, New Jersey, then transferring to a NJ Transit commuter line to Manhattan. The trip takes an extra 45 minutes, but the savings are considerable (about $28 each way). Amtrak also serves Philadelphia from points west, including Harrisburg, Pittsburgh, and Chicago.

SEPTA's network of commuter trains serves the city and its suburbs. The famous Main Line, a cluster of affluent suburbs, got its start—and its name—from the Pennsylvania Railroad route that ran westward from Center City. SEPTA commuter trains stop at 30th Street Station and connect to Suburban Station (16th Street and JFK Boulevard, near major hotels), and Jefferson Station (10th and Market Streets), which is close to historic Old City. Fares, which vary according to route and time of travel, range from $3.75 to $10 each way. These trains are your best bet for reaching neighborhoods to the northwest, like Manayunk, Germantown, and Chestnut Hill, as well as numerous suburbs, especially during rush hour.

The PATCO (Port Authority Transit Corporation) High Speed Line trains run from 16th and Locust Streets to Lindenwold, New Jersey. Trains stop underground at 12th and Locust, 9th and Locust, 8th and Market, and City Hall, then continue aboveground across the Delaware River to Camden. It's one way to get to the Adventure Aquarium or the BB&T Pavilion; round-trip fares range from $2.80 to $6.

## Trolley

Philadelphia once had an extensive trolley network, and a few good trolley lines are still in service and run by SEPTA. Route 10 begins west and north of Center City and ends on Market Street; Routes 11, 13, 34, and 36 each come from the west and south of Center City and also end on Market.

# Essentials

## 🍴 Dining

Philadelphia's dining landscape has had 20 years of amazing growth and shows no signs of slowing down, making it one of the country's buzziest, with a new generation of talented chefs, a thriving vegan scene, and some of the country's top-ranked restaurants. All cuisines are available, including Italian, Mexican, Thai, French, and Mediterranean. They are found throughout the city but are perhaps most highly concentrated in areas of South Philly.

Don't worry, though—Philly food purists can still find the country's best hoagies, cheesesteaks, and roast pork sandwiches at restaurants and delis throughout the city.

### RESERVATIONS AND DRESS

Aside from the numerous bistro-pubs that can boast some of the city's best food, reservations are often essential for most restaurants—though check for last-minute cancellations, as it's become the norm to book a reservation without being fully committed to going. Many top restaurants are typically booked a month ahead for weekend nights. Vetri is almost always booked two months ahead.

Few Philadelphia restaurants have a dress code, though folks will dress up on their own for a night on the town. Dress is mentioned in reviews only when men are required to wear a jacket or a jacket and tie.

### WINE, BEER, AND SPIRITS

Popular local beers include Victory, Flying Fish, Sly Fox, Nashaminy Creek Brewing, Philadelphia Brewing Company, and Yards, available in bottles and cans and at many bars in the city. Additional, mostly site-specific breweries to visit include Conshohocken Brewing Company, Attic Brewing, Chestnut Hill Brewing,

Wissahickon Brewing Company, Crime and Punishment, and Human Robot.

One happy development to come from Pennsylvania's arcane alcohol laws is the proliferation of BYOB restaurants, typically the cozier spots—where you can bring your own bottle(s) of wine, beer, or liquor and enjoy them with your meal free of corkage fees. In fact, do not assume a restaurant sells alcohol.

State-run liquor stores, called state stores, sell wine and other spirits. Beer is sold on a take-out basis by some bars and restaurants, and at some supermarkets and bottle shops.

| What it Costs in U.S. Dollars | | | |
|---|---|---|---|
| $ | $$ | $$$ | $$$$ |
| **RESTAURANTS** | | | |
| under $17 | $17–$24 | $25–$32 | over $32 |

## ➕ Health

Most travel restrictions, including vaccination and masking requirements, have been lifted across the United States except in healthcare facilities and nursing homes. Some travelers may still wish to wear a mask in confined spaces, including on airplanes, on public transportation, and at large indoor gatherings, but that is increasingly a personal choice. Be aware that some local mandates still exist and should be followed.

## 🛏 Lodging

Philadelphia has lodgings for every style of travel. Some midprice chains have moved into town or have spruced up their accommodations, and if you have

greater expectations, you need look no further than the city's handful of swank hotels, each with its own gracious character.

Budget, moderate, and luxury properties are spread throughout the downtown area. The Historic Area, on the east side of downtown, centers on Independence Hall and extends to the Delaware River, and is a good base for sightseeing. Old City and Society Hill lodgings are also convenient for serious sightseeing; Society Hill is the quietest of the three areas. For business-oriented trips, Center City encompasses the heart of the downtown business district, centered around Broad and Market Streets, and Rittenhouse Square hotels are also nearby.

If you prefer to keep your distance from the tourist throngs, check out the Benjamin Franklin Parkway–Museum Area along the parkway from 16th Street to the Philadelphia Museum of Art. There are also a couple of hotels in University City—just across the Schuylkill River in West Philadelphia and close to the University of Pennsylvania and Drexel University—a 5- to 10-minute drive or taxi ride from Center City.

### RESERVATIONS

Even with the large number of hotel rooms, advance reservations are advised. Home to several large, centrally located universities, Philadelphia hotels tend to book up during graduations and back-to-school times. Philadelphia has no real off-season, but many hotels offer discount packages when the demand from business travelers and groups subsides. Besides substantially reduced rates, these packages often include an assortment of freebies, such as breakfast, parking, cocktails, and the use of exercise facilities.

### PARKING

Most downtown hotels charge an average of $25 a night for parking, but some include it in the rate and it can be much higher at some hotels. You can find street parking, but it's probably not worth the effort. The best time to try is in the early morning or in the early evening, before the nightlife starts up. However, most streets have two-hour time limits until 10 pm, and the two-hour rule goes into effect at 8 am.

| What it Costs in U.S. Dollars | | | |
|---|---|---|---|
| $ | $$ | $$$ | $$$$ |
| **HOTELS** | | | |
| Under $175 | $175–$250 | $251–$350 | Over $350 |

##  Nightlife

Generally speaking, you can break down Philly's central nightlife hubs into four distinct areas.

Traditionally, South Street is "where all the hippies meet," according to the 1963 hit by Philly's own The Orlons. The area has become less artsy and less counterculture, with tourist-friendly attractions taking over for some independent businesses, but there's still much to see and do, particularly along the eastern half of the river-to-river street—packed bars and restaurants, tattoo parlors, sneaker stores, cafés, erotica shops, and more.

Home to the majority of Philadelphia's historical attractions, Old City is equally popular with party people come nightfall. Like South Street, it can get packed on the weekends, with various clubs, bars, and restaurants serving as draws. The crowd is a mix of tourists and locals. Columbus Boulevard features a high

# Essentials

concentration of large clubs and there are some open-air summer clubs on the river side of the avenue.

North of Old City lie Northern Liberties and Fishtown. Both neighborhoods have long been associated with Philly's bohemian crowd, a target for edgy artists, chefs, and musicians. More recently, however, both enclaves and the areas surrounding them have come into their own as legitimate cultural contenders citywide with great restaurants, bars, and breweries.

Finally, Rittenhouse Square, in the heart of Center City, is the premier hangout for Philly's moneyed crowd, with a slew of high-profile bars, restaurants, and clubs joining a scattering of under-the-radar gems both old-school and new-school.

Other neighborhoods of interest are University City, with all the standard (and not-so-standard) college-age bars and clubs, plus unique international options in greater West Philly like Baltimore Avenue from 47th to 51st Streets; East Passyunk, a hot strip featuring hip bars and restaurants commingling with South Philly's old-school Italian population; and Manayunk, a nightlife-heavy area to the northwest particularly popular with recent college grads.

Bars and clubs can sometimes close, change hands, or turn over with very short notice, so stay abreast of the latest by following the food and entertainment pages of the *Philadelphia Inquirer* (⊕ *inquirer.com*); the *Philadelphia Gay News* (⊕ *epgn.com*); and *Philadelphia* magazine (⊕ *phillymag.com*).

Last call for bars and clubs is 2 am, though a handful of places with special licenses have after-hours service. Cover charges can range from free to about $12. While Philly tends toward the casual in many of its nightlife venues, dress codes are enforced in some clubs. Check online to make certain if you're venturing into new territory.

People from outside the city might be surprised to see just how popular dancing is here. The persuasive DJ culture has permeated the city, especially in Old City, Northern Liberties/Fishtown, and on South Street.

Philadelphia has a rich jazz and blues heritage that includes such greats as the late, legendary jazz saxophonists John Coltrane and Grover Washington Jr. That legacy continues today in clubs such as South, Chris' Jazz Café, Time, and the more raucous Bob & Barbara's.

Though a number of Philly rock/pop venues are owned by Live Nation, a good variety of touring bands are represented on a nightly basis. And with Fishtown's thriving live-music scene at venues such as Johnny Brenda's, Kung Fu Necktie, and Union Transfer, plus MilkBoy and First Unitarian Church of Philadelphia in Center City and Theatre of Living Arts (TLA) in South Philly, a great variety of live music is available.

## 🎒 Packing

Philadelphia is a fairly casual city, although men will need a jacket and tie in some of the old-school upscale restaurants. Jeans and sneakers or other casual clothing is fine for sightseeing. You'll need a heavy coat and boots for winter, which can be cold and snowy. Summers are hot and humid, but women may wish to bring a shawl or light jacket for air-conditioned restaurants. Many areas are best explored on foot, so bring good walking shoes.

## Where Should I Stay?

| | VIBE | PROS | CONS |
|---|---|---|---|
| Old City and Historic Downtown | Old City is home to some of the oldest buildings, streets, and attractions. | Its walkability makes it easy to get around and the dining options make it easy to stay fueled. | These areas are busy during touristy months. Market Street on weekends can be overrun by partiers. |
| Society Hill and Penn's Landing | While Society Hill is largely residential, adjacent Penn's Landing promises parks, waterfront views, and high-energy festivals. | Some of the city's most celebrated pop-up parks are here, along with restaurants and waterfront attractions. | Busy Columbus Boulevard, which runs through the area, can feel busy and overwhelming at all hours of the day. |
| Center City East and Chinatown | Expect everything from designer-brand shopping to dining at the city's most authentic Chinese restaurants. | Centrally located, these neighborhoods can be explored by foot. There's plenty of restaurants, shopping, and more. | Panhandlers frequent Center City East due to its central location, and traffic can be very heavy. |
| Center City West and Rittenhouse Square | A mix of retail and residential, expect the historic and affluent with an array of restaurants, bars, and shops. | Centrally located with some of the city's best food, drinks, shopping, hotels, and museums within a stone's throw of each other. | Hotel accommodations and overnight parking can be expensive, and traffic can be a problem, especially during rush hour. |
| Parkway Museum District and Fairmount Park | Home to some of the country's best museums and the city's largest municipal park. | Beautiful, clean, safe, and walkable, there are excellent hotels, museums, restaurants, parks, and shops all within a small radius. | The attractions are a bit spread out and traffic can make some crossings daunting for pedestrians. It's also a festival hub. |
| South Philadelphia and East Passyunk | An old-school Italian neighborhood is now a diverse area with cuisines and residents from all over. | Something for everyone—from top restaurants to local pizza spots and toy stores and bookshops. | Parking is a challenge; it's so bad that people park in the middle of bustling Broad Street. |
| University City and West Philadelphia | It's an even mix of diverse West Philly and cutting-edge development. | Cultural diversity means international eateries and a multitude of languages and traditions. | West Philadelphia covers an enormous amount of real estate and some neighborhoods are not safe. |
| Northern Liberties, Kensington and Fishtown | Philly's hippest neighborhoods offer local shopping, global dining, and plenty of Instagrammable spots for hanging out. | The neighborhoods are full of energy and an array of things to do, including some of the city's best restaurants, bars, and festivals. | Bars can be rowdy and crowded. Certain areas in Kensington, a very large neighborhood, are where safety is a concern. |

# Essentials

## 🎭 Performing Arts

Of all the performing arts, it's music for which Philadelphia is perhaps most renowned with the Philadelphia Orchestra leading the way. The city also serves as a major stop for touring productions of shows from *Hello, Dolly!* to *Hamilton,* and the local theater scene, which supports more than two dozen regional and local companies, is thriving. Modern dance companies include BalletX, Philadanco, Rennie Harris Pure Movement, Koresh, and Brian Sanders' JUNK. The Philadelphia Ballet (formerly Pennsylvania Ballet) was founded by Balanchine protégée Barbara Weisberger in 1963 and is one of the top ballet companies in the country.

The Kimmel Center is Philadelphia's premiere concert venue and host to the Philadelphia Orchestra. The Academy of Music, the country's oldest opera house, remains open in all its finery hosting concerts and the Philadelphia Ballet and Opera Philadelphia; Penn Live Arts and FringeArts house everything from dance to theater to performance art and circus; FringeArts also runs the citywide Philadelphia Fringe Festival each September; the Mann Center (in West Philly) and the BB&T Pavilion (in Camden) are very popular outdoor amphitheaters. Temple and Drexel Universities and Bryn Mawr College also bring inspired programming to their performance spaces.

Classical music in Philadelphia begins with the world-renowned Philadelphia Orchestra, which, under music director Yannick Nézet-Séguin, has kept its remarkable pedigree. But there is also the Chamber Orchestra of Philadelphia, which is also housed in the glorious Kimmel Center; the Black Pearl Chamber Orchestra; and the talented students of the Curtis Institute, to round out the bill.

### INFORMATION AND TICKETS

For current performances and listings, the best guides to Philly's performing arts are the "Guide to the Lively Arts" in the daily *Philadelphia Inquirer,* the "Weekend" section of the Friday *Inquirer,* and the "Friday" section of the *Philadelphia Daily News.*

##  Shopping

Philadelphia has spawned some influential fashion retailers. The Urban Outfitters chain was born in a storefront in West Philadelphia. Its sophisticated sister, Anthropologie, also has its roots in Philadelphia. Lagos, the popular high-end jewelry line, was founded here, and all items are still produced locally. High-fashion boutiques Joan Shepp and Elle Lauri, in the Rittenhouse Square area, are well regarded by locals for designer clothing and accessories.

Some of the most spirited shopping in town is also pleasing to the palate. The indoor Reading Terminal Market and the outdoor Italian Market are bustling with urban dwellers buying groceries and visitors searching for the perfect Philadelphia cheesesteak. Equally welcoming is the city's quaint, cobblestone Antiques Row, a three-block stretch of Pine Street crammed with shops selling everything from estate jewelry to stained glass and vintage furniture. Also worth a trip is the Third Street Corridor in Old City, home to scads of independent, funky boutiques.

# $ Taxes

The main sales tax in Philadelphia and the surrounding areas is 8%. This tax also applies to restaurant meals. Various other taxes—including a 10% liquor tax—may apply. There's no sales tax on clothing. Hotel taxes are 8.5% in Philadelphia, 5% in Bucks County, and 3.9% in Lancaster County.

# Visitor Information

**Arts and Entertainment.** Billing itself as a guide to experiencing Philly like a local, **Uwishunu** (⊕ uwishunu.com) is an in-the-know blog extension of the city's more comprehensive visitor site. Written by a diverse staff with different interests, it lives up to its local point of view. **Visit Philly** (⊕ visitphilly.com) is a comprehensive guide to events throughout the year; it also includes new entries in Philly dining, attractions, and shopping. For events listings and more local blogging, visit *Philadelphia* magazine's website (⊕ phillymag.com), where staffers hold forth on everything from street style to restaurants to shopping. **Phindie** (⊕ phindie.com) is a site that covers a wide net of performing arts big and small. **Inquirer.com**, the online home of the *Philadelphia Inquirer,* also covers arts and happenings.

**Food.** Philly has its fair share of food blogs, which just shows you how important the dining scene is to Philadelphians. **Foobooz** (⊕ phillymag.com/foobooz), part of *Philadelphia* magazine, mixes news of restaurant openings and closings with food-industry gossip and restaurant reviews. It also acts as a clearinghouse for other online reviews. **Eater** (⊕ philly.eater.com) has a very active Philly branch. The **Philadelphia Inquirer** (⊕ inquirer.com/food) is particularly good in its food and beverage coverage.

## Tipping Guidelines for Philadelphia

| | |
|---|---|
| Bartender | $1 to $5 per round of drinks, depending on the number of drinks |
| Bellhop | $1 to $5 per bag, depending on the level of the hotel |
| Hotel Concierge | $5 or more, if he or she performs a service for you |
| Hotel Doorman | $1 to $2 if he helps you get a cab |
| Hotel Maid | $1 to $3 a day (either daily or at the end of your stay, in cash) |
| Hotel Room-Service Waiter | $1 to $2 per delivery, even if a service charge has been added |
| Porter at Airport or Train Station | $1 per bag |
| Skycap at Airport | $1 to $3 per bag checked |
| Taxi Driver | 15%–20%, but round up the fare to the next dollar amount |
| Tour Guide | 10% of the cost of the tour |
| Valet Parking Attendant | $2 to $3, but only when you get your car |
| Waiter | 15%–20%, with 20% being the norm at high-end restaurants; nothing additional if a service charge is added to the bill |
| Restroom and Coat-Check Attendant | Restroom attendants in more expensive restaurants expect some small change or $1. Tip coat-check personnel at least $1 to $2 per item checked unless there is a fee. |

# Contacts

##  Air

**AIRLINES Alaska Airlines.** ✉ *Philadelphia* ☎ *800/252–7522* ⊕ *www. alaskaair.com.* **American Airlines.** ✉ *Philadelphia* ☎ *800/433–7300* ⊕ *www. aa.com.* **Delta.** ✉ *Philadelphia* ☎ *800/221–1212* ⊕ *www.delta.com.* **Frontier Airlines.** ✉ *Philadelphia* ☎ *801/401–9000* ⊕ *www. flyfrontier.com.* **JetBlue.** ✉ *Philadelphia* ☎ *800/538– 2583* ⊕ *www.jetblue. com.* **Southwest Airlines.** ☎ *800/435–9792* ⊕ *www. southwest.com.* **Spirit Airlines.** ☎ *800/955–8771* ⊕ *www.spirit.com.* **Sun Country.** ✉ *Philadelphia* ☎ *651/905–2737* ⊕ *www. suncountry.com.* **United.** ☎ *800/864–8331* ⊕ *www. united.com.*

**AIRPORTS Newark Liberty International Airport.** (*EWR*). ✉ *3 Brewster Rd.* ☎ *973/961–6000* ⊕ *www. newarkairport.com.* **Philadelphia International Airport.** (*PHL*). ✉ *8500 Essington Ave., Southwest Philadelphia* ☎ *215/937–6937, 800/PHL–GATE automated flight information* ⊕ *www.phl.org.*

##  Bicycle

**Bicycle Coalition of Greater Philadelphia.** ✉ *Philadelphia* ☎ *215/242–9253* ⊕ *bicyclecoalition.org.* **Indego.** ✉ *Philadelphia* ☎ *844/446–3346* ⊕ *www. rideindego.com.* **Schuykill River Greenways.** ✉ *Philadelphia* ☎ *484/945-0200* ⊕ *www.schuylkillriver.org.*

## 🛥 Boat

**RiverLink Ferry.** ✉ *Columbus Blvd. and Walnut St.* ☎ *856/964–5465* ⊕ *www. delawareriverwaterfront. com/places/riverlink-ferry.*

## 🚌 Bus

**FlixBus.** ✉ *616 Market St., at South 6th St., Historic Area* ⊕ *www.flixbus.com.* **Megabus.** ⊕ *us.megabus. com.* **Philly PHLASH.** ☎ ⊕ *www.phlvisitorcenter. com/PHLASH.*

## 🚗 Car

**CAR RENTALS Avis.** ☎ *800/230–4898* ⊕ *www. avis.com.* **Budget.** ☎ *800/218–7992* ⊕ *www. budget.com.* **Hertz.** ☎ *800/654–3131* ⊕ *www. hertz.com.* **National Car Rental.** ☎ *888/826–6890* ⊕ *www.nationalcar.com.*

## 🚆 Train

**Amtrak.** ☎ *800/872–7245* ⊕ *www.amtrak.com.* **New Jersey Transit.** ☎ *973/275– 5555* ⊕ *www.njtransit. com.* **Port Authority Transit Corporation.** (*PATCO*). ☎ *215/922–4600* ⊕ *www. ridepatco.org.* **Southeastern Pennsylvania Transportation Authority.** (*SEPTA*). ☎ *215/580–7800* ⊕ *www. septa.org.*

## 📍 Visitor Information

**Center City District.** ✉ *Philadelphia* ⊕ *www.centercity-phila.org.* **Delaware River Waterfront.** ✉ *Philadelphia* ⊕ *www.delawareriverwaterfront.com.* **Discover Philadelphia.** ✉ *Philadelphia* ⊕ *www.discoverphl.com.* **East Passyunk Ave.** ✉ *Philadelphia* ⊕ *www.visiteastpassyunk.com.* **Friends of Rittenhouse Square.** ✉ *Philadelphia* ⊕ *www. friendsofrittenhouse.org.* **Manayunk.** ✉ *Philadelphia* ⊕ *manayunk.com.* **Old City District.** ✉ *Philadelphia* ⊕ *www.oldcitydistrict.org.* **Queen Village Neighbors Association.** ✉ *Philadelphia* ⊕ *www.qvna.org.* **University City District.** ✉ *Philadelphia* ⊕ *www.universityc-ity.org.* **Visit Philadelphia.** ✉ *Philadelphia* ⊕ *www. visitphilly.com.*

# What Did They Just Say?

The Philly accent is an interesting one. Water is wooder. The Eagles are the Iggles. And jeet? That's how Philadelphians ask if you've eaten (one syllable version of "Did You Eat?"). But there's a certain vocabulary that's used as well. We suggest familiarizing yourself with the list below.

■ **The Birds:** What Philadelphia Eagles fans call their football team.

■ **Blue Route:** Another name for 476, the highway that cuts through Philadelphia suburbs and connects with the Schuylkill (see below).

■ **ca've:** "Can I Have" as one syllable.

■ **CHOP:** Nickname for The Children's Hospital of Philadelphia.

■ **Go Birds:** Literally means "Go Eagles," but also used as an everyday greeting in place of "thank you" and "have a good day."

■ **gravy:** A South Philly term for red sauce.

■ **Gritty:** The googly-eyed Flyers mascot.

■ **hoagie:** A hero or sub sandwich.

■ **Iggles:** Also what Philadelphia Eagles fans call their football team.

■ **jawn:** A fill-in-the-blank word that can represent a person, place, or thing.

■ **jimmies:** Sprinkles (for ice cream) to almost everyone else.

■ **jimmy-jam:** Typically a contraption of some sort.

■ **The Linc:** Nickname for Lincoln Financial Field, where the Iggles play.

■ **Mummers:** Costumed musicians and partygoers who parade down Broad Street on New Year's Day.

■ **Passyunk:** Pronounced *pash-shunk*. Popular South Philadelphia neighborhood; also an avenue.

■ **Schuylkill:** Pronounced *skool-kil*. Another name for I–76; also referred to as "the Expressway."

■ **scrapple:** A breakfast meat product made of leftover pig scraps and spices.

■ **Shore:** This refers to the Jersey Shore (i.e., "I'm going down the shore"), a popular summer vacation spot for Philadelphians.

■ **water ice:** Pronounced *wood-er ahys*. A flavored ice treat, more like a thick slushie than Italian ice.

■ **Wawa:** A convenience store with reliable hoagies native to the Philadelphia region; it's a sacred spot for many Philadelphians.

■ **whiz:** a respected cheese option for cheesesteaks.

■ **wit/witout:** with or without onions on cheesesteaks; if you say wit, you're getting fried onions on your cheesesteak.

■ **Yo:** Greeting; used to get someone's attention.

■ **youse:** "You guys."

# A Historic Walk through the Old City

Touring through Old City, the neighborhood that encompasses the majority of Philly's Historic Downtown, doesn't have to begin and end with the Liberty Bell. Rely on this walk to make sure you hit all the highlights—and some under-the-radar locations as well.

## A JUMPING-OFF POINT

Start off with a stop at the **Independence Visitor Center,** where you can get your bearings, talk to park rangers and concierges, and take in two short films chronicling Philadelphia's Revolutionary War history. The Center also has a café, public restrooms, and free Wi-Fi.

## INDEPENDENCE NATIONAL HISTORIC PARK AND VICINITY

From here, it's off to the **Liberty Bell Center,** which is close by. Admission to lay eyes upon this gargantuan beacon of American freedom is free, but it's also very popular, so expect lines. You should also anticipate consistent crowds at **Independence Hall,** though there's quite a bit more to this portion of the Independence National Historical Park than the one-and-done Bell. Timed tours of the birthplace of both the Constitution and the Declaration of Independence are available free of charge; the most popular times are available on a first-come, first-served basis, though you can also reserve tickets over the phone or online for a small fee. Don't miss the other features of the park complex, including **Carpenter's Hall** (site of the First Continental Congress); and **Franklin Court,** Benjamin Franklin's former residence, featuring a mix of original architecture and restored features, including a fully operational post office and delightfully high-concept-for-the-1970s underground museum.

Walk a few blocks east down Market Street and you'll find **Christ Church,** the beautifully maintained circa-1695 house

## A Historic Walk through the Old City

**WHERE TO START**
Independence Visitor Center, 6th and Market Streets

**GETTING HERE**
It's a few minutes' walk from 30th Street Station to the visitor center, or you can park directly underneath it. Underground parking (41 N. 6th St.) costs $14 if you arrive before 9 and leave by 6, Monday–Friday. Otherwise, it's $23 for up to 24 hours.

**LENGTH**
Less than 2 miles (but seeing all the sights can take a full day).

**WHERE TO STOP**
If you continue beyond Elfreth's Alley, consider stopping at the Betsy Ross House (239 Arch St.), which is near the Constitution Center.

**BEST TIME TO GO**
When the weather is conducive to strolling outdoors.

**WORST TIME TO GO**
Sunday morning, when the National Constitution Center is closed, or on particularly cold or wet days, when walking isn't fun.

**WRITER'S CHOICE**
On weekends, Olde Bar is a good lunch stop, with happy hour starting at 4 pm. Royal Boucherie offers tasty French bistro bites and excellent cocktails.

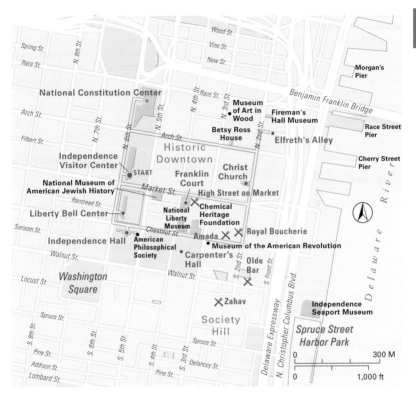

of worship that also happens to be Franklin's final resting place. Three blocks from here: the **National Constitution Center,** a gorgeous modern structure dedicated to the celebration and analysis of America's most important political document. One block northeast of the church sits **Elfreth's Alley,** one of the oldest "continuously inhabited" residential blocks in America. Two adjoined houses in the alley, which featured mostly hybrid business-residences in its heyday, serve as a museum and gift shop. Around the holidays, current residents host "Deck The Alley," an open-house fund-raiser with food, drink, and costumed revelry.

## BEYOND THE BIGGIES

There are plenty of other draws worthy of your attention besides the "big five." The **National Museum of American Jewish History,** the **American Philosophical Society, Betsy Ross House,** the **Independence Seaport Museum,** the **Museum of the American Revolution,** and the **Fireman's Hall Museum** are also historic/academic draws in the neighborhood—and the **Museum of Art and Wood** as well as numerous art galleries are nearby. Attractions like **Race Street Pier, Morgan's Pier, Cherry Street Pier,** and **Spruce Street Harbor Park** allow visitors to enjoy activities and chilling along the Delaware River.

# How to Spend 3 Days in Philadelphia

In a city with the wealth of museums, historical sites, parks, gardens, and more that you'll find in Philly, you risk seeing half of everything or all of nothing. With a day, you'll be hard-pressed to move beyond the city's primary historical sights, but three days is enough time to take in Philadelphia's cultural and historic highlights as well as spend some time exploring the appealing neighborhoods.

## Day 1: History

It's possible to get a good taste of what the city has to offer even if you only have a couple of days. You'll want to get the tour of the historic sights accomplished on Day 1.

There's no getting around the fact that colonial history is the primary reason most people visit Philadelphia, and most visitors will want to devote their first morning to exploring **Independence National Historical Park.** The two most popular sights are **Independence Hall** and the **Liberty Bell Center.** But don't neglect the **Independence Visitor Center,** where you must make a reservation (March through December) to tour Independence Hall; be sure to set aside 28 minutes from your schedule to see the film *Independence,* directed by John Huston, or the 20-minute *Choosing Sides.* There are usually lines to see the Liberty Bell, so do that while you wait for your tour time. If you have extra time, visit the Benjamin Franklin Museum on Franklin Court. Have lunch at nearby **Reading Terminal Market.** In the afternoon, you have a choice. You can keep up your historical pursuits, staying in Old Town to see more historic sights, including the **Carpenter's Hall,**

**Christ Church,** the **Betsy Ross House,** and **Elfreth's Alley,** or you can delve deeper into the Constitution at the **National Constitution Center** or the American Revolution at the aptly named **Museum of the American Revolution,** which have fascinating programs and interactive exhibits. At night, dinner and nightlife beckon in all the downtown neighborhoods.

## Day 2: Art and Museums

Philadelphia has more than enough museums to occupy a visitor for a full week, but it's worth spending one day to visit a couple that are particularly interesting. The **Philadelphia Museum of Art** on Benjamin Franklin Parkway, followed by lunch in the museum's lovely dining room, will be enjoyable to almost anyone; it's the city's widest-ranging art museum. But if your interest is impressionist, postimpressionist, and early modern American art, **the Barnes Foundation** may be a better destination (reservations required). In the afternoon you could visit **Eastern State Penitentiary Historic Site** for a tour of a former prison or the **Franklin Institute.** Another option is to explore one of Philadelphia's distinct neighborhoods. Stroll around **Rittenhouse Square** and stop in at the **Rosenbach Museum and Library,** which has a diverse collection ranging from the original manuscript of James Joyce's *Ulysses* to the works of beloved children's author Maurice Sendak. There's also Society Hill, Queen Village, and South Philadelphia for the **Mummer Museum** on 9th Street and the outdoor **Italian Market.** Set aside time to dine in one of the city's best restaurants or take in a concert.

# Day 3: Neighborhood Exploration

With more time, you can go deeper into your personal interests, whether they include art, shopping, history, the outdoors, or keeping your kids happy and occupied.

The best way to do that is to delve into more Philly neighborhoods. Check out Chinatown or Northern Liberties, or take a drive through Germantown, Mt. Airy, and Chestnut Hill (stopping at **Cliveden**). If the weather's nice, you can drive or bike to the northwestern tip of **Fairmount Park** and check out the **Wissahickon River**—a local favorite for all sorts of activities, from strolling to cycling. Afterward, head back into the city to check out the **Penn Museum of Archaeology and Anthropology** in University City and stroll down Locust Walk, the heart of University of Pennsylvania's leafy urban campus. In the evening, drive or take the SEPTA Market-Frankford line to Fishtown, where you can have dinner in one of the neighborhood's restaurants, and catch some live music afterwards.

# If You Only Have 1 Day in Philadelphia

If you only have one day to explore Philly, head to the **Independence National Historical Park Visitor Center** to sign up for a walking tour hosted by a National Park Service guide, or try a go-at-your-own-pace tour offered by **the Constitutional Audio Walking Tour** (⊕ *theconstitutional. com/app*). At the very least you'll want to see the **Liberty Bell, Independence Hall, Carpenter's Hall,** and **Franklin Court.** If you get started early, you can finish all that in about three or four hours. For lunch, visit **Reading Terminal Market,** where you can sample the cuisine Philadelphia is known for like cheesesteaks, soft pretzels, and Bassett's ice cream. If you're interested in art, you can visit **the Barnes Foundation** and its incredible collection of Renoirs, Cezannes, Matisses, and Picassos on Benjamin Franklin Parkway. Then walk nine blocks east on Arch Street to Old City; **Christ Church,** the **Betsy Ross House,** and **Elfreth's Alley** are all in close proximity. In the late afternoon, head back toward Independence Hall for a horse-drawn carriage ride and then have dinner in Old City.

# Best Tours

With a fine assortment of Colonial architecture, many museums, and some of the country's most significant historical artifacts and edifices, Philadelphia is perfect for a tour. In a relatively small area, the city offers history buffs, artisans, and architecture aficionados a wealth of fascinating material. The most-frequented tourist destination remains Old City, home to Independence Mall, which encompasses Independence Hall, the Liberty Bell, and the National Constitution Center, among other highlights. But there are many other historic and architectural tours to enjoy throughout the city. The mode of transportation largely dictates the type of tour, be it boat, bus, on foot, or horse and buggy, but you can explore everything from the cuisine of the city to the vast number of gorgeous giant art murals on the city's buildings.

## BICYCLE TOURS

**Indego.** Philly's bike-share program has docking stations scattered around the city. Electric bikes are available in selected spots. Day passes are available for $15. ⊠ *Philadelphia* ☎ *844/446–3346* ⊕ *www.rideindego.com.*

**Philly Bike Tour Co.** Tours range from the Classic City Tour with stops at the Rocky Steps, Liberty Bell, and Rittenhouse Park to the Murals & Public Art Tour to a history of brewing tour as well as private tours. All tours include a bicycle, helmet, and water. ⊠ *2015 Fairmount Ave., Philadelphia* ✛ *Near Eastern State Penitentiary and the Art Museum* ☎ *267/521–2150* ⊕ *www.phillybiketours.com* ⊒ *From $59.*

## BOAT TOURS

**Patriot Harbor Lines.** Between April and October, Patriot Harbor Lines offers cruises on both the Delaware and Schuylkill Rivers, including wine-centric events and a ride to Bartram's Garden, a National Historic Landmark in Philly's southwest.

⊠ *Philadelphia* ☎ *267/908–3876* ⊕ *www.phillybyboat.com.*

**Spirit of Philadelphia.** The *Spirit of Philadelphia* runs lunch and dinner cruises along the Delaware River. This three-deck ship leaves Penn's Landing for lunch, dinner, and a variety of specialty cruises. Dinner cruises include entertainment and music. ⊠ *Philadelphia* ☎ *800/459–8105* ⊕ *www.spiritcruises.com/philadelphia.*

## BUS AND TROLLEY TOURS

**Mural Arts Philadelphia.** For a different kind of Philly experience, these tours (some walking, some by trolley) visit some of the more than 2,000 public murals the city has to offer, including a new mural honoring the Cecil B. Moore Freedom Fighters, the mural depicting the History of the Philadelphia Fire Department, and two murals honoring John Coltrane. Self-guided tours are available on their website. ☎ *215/925–3633* ⊕ *www.muralarts.org.*

**Philadelphia Trolley Works.** Philadelphia Trolley Works offers narrated tours in buses designed to resemble Victorian-style open-air trolleys. Trolleys depart frequently from the corner of 5th and Market Streets; the $35 fare is an all-day pass, allowing unlimited stops. There are nearly 30 sights on a route covering the Historic Area, the Benjamin Franklin Parkway, the Avenue of the Arts, Fairmount Park, the Philadelphia Zoo, Eastern State Penitentiary, and Penn's Landing. ⊠ *Philadelphia* ☎ *215/389–8687* ⊕ *www.phillytour.com.*

**Philadelphia Trolley Works & 76 Carriage Company.** Started more than 40 years ago, 76 Carriage Company and its sister companies (Philadelphia Trolley Works, The Big Bus Company, and Connective Tours) offer a wide range of tour options including Hop On/Hop Off tours, seasonal tours (haunted and holiday lights), a Philly by Night tour, walking tours of Old City, and horse-drawn carriage tours. Numerous horse-drawn carriages wind their way through the narrow streets of the Historic Area. Tours last anywhere from 20 minutes to an hour and cost from $50 to $120 for up to four people. Carriages line up on 5th and Chestnut Streets near Independence Hall between 10:30 am and 3:30 pm and 6:30 pm and 10:30 pm Monday through Friday, and 10:30 am to 10:30 pm Saturday and Sunday. Carriages operate year-round, weather permitting. The Philly By Night Tour gives patrons a chance to see the city under the stars in the comfort of a double-decker open-top bus. ⊠ *Philadelphia* ☎ *215/923–8516 horse-drawn carriages, 215/389–8687 trolleys, Big Bus, and motor coaches* ⊕ *www.phillytour.com.*

## SEGWAY TOURS

**Philly by Segway.** Philly by Segway operates tours on motorized Segway scooters that travel throughout the city, allowing patrons to zip around the museum corridor, through historic Old City, and more. The tours, which run from two to three hours depending on destination, include hands-on Segway training. ⊠ *Philadelphia* ☎ *215/523–5827* ⊕ *phillybysegway.com* ✉ *From $55.*

## WALKING TOURS

**City Food Tours.** Tours include Flavors of Philly (yes that includes cheesesteaks and tomato pie), East Passyunk (a tour of one of the country's best foodie streets), Historic Happy Hour (history and food), and the Decadent Gourmet, which includes meet-and-greets with chefs and owners of multiple establishments, food tastings, and more. ⊠ *Philadelphia* ☎ *844/436–6336* ⊕ *www.cityfoodtours. com* ✉ *$49.*

**The Constitutional Walking Tour.** Founding Father fanatics should take the 75-minute Constitutional Walking Tour, which leads guests through Independence National Historical Park and stops at more than 20 historic sites, including the Liberty Bell and Independence Hall. ⊠ *Philadelphia* ⚓ *Tours meet in front of the National Constitution Center* ☎ *215/525–1776* ⊕ *www.theconstitutional.com* ✉ *$23.*

**Founding Footsteps.** Founding Footsteps offers highly rated tours of Independence Park led by informative and energetic guides. The Philly Phables tour has you literally retracing the footsteps of our Founding Fathers around Philadelphia; the BYOB tour aboard a trolley allows you to sip cold beer along the way. There's also a food and history tour with stops in Reading Terminal Market and the Italian Market, as well as the Bad Things Happen In Philly tour, which details some of the city's most disturbing crimes, and holiday light tours. ⊠ *Philadelphia* ☎ *609/795–1776* ⊕ *foundingfootsteps. com* ✉ *From $22.*

**Spirits of '76 Ghost Tour.** Mild scares can be found during the Spirits of '76 Ghost Tour (closed in the winter months), which begins at 4th and Chestnut Streets and guides its patrons through some of the ancient architecture of Old City, including famous film locations from spooky Philly-based films like *The Sixth Sense.* ⊠ *Philadelphia* ☎ *215/525–1776* ⊕ *www. spiritsof76.com* ✉ *$23; $41 combo with The Constitutional.*

# On the Calendar

## January

**Mummers Parade.** One of Philadelphia's most unique traditions, the annual New Year's Day celebration is a bacchanal of music, dance, and ridiculous costumes with roots in 17th-century European folk celebrations. The parade begins at City Hall and proceeds south down Broad Street. ⊕ *www.facebook.com/mummersparade*

## February

**Black History Month.** There are numerous events around the city celebrating Black History. ⊕ *www.visitphilly.com*

**Blue Cross RiverRink Winterfest.** Strap on your ice skates and glide around the seasonal pop-up that features a sprawling rink, a fire pit, warming cabins, and plenty of seasonal treats. ⊕ *delawareriverwaterfront.com/places/blue-cross-riverrink-winterfest*

## March

**Philadelphia Flower Show.** One of the city's most high-profile happenings, Philly's flower show is the world's oldest continuously running indoor floral exhibition. Attracting more than a quarter-million viewers, the show features rare and ornate displays, a judged competition, hands-on instruction, and live entertainment. ⊕ *phsonline.org*

**Philly Theatre Week.** Experience more than 100 events—including live performances, concerts, and panels—over 10 entertaining days. ⊕ *theatrephiladelphia.org*

## April

**Center City Jazz Festival.** Various performances are held throughout Center City. ⊕ *www.ccjazzfest.com*

**Cherry Blossom Festival.** The Japan Society of Greater Philadelphia organizes the city's take on the elaborate welcome-to-spring celebrations held in Japan and beyond, with events throughout the city and its suburbs. The occasion culminates with "Sakura Sunday," a vibrant celebration at the Horticulture Center of Fairmount Park. ⊕ *japanphilly.org*

**Penn Relays.** Established in 1895 by the University of Pennsylvania, the Penn Relays are among America's oldest athletic traditions, now an international affair that attracts teams from around the globe to race over a three-day period. Held at Penn's historic Franklin Field, it regularly draws six-figure crowds. ⊕ *pennrelays.com*

## May

**Jefferson Dad Vail Regatta.** More than 100 colleges and universities from the United States and Canada participate in North America's largest collegiate regatta. ⊕ *www.dadvail.org*

**Kensington Derby and Arts Festival.** People dress up in crazy costumes and ride bicycle-powered sculptures through various obstacles. Also features plenty of food, drink, and music. ⊕ *www.kensingtonkineticarts.org*

**Philadelphia Chinese Lantern Festival.** Held through mid-July, the festival features lantern displays, folk artists, and authentic Chinese performances. ⊕ *historicphiladelphia.org*

**Rittenhouse Row Spring Festival.** This annual festival, which takes place along the main vein of Walnut Street, high-lights all the neighborhood's offerings and includes food, drink, live music, and entertainment. It's a great way to roam the neighborhood. ⊕ *www.rittenhouse-row.org*

**Spruce Street Harbor Park.** One of the riverside attractions, from Memorial Day to Labor Day, includes a sampling of food trucks from established Philly restaurants, beer, entertainment, games, and hammocks for chilling along the Delaware River. ⊕ *www.delawareriver-waterfront.com*

## June

**Philly Beer Week.** Conceived as a way to bring together regional craft breweries and their out-of-town cohorts, this 10-day festival in early June has blossomed into one of the nation's largest and most ambitious brew-centric events. The schedule comprises hundreds of events (tastings, dinners, rare releases, meet the brewer, etc.) hosted at an equally diz-zying array of area bars, restaurants, and venues. ⊕ *www.phillylovesbeer.com*

**Philly Pride.** A community march through Center City culminates in a Pride festival in the Gayborhood. ⊕ *www.phlpridecol-lective.org*

**Roots Picnic.** Even though they're now the big-time house band for *The Tonight Show Starring Jimmy Fallon,* Philly's own The Roots still show a heavy amount of love for their hometown. Their annual music festival has attracted A-List talents like Erykah Badu, Snoop Dogg, Nas, and Vampire Weekend. The Roots, of course, make their way onstage, too. ⊕ *www.therootspicnic.com*

## July

**Wawa Welcome America Festival.** Wawa, the region's best-loved convenience store chain, sponsors this Independence Day celebration with a week of patriotic happenings, from a massive block party on Benjamin Franklin Parkway to free museum access and historical tours. It all culminates with a July 4th concert and fireworks extravaganza held on the parkway. ⊕ *welcomeamerica.com*

## August

**BlackStar Film Festival.** A weeklong festival that showcases new films by Black and Brown filmmakers. ⊕ *www.blackstarfest.org*

**Philadelphia Folk Festival.** Located in Salfordville, about an hour west of Phil-adelphia, this family-friendly festival has been entertaining folk fans for 60 years. Expect food, drink, hands-on educational activities, and entertainment, all with a backdrop of beautiful, bucolic country-side. ⊕ *pfs.org*

**2nd Street Festival.** An art, music, crafts, and food festival celebrating the Northern Liberties neighborhood. ⊕ *www.2ndst-festival.org*

## September

**Made in America.** Held over the long Labor Day weekend, the unofficial end of summer, Made in America is a multiday musical festival founded by Jay-Z. The event, which takes over the Benjamin Franklin Parkway, typically features world-renowned acts; past installments have seen Beyoncé, Pearl Jam, Drake, Calvin Harris, and Run-DMC grace the stage. ⊕ *madeinamericafest.com*

# On the Calendar

**Philadelphia Fringe Festival.** Taking place every September, the "Philly Fringe" is a celebration of cutting-edge and avant-garde theater and performance art. Inspired by Edinburgh's Fringe Festival, the Philly Fringe—run by the year-round FringeArts—has grown into a formidable cultural and artistic force, attracting talent from around the world to stage shows throughout the city over a four-week stretch. ⊕ *fringearts.com*

## October

**Head of the Schuylkill Regatta.** One of the world's largest rowing competitions takes place annually in Fairmount Park, attracting thousands of athletes and spectators. ⊕ *hosr.org*

**Philadelphia International Film Festival.** Organized by the Philadelphia Film Society, the city's annual film fest screens titles both high-profile and under-the-radar every fall. First established in 1991, the fest brings together a diverse slate of entries, with categories such as "World Narratives" (for global cinema), "Documentary," "Graveyard Shift" (horror and sci-fi), and "Filmadelphia" (films shot locally, or with a local connection). Screenings are held at theaters throughout the city. ⊕ *filmadelphia.org*

## November

**Franklin Square Holiday Festival.** Held through December, this free festival features the Electrical Spectacle light show with more than 75,000 lights. There's food and shopping, too. ⊕ *historicphiladelphia.org*

**Made in Philadelphia Holiday Market.** Situated in Dilworth Park, across the street from the Christmas Village at LOVE Park, more than 40 vendors showcase crafts, confections, and other gifts, all locally made. ⊕ *madeinphila.com/holiday-market*

**Philadelphia Marathon Weekend.** Started in 1994, this is one of the country's top marathons. ⊕ *philadelphiamarathon.com*

**The Rothman Institute Ice Rink.** This picturesque ice rink, sponsored by the local medical orthopedic center, is centrally located in Dilworth Park, on the northwest side of City Hall. A seasonal attraction running from November to February, it offers affordable admission as well as skate rentals; in the spring and summer it turns into a roller rink. ⊕ *centercityphila.org*

## December

**Christmas Village at LOVE Park.** Iconic LOVE Park is transformed into a festive outdoor market inspired by historic German Christmas markets and features a beer garden. Vendors sell ornaments, gifts, and seasonal treats like gingerbread and mulled wine. ⊕ *philachristmas.com*

**Macy's Christmas Light Show.** Throughout the month of December, Macy's Center City hosts a nostalgic show in which more than 100,000 LED lights take the shape of merry holiday motifs, accompanied by a holiday concert featuring the Wanamaker historic grand organ. Hokey but free and strangely delightful. ⊕ *visitmacysusa.com/philadelphia*

Chapter 3

# OLD CITY AND HISTORIC DOWNTOWN

Updated by
Marla Cimini

| ◉ Sights | 🍴 Restaurants | 🛏 Hotels | 🛍 Shopping | 🍸 Nightlife |
|----------|---------------|----------|-------------|-------------|
| ★★★★★ | ★★★★☆ | ★★★★☆ | ★★★★★ | ★★★★☆ |

# VISITING INDEPENDENCE NATIONAL HISTORICAL PARK

Independence Hall is one of the city's most popular sights.

Independence National Historical Park (INHP) welcomes more than 4 million visitors every year. Several of the country's most important historic sites are here, including the Liberty Bell, Congress Hall, the National Constitution Center, and Independence Hall (a UNESCO World Heritage site).

Your first stop should be the Independence Visitor Center, where you can buy tickets for tours and pick up maps and brochures. From here you can easily explore the park on your own; in each building, a park ranger can answer all your questions. In summer more than a dozen storytellers wander through the park, perching on benches to tell tales of the times. Special paid guided tours are also available through the Independence Visitor Center. ■TIP→ **Visitors are required to join a ranger-led tour to see Independence Hall, Congress Hall, Dolley Todd House, and the Bishop White House, as well as the Germantown White House in Germantown. Tours of Independence Hall last 30 to 45 minutes.**

## WHAT'S HERE

There are more than 20 sites in Independence National Historical Park (INHP), including Carpenters' Hall, Christ Church, Congress Hall, First Bank of the United States, Franklin Court, the National Constitution Center, and the President's House Site. Some of the lesser known sites include Declaration House, Dolley Todd House, Bishop White House, and the Merchants' Exchange Building. ■TIP→ The Germantown White House, in Germantown, is also part of the park.

## HOURS AND FEES

The Independence Visitor Center, Independence Hall, and the Liberty Bell Pavilion are open daily year-round 9–5 (except Christmas Day). In summer the closing times are often later. Other park buildings are also open daily, although their hours may vary from season to season. Call ☎ 800/537-7676, the 24-hour hotline, for hours plus a schedule of park programs; or visit ⊕ phlvisitorcenter.com.

Independence Hall timed entry tickets are free but required between March and December, and can be picked up for that day at the visitor center starting at 9 am. It's highly encouraged to get reserved tickets up to a year in advance (⊕ recreation.gov ☎ 877/444-6777); the cost is $1 each for the processing fee.

Most other attractions run by the park are free, but there are some exceptions, including the Benjamin Franklin Museum (🎟 $5) and the National Constitution Center (🎟 $14.50). To save, consider the NCC's discounted ticket packages bundled with sites outside the INHP's purview, such as the Museum of the American Revolution and the African American Museum.

The Commodore John Barry statue is found behind Independence Hall.

The President's House is located next to the Liberty Bell.

## WHEN TO GO

Visit America's birthplace on America's birthday for the annual Wawa Welcome America Festival (starting late June through July 4). There are more than 50 free events, including parades (the Mummers and an illuminated boat procession), outdoor concerts, historical reenactments, and fireworks. The rest of the summer is filled with plays, musicals, and parades.

If you want to avoid the crowds, plan your visit in the summer or winter, as much of the spring and fall sees heavy visitation from school field trips. Day of, prioritize the Liberty Bell Center and Independence Hall as your earliest stops for the most manageable crowds.

## HOW LONG TO STAY

Plan for a full day here. An early start lets you reserve timed tickets for a tour of the Todd and Bishop White houses and adjust your schedule to catch some of the daily special events at the visitor center. Allow about 40 minutes for the Independence Hall tour and an hour each at Franklin Court and the Todd and Bishop White houses. Plan for 30 minutes at Declaration House and the Visitor Center. You can view the Liberty Bell 24 hours a day, as it's enclosed in glass. Dine in the area before wrapping up for the day.

# NEIGHBORHOOD SNAPSHOT

## TOP EXPERIENCES

■ **African American Museum:** One of the nation's first museums created to commemorate black history, there's a deep focus here on the lives of African Americans in the nation's first century.

■ **Art, Boutiques, Shopping:** Old City is packed with history, but it also happens to be populated by an appealing concentration of art galleries and indie boutiques, including clothing and gift shops.

■ **Elfreth's Alley:** Stroll down this charming, cobblestone lane—the country's oldest continuously occupied street—and imagine yourself in Colonial times.

■ **Independence Hall:** The United States literally got its start in this modest redbrick building, where the Declaration of Independence was signed and the U.S. Constitution was adopted.

■ **Liberty Bell:** Yes, the bell really does have a giant crack, but more importantly, it still resonates as a symbol of the right of all Americans to be free.

■ **Museum of the American Revolution:** This relative newcomer to the Old City circuit offers a refreshing new perspective on the American Revolution.

## GETTING HERE

It's an easy walk from Center City—check out pedestrian-friendly City Hall along the way—but SEPTA's Blue Line is one way to get here fast. From Center City, ride the train east from 15th Street/City Hall to the 5th Street or 2nd Street stops. Rides are $2.50 each (have exact change if paying in cash). A number of SEPTA's bus routes, including the 9, 17, 21, and 42, will get you down here easily, too.

## PLANNING YOUR TIME

Old City is busy every day in high season; school months see plenty of student groups on weekdays in addition to the usual tourists. Visit iconic sites like Independence Hall and the Liberty Bell as early as possible to beat the rush, then break for lunch before more leisurely museum visits.

## QUICK BITES

■ **Cafe Ole.** This charming Euro-like café does a wide range of sandwiches, salads, and breakfast dishes, but it's best known for its *shakshuka*, the soulful tomato-and-egg stew made here in the Tunisian style. ✉ *147 N. 3rd St., Old City* ⊕ *www.facebook.com/ phillycafeole*

■ **Campo's.** Feeding Philly since the 1940s, Campo's is a respected name in the city's sandwich and cheesesteak game. ✉ *214 Market St., Old City* ⊕ *www.camposdeli.com*

■ **Sonny's Famous Steaks.** It doesn't enjoy the same notoriety of other shops, but connoisseurs know the friendly Sonny's slings a mean version of the iconic sandwich. ✉ *228 Market St., Old City* ⊕ *www.sonny-scheesesteaks.com*

## GOOD TO KNOW

■ If you've put on your walking shoes and are good at negotiating the cobblestones, you can wander through this area in about two hours. But the city's atmospheric historic district warrants a slower pace, and leave ample time for the many sights of interest. While there are plenty of parking lots and multilevel garages (with very few metered street spots), it's a busy neighborhood that's best explored on foot.

In Colonial days, wealthy folks in Society Hill derisively whispered of those who lived "north of Market," referencing the neighborhood between Front and 5th Streets and Chestnut and Vine Streets. This was traditionally a commercial district for industry and wholesale distributors, filled with wharves, warehouses, and taverns, plus the modest homes of craftsmen and artisans. Old City, so dubbed in 1972 to distinguish it from Independence National Historical Park, deserves its name: it's one of the nation's most historic neighborhoods, and millions visit from around the world each year to immerse themselves in the birthplace of modern democracy.

Despite its touristic heartbeat, Old City is still very much an artistic and residential neighborhood, with personality unto itself. It shares stylistic similarities with Manhattan's SoHo in its architectural mix. Many cast-iron building facades and ghost signs remain, while rugged old warehouses with telltale names like the Sugar Refinery and the Hoopskirt Factory now house modern loft space. There are numerous galleries, small theaters, boutiques, cafés, and restaurants. On the First Friday of each month, the Old City Arts Association coordinates a sprawling, ever-changing neighborhood-wide event that sees businesses extend hours, and host show openings, receptions, and special pop-ups. The First Friday sidewalk scene is equally lively with a creative class of street artists, vendors, and performers.

## ◉ Sights

Any visit to Old City, whether you have one day or several, should begin in the area that comprises Independence National Historical Park. Philadelphia was the birthplace of the United States, the home of the country's first government, and nowhere is the spirit of those early days—the audacious beginnings of a brand-new nation—more palpable than along these cobbled streets.

In the late 1940s, before civic-minded citizens banded together to save the area, the neighborhood was crowded with factories and run-down warehouses. The city, state, and federal governments finally took an interest. Some buildings were restored, while others were reconstructed on their original sites; several attractions were built for the 1976 Bicentennial celebration. In recent years, development has again spread across the area, with notable additions like an expanded Visitor Center, a more attractive home for the Liberty Bell, and museums examining the Constitution, the Revolution, African Americans, and Jewish Americans.

The neighborhood continues to grow, and it remains a vibrant destination for art and nightlife lovers. Within the National Park Service's 52-acre footprint and well beyond it, mindful development and renewal have ensured Old City will preserve its heritage and charm.

### African American Museum in Philadelphia

**HISTORY MUSEUM | FAMILY** | Opened in the Bicentennial year of 1976, this is the first museum of its kind funded and built by a city. The centerpiece is "Audacious Freedom: African Americans in Philadelphia 1776–1876," an interactive and immersive exhibit that uses technology to tell the stories of pioneers in the freedom movement. The list includes Frances Ellen Watkins Harper, a suffragist and conductor on the Underground Railroad; Thomas Morris Chester, the first black lawyer to argue before the U.S. Supreme Court; and Elizabeth Taylor Greenfield, a renowned singer who performed for Queen Victoria. Visiting and rotating exhibitions dive deep into the artistic, cultural, and political contributions of African Americans. The museum's gift shop stocks one of the city's widest selections of books on black culture, history, fiction, poetry, and drama, along with textiles, sculpture, jewelry, prints, and tiles. ✉ *701 Arch St., Old City* ☎ *215/574–0380* ⊕ *www.aampmuseum.org* 💲 *$14* ⊙ *Closed Mon.–Wed.*

### Arch Street Meeting House

**HISTORY MUSEUM** | This site has been home to a Quaker gathering place since 1682. The current simple-lined building, constructed in 1804 for the Philadelphia Yearly Meeting of the Society of Friends, is still used for that purpose, as well as for weekly services. Among the most influential members in the 19th century was Lucretia Mott (1793–1880), a leader in the women's suffrage, antiwar, and antislavery movements. A small museum in the building presents a series of dioramas and a slide show depicting the life and accomplishments of William Penn (1644–1718), who gave this land to the Society of Friends. Tours take place during the day April through October, and by appointment only November through March. ✉ *320 Arch St., at 4th St., Old City* ☎ *215/627–2667* ⊕ *www.historicasmh.org* 💲 *$5 suggested donation* ⊙ *Closed Mon.–Wed. and mid-Dec.–Feb.*

### Benjamin Franklin Bridge

**BRIDGE** | When the bridge opened in 1926, its 1,750-foot main span made it the longest suspension bridge in the world. Paul Cret, architect of the Rodin Museum, was the designer. The bridge, which crosses the Delaware River, is mainly used by cars and the PATCO commuter train which has several stops in Center City and Southern Jersey. The bridge is most impressive when it's lit at night. Start the 1¾-mile walk (one way) from either the Philadelphia side, two blocks north of the U.S. Mint, or the Camden, New Jersey, side, where there are metered parking lots. Enjoy stunning city views along the way, but know it's best to walk across on mornings or cooler days, as there's no shade. ✉ *5th* *and Vine Sts., Old City ☎ 215/218–3750 ⊕ www.drpa.org ⌁ Free ☞ Weather and construction conditions may restrict access to the walkway. For updates call 856/968–2255 or 215/218–3750 Ext. 2255 (weekdays 9–5). All other times call DRPA Police Radio at ☎ 856/968–3301 or ☎ 215/218–3750 Ext. 3301.*

### The Benjamin Franklin Museum
(*Franklin Court*)

**HISTORIC HOME** | **FAMILY** | This museum built on the site that was Benjamin Franklin's first permanent home in Philadelphia was thoroughly renovated in 2013, reopening as the Benjamin Franklin Museum. The exhibits combine the latest touch-screen displays and computer-generated animation with a chess set, eyeglasses, and other items actually used by the Renaissance man. Franklin's multifaceted roles as scientist, inventor, philosopher, writer, politician, and businessman are represented in various rooms via interactive displays. Franklin, publisher of *Poor Richard's Almanac,* helped draft the Declaration of Independence and negotiate peace with Great Britain. He also helped found Pennsylvania Hospital, the University of Pennsylvania, the Philadelphia Contributionship, and the American Philosophical Society. In the courtyard adjacent to the museum, architect Robert Venturi erected a steel skeleton of Franklin's former home. You can peek through "windows" into cutaways to see wall foundations, outdoor privies, and other original elements uncovered during excavation. At the Market Street side are several houses, now exhibition halls, that Franklin rented in addition to his main home. Here, too, you can find a restoration of a Colonial-era print shop and an operational post office. Don't forget to get a letter hand-stamped with a "b. free franklin" cancellation. ⊠ *314–322 Market St., or enter from Chestnut St. walkway, Old City* ☎ *267/514–1522* ⊕ *www.nps. gov* ⌁ *$5.*

### Betsy Ross House

**HISTORIC HOME** | **FAMILY** | It's easy to find this little brick house with the gabled roof: just look for the 13-star flag displayed from its second-floor window. Whether Betsy Ross, also known as Elizabeth Griscom Ross Ashbourn Claypoole (1752–1836), actually lived here and whether she really made the first Stars and Stripes is debatable. Nonetheless, the house, built around 1740, is a splendid example of a Colonial Philadelphia home. The eight-room house overflows with artifacts such as a family Bible and Ross's chest of drawers and reading glasses. You may have to wait in line, as this is one of the city's most popular attractions. The house, with its winding narrow stairs, is not accessible to people with disabilities. Alongside the house is a courtyard with a fountain, as well as the graves of Ross and her third husband, John Claypoole. Visitors can meet Betsy in her upholstery shop (the only working Colonial upholstery shop in the country) and enjoy interactive historical programming. ⊠ *239 Arch St., Old City* ☎ *215/629–5801* ⊕ *www. historicphiladelphia.org/betsy-ross-house/ what-to-see* ⌁ *$8.*

### Bishop White House

**HISTORIC HOME** | Built in 1787, this restored upper-class house embodies Colonial and Federal elegance. It was the home of Bishop William White (1748–1836), rector of Christ Church, first Episcopal bishop of Pennsylvania and spiritual leader of Philadelphia for 60 years. White, a founder of the Episcopal Church after the break with England, was chaplain to the Continental Congress and entertained many of the country's first families, including Washington and Franklin. The second-floor study still contains much of the bishop's own library. The building is currently not open to the public. ⊠ *309 Walnut St., Old City* ☎ *215/965–2305* ⊕ *www.nps. gov/inde/learn/historyculture/places-bishopwhitehouse.htm* ⌁ *Free.*

# Old City and
# Historic Downtown

**KEY**

- 1 Sights
- 1 Restaurants
- 1 Quick Bites
- 1 Hotels

③ Benjamin Franklin Bridge

Delaware River

0       500 M

0       1,000 ft

## Carpenters' Hall

HISTORIC SIGHT | This handsome, patterned red-and-black brick building dating from 1770 was the headquarters of the Carpenters' Company, a guild founded to support carpenters, who were both builders and architects in this era, and to aid their families. In September 1774 the First Continental Congress convened here and addressed a declaration of rights and grievances to King George III. 2024 marks the 300th anniversary of The Carpenters' Company and the 250th anniversary of the First Continental Congress. The Carpenters' Company still owns and operates the building. Today re-creations of Colonial settings include original Windsor chairs and candle sconces and displays of 18th-century carpentry tools. ⊠ *320 Chestnut St., Old City* ☎ *215/925–0167* ⊕ *www.carpentershall.org* ✉ *Free; donations accepted* ☉ *Closed Mon. Mar.–Dec.; closed Mon. and Tues. in Jan. and Feb.*

## Christ Church

CHURCH | The Anglicans of the Church of England built a wooden church on this site in 1697. When they outgrew it, they erected a new church, the most sumptuous in the colonies, probably designed by Dr. John Kearsley and modeled on the work of famed English architect Sir Christopher Wren. The symmetrical, classical facade with arched windows, completed in 1754, is a fine example of Georgian architecture; the church is one of the city's treasures. The congregation included 15 signers of the Declaration of Independence. The bells and the soaring 196-foot steeple, the tallest in the colonies, were financed by lotteries run by Benjamin Franklin. Brass plaques mark the pews of George and Martha Washington, John and Abigail Adams, Betsy Ross, and others. Two blocks west of the church is Christ Church Burial Ground. Guided tours are available throughout the day. ⊠ *20 N. American St., 2nd St. north of Market St., Old City* ☎ *215/922–1695* ⊕ *www.christchurchphila.org* ✉ *$5 for Christ Church admission and guided tour, $8 for Burial Ground admission and guided tour* Ⓜ *2nd and Market Sts.*

## Christ Church Burial Ground

CEMETERY | Weathered gravestones fill the resting place of five signers of the Declaration of Independence and other Colonial patriots. The best known is Benjamin Franklin; he lies alongside his wife, Deborah, and their son, Francis, who died at age four. According to local legend, throwing a penny onto Franklin's grave will bring you good luck. The burial ground is open to the public—except in January and February—for regular visits. ⊠ *5th and Arch Sts., Old City* ☎ *215/922–1695* ⊕ *www.christchurchphila.org* ✉ *$3, $8 with guided tour* ☉ *Closed Jan. and Feb.*

## Congress Hall

HISTORIC SIGHT | Congress Hall was the meeting place of the U.S. Congress from 1790 to 1800, one of the most important decades in our nation's history. Here the Bill of Rights was added to the Constitution; Alexander Hamilton's proposals for a mint and a national bank were enacted; and Vermont, Kentucky, and Tennessee became the first new states after the original colonies. On the first floor you can find the House of Representatives, where President John Adams was inaugurated in 1797. On the second floor is the Senate chamber, where in 1793 George Washington was inaugurated for his second term. Both chambers have been authentically restored. ⊠ *520 Chestnut St., at 6th St., Old City* ☎ *215/965–2305* ⊕ *www.nps.gov/inde* ✉ *Free* ☞ *Admission is on a first-come, first-served basis.*

## Curtis Center

PUBLIC ART | The lobby of the Curtis Publishing Company building has a great treasure: a 15-by-50-foot glass mosaic mural, *The Dream Garden,* based on a Maxfield Parrish painting. It was executed by the Louis C. Tiffany Studios in 1916. The work's 260 colors and 100,000 pieces of opalescent hand-fired glass laced with gold leaf make it perhaps the finest Tiffany mural in the world. The beautiful mural was also designated a "historic object" by the Philadelphia Historical Commission after its owner, the estate of a local art patron, put it up for sale for $9 million in 1998; the designation, the first in the city's history, stopped the sale and the mural remains in public view, under the auspices of the Pennsylvania Academy of the Fine Arts. ⊠ 601–45 Walnut St., at 6th St., Old City ☎ 215/627–7280 ⌨ Free ☞ The mural is open to the public whenever the building is open.

### Declaration House

**HISTORIC SIGHT** | Thomas Jefferson and his enslaved servant Robert Hemings lived and worked in Philadelphia in the summer of 1776. Jefferson rented rooms on the second floor of the home of bricklayer Jacob Graff, where he drafted the Declaration of Independence; Hemings likely lived in the attic. The home was reconstructed for the Bicentennial celebration; the bedroom and parlor in which Jefferson lived that summer were re-created with period furnishings. The first floor has a Jefferson exhibition. The display on the Declaration of Independence shows some of the changes Jefferson made while writing it. You can see Jefferson's original version—which would have abolished slavery had the passage not been stricken by the committee that included Benjamin Franklin and John Adams. ⊠ 701 Market St., at 7th St., Old City ☎ 215/965–2305 ⊕ www.nps.gov/inde ⌨ Free ☉ Call for hrs.

### Dolley Todd House

**HISTORIC HOME** | Built in 1775 by John Dilworth, Todd House has been restored to its 1790s appearance, when its best-known resident, Dolley Payne Todd (1768–1849), lived here. She lost her husband, the Quaker lawyer John Todd, to yellow fever in 1793. The widow later married James Madison, our fourth president. Her time as a hostess in the White House was quite a contrast to her years in this simple home. There's an 18th-century garden next to Todd House. ■ **TIP➜ Open by tour only; free tickets available at the Independence Visitor Center in advance.** ⊠ 400 Walnut St., at 4th St., Historic Area ☎ 215/965–2305 ⊕ www.nps.gov/inde/learn/historyculture/places-dolleytoddhouse.htm ⌨ Free ☞ Tickets are required for tours and available on a first-come, first-served basis at the Independence Visitor Center; limit 10 adults per tour.

### ★ Elfreth's Alley

**HISTORIC SIGHT** | This alley is the oldest continuously occupied residential street in America, dating back to 1702. Much of Colonial Philadelphia resembled this area, with its cobblestone streets and narrow two- or three-story brick houses. These were modest row homes rented by craftsmen, such as cabinetmakers, silversmiths, pewterers, and those who made their living in the shipping industry. The earliest houses have pent eaves; taller houses, built after the Revolution, show the influence of the Federal style. The Elfreth's Alley Museum includes two homes that have been restored by the Elfreth's Alley Association: No. 124, home of a Windsor chair maker, and No. 126, a Colonial dressmaker's home, with authentic furnishings and a Colonial kitchen. In early June residents celebrate Fete Day, when some of the 30 homes are open to the public for tours hosted by guides in Colonial garb. In December, residents again welcome visitors for "Deck the Alley," a holiday-themed celebration. Both of these special events require advance tickets. You can stop at the museum and purchase an audio tour or simply stroll down the street anytime. ⊠ Front and 2nd Sts. between Arch and Race Sts., 124–126 Elfreth's Alley, Old City ☎ 215/627–8680 ⊕ www.elfreth-salley.org ⌨ $3 for self-guided Museum House tour, $8 for guided tour.

### Fireman's Hall Museum

**HISTORY MUSEUM** | **FAMILY** | Housed in an authentic 1876 firehouse, this museum traces the history of firefighting, from the volunteer company founded in Philadelphia by Benjamin Franklin in 1736 to the professional departments of the 20th century. The collection includes early hand- and horse-drawn fire engines, such as a 1796 hand pumper, an 1857 steamer, and a 1907 three-horse Metropolitan steamer; fire marks (18th-century building signs marking them as insured for fire); uniforms; other memorabilia; and a 9/11 memorial. There is also a gift shop on-site and online. ⊠ *147 N. 2nd St., Old City* ☎ *215/923–1438* ⊕ *www.firemanshall.org* ✆ *Free; donations requested* ⊘ *Closed Sun. and Mon.*

### First Bank of the United States

**GOVERNMENT BUILDING** | A fine example of Federal architecture, the oldest bank building in the country was the headquarters of the government's bank from 1797 to 1811. Designed by Samuel Blodget Jr., it was an imposing structure in its day, exemplifying strength, dignity, and security. It's closed to the public; head to the right to find a wrought-iron gateway topped by an eagle. Pass through it into the courtyard, and you magically step into Colonial America. Before you do so, check out the bank's pediment. Executed in 1797 by Clodius F. Legrand and Sons, its cornucopia, oak branch, and American eagle are carved from mahogany—a late-18th-century masterpiece that has withstood weather better than the bank's marble pillars. ⊠ *120 S. 3rd St., Old City.*

### Franklin Square

**CITY PARK** | **FAMILY** | One of five squares William Penn placed in his original design, this park is now a family-friendly destination. In addition to the water-dancing fountain, there's a modern playground and carousel; a food stand with burgers, fries, and shakes; and an 18-hole miniature golf course boasting scale models of Independence Hall, the Philadelphia Museum of Art, Ben Franklin Bridge, and other local landmarks. The park also plays host to numerous events throughout the year including the Philadelphia Chinese Lantern Festival and Winter in Franklin Park. ⊠ *200 N. 6th St., at Race St., Old City* ☎ *215/629–4026* ⊕ *www.historicphiladelphia.org* ✆ *Park free; attraction prices vary.*

### Free Quaker Meeting House

**HISTORIC SIGHT** | This was the house of worship for the Free "Fighting" Quakers, a group that broke away from the Society of Friends to support the cause against the British during the Revolutionary War. The building was designed in 1783 by Samuel Wetherill, one of the original leaders of the group, after they were disowned by their pacifist flock. Among the 100 members were Betsy Ross and Timothy Matlack, colonel in Washington's Army and assistant secretary of the Continental Congress. After the Free Quaker group dissolved, the building was used as a school, library, and warehouse. The meetinghouse, built in the Quaker plain style with a brick front and gable roof, has been carefully restored. ∎ **TIP→ No tickets are required, but call the Independence National Historical Park to check on availability.** ⊠ *500 Arch St., at 5th St., Old City* ☎ *215/965–2305* ⊕ *www.nps.gov/inde/learn/historyculture/places-freequaker.htm* ✆ *Free* ⊘ *Call for schedule.*

### ★ Independence Hall

**HISTORIC SIGHT** | The birthplace of the United States, this redbrick building with its clock tower and steeple is one of the nation's greatest icons. It was constructed in 1732–56 as the Pennsylvania State House. What happened here between 1775 and 1787 changed the course of American history—and the name of the building to Independence Hall. The delegates to the Second Continental Congress met in the Assembly Room in May 1776, united in anger over British troops firing on citizens in Concord, Massachusetts. In this same room, George

Home to the annual Philadelphia Chinese Lantern Festival, family-friendly Franklin Square also has a carousel and an 18-hole Philly-inspired mini-golf course.

Washington was appointed commander in chief of the Continental Army, Thomas Jefferson's eloquent Declaration of Independence was signed, and later the Constitution of the United States was adopted. Here the first foreign minister to visit the United States was welcomed; the news of Cornwallis's defeat was announced, signaling the end of the Revolutionary War; and, later, John Adams and Abraham Lincoln lay in state. The memories this building holds linger in the collection of polished muskets, the silver inkstand used by delegates to sign the Declaration of Independence, and the "Rising Sun" chair in which George Washington sat. (After the Constitution was adopted, Benjamin Franklin said about the carving on the chair: "I have the happiness to know that it is a rising and not a setting sun.")

In the **East Wing**—attached to Independence Hall by a short colonnade—you can embark on free tours that start every 15 to 20 minutes and last 35 minutes. Admission is first-come, first-served; pick up free, timed tickets from the visitor center to avoid waiting in line. The **West Wing** of Independence Hall contains an exhibit of our nation's founding documents: the final draft of the Constitution, a working copy of the Articles of Confederation, and the first printing of the Declaration of Independence.

In front of Independence Hall, next to the statue of George Washington, note the plaques marking the spots where Abraham Lincoln stood on February 22, 1861, and where John F. Kennedy delivered an address on July 4, 1962. With Independence Hall in front of you and the Liberty Bell behind you, this is a place to stand for a moment and soak up a sense of history. From March through December and on major holidays, free, timed tickets from the Independence Visitor Center are required for entry. Tickets also can be reserved online. ⊠ *520 Chestnut St., between 5th and 6th Sts., Old City* ☎ *215/965–2305, 877/444–6777 advance tickets* ⊕ *www.nps.gov/inde* ⊠ *Free.*

# Philadelphia's Place in American History

William Penn founded the city in 1682, and chose to name it Philadelphia—Greek for "brotherly love"—after an ancient Syrian city, site of one of the earliest and most venerated Christian churches. Penn's Quakers settled on a tract of land he described as his "greene countrie towne." After the Quakers, the next waves of immigrants to arrive were Anglicans and Presbyterians (who had a running conflict with the "stiff Quakers" and their distaste for music and dancing). The new residents forged traditions that remain strong in parts of Philadelphia today: united families, comfortable houses, handsome furniture, and good education. From these early years came the attitude Mark Twain summed up as: "In Boston, they ask: 'What does he know?' In New York, 'How much does he make?' In Philadelphia, 'Who were his parents?'"

The city became the queen of the English-speaking New World from the late 1600s to the early 1800s. In the latter half of the 1700s Philadelphia was the largest city in the colonies, a great and glorious place. So when the delegates from the colonies wanted to meet in a centrally located, thriving city, they chose Philadelphia. They convened the First Continental Congress in 1774 at Carpenters' Hall. It is here that the Declaration of Independence was written and adopted, the Constitution was framed, the capital of the United States was established, the Liberty Bell was rung, the nation's flag was sewn by Betsy Ross (though scholars debate this), and George Washington served most of his presidency.

## Independence Square

**PLAZA/SQUARE** | Independence Square is located within the larger Independence Park. On July 8, 1776, the Declaration of Independence was first read in public here. You can imagine the impact the reading had on the colonists. There are several buildings you can visit within this square, including Independence Hall, Congress Hall, Old City Hall, and the Museum of the American Philosophical Society in Philosophical Hall. ⊠ *Bounded by Walnut and Chestnut Sts. and 5th and 6th Sts., Old City* ⊕ *www.nps.gov/ inde* ⊠ *Free* ☞ *Visitors may have to pass through a security checkpoint at 5th and Chestnut Sts.*

## ★ Independence Visitor Center

**VISITOR CENTER** | This is the city's official visitor center as well as the gateway to Independence National Historical Park. Here, you'll find a fully staffed concierge-and-trip-planning desk, which provides information on the Park, the Philadelphia Museum of Art, the Philadelphia Zoo, and other attractions, as well as a reservation and ticketing service. Before you set off on a walking tour, acquaint yourself with Colonial American history by watching the Founding Fathers come to life in the 30-minute movie *Independence*, one of the films shown in the center's two theaters. On the mezzanine level upstairs, there's Liberty Terrace, a great outdoor platform with views of Independence Mall. (In warmer months, you can dine at the Terrace on Tap.) There's also a café operated by the Hershey's brand, accessible restrooms, and an excellent gift shop, where you can stock up on books, videos, brochures, prints, wall hangings, and souvenirs of historic figures and events. An atrium connects the visitor center to a renovated underground parking area. ⊠ *1 N.*

*Independence Mall W, 6th and Market Sts., Old City* ☎ *215/965–7676, 800/537–7676* ⊕ *www.independencevisitorcenter.com* ☞ *Hrs may be extended during holidays and peak seasons.*

## ★ Liberty Bell Center

**PUBLIC ART** | The bell fulfilled the words of its inscription when it rang to "proclaim liberty throughout all the land unto all the inhabitants thereof," beckoning Philadelphians to the State House yard to hear the first reading of the Declaration of Independence. Ordered in 1751 and originally cast in England, it cracked during testing and was recast in Philadelphia by Pass and Stow two years later. To keep it from falling into British hands during the Revolution—they would have melted it down for ammunition—it was spirited away by horse and wagon to Allentown, 60 miles to the north. The Liberty Bell is the subject of much legend; one story says it cracked when tolled at the funeral of Chief Justice John Marshall in 1835. Actually, the bell cracked slowly over a period of years. It was repaired but cracked again in 1846 and was then forever silenced. It was called the State House Bell until the 1830s, when a group of abolitionists adopted it as a symbol of freedom and renamed it the Liberty Bell.

After more than 200 years inside Independence Hall, the bell was moved to a glass-enclosed pavilion for the 1976 Bicentennial, which for many seemed an incongruous setting for such a historic object. In mid-2003 it once again moved to another glass-enclosed pavilion with redbrick accents. This time, great care was taken to improve access and viewing of its former home at Independence Hall, which is seen against the backdrop of the sky—rather than 20th-century buildings. The Liberty Bell complex houses a bell chamber, an interpretive exhibit area with historic displays and memorabilia, and a covered area for waiting in line. The bell is clearly visible from outside day or night, so if time is an issue

(or if the lines are very long), you can see it without entering the building.

During construction for the bell's current home, the foundation and other archaeological remains of The President's House, the home of the nation's chief executives before the capital shifted to Washington, D.C., were discovered, as well as evidence of slaves owned by President George Washington who lived there during his time in office. A new permanent installation includes a series of video panels focusing on the stories of the nine enslaved African Americans, as well as glass panels through which you can view the remains of the structure's foundation. ✉ *6th and Chestnut Sts., 526 Market St., Old City* ☎ *215/965–2305* ⊕ *www.nps.gov/inde/liberty-bell-center.htm* ☜ *Free.*

### Library Hall

**HISTORIC SIGHT** | This 20th-century building is a reconstruction of Franklin's Library Company of Philadelphia, the first public library in the colonies. The American Philosophical Society, one of the country's leading institutions for the study of science, has its library here. The vaults contain such treasures as a copy of the Declaration of Independence handwritten by Thomas Jefferson, William Penn's 1701 Charter of Privileges, and journals from the Lewis and Clark expedition of 1803–06. The library's collection also includes first editions of Newton's *Principia Mathematica,* Franklin's *Experiments and Observations,* and Darwin's *On the Origin of Species.* The APS also offers a small, rotating exhibit of its rare books and manuscripts in the lobby of its first floor. ✉ *105 S. 5th St., Old City* ☎ *215/440–3400* ⊕ *www.amphilsoc.org* ☜ *Free* Ⓜ *5th and Market Sts.*

### Loxley Court

**HISTORIC HOME** | One of the restored 18th-century houses in this lovely court was once home to Benjamin Loxley, a carpenter who worked on Independence Hall. The court's claim to fame, according to its residents, is as the spot where

Benjamin Franklin flew his kite in his experiment with lightning; the key tied to it was the key to Loxley's front door. Peer through the icon gates to see the home, as it is private and can be admired only from the outside. ⊠ *321–323 Arch St., Old City* ⊘ *Closed to public.*

## Mikveh Israel

SYNAGOGUE | Nathan Levy, a Colonial merchant whose ship, the *Myrtilla*, brought the Liberty Bell to America, helped found this Jewish congregation in 1740, making it the oldest in Philadelphia and the second oldest in the United States. The original synagogue was at 3rd and Cherry Streets; the congregation's current space, where it has been since 1976, is in the Sephardic style (following Spanish and Portuguese Jewish ritual). The synagogue's Spruce Street Cemetery (about eight blocks away, beyond Old City) dates from 1740 and is the oldest surviving Jewish site in Philadelphia. It was the burial ground for the Spanish-Portuguese Jewish community. Guided tours of the synagogue and the cemetery are available by appointment. ⊠ *44 N. 4th St., Old City* ☎ *215/922–5446* ⊕ *www.mikvehisrael.org* ✉ *Free; donations accepted* ☞ *The daily minyan (weekdays 7:30 am, Sun. and holidays 8:30 am) and Shabbat services (Fri. 7:15 pm, Sat. 9 am) are open to all.*

## Museum for Art in Wood

ART MUSEUM | This stunning destination for the international wood-art community cultivates and promotes education and creative expression of the form. Rebranded in 2023 to include the word "museum" in its name, this space features a two-floor, light-filled museum showcasing more than a thousand beautiful pieces of artwork all made from wood. The on-site gift shop is stocked with gorgeous, handmade works, some by accomplished artists whose works are on display, including those who are a part of the organization's annual Windgate Wood Arts Residency Program (WARP). ⊠ *141 N. 3rd St., Old City* ☎ *215/923–8000* ⊕ *www.centerforartinwood.org* ✉ *$5 requested donation* ⊘ *Closed Sun. and Mon.*

## ★ Museum of the American Revolution

HISTORY MUSEUM | FAMILY | Within walking distance of the Liberty Bell, Independence Hall, the Constitution Center, and the First Bank of the United States, the Museum of the American Revolution resides in the heart of historic Philadelphia. Divided into four parts—Road to Independence (1760–75), The Darkest Hour (1776–78), A Revolutionary War (1778–83), A New Nation (1783–present)—the museum's impressive collection has been in the making for more than a century. Several thousand artifacts, many of which have never been shown before, include General George Washington's actual tent that he used as his war headquarters; a pair of English holster pistols carried throughout the war by a German American brigadier general; an early-19th-century summer coat worn by a Revolutionary War soldier; and a pair of infant shoes crafted from the stolen coat of a British soldier. Many of the exhibits are interactive and family-friendly, too. ⊠ *101 S. 3rd St., Old City* ☎ *215/253–6731* ⊕ *www.amrevmuseum.org* ✉ *$25.*

## ★ National Constitution Center

HISTORY MUSEUM | This 160,000-square-foot attraction brings the U.S. Constitution to life with exhibits tracing the development and adoption of the nation's guiding document. The interactive "The Story of We the People" takes you from the American Revolution through the Constitution's ratification to major events in the nation's constitutional history, including present-day events like the inauguration of President Barack Obama, Hurricane Katrina, and the recent economic crisis. Later, you can play the role of a Supreme Court justice deciding an important case, walk among the framers in Signers' Hall, and add your signature to the list of Founding Fathers. The facility

# William Penn and His Legacy

William Penn was a rebel with a cause. Born in London in 1644 into a nobleman's family, he attended Oxford University, studied law, and tried a military career (in emulation of his father, an admiral in the British Navy). It was at Oxford that Penn first heard Quaker preachers professing that each life is part of the Divine spirit, and that all people should be treated equally. At age 23, Penn joined the Religious Society of Friends (Quakers), who at the time were considered religious zealots.

Penn was imprisoned in the Tower of London for his heretical pamphlets, but he was spared worse persecution because of his father's support of King Charles II. He petitioned the king to grant him land in the New World for a Quaker colony; he was given a 45,000-square-mile tract along the Delaware River in payment of a debt Charles owed to his late father. Indeed, the king named the land Pennsylvania in honor of the admiral.

On Penn's first visit to his colony, from 1662 to 1664, he began his "Holy Experiment," establishing his haven for Quakers. His laws guaranteed religious freedom and an elected government. He bought land from the Native Americans and established a peace treaty that lasted for 70 years.

Penn was called back to England in 1684 and remained there until 1699, caring for his ill wife, Gulielma Maria Springett, who would die without seeing his beloved Pennsylvania. Penn was suspected of plotting with the former Catholic king, James II, to overthrow the Protestant monarchy of William and Mary, who revoked his charter in 1692 for 18 months.

Penn made his second trip to America with his second wife, Hannah Callowhill Penn, in 1699. The couple moved into Pennsbury Manor along the upper Delaware River, where, while preaching about a life of simplicity, he lived in luxury. Penn issued a new frame of government, the Charter of Privileges, which became a model for the U.S. Constitution. He had to return to England yet again in 1701; there he was consumed by the political and legal problems of his colony, a term in prison for debt, and then illness. Penn died before he could return to Pennsylvania. After his death, his wife honored him by assuming the governorship for nine years.

Although Penn spent only 4 of his 74 years in Pennsylvania, his legacy is profound. As a city planner, he mapped out a "greene countrie towne" with broad, straight streets. He positioned each house in the middle of its plot, so that every child would have play space; he named its streets—Walnut, Spruce, Chestnut—for trees, not for men. His original city plan has survived. As a reformer, Penn replaced dungeons with workhouses; established the right of a jury to decide a verdict without harassment by a judge; provided schools where boys—and girls—could get a practical education; and limited the death penalty to two offenses—murder and treason—rather than the 200 mandated by English criminal law. Visitors to Philadelphia can see the bronze statue of William Penn perched atop the City Hall building, which was once the tallest in the city.

Located on Independence Mall, the interactive National Constitution Center is a great place to learn about the U.S. Constitution.

has 100-plus exhibits and plays host to many events with major historians, authors, and political figures. ✉ *525 Arch St., Independence Mall, Historic Area* ☎ *215/409–6700* ⊕ *www.constitution-center.org* ✉ *$14.50 (with extra charges for some special exhibits)* ⊘ *Closed Mon. and Tues.* ⚓ *Advance tickets recommended* Ⓜ *SEPTA; the Market-Frankfurt subway line stops 1 block from the Center at 5th and Market Sts.*

### National Liberty Museum

**HISTORY MUSEUM** | Using interactive exhibits, video, and works of art, the museum aims to combat bigotry in the United States by putting a spotlight on the nation's rich traditions of freedom and diversity. Galleries celebrate outstanding Americans and contemporaries abroad. The "Heroes from around the World" exhibit celebrates everyday heroes, including teachers, first responders, and extraordinary children working to better their communities. The museum's collection of glass art is symbolic of the fragility of peace; its highlight is Dale Chihuly's 21-foot-tall red glass sculpture *Flame of Liberty*. Sandy Skoglund's colorful *Jelly Bean People* are a reminder that many of our differences are only skin-deep. ✉ *321 Chestnut St., Historic Area* ☎ *215/925–2800* ⊕ *www.libertymuseum.org* ✉ *$12* ⊘ *Closed Tues. and Wed.*

### New Hall Military Museum

**HISTORY MUSEUM** | When it was originally built in 1791, this building housed the U.S. Department of War. Today's reconstruction outlines early American military history and the formation of the Army, Navy, and Marine Corps. On display are Revolutionary uniforms, medals, and authentic weapons, including powder horns, swords, and a blunderbuss. Dioramas depict highlights from the Revolutionary War through the late 18th century, and there are several scale models of warships and frigates, as well. This museum is typically open for special events and occasions only. ✉ *320 Chestnut St., east of 4th St., Old City* ☎ *215/965–2305* ⊕ *www.nps.gov/inde/*

learn/historyculture/places-newhallmilitarymuseum.htm ⬛ Free.

### Old City Hall

**HISTORIC SIGHT** | Independence Hall is flanked by Congress Hall to the west and Old City Hall to the east: three distinctive Federal-style buildings erected to house the city's growing government. But when Philadelphia became the nation's capital in 1790, the just-completed city hall was lent to the federal government. It housed the U.S. Supreme Court from 1791 to 1800; John Jay was the Chief Justice. Later, the boxlike building with a peaked roof and cupola was used as the city hall. Today an exhibit presents information about the early days of the federal judiciary. ✉ 5th and Chestnut Sts., Historic Area ☎ 215/965–2305 ⊕ www.nps.gov/inde/planyourvisit/oldcityhall.htm ⬛ Free.

### Philadelphia Merchant's Exchange

**NOTABLE BUILDING** | Designed by the well-known Philadelphia architect William Strickland and built in 1832, this impressive Greek Revival building served as the city's commercial center for 50 years. It was both the stock exchange and a place where merchants met to trade goods. In the tower a watchman scanned the Delaware River and notified merchants of arriving ships. The exchange stands behind Dock Street, a cobblestone thoroughfare. The building houses a small exhibit on its history and now serves as the headquarters for Independence National Park. ✉ 143 S. 3rd St., Historic Area ☎ 215/965–2305 ⊕ www.nps.gov/inde/learn/historyculture/places-merchantsexchange.htm ⬛ Free ☺ Closed weekends.

### Philosophical Hall

**NOTABLE BUILDING** | This is the headquarters of the American Philosophical Society, founded by Benjamin Franklin in 1743 to promote "useful knowledge." The members of the oldest learned society in America have included Washington, Jefferson, Lafayette, Emerson, Darwin, Edison, Churchill, and Einstein. Erected between 1785 and 1789 in what has been called a "restrained Federal style" (designed to complement, not outshine, adjacent Independence Hall), Philosophical Hall is brick with marble trim, has a handsome arched entrance, and houses the Society's museum, open to the public Friday to Sunday. The society's library is across the street in Library Hall. ✉ 104 S. 5th St., Historic Area ☎ 215/440–3400 ⊕ www.amphilsoc.org ⬛ $2 suggested donation ☺ Closed Mon.–Thurs. and Jan.–mid-Apr.

### The President's House

**RUINS** | This site commemorates the location of the home of U.S. presidents George Washington and John Adams from 1790 to 1800, as well as nine enslaved Africans who worked as household staff. The outdoor monument, which is open 24 hours a day, shows video clips that bring the house's history alive. Inside, take note of the bow window, which is thought to have inspired the shape of the Oval Office at the White House, as well as the remains of a passage torn down in 1832 that connected the main house to the slave quarters. ✉ 600 Market St., Historic Area ☎ 215/965–2305 ⊕ www.nps.gov/inde/learn/historyculture/places-presidentshousesite.htm ⬛ Free ☞ The outdoor site is accessible at all times, but the interactive exhibits run concurrent with the Liberty Bell Pavilion hrs.

### Second Bank of the United States

**HISTORIC SIGHT** | When Second Bank president Nicholas Biddle held a design competition for a new building, he required all architects to use the Greek style; William Strickland, one of the foremost architects of the 19th century, won. Built in 1824, the bank, with its Doric columns, was based on the design of the Parthenon and helped establish the popularity of Greek Revival architecture in the United States. The interior hall, though, was Roman, with a dramatic barrel-vault ceiling. Housed here are portraits of prominent Colonial Americans by noted artists such as Charles Willson Peale, William Rush, and Gilbert Stuart. Don't miss Peale's portraits of Jefferson and Lewis and Clark: the former is the only one that shows the third president with red hair, and the latter is the only known portrait of the famous explorers. The permanent exhibition, "The People of Independence," has a life-size wooden statue of George Washington by William Rush; a mural of Philadelphia in the 1830s by John A. Woodside Jr.; and the only known likeness of William Floyd, a lesser-known signer of the Declaration of Independence. ⊠ *420 Chestnut St., Old City* ☎ *215/965–2305* ⊕ *www.nps. gov/inde/learn/historyculture/places-sec- ondbank.htm* ☒ *Free* ⟳ *Call ahead for availability.*

### United States Mint

**NOTABLE BUILDING** | The first U.S. mint was built in Philadelphia at 16th and Spring Garden Streets in 1792, when the Bank of North America adopted dollars and cents instead of shillings and pence as standard currency; the current mint was built in 1971. During a self-guided tour you can see blank disks being melted, cast, and pressed into coins, which are then inspected, counted, and bagged. Historic artifacts such as the Key to the First Mint and the gold medal awarded to General Anthony Wayne for his capture of Stony Point during the Revolutionary War are displayed. Seven Tiffany glass tile mosaics depict coin making in ancient Rome. A shop in the lobby sells special coins and medals—in mint condition. ⊠ *151 N. Independence Mall E, 5th and Arch Sts., Old City* ☎ *215/408–0112* ⊕ *www.usmint.gov* ☒ *Free* ⟳ *No tours Sept.–May weekends, June–Aug. Sun.* ☞ *The mint is subject to U.S. Homeland Security rules. If the Homeland Security threat is raised to "orange," no public tours will be allowed.*

### Weitzman National Museum of American Jewish History

**HISTORY MUSEUM** | **FAMILY** | Established in 1976, this museum moved in 2010 to a new, James Polshek–designed, contemporary building near Independence Hall. The 100,000-square-foot facility, via multimedia displays, historic objects, and ephemera, traces the history of American Jews from 1654 to the present. Highlights include "Only in America," a showcase of the accomplishments of famed Jewish Americans, including Jonas Salk, Barbra Streisand, and Irving Berlin; a three-level timeline covering immigration, the formation of Israel, and the civil rights movement; *Seinfeld*; a Contemporary Issues Forum, where you can share your views on Post-it-style notes that are electronically scanned and displayed; and "It's Your Story," where you can record clips about your family history. The museum's exterior offers two contrasting sculptures symbolizing how American Jewish history is intertwined with the nation's story: a 19th-century marble monument dubbed *Religious Liberty* and a sculpture by contemporary artist Deborah Kass. ⊠ *5th and Market Sts., 101 S. Independence Mall E, Old City* ☎ *215/923–3811* ⊕ *www.nmajh.org* ☒ *$15* ⟳ *Closed Mon.–Thurs.*

### Welcome Park

**PLAZA/SQUARE** | A scale model of the William Penn statue that tops City Hall sits on a 60-foot-long map of Penn's Philadelphia, carved in the pavement of Welcome Park. (The *Welcome* was the ship that transported Penn to America.) The wall surrounding the park displays a timeline of Penn's life, with information about his philosophy and writings. The park was the site of the slate-roof house where Penn lived briefly and where he granted the Charter of Privileges in 1701, which served as Pennsylvania's constitutional framework until 1776; the Liberty Bell was commissioned to commemorate the charter's 50th anniversary. ⊠ *129 Sansom Walk, 2nd St. and Sansom Walk,*

*Historic Area* 🌐 *www.ushistory.org/tour/welcome-park.htm* 🎟 *Free.*

## 🍴 Restaurants

### ★ Amada

$$ | **SPANISH** | At Amada, the first of chef-restaurateur Jose Garces's restaurants, the Ecuadorian-American chef reinterprets regional cuisine with choice ingredients and a modern touch that feature in more than 50 tapas, from the crab-stuffed peppers with toasted almonds to the flatbread topped with artichoke, black truffle, and manchego. Ingredients—including even more glorious cheeses—are sourced from northern Spain, the main inspiration for the menu. **Known for:** Andalusian cuisine; Spanish meats and cheeses; lively scene. [$] *Average main: $22* ✉ *217–19 Chestnut St., Old City* ☎ *215/398–6968* 🌐 *www.amadarestaurant.com* 🕓 *No lunch weekdays.*

### Buddakan

$$ | **ASIAN** | This Stephen Starr restaurant is presided over by a 10-foot-tall gilded Buddha who seems to approve of the fusion food that pairs Pan-Asian ingredients with various cooking styles. The truffled edamame dumplings and tuna tartare spring rolls are tasty, but much of the appeal is in the theatrical decor and people-watching, also prevalent at Buddakan's outposts in New York and Atlantic City. **Known for:** creative Pan-Asian cooking; eye-catching decor; lively scene. [$] *Average main: $31* ✉ *325 Chestnut St., Old City* ☎ *215/574–9440* 🌐 *www.buddakan.com* 🕓 *No lunch.*

### Cuba Libre

$$$ | **LATIN AMERICAN** | People who have been to Havana swear this place is a dead ringer; in any event, it's lovely, with balconies and fancy streetlights, and even a leaded-glass window on the interior. An entire drinks menu is devoted to rum from everywhere in the Caribbean and Central and South America, including Cuba Libre's own brand, and of course, the mojitos are excellent. **Known for:** Cuban cuisine; mojitos; salsa dancing. [$] *Average main: $27* ✉ *10 S. 2nd St., Old City* ☎ *215/627–0666* 🌐 *www.cubalibrerestaurant.com* 🕓 *No lunch weekdays.*

### ★ Fork

$$$$ | **AMERICAN** | Happy sounds are always emanating from eaters at this comfortable, elegant eatery, one of Old City's most respected and longest-running dinner destinations. For more than 25 years, this award-winning kitchen has been known for its innovative pastas, delectable dishes, in-house fermentation, and the celebration of local meats and produce. **Known for:** creative new American food; excellent service; elegant dining room. [$] *Average main: $38* ✉ *306 Market St., Old City* ☎ *215/625–9425* 🌐 *www.forkrestaurant.com* 🕓 *Closed Mon. and Tues. No lunch Wed.–Fri.*

### ★ Forsythia

$$$ | **FRENCH** | Well traveled and well trained, chef Christopher Kearse presents his unique take on French cuisine at the modern Forsythia. Start with shareable canapés, like smoked trout rillettes or sweet-and-sour crispy pig tails, before digging into small plates, pastas, and shareable mains (try the tuna collar amandine) that split the difference between edgy and accessible. **Known for:** modern French cuisine; beautiful room; bar scene. [$] *Average main: $32* ✉ *233 Chestnut St., Old City* ☎ *215/644–9395* 🌐 *www.forsythiaphilly.com* 🕓 *Closed Mon. and Tues. No lunch weekdays.*

### Franklin Social Kitchen and Bar

$$ | **AMERICAN** | **FAMILY** | Located at street level, just off the lobby of the Renaissance Hotel Philadelphia Downtown, the Franklin Social features a menu of comfort food favorites that include chicken quesadillas, French onion soup, and the Benjamin Burger (named after you-know-who), topped with cheese and a special sauce. Open all day, this lively restaurant also offers small plates, soups, salads, and sandwiches as well as a creative

Stop by Franklin Fountain for scoops of house-made ice cream in flavors like fresh peach, mint chocolate chip, and caramelized banana.

cocktail menu and plenty of wines by the glass. **Known for:** American-style menu with something for everyone; large and small plates; convenient location that's open all day. [$] *Average main: $24* ✉ *401 Chestnut St., Old City* ☎ *215/931–4260* 🌐 *www.franklinsocialphilly.com.*

**★ High Street on Market**
**$$$ | AMERICAN** | This sunny younger sibling of perennial favorite Fork is half clubhouse for Old City neighbors, half food-tourist magnet. Grain-brained High Street will take you from cortados (an espresso drink) and *kouign-amann* (a French pastry) and other especially uniques breads in the morning to beet-cured salmon sandwiches in the afternoon to creative alt-flour pastas—spelt pappardelle, anyone?—at night. **Known for:** all-day service; creative breads; innovative pastas. [$] *Average main: $29* ✉ *308 Market St., Old City* ☎ *215/625–0988* 🌐 *www.highstreetonmarket.com.*

**The Olde Bar**
**$$$ | SEAFOOD** | This Jose Garces spot is located in the historic bones of Old Original Bookbinders, a famous seafood restaurant that catered to politicians, bigwigs, and celebrities in its day. The menu isn't elaborate but manages well with pristine East and West Coast oysters and updates on classics like snapper soup and lobster rolls, but the deep catalog of cocktails both classic and nouveau is the real reason to come—seasonal Old Fashioneds, elaborate swizzles, and sours as foamy as the ocean surf satisfy tipplers of all tastes. **Known for:** raw bar; great list of new and classic cocktails; historic atmosphere. [$] *Average main: $25* ✉ *125 Walnut St., Old City* ☎ *215/253–3777* 🌐 *www.theoldebar.com* ⏲ *No lunch weekdays.*

**Panorama**
**$$$ | ITALIAN** | The name refers to a lovely mural rather than a window view from this lively spot inside the Penn's View Hotel. The restaurant has the largest wine cruvinet (storage system) in the

country. **Known for:** Italian cuisine; relaxed atmosphere; wide wine selection. $ *Average main: $32* ✉ *Penn's View Hotel, 14 N. Front St., Old City* ☎ *215/922–7800* ⊕ *www.pennsviewhotel.com* ⊗ *No lunch weekdays.*

### Plough and the Stars
**$$ | IRISH** | Owned by husband-and-wife restaurateurs Kevin and Janet Meeker, the cheery first floor of a renovated bank feels like a genuine Irish pub. The eatery's long bar features a dozen taps—invariably spouting several imported and a few local brews—and the menu includes good Irish smoked salmon on grainy bread as well as a panoply of worldly appetizers, salads, and main courses. **Known for:** Irish hospitality; the place to get a Guinness poured the correct way; Irish music. $ *Average main: $24* ✉ *123 Chestnut St., enter on 2nd St., Old City* ☎ *215/733–0300* ⊕ *www.ploughstars.com.*

### Positano Coast by Aldo Lamberti
**$$$$ | ITALIAN** | This second-floor, Amalfi coast–inspired restaurant is surrounded by floor-to-ceiling windows that offer guests a great view of Old City; the decor is inspired by the owner's seaside home in Italy. The menu includes something for everyone—there's an array of zesty homemade Italian specialties, including pastas; grilled octopus and shrimp scampi appetizers; a selection of fresh salads; and entrée favorites like zucchini crab cakes and a pan-seared pork chop. **Known for:** lively, upscale ambience with an Old City view; authentic Italian coastal cuisine; consistent food offerings. $ *Average main: $35* ✉ *212 Walnut St., Old City* ☎ *215/238–0499* ⊕ *www.positanocoast. net* ⊗ *Closed Mon.*

### Royal Boucherie
**$$$ | FRENCH** | A collaboration between award-winning chef Nicholas Elmi and the owners of local favorites Royal Tavern, Cantina Los Caballitos, and Khyber Pass Pub, Royal Boucherie is a polished operation set in a moody and intimate bi-level 2nd Street space. A classic brasserie in approach, it specializes in luscious raw-bar selections, house-made charcuterie, and rib-sticking plates like steak au poivre, pork schnitzel, and handwrought pastas. **Known for:** raw bar; cocktails; intimate space. $ *Average main: $27* ✉ *52 S. 2nd St., Old City* ☎ *267/606–6313* ⊕ *www.royalboucherie. com* ⊗ *No lunch weekdays.*

### Tuna Bar
**$$$$ | JAPANESE** | Exceptional Japanese cuisine and creative sushi attracts neighborhood foodies as well as visitors to owner and chef Kenneth Sze's Tuna Bar. Fresh specialties made from locally sourced seafood and other ingredients include favorites such as hand rolls, seaweed salad, and shrimp tempura, along with some unique house specialties that showcase a delectable mix of Japanese flavors and textures. **Known for:** upscale sushi in a chic environment; unique and modern take on sushi rolls and house specialties; extensive sake and wine list. $ *Average main: $28* ✉ *205 Race St., Old City* ☎ *215/238–8862* ⊕ *www.tunabar. com* ⊗ *Closed Mon.*

## ☕ Coffee and Quick Bites

### The Bourse Food Hall
**$ | INTERNATIONAL** | Built in 1895 as a stock, maritime, and commodities exchange, the Bourse building is an icon of Philadelphia commerce that now features a casual, light-filled food hall with local roots, ideal for a quick lunch. Stop in for a gourmet coffee from Menagerie, Mexican specialties from Rebel Taco, tasty Freebyrd chicken, creative comfort food from Grubhouse, and several other lunch and early-dinner options. **Known for:** historic architecture; wide culinary options; space for big groups. $ *Average main: $12* ✉ *111 S. Independence Mall E, at 5th St. across from Liberty Bell Pavilion, Philadelphia* ☎ *215/625–0300* ⊕ *www.theboursephilly.com.*

### ★ Franklin Fountain

$ | **CAFÉ** | **FAMILY** | You can't throw a wet walnut in Philly without hitting an artisanal-ice-cream maker these days, but brothers Ryan and Eric Berley and their charming Colonial-inspired scoop shop have newcomers beat by years. On summer nights, long lines ripple out the door into the warm Old City night, but the wait (half an hour isn't uncommon in summer) is worth it for the house-made seasonal flavors like fresh peach, brooding black raspberry, and honeycomb made with booty from the Fountain's rooftop hives. **Known for:** old-timey uniforms and decor; handmade ice cream; long lines. [$] *Average main: $10* ✉ *116 Market St., Old City* ☎ *215/627–1899* 🌐 *www.franklinfountain.com.*

### Istanbul Cafe

$ | **CAFÉ** | A modern oasis in Old City, this café and bakery serves up homemade pastries and light bites, along with a variety of locally roasted coffees (including Turkish coffee) and other hot and cold beverages. Owned by brothers Engin and Emre from Istanbul, this light-filled corner café has seating along the windows which is a great place for a short break while still enjoying the busy sidewalks at this Old City intersection. **Known for:** Turkish coffee; quick snack in the middle of Old City; homemade pastries. [$] *Average main: $12* ✉ *301 Market St., Old City* ☎ *267/639–4594.*

### La Colombe Coffee Roasters

$ | **CAFÉ** | Across the street from Independence Mall and steps away from many historical sights, this Philly-based company offers a variety of coffee and beverage options as well as pastries and light snacks. There's ample seating inside, with additional outdoor seating during warmer months, which makes it a great place for a break while visiting the city's most popular sights. **Known for:** exceptional coffee with large selection of options; a variety of pastries and snacks; spacious café. [$] *Average main: $9* ✉ *100 S. Independence Mall W, Old City* ☎ *267/479–1650* 🌐 *www.lacolombe.com.*

## Hotels

### ★ Hotel Monaco Philadelphia

$$$ | **HOTEL** | Located in the heart of Philly's historic center, this LEED-certified property offers style and sass, along with the beloved perks of the Kimpton brand, including free bike rentals, yoga mats in every room, complimentary evening wine hours nightly from 5 to 6 pm, and pet-friendly accommodations. **Pros:** central location; lots of great perks and freebies; popular on-site dining and drinking. **Cons:** note that it's pet-friendly, if you have allergies; crowded part of town; pricey valet parking. [$] *Rooms from: $286* ✉ *433 Chestnut St., Old City* ☎ *215/925–2111* 🌐 *www.monaco-philadelphia.com* 🛏 *268 rooms* 🍴 *No Meals.*

### Independence Park Hotel, BW Premier Collection

$$$ | **HOTEL** | Newly renovated and reopened in 2022, the five-story building, a Best Western "Premier Collection" property, is located in the heart of Old City surrounded by key historic sites; built in 1856, it's included on the National Register of Historic Places. **Pros:** free hot breakfast; newly renovated in 2022; intimate boutique hotel near restaurants, nightlife, and tourist attractions. **Cons:** can be noisy at night; no parking on-site; some rooms are small. [$] *Rooms from: $263* ✉ *235 Chestnut St., Old City* ☎ *215/922–4443, 800/624–2988* 🌐 *www.theindependenceparkhotel.com* 🛏 *41 rooms* 🍴 *Free Breakfast.*

### Lokal Hotel

$$$$ | **HOTEL** | A unique boutique hotel that stands out from Old City's numerous big-brand options, Lokal is owned by a husband-and-wife team that preaches the merits of "invisible service"—no front desks or on-site staff, with check-ins, deliveries, and the like handled by the guest via tech innovations and mobile

apps. **Pros:** private boutique feel; fully equipped kitchens; in-suite washer and dryer. **Cons:** no elevator; not wheelchair accessible; pricier than traditional hotels. [$] *Rooms from: $430* ✉ *139 N. 3rd St., Old City* ☎ *267/702–4345* 🌐 *www.staylokal.com* 🛏 *6 rooms* 🍴 *No Meals.*

**Penn's View Hotel**

$$$ | **HOTEL** | This cosmopolitan little hotel in a refurbished 19th-century commercial building on the fringe of Old City offers its own brand of urban charm. **Pros:** away from main area of Old City; generous continental breakfast including waffles; romantic atmosphere. **Cons:** gym is tiny; rooms facing I–95 can be noisy; slightly dated decor. [$] *Rooms from: $259* ✉ *14 N. Front St., Old City* ☎ *215/922–7600* 🌐 *www.pennsviewhotel.com* 🛏 *53 rooms* 🍴 *Free Breakfast.*

**Renaissance Philadelphia Downtown Hotel**

$$$ | **HOTEL** | **FAMILY** | An ornate fireplace dominates the breathtaking marble lobby of this towering Marriott-member hotel in the historic district; its location makes it a pleasant base for visiting the nearby art galleries and cafés, as well as the Liberty Bell, Independence Hall, and other sights. **Pros:** boutique feel with good service; excellent location for historic touring and Old City sights; nice views; known to offer good sale rates. **Cons:** crowded part of town; surrounding area can be noisy; pricey valet parking. [$] *Rooms from: $269* ✉ *401 Chestnut St., Old City* ☎ *215/925–0000* 🌐 *renaissance-hotels.marriott.com/renaissance-philadelphia-downtown-hotel* 🛏 *152 rooms* 🍴 *No Meals.*

**Thomas Bond House**

$$ | **B&B/INN** | This bed-and-breakfast in the heart of Old City is great for travelers who want an authentic taste of historic Philadelphia—built in 1769 by a prominent local physician (an enormous family tree detailing his descendents hangs from a wall in a common living room), the four-story Georgian house has undergone a faithful, meticulous revival. **Pros:** historic home; good service; complimentary wine and snacks. **Cons:** some guests complain of noise when nearby bars let out at 2 am; rooms are small; no elevator. [$] *Rooms from: $225* ✉ *129 S. 2nd St., Old City* ☎ *215/923–8523, 800/845–2663* 🌐 *www.thomasbondhousebandb.com* 🛏 *12 rooms* 🍴 *Free Breakfast.*

**Wyndham Philadelphia Historic District**

$$ | **HOTEL** | This eight-story hotel sits within what is billed as the country's "most historic square mile," and it's a block and a half from Old City's major historical attractions, including the Liberty Bell and Independence Hall. **Pros:** convenient and walkable location; 24-hour gym; rooftop swimming pool in summer. **Cons:** lots of tourists and large groups; rates very high in busy seasons; noisy part of town. [$] *Rooms from: $209* ✉ *400 Arch St., Old City* ☎ *215/923–8660, 800/843–2355* 🌐 *www.phillydowntownhotel.com* 🛏 *371 rooms* 🍴 *No Meals.*

## 🍸 Nightlife

**Khyber Pass Pub**

**BARS** | Operated as a saloon since 1876, this bi-level pub was a popular punk rock club from the 1970s through the 1990s. It has since been reinvented as a restaurant serving authentic New Orleans cuisine (try the po'boys and gumbo) alongside a serious craft beer selection (22 taps). The upstairs space still plays host to a wide slate of live performances, featuring local and lesser-known bands; musical artists; and special events with plenty of room for dancing. ✉ *56 S. 2nd St., Old City* ☎ *215/238–5888* 🌐 *www.khyberpasspub.com.*

**★ Sassafras**

**BARS** | A classic and classy Old City watering hole, Sassafras is a stately stop for a well-made cocktail; it's a cozy hideaway for grown-ups among the neighborhood's more boisterous and youthful hangouts. Known for its sophisticated ambience and great service, it also offers light lunch and small bites. In addition to drinks and dinner, it hosts live jazz musicians Sunday to Thursday. ⊠ *48 S. 2nd St., Old City* ☎ *215/925–2317* ⊕ *www.sassafrasbar.com.*

 # Shopping

Lofts, art galleries, furniture stores, and unique home-decor shops line the streets of the Old City in the Historic Downtown; there are also wonderful clothing stores with work by local up-and-coming designers. One of the best times to explore Old City's gallery scene is during First Friday. As the name implies, on the first Friday of each month Old City galleries are open to the public late into the evening. Many offer refreshments, and the street scene becomes quite festive (and often crowded, too).

## ART GALLERIES

### Muse Gallery

**ART GALLERIES** | Established in 1978 by the Muse Foundation for the Visual Arts, this gallery is an artists' cooperative committed to increasing the visibility of local artwork and presenting experimental work in a variety of mediums displayed in a variety of exhibitions throughout the year. ⊠ *52 N. 2nd St., Old City* ☎ *215/627–5310.*

### Wexler Gallery

**ART GALLERIES** | This gallery is known for specializing in historic and contemporary glass, but it always has an interesting mix of 20th- and 21st-century handcrafted furnishings and art. ⊠ *201 N. 3rd St., Old City* ☎ *215/923–7030* ⊕ *www. wexlergallery.com.*

## GIFTS AND SOUVENIRS

### Art in the Age

**OTHER SPECIALTY STORE** | A one-stop shop for craft cocktail enthusiasts, Art in the Age stocks a curated selection of spirits, including locally distilled whiskies and its own line of unique products (black trumpet/blueberry cordial; chicory root vodka). In addition to cocktail books, tools, gift items, and accessories, there's a full bar in the rear that accommodates tastings and pre-purchase sampling; it's regularly used for special events, cocktail workshops, and parties. (They serve coffee and sometimes snacks at the bar, too.) ⊠ *116 N. 3rd St., Old City* ☎ *215/922–2600* ⊕ *www. artintheage.com.*

### Art Star

**SOUVENIRS** | Tucked away near the Bourse Food Hall's entrance, this locally owned shop sells souvenirs made by area artists. You can purchase unique Philly-focused items (and beyond), such as clothing for kids and adults, ornaments, stickers, pictures, cards, jewelry, and much more. You'll need to enter the Bourse building to see the shop, but it's worth a look. Also, be sure to grab a snack while you're here, as the food hall is an ideal spot for a break and it's near all the historical sights. ⊠ *Bourse Food Hall, 111 S. Independence Mall E, Old City* ⊕ *www.artstarphilly.com.*

### Philadelphia Independents

**SOUVENIRS** | This unique and fascinating shop is a true Philly gem featuring only locally made items from more than 50 artisans. Browse through an abundance of handmade gifts, jewelry, home decor, baby items, clothing, artwork, and pet accessories, many of which can only be purchased at this location. ⊠ *35 N. 3rd St., Old City* ☎ *267/773–7316* ⊕ *www. philadelphiaindependents.com.*

### ★ Shane Confectionery

**CANDY** | **FAMILY** | America's oldest candy shop is truly a wonderland of sweet treats with a wide assortment of beautifully made hand-crafted delights, such as chocolate assortments, clear "toy" candy, seasonal goodies, and candy-filled gift boxes. (They also have an incredibly rich hot chocolate during the colder months.) While perusing, you can learn all about the history of this lovely shop that first opened in the 1800s. ⊠ *110 Market St., Old City* ☎ *215/922–1048* ⊕ *www. shanecandies.com.*

# Chapter 4

# SOCIETY HILL AND PENN'S LANDING

Updated by
Marla Cimini

| ◉ Sights | 🍴 Restaurants | 🛏 Hotels | 🛍 Shopping | 🍸 Nightlife |
|----------|--------------|-----------|-------------|-------------|
| ★★★★★ | ★★☆☆☆ | ★★★★☆ | ★★★☆☆ | ★★☆☆☆ |

# NEIGHBORHOOD SNAPSHOT

## TOP EXPERIENCES

- **Battleship *New Jersey:*** Walk the decks of this World War II–era ship, one of the U.S. Navy's most decorated military vessels (take a ferry to NJ).

- **Headhouse Shambles:** Peruse the wares at this historic open-air marketplace.

- **House museums:** See how the Colonial era's high society lived at two of the city's most gracious residences, the Hill-Physick and Powel houses.

- **Mother Bethel A.M.E. Church:** This historic house of worship was also an Underground Railroad stop.

- **Race Street Pier:** This reimagined pier along Philly's waterfront offers free Wi-Fi and water views.

- **Washington Square:** One of William Penn's original squares, it's a great place to picnic or people-watch.

## GETTING HERE

Society Hill is easy to reach on foot for those staying in Center City. Stroll eastward along Locust, Spruce, or Pine Streets for an enjoyable pedestrian experience (i.e., sightseeing, snacking, and shopping). SEPTA's 12 bus goes from Rittenhouse Square to Society Hill in about 15 minutes.

Penn's Landing is also within walking distance of Old City and Society Hill, or can be accessed by SEPTA. To reach it, cross the Walnut Street Bridge at Front Street, which deposits you at the Independence Seaport Museum. The RiverLink Ferry connects Penn's Landing to Camden, New Jersey (summer).

## PLANNING YOUR TIME

It's about one hour to walk through Society Hill, more if you tour the Powel and Physick houses. However, you can easily spend a whole day in Penn's Landing. If kids are in tow, allow an hour and a half for the Independence Seaport Museum and its historic boats and another two or three hours for the ferry ride across the Delaware to visit the Adventure Aquarium in Camden, NJ, followed by a tour of the battleship *New Jersey.*

## QUICK BITES

- **Cavanaugh's.** A traditional sports bar, Cav's is worth a drop-in for a casual bite or drink, as this multi-level, multi-room tavern has been serving up pub grub since the 1780s (try the wings). ⊠ *421 S. 2nd St., Society Hill* ⊕ *www.cavshead-house.com*

- **Bodhi Coffee.** This cozy neighborhood café serves a variety of gourmet coffees, tea, breakfast sandwiches and locally made pastries in a friendly atmosphere. ⊠ *410 S. 2nd St., Society Hill* ⊕ *www.face-book.com/bodhicoffee*

- **The Victoria Freehouse.** This U.K.-inspired pub on Front Street serves proper pub fare (shepherd's pie, bangers, and mash) and authentic cask ales; it's a popular hangout for fans of English soccer. ⊠ *10 S. Front St., Penn's Landing* ⊕ *www.victoriafreehouse.com*

## GOOD TO KNOW

- If walking is your preference, be sure to visit this area on a warm day, because it can be quite windy along the waterfront. On summer weekends, revitalized Penn's Landing bustles with festivals, music, and pop-up parks, and Headhouse Square turns into a farmers' market with locally grown products and baked goods.

The Historic District teaches us what the earliest Philadelphians did; Society Hill shows us how they lived. This residential neighborhood offers a postcard-perfect view of post-Colonial America, with cobblestone streets, historic private residences, and centuries-old churches. And thanks to its central location, exploring the area is easy.

Comprising the far edge of Society Hill and overlapping with Old City, Penn's Landing refers to the sliver of land separating the easternmost neighborhoods of Center City with the Delaware River, which in turn separates Philadelphia from Camden, New Jersey. Long in developmental flux as the civic powers that be determine how to capitalize on this waterfront entertainment district, Penn's Landing has enjoyed recent enhancements—and many points of interest ready to explore right now.

## Society Hill

During the 18th century Society Hill was Philadelphia's showplace. A carefully preserved district, it remains the city's most photogenic neighborhood, filled with hidden courtyards, delightful decorative touches such as chimney pots and brass door knockers, wrought-iron foot scrapers, and other remnants from the days of horse-drawn carriages and muddy, unpaved streets. Here, time has not quite stopped, but meanders down the cobblestone streets, whiling away the hours.

A trove of Colonial- and Federal-style brick row houses, churches, and narrow streets, Society Hill stretches from the Delaware River to 8th Street, south of Independence National Historical Park. Those homes built before 1750 in the Colonial style generally have 2½ stories and a dormer window jutting out of a steep roof. The less heavy, more graceful houses built after the Revolution were often in the Federal style, popularized in England during the 1790s.

Here lived the "World's People," wealthier Anglicans who arrived after William Penn and loved music and dancing—pursuits the Quakers shunned when they set up their enclave in Old City, north of Market Street, in a less desirable commercial area. The "Society" in the neighborhood's moniker refers, however, to the now-defunct Free Society of Traders, a group of business investors who settled here on William Penn's advice.

Today many Colonial homes in this area have been lovingly restored by modern pioneers who moved into the area about 50 years ago and rescued Society Hill from becoming a slum. Inspired urban renewal efforts have transformed vast empty factory spaces into airy lofts; new town houses were carefully designed to blend in with the old. As a result, Society Hill is not just a showcase for historic churches and mansions but a living, breathing neighborhood.

##  Sights

### Athenaeum of Philadelphia

**LIBRARY** | Housed in a national landmark Italianate Revival brownstone built in the mid–19th century, the Athenaeum is a research library specializing in architectural history and design with a collection that features millions of items. The library, founded in 1814, was refurbished in 2022 and contains significant materials on the French in America and on early American travel, exploration, and transportation. Besides books, the Athenaeum has notable paintings and period furniture; changing exhibits are presented in the gallery. Research is by appointment only. ⊠ *219 S. 6th St., Society Hill* ☎ *215/925–2688* ⊕ *www.philaathenaeum.org* ☾ *Closed Sun. and most holidays* Ⓜ *4 blocks from the 5th and Market stop.*

### Bouvier's Row

**HISTORIC SIGHT** | Three of the Victorian brownstones on a stretch of 3rd Street near Locust Street, often called Bouvier's Row, were once owned by the late Jacqueline Kennedy Onassis's ancestors. Michel Bouvier, her great-great-grandfather—the first of the family to come from France—and many of his descendants lie in the family vault at Old St. Mary's Church, a few blocks away on 4th Street. These are private residences and can be viewed from the outside only. ⊠ *258–262 S. 3rd St., Society Hill.*

### ★ Headhouse Square

**PLAZA/SQUARE** | This open-air Colonial marketplace, extending from Pine Street to Lombard Street, is a reminder of the days when people went to central outdoor markets to buy food directly from farmers. It was first established as New Market in 1745, and George Washington was among those who came here to buy butter, eggs, meat, fish, herbs, and vegetables. The Head House, a boxy building with a cupola and weather vane, was built in 1803 as the office and home of the market master, who tested the quality of the goods. Today it's the site of a year-round farmers' market, featuring dozens of vendors selling local, seasonal produce, plus everything from honey and flowers to pickles and pastries. On some summer weekends, the square is also home to an arts-and-crafts fair featuring the work of Delaware Valley artists. ⊠ *200 Pine St., Society Hill* ☎ *215/413–3713* ⊕ *www.southstreet.com.*

### Hill-Physick House

**HISTORIC HOME** | Built in 1786, this is one of the oldest freestanding houses in Society Hill, with elegantly restored interiors and some of the finest Federal and Empire furniture in Philadelphia. Touches of Napoléon's France are everywhere—the golden bee motif woven into upholstery; the magenta-hue Aubusson rug; and stools in the style of Pompeii, the Roman city rediscovered at the time of the house's construction. Upstairs in the parlor, there's an inkstand that retains Benjamin Franklin's actual fingerprints. Originally built by a wealthy wine importer, the house's most famous owner was Philip Syng Physick, the "Father of American Surgery" and a leading physician in the days before anesthesia. His celebrated patients included President Andrew Jackson and Chief Justice John Marshall. The garden planted outside the house is filled with plants common during the 19th century; complete with an Etruscan sarcophagus, a natural grotto, and antique cannon, it's one of the city's loveliest. Tour times change throughout the year, so check in advance. ⊠ *321 S. 4th St., Society Hill* ☎ *215/925–7866* ⊕ *www.philalandmarks. org/physick-house* ⊠ *$8* ☾ *Closed Mon. and Tues.* ☞ *Tours Thurs.–Sat. Apr.–Nov. and weekends Mar. and Dec.*

With hidden courtyards, cobblestone streets, and brass door knockers, the carefully preserved Society Hill district is the city's most photogenic neighborhood.

### Mother Bethel A.M.E. Church

**CHURCH** | In 1787, Rev. Richard Allen, a former slave, galvanized fellow black congregants who left St. George's Methodist Church in a protest against segregated worship. Allen purchased this site in 1791, and it's believed to be the country's oldest parcel of land continuously owned by African Americans. When the African Methodist Episcopal Church, America's first black congregation, was formed in 1816, Allen was its first bishop. The current church is an example of the 19th-century Romanesque Revival style, with broad arches, opalescent stained glass, and stunning woodwork. An earlier building on these grounds was a stop on the Underground Railroad. Allen's tomb and a small museum are on the lower level. ⊠ *419 S. 6th St., Society Hill* 🕾 *215/925–0616* ⊕ *www.facebook.com/motherbethel* 🖾 *Donation requested.*

### Old Pine Street Presbyterian Church

**CHURCH** | Designed by Robert Smith in 1768, Old Pine is the only remaining Colonial Presbyterian church and churchyard in Philadelphia. Badly damaged during the Revolution, it served as a hospital and then a stable. In the mid–19th century, its exterior had a Greek Revival face-lift that introduced Corinthian columns. In the 1980s, the interior walls and ceiling were stenciled with thistle and wave motifs, a reminder of Old Pine's true name—Third, Scots, and Mariners Presbyterian Church, which documented the congregation's mergers. The beautifully restored church is painted in soft shades of periwinkle and yellow. In the churchyard are the graves of 100 Hessian soldiers from the Revolution; and that of Eugene Ormandy, former conductor of the Philadelphia Orchestra. ⊠ *412 Pine St., Society Hill* 🕾 *215/925–8051* ⊕ *www.oldpine.org* 🖾 *Free; donations accepted* ☞ *Guided tours by appointment.*

### Old St. Joseph's Church

**CHURCH** | In 1733 a tiny chapel was established by Jesuits for Philadelphia's 11 Catholic families. It was one of the first places in the English-speaking colonies

# Society Hill

**KEY**

- ① Sights
- ① Restaurants
- ⑪ Quick Bites
- ① Hotels

Delaware River

Penn's Landing

Independence Square National Historic Park

0 ———— 1,000 ft
0 ———— 200 m

**Sights**

1 Athenaeum of
  Philadelphia................**D1**
2 Bouvier's Row................**E2**
3 Headhouse Square........**E3**
4 Hill-Physick House........**D2**
5 Mother Bethel
  A.M.E. Church..............**C3**
6 Old Pine Street
  Presbyterian Church.....**D3**
7 Old St. Joseph's
  Church.........................**E2**
8 Old St. Mary's Church....**D2**
9 Pennsylvania Hospital ...**B2**
10 The Philadelphia
   Contributionship...........**D1**
11 Powel House.................**E2**
12 St. Peter's
   Episcopal Church.........**E3**
13 Thaddeus Kosciuszko
   National Memorial........**E2**
14 Washington Square ......**C1**

**Restaurants** ▶

1 Bistro Romano.............**F3**
2 Bloomsday Cafe...........**E3**
3 Pizzeria Stella.............**E3**
4 Twisted Tail................**E3**
5 Zahav.........................**E2**

**Quick Bites** ▶

1 Bodhi Coffee...............**E3**
2 Cavanaugh's
  Headhouse..................**E3**
3 Lombard Cafe..............**C3**
4 Puyero Venezuelan
  Flavor........................**D3**

**Hotels** ▶

1 Morris House Hotel.......**C1**
2 Philadelphia Marriott
  Old City......................**F2**

where Catholic mass could be legally celebrated, a right granted under William Penn's 1701 Charter of Privileges, which guaranteed religious freedom. But freedom didn't come easy; on one occasion Quakers had to patrol St. Joseph's to prevent a Protestant mob from disrupting services. The present church, built in 1839, is the third on this site. The late-19th-century stained-glass windows are notable. ⊠ *321 Willings Alley, Society Hill* ☎ *215/923–1733* ⊕ *www.oldstjoseph. org* ✉ *Free* ☞ *A free, self-guided audio tour is available for download on the church's website.*

### Old St. Mary's Church

CHURCH | The city's second-oldest Catholic church, circa 1763, became its first cathedral when the city's archdiocese was formed in 1810. Though the interior was renovated in the 1960s, the stained-glass windows and brass chandeliers that once hung in the Founders Room of Independence Hall are historic highlights. Commodore John Barry, a Revolutionary War naval hero, and other famous Philadelphians are buried in the small churchyard. ⊠ *252 S. 4th St., Society Hill* ☎ *215/923–7930* ⊕ *www.oldstmary.com* ✉ *Free* ☞ *Mass weekdays 7:30 am, Sat. 4:30 pm, Sun. 10 am.*

### Pennsylvania Hospital

HOSPITAL | Inside the fine 18th-century original buildings of the oldest hospital in the United States are the nation's first medical library and first surgical amphitheater (an 1804 innovation, with a skylight). The hospital also has a portrait gallery, early medical instruments, art objects, and a rare-book library with items dating from 1762. The artwork includes the 1817 Benjamin West painting *Christ Healing the Sick in the Temple.* Today Pennsylvania Hospital is a full-service modern medical center four blocks southwest of the Athenaeum. Guided tours are available on weekdays and by appointment (via phone) only. ⊠ *800 Spruce St., at 8th St., Society Hill*

☎ *215/829–3370* ⊕ *www.pennmedicine. org/for-patients-and-visitors/penn-medicine-locations/pennsylvania-hospital* ⊘ *Closed weekends.*

### The Philadelphia Contributionship

NOTABLE BUILDING | The Contributionship, the nation's oldest fire insurance company, was founded by Benjamin Franklin in 1752; the present Greek Revival building with fluted marble Corinthian columns dates from 1836 and has some magnificently elegant salons (particularly the boardroom, where a seating plan on the wall lists Benjamin Franklin as the first incumbent of seat Number One). The architect, Thomas U. Walter, was also responsible for the dome and House and Senate wings of the U.S. Capitol in Washington, D.C. This is still an active business, but a small museum is open to the public by appointment. ⊠ *210 S. 4th St., Society Hill* ☎ *215/627–1752 Ext. 1286 to arrange a tour* ⊕ *www.1752.com* ✉ *Free.*

### Powel House

HISTORIC HOME | Built in 1765 and later purchased by Samuel Powel, the last mayor of Philadelphia under the Crown and the first in the new republic, this brick Georgian house remains one of the city's most elegant historic homes. It's furnished with important pieces of 18th-century furniture. A mahogany staircase from Santo Domingo embellishes the front hall, and there is a signed Gilbert Stuart portrait in the parlor. In the second-floor ballroom, renowned hostess Mrs. Powel served floating islands and whipped syllabubs to distinguished guests (Adams, Franklin, Lafayette) on Nanking china that was a gift from George and Martha Washington. Today the ballroom can be rented for parties and special events. ⊠ *244 S. 3rd St., Society Hill* ☎ *215/627–0364* ⊕ *www. philalandmarks.org/powel-house* ✉ *$8* ⊘ *Closed Mon.–Wed.* ☞ *Tours offered Thurs.–Sat. Apr.–Nov. and weekends Mar. and Dec.*

### St. Peter's Episcopal Church

**CHURCH** | St. Peter's Church has been in continuous use since its first service on September 4, 1761. The brick Palladian-style building was designed by Scottish architect Robert Smith, also responsible for Carpenters' Hall and the steeple on Christ Church. William Strickland's simple steeple, a Philadelphia landmark, was added in 1842. Notable features include the grand Palladian window on the chancel wall, high-back box pews that were raised off the floor to eliminate drafts, and the unusual arrangement of altar and pulpit at either end of the main aisle. The design has been called "restrained," but what is palpable on a visit is the silence and grace of the stark white interior. In the churchyard lie Commodore John Hazelwood, a Revolutionary War hero; painter Charles Willson Peale; and seven Native American chiefs who died of smallpox on a visit to Philadelphia in 1793. A guide may be on hand Saturday from 11 to 1 and on Sunday from 1 to 3. ✉ *313 Pine St., Society Hill* ☎ *215/925–5968, 215/554–6161 for audio tour of the church* 🌐 *www.stpetersphila.org* 🎟 *Free; donations accepted* 🕒 *Closed Sat.* [M] *SEPTA buses 12, 40, and 57 all stop alongside St. Peter's campus.*

### Thaddeus Kosciuszko National Memorial

**HISTORIC HOME** | A Polish general who later became a national hero in his homeland, Kosciuszko came to the United States in 1776 to fight in the Revolution, one of the first foreign volunteers in the war. The plain three-story brick house, built around 1776, features a series of exhibits that feature artifacts from six Polish museums, depicting Kosciuszko's life in his homeland as well as some of his original possessions. An eight-minute film (in English and Polish) portrays the general's activities during the Revolution. ✉ *301 Pine St., Society Hill* ☎ *215/965–2305 Independence Visitor Center (call to check availability)* 🌐 *www.nps.gov/thko* 🎟 *Free* 🕒 *Closed Nov.–Mar., and weekdays Apr.–Oct.*

### Washington Square

**PLAZA/SQUARE** | This leafy area resembling a London park has been through numerous incarnations since it was set aside by William Penn. From 1705 until after the Revolution, the square was lined on three sides by houses and on the fourth by the Walnut Street Prison. The square served as a burial ground for victims of the 1793 yellow fever epidemic and for 2,600 British and American soldiers who perished during the Revolutionary War. The square holds a Tomb of the Unknown Soldier, erected to commemorate those lost in that conflict. By the 1840s the square had gained prestige as the center of the city's most fashionable neighborhood. It later became the city's publishing center. Today, it features a fountain and is a lovely place to stroll in the warmer months with benches to rest and remember the incredible history that took place in and around this small city square. ✉ *Bounded by 6th and 7th Sts. and Walnut and Locust Sts., Society Hill* 🌐 *www.nps.gov/inde/learn/historyculture/places-washingtonsquare.htm* 🎟 *Free.*

## 🍴 Restaurants

### Bistro Romano

**$$$$ | ITALIAN | FAMILY** | Copious portions of regional Italian cuisine are served in the cozy brick-walled dining room of this historic early 18th-century granary. The menu showcases a number of old-world classics, alongside modern versions of pastas, and seafood and meat dishes like rack of lamb, grilled swordfish, and veal saltimbocca. **Known for:** hearty Italian cuisine; Caesar salad made table-side; extensive wine menu. [$] *Average main: $33* ✉ *120 Lombard St., Society Hill* ☎ *215/925–8880* 🌐 *www.bistroromano.com* 🕒 *Closed Mon. and Tues. No lunch.*

### Bloomsday Cafe

**$$ | AMERICAN** | Located along Philly's legendary Headhouse Square, Bloomsday's modern, eclectic menu features a wide assortment of large and small plates suitable for sharing, as well as hearty, seasonal, and farm-to-table specialties like baba ghanoush, sweet-and-spicy wings, fish-and-chips, and beef stew. Fans keep returning to this friendly, stylish restaurant for the Bloomsday dry-aged burger and an array of tinned fish plates, which include sardines, tuna, mussels, and octopus. **Known for:** wine shop on the premises; eclectic menu with shareable plates; seasonal, farm-to-table cuisine. $\boxed{S}$ *Average main: $24 ⊠ 414 S. 2nd St., Society Hill* ☎ *267/319–8018* ⊕ *www.bloomsdaycafe.com* ⊘ *Closed Mon. and Tues. No dinner Sun.*

### Pizzeria Stella

**$$** | **PIZZA** | **FAMILY** | Restaurateur Stephen Starr logged countless hours researching how to make the very best pizza, agonizing over the dough, oven type, ideal temperature, and every other conceivable variable. The resulting artisanal, 12-inch rounds, with ingredients like black truffle, fresh prosciutto, and earthy chanterelles, keep this cozy 80-seater overflowing with neighborhood duos and families; the no-reservations policy necessitates getting here early or late if you don't want to wait. **Known for:** Neapolitan pizza; outdoor seating; charming location. $\boxed{S}$ *Average main: $19 ⊠ 420 S. 2nd St., Society Hill* ☎ *215/320–8000* ⊕ *www.pizzeriastella. net.*

### Twisted Tail

**$$** | **SOUTHERN** | Specializing in Southern specialties cooked on a charcoal grill, this Headhouse Square restaurant's extensive menu offerings include fried chicken, barbecue smoked ribs, shrimp and grits, and grilled swordfish. This fun, lively hot spot also has a busy bar, including a robust wine list and American whiskey selection, with mixologists pouring craft cocktails. **Known for:** centrally located on Headhouse Square; live music most nights; Southern cuisine. $\boxed{S}$ *Average main: $24 ⊠ 509 S. 2nd St., Society Hill* ☎ *215/558–2471* ⊕ *www.thetwistedtail. com* ⊘ *No lunch weekdays.*

### ★ Zahav

**$$$** | **MEDITERRANEAN** | Chef Michael Solomonov's Zahav is steeped in the milk and honey and hummus and lamb of his native Israel, as well as the cultures that have left a mark on that Promised Land. Taking advantage of its dramatic perch above one of the city's oldest streets, this James Beard award–winning restaurant relies on picture windows and soaring ceilings to create spectacle, but the open kitchen is the true stage. **Known for:** Israeli cuisine; creative cocktails; hopping dining room. $\boxed{S}$ *Average main: $25 ⊠ 237 St. James Pl., Society Hill* ☎ *215/625–8800* ⊕ *www.zahavrestaurant.com* ⊘ *No lunch.*

## ☕ Coffee and Quick Bites

### Bodhi Coffee

**$** | **CAFÉ** | This cute café serves up a variety of gourmet coffees, teas, breakfast sandwiches, and locally made pastries in a friendly atmosphere. Run by the same owner of Federal Donuts, this shop is sustainability-minded, and they make their own nondairy milk in-house with locally sourced oats. **Known for:** excellent gourmet coffee selection; oat milk made with locally sourced oats; small bits and light fare. $\boxed{S}$ *Average main: $7 ⊠ 410 S. 2nd St., Society Hill* ⊕ *bodhicoffee.com.*

### Cavanaugh's Headhouse

**$$** | **AMERICAN** | A traditional sports bar, this popular spot is worth dropping in for a casual bite or drink, as this multi-level, multi-room tavern has been serving pub grub since the 1780s. The menu has all the pub food you could want, but be sure to try the wings; they are dry-rubbed and fried to order and come hot, mild, or 3rd degree. **Known for:** wings; plenty of TVs to watch whatever game you're looking for; location on the historic Headhouse Square. $\boxed{S}$ *Average main: $20 ⊠ 421 S. 2nd St., Society Hill* ☎ *215/928–9307* ⊕ *www.cavsheadhouse.com* ⊘ *No lunch Mon.–Thurs.*

### Lombard Cafe

$ | **CAFÉ** | This cute and cozy neighborhood gem has exceptional coffees, lattes, iced teas, and other hand-crafted beverages. They also sell a selection of locally made baked goods (try the cinnamon rolls); it's a solid spot for a coffee break while exploring the area. **Known for:** locally roasted coffee; friendly ambience; variety of tasty light bites and sandwiches. [$] *Average main: $10* ✉ *542 Lombard St., Society Hill* ☎ *267/455–0327* 🌐 *www.facebook.com/lombardcafe.*

### Puyero Venezuelan Flavor

$ | **SOUTH AMERICAN** | Owned by a team of young Venezuelans, the vibrant Puyero offers a fun fast-casual take on their country's cuisine. The main focus is crispy cornmeal arepas filled with a variety of meats, cheeses, and veggies; they also offer *patacones* (fried plantain sandwiches), *cachacas* (thinner cornmeal pancakes), and rotating specials. **Known for:** traditional arepas; Venezuelan food; fun environment. [$] *Average main: $11* ✉ *524 S. 4th St., Society Hill* ☎ *267/928–4584* 🌐 *www.puyeroflavor.com* 🕒 *Closed Wed.*

## Hotels

### Morris House Hotel

$$ | **B&B/INN** | A lovely bed-and-breakfast in leafy Society Hill, Morris House is within walking distance of historic Old City, the Pine Street shopping corridor, and Center City to the north, but it's away from other hotels and touristy spots, giving visitors an authentic neighborhood experience. **Pros:** great, low-key location; a National Historic Landmark built in 1787; outdoor courtyard. **Cons:** no elevator; no parking; not a good fit for families. [$] *Rooms from: $244* ✉ *225 S. 8th St., Society Hill* ☎ *215/922–2446* 🌐 *www.morrishousehotel.com* 🛏 *17 rooms* 🍴 *Free Breakfast.*

### Philadelphia Marriott Old City

$$ | **HOTEL** | Convenient to downtown sights, this Colonial-style building is two blocks from Penn's Landing, three blocks from Headhouse Square, and four blocks from Independence Hall. **Pros:** pleasant, airy lobby; newly updated fitness center; within walking distance of Old City nightlife. **Cons:** pricey valet parking; noise from traffic may be bothersome; removed from main attractions. [$] *Rooms from: $239* ✉ *1 Dock St., Society Hill* ☎ *215/238–6000, 800/325–3535* 🌐 *www.marriott.com* 🛏 *364 rooms* 🍴 *No Meals.*

# Penn's Landing

Named in honor of Philadelphia founder William Penn's first steps ashore in 1682—the actual spot is in nearby Chester—Penn's Landing runs along the western bank of the Delaware River, providing views of moored pleasure boats and chugging cargo ships alike. Attractions along the stretch of Penn's Landing adjacent to Old City include the world's largest four-masted tall ship, the *Moshulu,* which doubles as a restaurant. The waterfront is also the scene of July 4 fireworks as well as jazz and big-band concerts, cultural festivals, and children's events. Recent years have seen the development of the walkable Race Street Pier, where you can take in views of the Benjamin Franklin Bridge looming overhead. There's also the mixed-use Cherry Street Pier, and seasonal gathering places like Spruce Street Harbor Park, Morgan's Pier, and the Blue Cross RiverRink Winterfest and Summerfest, all popular places for strolling, snacking, sipping, and family-friendly recreation. An ambitious, multimillion-dollar redevelopment of this area, which will introduce a cap park connecting Old City with its riverfront, is expected to be completed by 2024.

Penn's Landing's Irish Memorial honors those who lost their lives during the Great Famine and well as those who were forced to emigrate.

## GETTING HERE AND AROUND

The RiverLink Ferry makes a 15-minute trip across the Delaware River, traveling between the Philadelphia side and waterfront attractions in Camden, New Jersey, including the Adventure Aquarium, the Camden Children's Museum, Freedom Mortgage Pavilion (formerly BB&T Pavilion), and the battleship *New Jersey*. It operates seasonally, and round-trip tickets cost $10. Though the closest access point is at 8th and Market Streets, about a 15-minute walk from Penn's Landing, the PATCO Speedline is another efficient and affordable means of transportation between both sides of the Delaware River. Round-trip fares are $6. (A new PATCO station at Franklin Square is scheduled to re-open in 2024.)

**CONTACT RiverLink Ferry.** ⊠ *Penn's Landing, Columbus Blvd. and Walnut St., Penn's Landing* ✛ *Near Independence Seaport Museum* ☎ *856/964–5465* ⊕ *www.delawareriverwaterfront.com/ places/riverlink-ferry.*

##  Sights

Penn's Landing attractions include historic vessels like the *Moshulu,* the world's largest four-masted tall ship. The Cherry Street Pier, Spruce Street Harbor Park, and the Independence Seaport Museum are along the Delaware River, too. There's also access to Camden's waterfront attractions, including the Adventure Aquarium, the Camden Children's Museum, the Freedom Mortgage Pavilion, and the battleship *New Jersey* via the RiverLink Ferry.

### Adventure Aquarium

**AQUARIUM | FAMILY** | This high-tech, hands-on science education center is the home of "Shark Realm," a 550,000-gallon tank stretching two stories high and thick with sharks, stingrays, and sawfish. The daring can traverse "Shark Bridge," a V-shaped rope suspension bridge just above the exhibit. In the "Hippo Haven," hippopotamuses cohabitate with birds, lizards, and tortoises also native to Africa. There are also up-close "animal experiences,"

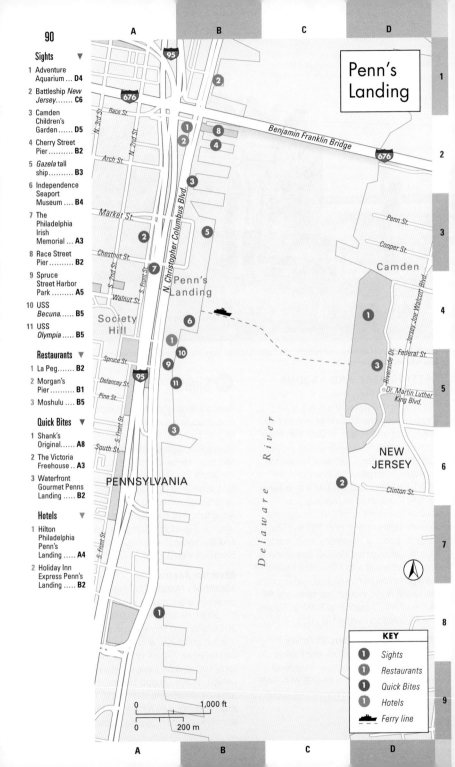

90

Penn's Landing

### Sights ▼

1  Adventure Aquarium ... **D4**
2  Battleship *New Jersey*....... **C6**
3  Camden Children's Garden ...... **D5**
4  Cherry Street Pier .......... **B2**
5  *Gazela* tall ship .......... **B3**
6  Independence Seaport Museum .... **B4**
7  The Philadelphia Irish Memorial ... **A3**
8  Race Street Pier .......... **B2**
9  Spruce Street Harbor Park ......... **A5**
10  USS *Becuna*...... **B5**
11  USS *Olympia* ..... **B5**

### Restaurants ▼

1  La Peg....... **B2**
2  Morgan's Pier .......... **B1**
3  Moshulu .... **B5**

### Quick Bites ▼

1  Shank's Original...... **A8**
2  The Victoria Freehouse .. **A3**
3  Waterfront Gourmet Penns Landing ..... **B2**

### Hotels ▼

1  Hilton Philadelphia Penn's Landing ..... **A4**
2  Holiday Inn Express Penn's Landing ..... **B2**

### KEY

- **1** Sights
- **1** Restaurants
- **1** Quick Bites
- **1** Hotels
- Ferry line

Race St.

Arch St.

Market St.

Chestnut St.

Walnut St.

Spruce St.

Delancey St.

Pine St.

South St.

N. 2nd St.

N. 2nd St.

S. 2nd St.

S. Front St.

S. Front St.

N. Christopher Columbus Blvd.

N. Christopher Columbus Blvd.

Benjamin Franklin Bridge

Penn's Landing

Society Hill

PENNSYLVANIA

Delaware River

Penn St.

Cooper St.

Camden

Jersey Joe Walcott Blvd.

Riverside Dr.

Federal St.

Dr. Martin Luther King Blvd.

Clinton St.

NEW JERSEY

0    1,000 ft

0    200 m

penguin feedings, live animal talks, and immersive 3-D theater presentations. The aquarium features a coffee shop, an eco-friendly marketplace and a beer garden (with outdoor seating during the warmer months). To get here, drive or take the ferry from Penn's Landing. Tickets are cheaper if you purchase online ahead of time. ⊠ *Camden Waterfront, 1 Riverside Dr., Camden* ☎ *844/474–3474* ⊕ *www.adventureaquarium.com* 🎫 *From $27.*

### Battleship *New Jersey*
**NAUTICAL SIGHT | FAMILY** | The World War II–era USS *New Jersey,* one of the most decorated battleships in the history of the U.S. Navy, is now a floating museum. It's docked in Camden, New Jersey, just south of the Freedom Mortgage Pavilion amphitheater. A 90-minute guided tour takes you around the upper and lower decks of the ship, or you can explore this fascinating vessel on your own. Some recently launched tours include evening small-group tours of the engine room and other specific areas; and families and groups can arrange to tour, dine, and sleep on the vessel overnight. ⊠ *62 Battleship Pl., Camden Waterfront, Camden* ☎ *866/877–6262* ⊕ *www.battleshipnewjersey.org* 🎫 *Self-guided tours $25; guided tours $35.*

### Camden Children's Garden
**GARDEN | FAMILY** | Located adjacent to the Adventure Aquarium on the Camden waterfront, this delightful 4-acre garden is an interactive horticultural playground with theme exhibits located in Wiggins Park. You can smell, hear, touch, and even taste some of the elements in the Dinosaur, Cityscapes, Picnic, and Storybook exhibits, as well as in the gardens and the Butterfly House. Other attractions include Amaze, Carousel, Train Ride, Tree House, and more. To get here, drive or take the ferry from Penn's Landing. ⊠ *Camden Waterfront, 3 Riverside Dr., Camden* ☎ *856/365–8733*

⊕ *www.camdenchildrensgarden.org* 🎫 *$9* ⊗ *Closed weekdays.*

### Cherry Street Pier
**MARINA/PIER** | Spread out across 55,000 square feet, the multiuse Cherry Street Pier is among the newer gems of Philadelphia's slow but gradual Delaware River revitalization efforts. It's a great place to explore and soak in views of the Ben Franklin Bridge, waterfront scenery, and beyond, especially during the warmer months. It's free to walk around, but there's plenty to purchase here, as it's home to artists' studios, artisan craft fairs, and continually changed exhibits throughout the versatile space. There's a diversity of snacks, too. Popular concessions include a variety of sweets, local brews, and comfort foods. ⊠ *121 N. Columbus Blvd., Penn's Landing* ☎ *215/923–0818* ⊕ *www.cherrystreetpier.com.*

### *Gazela* Tall Ship
**NAUTICAL SIGHT | FAMILY** | Built in 1883 and formerly named *Gazela Primeiro,* this 177-foot square-rigger is the last of a Portuguese fleet of cod-fishing ships, retired from regular service in 1969. As the Port of Philadelphia's ambassador of goodwill, the *Gazela* sails from June to October to participate in harbor festivals and celebrations up and down the Atlantic coast. She's also a ship school and a museum, and has been featured in movies like *Interview with the Vampire.* An all-volunteer crew works on maintenance while the vessel is in port. While visiting, you can also admire the tugboat, *Jupiter,* the oldest tugboat in existence that was built in Philadelphia. ⊠ *101 S. Christopher Columbus Blvd., Penn's Landing* ☎ *215/238–0280* ⊕ *www.philashipguild.org.*

### Independence Seaport Museum
**HISTORY MUSEUM | FAMILY** | Philadelphia's maritime museum houses many nautical artifacts, figureheads, and ship models, as well as interactive exhibits that convey just what the Delaware and Schuylkill

rivers have meant to the city's fortunes over the years. You can climb in the gray, cold, wooden bunks used in steerage; unload cargo from giant container ships with a miniature crane; or even try your hand at designing your own boat. Enter the museum by passing under the three-story replica of the Benjamin Franklin Bridge, and be sure to check out the Seaport Boat Shop and Ship Model Shack, where members of the Philadelphia Ship Model Society put together scale-model ships in front of visitors' eyes. Tickets to tour the USS *Becunia* in addition to the museum cost slightly more. During summer season only, visitors can dine at the adjacent Liberty Point restaurant. ⊠ *211 S. Columbus Blvd., at Walnut St., Penn's Landing* 🕾 *215/413–8655* ⊕ *www.phillyseaport.org* 🖾 *$18 for museum and USS Olympia.*

### The Philadelphia Irish Memorial

**PUBLIC ART** | Erected in 2003 to honor the victims of the Irish Famine (1845–1849), the memorial features 35 life-size bronze figures that depict the famine in Ireland, as well as people moving to and arriving in America; more than 1 million people died in the famine and more than 1 million people left the country. The memorial was designed by Glenna Goodacre. ⊠ *100 Chestnut St., Penn's Landing* ⊕ *www.irishmemorial.org.*

### Race Street Pier

**PROMENADE** | The first in a planned series of parks along the Delaware River, this green space offers dramatic views of the overhead Benjamin Franklin Bridge and allows for up-close views of the river itself. Designed by the same firm behind New York's popular High Line, the terraced promenade features lush plantings, including some three dozen trees and many perennials, as well as amphitheater-style seating near the river's edge, plenty of benches and green lawns for relaxing, and regular donation-based yoga classes during the summer months. ⊠ *N. Columbus Blvd. and Race St.,*

*Penn's Landing* 🕾 *215/922–2386* ⊕ *www.delawareriverwaterfront.com/places/race-street-pier* 🖾 *Free.*

### Spruce Street Harbor Park

**PROMENADE** | **FAMILY** | This seasonal oasis—referred to by some as an urban beach—is a combination of three landscaped barges, a hammock lounge, and floating gardens that hug the Delaware River. More than 50 hammocks are strung throughout the park, and there's an award-winning beer garden that pours more than 15 local brews. You can get food from the Franklin Fountain and Chickie's & Pete's as well as pizza, classic boardwalk foods, and more. There's even a boardwalk that's lined with swings, hammocks, bocce courts, Ping-Pong, shuffleboard, and shipping containers that have been converted into an arcade with skeeball, air hockey, and other classic games. ⊠ *Marina at Penn's Landing, 301 S. Christopher Columbus Blvd., Penn's Landing* 🕾 *215/922–2386* ⊕ *www.sprucestreetharborpark.com* 🕙 *Closed Oct.–Apr.*

### USS *Becuna*

**NAUTICAL SIGHT** | **FAMILY** | You can tour this 307-foot-long Balao-class submarine (with a "guppy" conversion), that was launched in 1944 and conducted search-and-destroy missions in the South Pacific. A free audio tour, available with the price of admission, tells amazing stories of what life was like for a crew of 80 men, at sea for months at a time, in these claustrophobic quarters. Then you can step through the narrow walkways, climb the ladders, and glimpse the torpedoes in their firing chambers. Tickets are available at the Independence Seaport Museum. ⊠ *211 S. Columbus Blvd., at Walnut St., Penn's Landing* 🕾 *215/413–8655* ⊕ *www.phillyseaport.org/submarine-becuna* 🖾 *$12; Independence Seaport Museum admission ($18) separate* ☞ *Tickets can only be purchased in-person at the Seaport Museum.*

**USS *Olympia***

**NAUTICAL SIGHT** | **FAMILY** | Commodore George Dewey's flagship at the Battle of Manila in the Spanish-American War is the oldest still-afloat steel warship in the world. Dewey entered Manila Harbor after midnight on May 1, 1898. At 5:40 am he told his captain, "You may fire when you are ready, Gridley," and by 12:30 they had destroyed the entire Spanish fleet. You can tour the entire restored ship, including the officers' staterooms, galley, gun batteries, and pilothouse. Admission is included with your ticket to the Independence Seaport Museum. ✉ *211 S. Columbus Blvd., at Walnut St., Penn's Landing* ☎ *215/413–8655* 🌐 *www.phillyseaport.org/cruiser-olympia* 🎟 *$18 for museum admission and USS Olympia* ☞ *Tickets to other historic vessels are an additional fee.*

## 🍴 Restaurants

**La Peg**

**$$$** | **AMERICAN** | Peter Woolsey, whose tenured Bella Vista bistro, La Minette, is beloved by Francophiles, bet big on an out-of-the-way Penn's Landing sequel named for his wife, Peggy. Housed in a former water pumping station, the digs are catnip for engineering and architecture nerds—rivet-studded I-beams crisscross the ceiling like a catwalk, and soaring arched windows overlook the brontosaurus hoof–like supports of the Ben Franklin Bridge—but foodies love the comfort-food-heavy, Gallic-influenced menu with items like New England clam chowder, pot roast, and chicken and dumplings. **Known for:** waterfront views; impressive architecture; theatrical touches. [$] *Average main: $30* ✉ *140 N. Christopher Columbus Blvd., Penn's Landing* ☎ *215/375–7744* 🌐 *www.facebook.com/lapegatfringe* 🕒 *Closed Tues. and winter months. No lunch weekdays.*

**Morgan's Pier**

**$** | **AMERICAN** | This waterfront open-air beer garden has made a splash every year since its 2012 debut, offering exciting new eats with each new season—the "chef-in-residence" program, which sees a new chef shaping the culinary approach at the start of each spring season, keeps things fresh. Expect a high-low approach, mixing beer-friendly snacks with more creative fare. **Known for:** craft cocktails; casual alfresco dining; craft beer. [$] *Average main: $14* ✉ *221 N. Columbus Blvd., Penn's Landing* ☎ *215/279–7134* 🌐 *www.morganspier.com* 🕒 *Closed in winter months.*

**Moshulu**

**$$$$** | **AMERICAN** | The altogether unexpected restaurant set aboard the *Moshulu,* the oldest and biggest still-floating rigged-sail vessel in the world, offers one of the city's more unique atmospheres. The 359-foot ship, built in 1904, once transported coal and other natural resources all over the world, but today it focuses on serving high-end (and often pricey) new American cuisine, with attention paid to seafood and local, seasonal produce. **Known for:** unique atmosphere; creative seafood; wine. [$] *Average main: $42* ✉ *401 S. Columbus Blvd., Penn's Landing* ☎ *215/923–2500* 🌐 *www.moshulu.com* 🕒 *No lunch weekdays.*

## ☕ Coffee and Quick Bites

**Shank's Original**

**$** | **ITALIAN** | A South Philly staple for decades, the relocated Shank's now slings its signature sandwiches on the waterfront. A cheesesteak is always a solid order, but longtime customers sing the praises of lesser-publicized signatures, such as the chicken cutlet "Italiano" (pick broccoli rabe or spinach) and vegetarian eggplant Parmesan. **Known for:** cheesesteaks; roast pork sandwiches; chicken cutlet sandwiches. [$] *Average main: $12* ✉ *Pier 40, 901 S. Columbus Blvd., Penn's*

*Landing* ☎ *215/218–4000* 🌐 *www.shanksoriginal.com* ⏲ *Closed Mon.*

**The Victoria Freehouse**
$ | **BRITISH** | This U.K.-inspired pub on Front Street serves proper hearty pub fare (shepherd's pie, bangers and mash) and authentic cask ales. It's also a popular hangout for fans of English soccer. **Known for:** Sunday roast; craft beer and cask ale; weekend brunch. [$] *Average main: $15* ✉ *10 S. Front St., Penn's Landing* ☎ *215/543–6089* 🌐 *www.victoriafreehouse.com* ⏲ *No lunch weekdays.*

**Waterfront Gourmet Penns Landing**
$ | **CAFÉ** | **FAMILY** | A small sandwich shop and deli, Waterfront Gourmet has a variety of breakfast items, sandwiches, salads, coffees, and more light bites for a quick meal. There are even vegan and vegetarian options available like the veggie panini and avocado toast. **Known for:** generously sized sandwiches; Delaware River views; vegan, vegetarian and healthy options. [$] *Average main: $12* ✉ *5 N. Christopher Colombus Blvd., Penn's Landing* ☎ *267/227–1994* 🌐 *www.waterfrontgourmet.com.*

## Hotels

**Hilton Philadelphia Penn's Landing**
$$$ | **HOTEL** | **FAMILY** | The theme here is "room with a view," as this hotel on the banks of the Delaware offers dramatic river views from the 22-story tower; southern-facing rooms have views of both the river and the city. **Pros:** nice indoor pool with option to sit outside; great views; kid-friendly. **Cons:** separated from Old City by I–95; rooms showing some wear and tear; expensive valet parking. [$] *Rooms from: $299* ✉ *201 S. Columbus Blvd., Penn's Landing* ☎ *215/521–6500* 🌐 *www.hiltonpennslanding.com* 🛏 *350 rooms* 🍴 *No Meals.*

**Holiday Inn Express Penn's Landing**
$$ | **HOTEL** | Situated on a busy corner, the 10-story location can be noisy, but the affordable rates are the main attraction; if you have a room on an upper floor facing the Delaware River you can enjoy excellent views of the Benjamin Franklin Bridge. **Pros:** cheaper alternative to staying in Old City; nice views of the river and Benjamin Franklin Bridge; free shuttle to Center City. **Cons:** isolated from Center City; immediate area can be desolate; can be noisy due to traffic. [$] *Rooms from: $198* ✉ *100 N. Columbus Blvd., Penn's Landing* ☎ *215/627–7900* 🌐 *www.ihg.com/holidayinnexpress/hotels/us/en/philadelphia/phlpl/hoteldetail* 🛏 *184 rooms* 🍴 *Free Breakfast.*

## Performing Arts

**Freedom Mortgage Pavilion**
**CONCERTS** | Across the Delaware River in Camden, New Jersey, this urban amphitheater (formerly called BB&T Pavilion) programs everything from classical to hip-hop and rock in an adaptable space. Between the outdoor lawn and seated pavilion, it can host crowds as large as 25,000, with the indoor portion able to accommodate 7,000. Best reached from Philadelphia by car, PATCO, or ferry (during summer). ✉ *1 Harbor Blvd., Camden* ☎ *856/365–1300 ticket information and directions* 🌐 *www.waterfrontamphitheater.com.*

**PECO Multicultural Series**
**FESTIVALS** | **FAMILY** | PECO, Philadelphia's primary electric provider, sponsors a series of free-to-attend summer festivals along Penn's Landing. Each installment focuses on a different cultural tradition, welcoming food, music, dance, and vendors from around the world. Programming changes yearly, but recent slates have included ACANAfest, by the African Cultural Alliance of North America; Brazilian and Mexican independence celebrations; the Philadelphia Irish Festival; and the Islamic Heritage Festival. ✉ *Great Plaza at Penn's Landing, 101 Columbus Blvd., at Chestnut St., Penn's Landing* ☎ *215/922–2386* 🌐 *www.delawareriverwaterfront.com* 🎟 *Free.*

# CENTER CITY EAST, MIDTOWN VILLAGE AND THE GAYBORHOOD, AND CHINATOWN

Updated by
Maddy Sweitzer-Lamme

 Sights
★★★★☆

 Restaurants
★★★★★

 Hotels
★★★★☆

 Shopping
★★★☆☆

 Nightlife
★★★☆☆

# READING TERMINAL MARKET 101

The market's many stalls are a great place to grab a bite.

The roots of the Reading Terminal Market date to 1890, when the Reading Railroad Company, wishing to build a grand terminal at 1100 Market Street, struck a deal with existing merchants on the block to construct a new home for them to vend. The market you see today opened for business in 1893, and though much has changed, it still provides a throwback experience to an older, simpler Philadelphia. And yes, there is free Wi-Fi throughout the Market.

## WHAT TO EXPECT

There are more than 80 stalls in the market. Pennslyvannia Dutch merchants from Lancaster County sell baked goods and produce straight from their farms, alongside butchers, bakers, fishmongers, candymakers, cheese specialists, and many other artisan makers. Breakfast and lunch options abound, with everything from cheesesteaks, Cajun cuisine, and a Jewish deli to vegetarian dishes, sushi, and soul food.

## NON-FOOD VENDORS

It's not all about food at the Reading Market. Retail vendors sell exotic spices, flowers, crafts, jewelry, clothing, gifts, and local spirits.

## WHAT NOT TO MISS

Don't miss Miller's Twist for piping-hot, freshly rolled soft pretzels; Bassetts, America's oldest ice-cream makers; Metropolitan Bakery, for hearty breads and light pastries; and Down Home Diner for affordable Southern-style fare. And while arguing over food is a time-honored pastime in Philly, pretty much everyone agrees on pancakes and scrapple at the Dutch Eating Place, roast pork sandwiches at DiNic's, whoopie pies at Flying Monkey, and chocolate chip cookies at Famous 4th Street. Sami Somi will make you a traditional Georgian *khachapuri* (cheese-filled bread), Hershel's East Side Deli has your reliable corned beef and pastrami fix; Fox & Son will fix you a high-end corndog, while Beiler's big ol' doughnuts and fritters draw long lines daily. And if you need a drink to calm the nerves enough to navigate the madness, stop by the friendly Molly Malloy's; they'll pour you a brew in a to-go cup you can sip as you stroll around and shop.

### WHEN TO GO

The market is open daily 8 am to 6 pm, but some vendors close earlier, and popular items often sell out before the end of the day, so if there's something specific you're after, go early. If you want to avoid the crowds, your best bet is to visit on weekdays before 11 am or after 2 pm.

■ TIP→ **All Pennsylvania Dutch merchants are closed on Sundays.**

Hot dogs and hot beef sausages wrapped in pastry. Yum.

If you love food, plan to spend a few hours exploring the market's stocked shelves.

### CONTACT INFO

✉ 51 N. 12th St., at Arch St.
☎ 215/922–2317 ⊕ www.readingterminalmarket.org

### OTHER MARKETS WORTH VISITING

Though Reading Terminal Market has a tourist-friendly reputation, note that it is also a popular destination with everyday Philadelphians looking to do their weekly grocery shopping, given the high number of affordable produce, meat, and seafood purveyors. For a slightly different glimpse into how locals shop, check out the **Rittenhouse Farmers' Market** (✉ 18th and Walnut Sts., Rittenhouse Square ⊕ friendsofrittenhouse.org), held every Saturday morning year-round, along with Tuesdays on a seasonal basis; the **Headhouse Farmers Market** (✉ 2nd and Lombard Sts., Society Hill ⊕ thefoodtrust.org), which operates on Sunday mornings year-round; and the **South 9th Street Italian Market** (✉ 9th St., between Fitzwater St. and Wharton St., South Philadelphia ⊕ www.italianmarketphilly.org), another year-round option (⇨ *see Chapter 8 for more details*).

# NEIGHBORHOOD SNAPSHOT

## TOP EXPERIENCES

■ **Reading Terminal Market:** Sample a wide range of cuisines at dozens of stalls at this bustling market.

■ **City Hall:** Take the elevator to the observation deck for commanding views of the city.

■ **The Comcast Center:** The city's tallest building offers a seasonal sidewalk café and an entertaining video installation in its lobby.

■ **Macy's:** The Wanamaker Building is a city landmark. It's home to Macy's, the world's largest pipe organ, and a spectacular holiday light show.

■ **Pennsylvania Academy of the Fine Arts:** The High Victorian building housing this collection of American art is worth a visit in itself.

■ **Chinatown:** Stop by this colorful district to sample authentic Asian cuisine or shop for ingredients to make your own meal at home.

## GETTING HERE

The heart of Center City is an easy 10- to 15-minute stroll from the Historic Area, or about a 20- to 25-minute walk from Penn's Landing. To orient yourself, Broad Street (the name for what would be 14th Street) serves as a delineation for Center City East and Center City West, while City Hall, located at Broad and Market Streets, is the dividing line for north–south addresses on the numbered streets. You also can use SEPTA bus lines on Market or Walnut Streets, or the underground Blue Line on Market Street, to reach points west of the Historic Area, or take the seasonal PHLASH. The City Hall SEPTA station is a major hub that includes connections for the north–south Orange Line, as well as the east–west Blue and Green Lines.

Chinatown is easily reached by foot from anywhere in greater Center City, or by riding the Blue Line east to the 11th or 8th Street stations. Street parking is available, but it's often challenging; opt for a pay lot, or leave the vehicle behind at your hotel or garage.

## QUICK BITES

■ **Merkaz.** Zahav chef Michael Solomonov's quick-serve whips up Israeli-style lunch, fresh hot pitas filled with tasty meat and veg. ✉ 1218 Sansom St., Center City East ⊕ merkazphilly.com

■ **Kanella Grill.** Popular for lunch and dinner, this casual Cypriot corner spot offers killer Mediterranean cuisine. ✉ 1001 Spruce St., Center City East ⊕ kanellarestaurant.com

■ **Greenstreet Coffee Co.** What this minute shop lacks in size it makes up for in expertly pulled espresso. ✉ 1101 Spruce St., Center City East ⊕ greenstreetcoffee.com

## PLANNING YOUR TIME

■ To get a feel for the city at work, save exploring City Center East for a weekday, when the streets are bustling; but even on weekends you'll encounter plenty of people strolling and shopping. Besides, the City Hall Observation Tower is open weekdays only, and the Masonic Temple is closed on Sunday and Monday. You could walk through the neighborhood in 45 minutes, but reserve about half a day, with an hour each at the Masonic Temple, City Hall Tower, and the Pennsylvania Academy of the Fine Arts.

City Hall is the heart of Philadelphia, geographically and culturally. The densely packed surrounding blocks, especially those east of Broad Street, are home to the buildings, businesses, and people that make Philly tick. From historic landmarks and the humming nightlife scene of 13th Street to vibrant Chinatown, this area exudes urban energy.

The story behind Philadelphia's skyline begins with City Hall, which reaches 40 stories and was the tallest structure in the metropolis until 1987. No law prohibited taller buildings, but the tradition sprang from a gentleman's agreement not to build higher. In May 1984, when a developer introduced plans to build two office towers that would break the 491-foot barrier, it became evident how entrenched this tradition was: the proposal provoked a public outcry. Traditionalists contended that the height limitation made Philadelphia a city of human scale, gave character to its streets and public places, and showed respect for tradition. Those opposed thought a dramatic new skyline would shatter the city's conservative image and encourage economic growth. After much debate, the go-ahead was granted. In short order midtown became the hub of the city's commercial center, Market Street west of City Hall became a district of high-rise office buildings, and the area became a symbol of the city's ongoing transformation from a dying industrial town to a center for service industries. Here, too, are a number of museums, the Reading Terminal Market and the convention center, and Chinatown.

## Center City East

Though geographically accurate, Center City East is not the name Philadelphians use to refer to this zone, bounded by Broad Street to the west and Old City to the east. Instead, you might hear them name-drop sub-neighborhoods, like Midtown Village, a dining-and-shopping juggernaut that has grown up along formerly derelict 13th Street. Or the Gayborhood, the historic HQ for LGBTQ Philly, where the street signs are etched in rainbows. Or Washington Square West, a larger catchall for the area. There's a lot of overlap between the interloping districts of Center City East, but no matter what you call it, its core is leafy Washington Square, the eastern mirror to Rittenhouse Square across Broad. Thomas Jefferson University Hospital has claimed a lot of real estate here, so it's not uncommon to see flocks of eds and meds buzzing around the area in teal scrubs.

Sights

**Avenue of the Arts**

STREET | Broad Street, the city's main north–south thoroughfare, has been reinvented as a performing arts district. Although most of the cultural institutions are situated along South Broad Street from City Hall to Spruce Street, the avenue's cultural, education, and arts organizations reach as far south as Washington Avenue in South Philadelphia and as far north as Dauphin Street in North Philadelphia. The main venue is the Kimmel Center for the Performing Arts, at Broad and Spruce Streets, which includes a 2,500-seat concert hall designed for the Philadelphia Orchestra. The newest addition is the Suzanne Roberts Theatre, a 365-seat facility that is home to the Philadelphia Theatre Company. ⊠ *408 S. Broad St., Center City East* ☎ *215/731–9668* ⊕ *www.avenueofthearts.org.*

★ **City Hall**

GOVERNMENT BUILDING | Topped by a 37-foot bronze statue of William Penn, City Hall provides an opportunity to study the trappings of government and get a panoramic view of the city. With close to 700 rooms, it's the largest city hall in the country and the tallest masonry-bearing building in the world: no steel structure supports it. Designed by architect John McArthur Jr., the building took 30 years to build (1871–1901). The result has been called a "Victorian wedding cake of Renaissance styles." Placed about the facade are hundreds of statues by Alexander Milne Calder, who also designed the statue of Penn, a 27-ton cast-iron work that is the largest single piece of sculpture on any building in the world. City Hall is also the center of municipal and state government. Many of the magnificent interiors—splendidly decorated with mahogany paneling, gold-leaf ceilings, and marble pillars—are patterned after the Second Empire salons of part of the Louvre in Paris. On a tour each weekday at 12:30 you can see the

## The Original Centre Square

Philadelphia's founder, William Penn, designed the city around five main squares including Centre Square, which became the site of the city's magnificent City Hall. Today, Dilworth Park, at the foot of City Hall, re-creates the original Centre Square's goal of being a public gathering point for the community.

Conversation Hall, the Supreme Court of Pennsylvania, the City Council chambers, and the mayor's reception room. You can attend City Council meetings, held each Thursday morning at 10. To top off your visit, take the elevator from the seventh floor up the tower to the observation deck at the foot of William Penn's statue for a 30-mile view of the city and surroundings. The elevator holds only six people per trip and runs every 15 minutes; the least crowded time is early morning. The 90-minute building tour, including a trip up the tower, steps off weekdays at 12:30. The tour office is in Room 121. ⊠ *Broad and Market Sts., Center City East* ☎ *215/686–2840, 215/686–2840 tour information* ⊕ *www.phlvisitorcenter.com/cityhallInteriorexterior* ⏍ *$18 for interior and tower tour, $10 for tower tour only.*

**Fabric Workshop and Museum**

ARTS CENTER | A nonprofit arts organization runs this center and store dedicated to creating new work in fabric and other materials, working with emerging and nationally and internationally recognized artists. ⊠ *1214 Arch St., Center City East* ☎ *215/561–8888* ⊕ *www.fabricworkshopandmuseum.org* ☞ *Suggested donation $5.*

Guided tours of City Hall, the country's largest municipal building, include a trip to the observation deck which provides amazing panoramic city views.

## Fashion District Philadelphia

**STORE/MALL** | An elaborate revamp of the long-standing Gallery shopping complex, the Fashion District consists of more than 800,000 square feet of shopping, dining, and entertainment destinations. Big-name retailers include Primark, Eddie Bauer, H&M, Levi's, and Nike. There's a state-of-the-art AMC movie theater, the large-scale City Winery as well as smaller, more affordable dining options, and Round1, a multi-entertainment facility that has bowling, billiards, karaoke, and more than 250 arcade games. Wonderspaces is an art installation space and there are rotating Instagram-friendly interactive exhibits like Banksy Was Here. ✉ *901 Market St., Center City East* ☎ *215/925–7162* ⊕ *www.fashiondistrict-philadelphia.com.*

## Masonic Temple

**NOTABLE BUILDING** | One of the city's architectural jewels, this temple remains a hidden treasure even to many Philadelphians. Historically, Freemasons were skilled stoneworkers who relied on secret signs and passwords. Their worldwide fraternal order—the Free and Accepted Masons—included men in the building trades, plus many honorary members; the secret society prospered in Philadelphia during Colonial times. Brother James Windrim designed this elaborate temple as a home for the Grand Lodge of Free and Accepted Masons of Pennsylvania. The ceremonial gavel used here at the laying of the cornerstone in 1868, while 10,000 brothers looked on, was the same one that Brother George Washington used to set the cornerstone of the U.S. Capitol. The temple's ornate interior consists of seven lavishly decorated lodge halls built to exemplify specific styles of architecture: Corinthian, Ionic, Italian Renaissance, Norman, Gothic, Oriental, and Egyptian. The Egyptian hall, with its accurate hieroglyphics, is the most famous. The temple also houses an interesting museum of Masonic items, including Benjamin Franklin's printing of the first book on Freemasonry published in America and George Washington's Masonic

# Center City East, and Midtown Village and the Gayborhood

5

## Sights ▼
1 Avenue of The Arts ................**C4**
2 City Hall .............................**C4**
3 Fabric Workshop and Museum ...**E3**
4 Fashion District Philadelphia.....**G4**
5 Masonic Temple .................. **D3**
6 Pennsylvania
   Convention Center .................**E2**
7 Reading Terminal Market .........**E3**
8 Wanamaker Building..............**D4**

## Restaurants ▼
1 Barbuzzo............................**D5**
2 Mercato.............................**D7**
3 Paulie Gee's
   Soul City Slice Shop...............**C8**
4 Pearl & Mary Oyster Bar .........**D5**
5 Sampan .............................**D5**
6 Seorabol Center City .............**D7**
7 Talula's Garden....................**H7**
8 Vedge ..............................**D6**
9 Vetri Cucina .......................**D7**

## Quick Bites ▼
1 Greenstreet Coffee Co. ...........**E7**
2 Kanella Grill ........................**F7**
3 Merkaz..............................**D5**
4 Middle Child........................**E7**
5 Van Leeuwen Ice Cream..........**D5**

## Hotels ▼
1 Alexander Inn .......................**E7**
2 Canopy by Hilton Philadelphia
   Center City...........................**E5**
3 DoubleTree by Hilton Philadelphia
   Center City...........................**C6**
4 Four Points by Sheraton
   Philadelphia City Center ..........**E2**
5 Guild House Hotel .................**D6**
6 Hampton Inn Philadelphia
   Center City-Convention Center....**E2**
7 Hilton Garden Inn Philadelphia
   Center City...........................**F3**
8 Holiday Inn Express Midtown....**D6**
9 Loews Philadelphia Hotel..........**E5**
10 The Notary Hotel...................**D4**
11 Philadelphia Mariott
   Downtown...........................**E4**
12 Residence Inn by Marriott
   Philadelphia Center City ..........**D4**
13 Roost East Market.................**E4**

apron. ⊠ *1 N. Broad St., Center City East* ☎ *215/988–1917* ⊕ *www.pamasonictemple.org* ✉ *$7 for library and museum only; tours $15* ⊙ *Closed Sun. and Mon.*

### Pennsylvania Convention Center

**CONVENTION CENTER** | It's big: a massive expansion completed in 2011 covers 20 acres of central Philadelphia. And it's beautiful: the 2.3 million square feet of space are punctuated by the largest permanent collection of contemporary art in a building of its kind. Many city and state artists are represented in the niches, nooks, and galleries built to house their multimedia works. To see the architectural highlight of the building—the Reading Terminal's magnificently restored four-story-high Victorian train shed, which has been transformed into the Convention Center's Grand Hall—enter the building through the century-old Italian Renaissance Headhouse structure on Market Street between 11th and 12th Streets and ride up the escalator. ⊠ *1101 Arch St., Center City East* ☎ *215/418–4700* ⊕ *www.paconvention.com* ✉ *Free.*

### ★ Reading Terminal Market

**MARKET** | The roots of the Reading Terminal Market date to 1892, when the Reading Railroad commissioned a food bazaar to be built in the train shed's cellar as part of its grand expansion plans. Today, the entire building is a National Historic Landmark, and the Reading Railroad train shed is a National Engineering Landmark. The sprawling market—a food heaven for Philadelphians and visitors alike—has more than 80 food stalls and other shops, selling items from hooked rugs and handmade jewelry to South American and African crafts. Try not to miss Miller's Twist for piping hot, freshly rolled soft pretzels; Bassetts Ice Cream, America's oldest ice-cream makers; Metropolitan Bakery, for hearty breads and light pastries; and the Down Home Diner for affordable Southern-style fare; you can also nibble on Greek, Mexican, Thai, and Indian foods. The Pennsylvania

Dutch merchants from Lancaster County (closed on Sundays) bring in their specialties like Lebanon bologna, shoofly pie, and scrapple. Many stalls have their own counters with seating; there's also a central eating area. An open kitchen offers regular demonstrations by some of the region's top chefs. The market is open daily 8–6. ⊠ *51 N. 12th St., at Arch St., Center City East* ☎ *215/922–2317* ⊕ *www.readingterminalmarket.org* Ⓜ *SEPTA's Blue Line subway.*

### ★ Wanamaker Building

**NOTABLE BUILDING** | The former John Wanamaker department store is almost as prominent a Philadelphia landmark as the Liberty Bell. Wanamaker began with a clothing store in 1861, and became one of America's most innovative and prominent retailers. The massive building was designed by Chicago architect Daniel H. Burnham; its focal point is a 2,500-pound statue of an eagle, a remnant of the 1904 Louisiana Purchase Exposition in St. Louis. Today, the building is home to Macy's and the store's 30,000-pipe organ—the largest ever built—which is used for free concerts every day but Sunday. There's a spectacular holiday light show in the atrium between Thanksgiving and New Years, as well as Macy's Dickens Christmas Village. ⊠ *1300 Market St., at 13th St., Center City East* ☎ *215/241–9000* ⊕ *thewanamakerbuilding.com.*

## 🍴 Restaurants

In Center City East (meaning the blocks east of Broad Street), most restaurants are near Washington Square and a few blocks west, along the bustling 13th Street corridor.

### Paulie Gee's Soul City Slice Shop

**$** | **PIZZA** | It's rare for Philadelphians to take to outsiders, but Paulie Gee's, an import from New York, has been happily embraced. That's partly because it's one of the very few great pizza shops that offer slices, and partially because it stays

## Philadelphia Flower Show

It takes one week; 7,000 Belgian blocks; 3,500 volunteers; thousands of plumbers, carpenters, and electricians; more than a million plants; and 50 tractor-trailer loads of mulch to transform the Pennsylvania Convention Center into the annual Philadelphia Flower Show (🌐 *phsonline.org*), the world's largest indoor horticultural event. But the exhibitors—nursery owners, landscapers, and florists from the region and from Africa, Japan, and Europe—spend the better part of a year planning their displays. Each year the show has a theme, and the show's designers think big, very big. The astonishing, fragrant results of their efforts arrive in the city as a touch of spring in early March.

It's a fitting tribute to William Penn that Philadelphia hosts this extravaganza, for this was Penn's "greene countrie town," which he laid out on a grid punctuated with tree-lined streets, pocket parks, small squares, and large public parks. It's also appropriate that this city gave root to the Pennsylvania Horticultural Society, the nation's first such organization. In 1829, two years after its founding, the society hosted its first show at the Masonic Hall in an 82-by-69-foot exhibition space; 25 society members showed off their green thumbs.

Today the show fills 10 acres of exhibition space at the convention center and spills throughout the area as local restaurants, hotels, and attractions offer special deals. (The show's website may have discounts and coupons.) Along with the more than 50 major exhibits, amateur gardeners contribute more than 2,000 entries in 330 competitive categories—from pressed plants and miniature settings to spectacular jewelry designs that use flowers. There are free cooking and gardening demonstrations, lectures, and an area where you can try out the latest gardening gadgets. Hundreds of vendors sell plants, birdhouses, topiaries, watering systems, botanical prints, and more.

Many people plan trips to Philadelphia during the run of the flower show, so be sure to make reservations early. Wear good walking shoes, check your coat, and bring spending money for the many horticultural temptations. To avoid crowds, which can be daunting, arrive after 4 on weekdays and stay until the 9 pm closing, or show up when the doors open on weekend mornings at 8.

open until 2 am on the weekends serving food and drinks. **Known for:** open until 2 am on weekends; Sicilian-style pies; vegan pizza options. [$] *Average main: $4* ✉ *412 S. 13th St., Center City East* ☎ *267/239–5761* 🌐 *www.pauliegee.com/soul-city.*

### ★ Talula's Garden

**$$$$** | **AMERICAN** | Aimee Olexy's Talula's Table in Kennett Square was an unlikely phenomenon; the little country market had a months-long backlog of reservations for its lone farmhouse table. Olexy's urban extension of that runaway success is a sprawling, high-ceilinged space decorated with Alice Waters quotations printed on the walls, a charming outdoor courtyard with a garden that glows under twinkly lights, and an elegant seasonal menu. **Known for:** farm-to-table cuisine; charming courtyard; cheese boards. [$] *Average main: $34* ✉ *210 W. Washington Sq., Center City East*

Located in the Wanamaker Building which is now the home of Macy's, the 30,000-pipe organ—the largest ever built—is used for free concerts every day but Sunday.

*☎ 215/592–7787 🌐 www.talulasgarden.com 🕓 No lunch Mon.–Sat.*

## Coffee and Quick Bites

**Greenstreet Coffee Co.**

$ | **CAFÉ** | What this minute shop lacks in size it makes up for in expertly pulled espresso. The tiny neighborhood café is the public-facing portion of the locally owned Greenstreet, which imports its beans from around the world and roasts and packages them in a South Philadelphia facility. **Known for:** international coffee selection; espresso drinks; cozy seating. *[$] Average main: $5 ✉ 1101 Spruce St., Center City East ☎ 610/504–3934 🌐 greenstreetcoffee.com 🕓 No dinner.*

**Kanella Grill**

$ | **MEDITERRANEAN** | Popular for lunch and dinner, this casual Cypriot corner spot offers killer Mediterranean cuisine. Center City workers on their lunch breaks and bottle-toting evening groups alike (BYOB) enjoy the ever-changing "dips of the day," with warm pita; a remarkable rendition of Greek salad; and kebabs of pork loin, lamb kofta, or seiftalia, Cypriot lamb-and-pork sausages made in-house. **Known for:** Cypriot cooking; charming dining room; Mediterranean flavors. *[$] Average main: $12 ✉ 1001 Spruce St., Center City East ☎ 267/928–2058 🌐 kanellarestaurant.com 🕓 Closed Mon.*

**Middle Child**

$ | **CAFÉ** | In Midtown Village, Middle Child represents the new guard in the land of hoagies and cheesesteaks. Their So Long Sal—with spicy lemon artichoke spread, Duke's mayo, meat, cheese, and arugula on a Sarcone's roll—draws lines out the door, as does their vegan, hoisin-eggplant Phoagie, but don't miss out on the breakfast options either. **Known for:** phone in your order if you're in a rush; weekends get crowded; sandwiches like the So Long Sal and the Phoagie. *[$] Average main: $12 ✉ 248 S. 11th St., Center City East ☎ 267/930–8344 🌐 www.middlechildphilly.com 🕓 Closed Mon. No dinner.*

## Hotels

**Alexander Inn**

$ | **HOTEL** | The well-maintained rooms at this small hotel have an art deco feel, while location puts you close to the Pennsylvania Convention Center, Avenue of the Arts, and most downtown attractions. **Pros:** excellent location between Rittenhouse Square and historic district; great service; cheap parking. **Cons:** tiny gym; no laundry facilities or services; bar downstairs can get noisy. [$] *Rooms from: $169* ✉ *301 S. 12th St., Center City East* ☎ *215/923–3535* 🌐 *www.alexanderinn.com* 🛏 *48 rooms* 🍴 *Free Breakfast.*

**Four Points by Sheraton Philadelphia City Center**

$$$ | **HOTEL** | With its understated boutiquelike charms, this Four Points offers a practical yet homey alternative to some of its larger neighbors in the Pennsylvania Convention Center area. **Pros:** 24-hour gym; free Wi-Fi; modern yet intimate. **Cons:** no tub for those who like baths; better dining outside hotel; block can be desolate at night. [$] *Rooms from: $340* ✉ *1201 Race St., Center City East* ☎ *215/496–2700* 🌐 *www.marriott.com* 🛏 *92 rooms* 🍴 *No Meals.*

**Hampton Inn Philadelphia Center City-Convention Center**

$ | **HOTEL** | This hotel bills itself as the "best value hotel in Center City" and backs it up with a gym, business center, and, weather permitting, complimentary breakfast on a patio facing 13th Street. **Pros:** excellent value for convention center events; friendly service; recently renovated. **Cons:** immediate area can be desolate at night; pricey parking; small guest laundry. [$] *Rooms from: $159* ✉ *1301 Race St., Center City East* ☎ *215/665–9100, 800/426–7866* 🌐 *www.hamptoninn.com* 🛏 *250 rooms* 🍴 *Free Breakfast.*

**Hilton Garden Inn Philadelphia Center City**

$$$ | **HOTEL** | This hotel is an affordable alternative to other hotels near the Pennsylvania Convention Center. **Pros:** nice rooms; good value; indoor pool. **Cons:** neighborhood can be desolate at night; pricey parking; area can be noisy. [$] *Rooms from: $296* ✉ *1100 Arch St., Center City East* ☎ *215/923–0100, 800/774–1500* 🌐 *www.hilton.com* 🛏 *279 rooms* 🍴 *No Meals.*

**The Notary Hotel**

$$$ | **HOTEL** | This hotel is in the historic City Hall Annex, and the brass, copper, and bronze details, as well as the lobby's ceiling and chandelier, are original from 1926. **Pros:** centrally located; architecturally beautiful; good service. **Cons:** central location can make for difficulty in picking up and dropping off car; no complimentary breakfast; old elevators are slow. [$] *Rooms from: $299* ✉ *21 N. Juniper St., Center City East* ☎ *215/496–3200* 🌐 *www.marriott.com* 🛏 *499 rooms* 🍴 *No Meals.*

**Philadelphia Marriott Downtown**

$$ | **HOTEL** | This bustling convention hotel fills an entire city block, and for an intrinsically impersonal type of place, the Marriott tries hard to meet special needs; it also offers some of the lowest rates in its price category. **Pros:** centrally located; clean rooms; good for traveling families or businesspeople. **Cons:** crowds, crowds, and more crowds; parking is a whopping $56 or more a night; the sheer size can be impersonal. [$] *Rooms from: $249* ✉ *1201 Market St., Center City East* ☎ *215/625–2900* 🌐 *www.philadelphiamarriott.com* 🛏 *1,408 rooms* 🍴 *No Meals.*

**Residence Inn by Marriott Philadelphia Center City**

$$ | **HOTEL** | **FAMILY** | Originally the Market Street National Bank, this building from the 1920s has a beautifully restored art deco facade; most rooms (studios or one-bedroom suites) have full kitchens,

living rooms, and work areas. **Pros:** centrally located; novel amenities; nice option for families. **Cons:** pricey parking; central location makes it hard to drop off and pick up your car; no on-site dinner option. $ *Rooms from: $209* ✉ *1 E. Penn Sq., corner of Market and Juniper Sts., Center City East* ☎ *215/557–0005, 800/331–3131* ⊕ *www.residenceinn.com* ⇥ *324 rooms* ⊙ *Free Breakfast.*

 Nightlife

**Fergie's Pub**

**BARS** | Fergus "Fergie" Carey is the jovial proprietor of this casual, cozy, and beloved bar, which has been around longer than most establishments of its ilk in Philly. The taproom, which serves solid craft beer and comfort food, hosts regular entertainment, including music, poetry, Quizzo, and even live theater. There are no televisions on the premises, as Carey believes in the lost art of conversation. ✉ *1214 Sansom St., Center City East* ☎ *215/928–8118* ⊕ *www. fergies.com.*

**MilkBoy**

**LIVE MUSIC** | One of two public outposts of MilkBoy recording studios in North Philly, this space features a down-to-earth café and bar on the street level, with a narrow, intimate performance space up top. It attracts mostly indie rock acts, both locals and touring outfits. ✉ *1100 Chestnut St., Center City East* ☎ *215/925–6455* ⊕ *www.milkboyphilly.com.*

**Philadelphia Clef Club of Jazz & Performing Arts**

**MUSIC** | Dedicated solely to jazz, including its history and instruction, the Clef Club boasts a 240-seat theater for live concerts, celebrating both the present and past of Philly jazz. ✉ *738 S. Broad St., Center City East* ☎ *215/893–9912* ⊕ *www.clefclubofjazz.org.*

 Performing Arts

## FILM FESTIVALS
**Philadelphia Film Festival**

**FESTIVALS** | This two-week extravaganza in late October organized by the Philadelphia Film Society is filled with screenings, seminars, and events attended by critics, scholars, filmmakers, and cinema buffs. It's held at various venues around the city. ✉ *Philadelphia* ⊕ *www.filmadelphia.org.*

**qFLIX Philadelphia**

**FESTIVALS** | This annual festival of contemporary LGBTQ+ cinema takes place in a variety of venues around the city. qFLIX Philadelphia hosts other film-related events throughout the year. ✉ *Philadelphia* ⊕ *www.facebook.com/qflixfestivals.*

## THEATER
**Walnut Street Theatre**

**THEATER** | Founded in 1809, this is the oldest English-language theater in continuous use in the United States. The schedule includes musicals, comedies, and dramas in a lovely 1,084-seat auditorium where almost every seat is a good one. Smaller stages showcase workshop productions of new plays, and are rented by other theater companies. ✉ *825 Walnut St., Center City East* ☎ *215/574–3550* ⊕ *www.walnutstreettheatre.org.*

## Shopping

Pine Street from 9th Street to 12th Street has long been Philadelphia's Antique Row. The three-block area has a good number of antique stores and curio shops, many specializing in expensive period furniture and Colonial heirlooms.

Centered on Sansom Street between 7th and 8th Streets, and on 8th between Chestnut and Walnut Streets, Jewelers' Row is one of the world's oldest and largest markets of precious stones: more than 350 retailers, wholesalers, and craftspeople operate here. The 700 block of Sansom Street is a brick-paved enclave occupied almost exclusively by jewelers.

## ANTIQUES

### Arader Galleries

**ANTIQUES & COLLECTIBLES** | This is the flagship store of a highly respected national chain that stocks the world's largest selection of 16th- to 19th-century prints and maps, specializing in botanicals, birds, and the American West. ⊠ *1308 Walnut St., Center City East* ☎ *215/735–8811* ⊕ *www.aradergalleries.com.*

### M. Finkel & Daughter

**ANTIQUES & COLLECTIBLES** | The country's leading dealer of antique needlework samplers, M. Finkel & Daughter also specializes in carefully selected furniture and folk art, making this an important outpost for lovers of Americana. Call ahead of visiting, as public hours of operation can vary. ⊠ *936 Pine St., Center City East* ☎ *215/627–7797* ⊕ *www.samplings.com.*

## BOOKSTORES

### Philly AIDS Thrift @ Giovanni's Room

**BOOKS** | Although longtime owner Ed Hermance retired and closed this historic bookstore in 2014, Philly AIDS Thrift, now owner of both the business and building, revived it for a new generation interested in LGBTQ fiction and nonfiction. Focusing on books dealing with gay, lesbian, and feminist topics, Giovanni's Room stocks an extensive inventory and sponsors many author appearances. This inventory is paired with a selection of clothing, home goods, and art. ⊠ *345 S. 12th St., Center City East* ☎ *215/923–2960* ⊕ *www.queerbooks.com* Ⓜ *Walnut–Locust on the Broad St. Line.*

## CLOTHING

### Kin Boutique

**WOMEN'S CLOTHING** | Boutique owner Joey Clark designed the store to look like a closet, highlighting her effort to make the shopping experience feel comfortable and relaxed. Expect pieces from Citizens of Humanity, Third Form, and Steve Madden, and more, in styles that range from casual to cocktail. There's also a men's store a few doors down, and personal styling appointments are available. ⊠ *1010 Pine St., Center City East* ⊕ *www.shop-kin.com.*

## DEPARTMENT STORES

### Macy's

**DEPARTMENT STORE** | Macy's displays the chain's classic merchandise in the spacious former John Wanamaker department store, a Philadelphia landmark. Its focal point is the nine-story grand court with its nearly 30,000-pipe organ—the largest ever built—and a 2,500-pound statue of an eagle, both remnants of the 1904 Louisiana Purchase Exposition in St. Louis. During Christmastime, the space is filled with families and office workers gazing (and listening) in awe at the store's legendary holiday sound-and-light show and organ performances. ⊠ *1300 Market St., surrounded by 13th, Juniper, Market, and Chestnut Sts., Center City East* ☎ *215/241–9000* ⊕ *l.macys.com/philadelphia-pa.*

## GIFTS AND SOUVENIRS

### Duross & Langel

**OTHER HEALTH & BEAUTY** | This shop makes eco-friendly soaps, organic scrubs, shampoos, and other skin- and hair-care products locally and infuses them with scents like cherry almond bark and coconut lime. They have also expanded their product line into hand-poured candles, natural perfumes, and a variety of giftable selections. ⊠ *240 S. 11th St., Center City East* ☎ *215/592–7627* ⊕ *www.durossandlangel.com.*

### Show of Hands

**ART GALLERIES** | You'll find one-of-a-kind artisan crafts—exquisite jewelry, colorful vases, textiles, Murano glass, and unique lamps—in a wide range of price points here. The friendly owner is on hand to answer questions and encourages you to handle the fragile objects. ⊠ *1006 Pine St., Center City East* ☎ *215/592–4010.*

**Verde**

**SOUVENIRS** | If you're hunting for a gift that makes you look thoughtful, this is the place to go—here you'll find jewelry, scarves, and handbags with a handcrafted look. This is also the home of Marcie Blaine Artisanal Chocolates, which offers delicious custom chocolates, caramels, and barks with unique flavor combinations. ✉ *108 S. 13th St., Center City East* ☎ *215/546–8700* 🌐 *www.verdephiladelphia.com.*

## HOME DECOR

**Open House**

**HOUSEWARES** | This modern, hip, urban home boutique strikes the balance between edgy hipster and hip hostess. The furniture, baby clothes, jewelry, candles, and soaps all manage to be clever and quirky. It's as fun to browse as it is to buy, as there's no pressure from the friendly sales staff. ✉ *107 S. 13th St., Center City East* ☎ *215/922–1415* 🌐 *www.openhouseliving.com.*

**Ten Thousand Villages**

**CRAFTS** | Woven rugs, pottery, carvings, and other handcrafted gifts made by skilled artisans in 38 countries such as Kenya, Thailand, and India make this fair-trade store a favorite for innovative gifts with a social conscience. ✉ *The Philadelphia Building, 1315 Walnut St., Center City East* ☎ *445/444–0632* 🌐 *www.tenthousandvillages.com/philadelphia.*

## JEWELRY

**Halloween**

**JEWELRY & WATCHES** | If the sheer quantity of baubles crammed into this tiny shop doesn't take your breath away, the gorgeous, one-of-a-kind designs will. The shelves, drawers, displays, and even the second-floor balcony overflow with rings, necklaces, earrings, bracelets, pins, and much more. The jewelry ranges from classic pearls to mystical amber. Owner Henri David (who designs some pieces) is well known for his lavish and outrageous Halloween fetes. He can do custom work, such as creating mates for single earrings. Proudly old-fashioned, the shop does not have a website, and does not accept credit cards. ✉ *1329 Pine St., Center City East* ☎ *215/732–7711* 🕒 *Closed Sun. and Mon.*

# Midtown Village and the Gayborhood

Just East of Broad Street, 13th Street is the center point of Midtown Village and the Gayborhood, a bustling few blocks of Philly where throngs of people fill the streets every weekend. Since the 1930s, the area has served as a safe haven for the LGBTQ+ community, with the height of its development happening in the '70s and '80s. In the early 2000s, the arrival of new restaurants and bars began to make the area a destination for all kinds of people. These days, just about anyone can find their place here, whether they're looking for a leather bar, a nice glass of wine, or both.

## 🍴 Restaurants

**Barbuzzo**

**$$ | MEDITERRANEAN** | This buzzing Mediterranean tapas joint has inspired an almost religious devotion among nearly every demographic of Philadelphian. Diners happily stuff themselves into the cramped tables at this long, narrow eatery for a fix of the cheese boards, the egg-and-truffle pizza, and the house-made charcuterie. **Known for:** creative pizzas; caramel budino; lively crowd. [$] *Average main: $19* ✉ *110 S. 13th St., Midtown Village & The Gayborhood* ☎ *215/546–9300* 🌐 *www.barbuzzo.com* 🕒 *No lunch Sun.*

**Mercato**

**$$ | ITALIAN** | This BYOB in a former corner market is noisy, cramped, and cash-only, but they have started taking reservations and keep packing them in. You may ask why, and it's because of the Italian–new

American bistro's attention to detail, visible in the exquisite artisanal cheese plate, the perfectly seared scallops, whole grilled artichoke, and the homemade triangle-shaped pasta. **Known for:** pasta dishes; classic Italian; close quarters. $ *Average main: $24* ⊠ *1216 Spruce St., Midtown Village & The Gayborhood* ☎ *215/985–2962* ⊕ *www.mercatobyob. com* ⊟ *No credit cards* ⊘ *No lunch.*

### Pearl & Mary Oyster Bar
$$$ | **AMERICAN** | The raw bar is the star of the show at Pearl & Mary, where piles of oysters, clusters of crab claws, and bright lobster tails are tough to resist. Build your perfect seafood order, paired with one of their sparkling wine cocktails, and then round out the meal with a crudo (raw fish or seafood with citrus juice), a platter of fish-and-chips, or a whole grilled snapper. **Known for:** sparkling cocktails; piles of oysters; happy hour. $ *Average main: $27* ⊠ *114 S. 13th St., Midtown Village & The Gayborhood* ☎ *215/330–6786* ⊕ *www.pearlandmary.com* ⊘ *No lunch weekdays.*

### Sampan
$ | **ASIAN** | One of the city's busiest happy hour spots, Sampan serves up delicious small plates like cheesesteak bao buns and crispy tuna rice crackers, Asian-inspired cocktails, and a clubby environment. Dinner service also sees a lot of action, so book ahead, especially on the weekends. **Known for:** cheesesteak bao buns; happy hour specials; chef's tasting menu. $ *Average main: $16* ⊠ *124 S. 13th St., Midtown Village & The Gayborhood* ☎ *215/732–3501* ⊕ *www.sampanphilly.com* ⊘ *No lunch.*

### Seorabol Center City
$$$ | **KOREAN** | Chef Chris Cho grew up around his family's Korean restaurant of the same name, still a staple restaurant in the North Philly neighborhood of Olney. In 2018, he opened his own spot on Spruce Street, where the menu is a mix of classic Korean foods like bibimbap, *budae jigae* (a rich spicy stew), and *japchae* (springy,

stir-fried sweet potato noodles), and more new-school items inspired by his childhood in Philadelphia's Korean community like General CHO Chicken, a play on that Chinese-American staple, Generals Tso's chicken. **Known for:** General CHO Chicken (a play on the Chinese-American staple Generals Tso's); dumplings; Korean classics. $ *Average main: $25* ⊠ *1326 Spruce St., Midtown Village & The Gayborhood* ☎ *215/608–8484* ⊕ *www.srbtogo.com* ⊘ *Closed Mon.*

### Vedge
$$ | **MODERN AMERICAN** | Less a restaurant than a roving dinner party spread among several rooms in a tony Center City brownstone, Vedge marked a shift for chefs Rich Landau and Kate Jacoby. At their longtime vegan spot, Horizons, the focus was on making non-meat look and taste like meat, but at Vedge, it's a true celebration of vegetables, many of them sourced from nearby farms. **Known for:** elevated vegan cuisine; local/seasonable produce; creative desserts. $ *Average main: $18* ⊠ *1221 Locust St., Midtown Village & The Gayborhood* ☎ *215/320–7500* ⊕ *www.vedgerestaurant.com* ⊘ *No lunch.*

### Vetri Cucina
$$$$ | **ITALIAN** | Philadelphia's foremost practitioner of Italian cooking, Marc Vetri, can still be found at his eponymous ristorante just off Broad Street. In this lovely, sepia-toned town house (the original home of the late Le Bec-Fin) you can expect exquisite but superexpensive custom-built tasting menus (no à la carte) that may involve freshly milled alt-grain pastas, quivering buffalo-milk mozzarella flown in from Campania, and long-standing classics like the golden onion crepe and roasted suckling goat. **Known for:** elaborate tasting menus (no à la carte options); elegant pastas; top-tier service. $ *Average main: $165* ⊠ *1312 Spruce St., Midtown Village & The Gayborhood* ☎ *215/732–3478* ⊕ *vetricucina.com* ⊘ *No lunch.*

## Coffee and Quick Bites

**Merkaz**
$ | **ISRAELI** | Zahav chef Michael Solomonov's colorfully appointed quick-serve concept serves up Israeli-style breakfast and lunch, featuring fresh hot pitas filled with tasty meat and veg. Must-orders include the zesty shakshuka, served daily before 11 am; and the fried eggplant and Jerusalem Grill sandwiches. **Known for:** coffee; Israeli cuisine; fresh-baked pita. [$] *Average main: $11* ✉ *1218 Sansom St., Midtown Village & The Gayborhood* ☎ *267/768–8111* 🌐 *merkazphilly.com.*

**Van Leeuwen Ice Cream**
$ | **ICE CREAM** | This Gotham ice cream superpower now has three locations in the City of Brotherly Love (there's also one in Rittenhouse Square and Fishtown). It's a great spot to satisfy your sweet tooth with classic ice cream flavors like cookies and cream and mint chip or more inventive options like Earl Grey and honeycomb; there are vegan flavors, too, as well as chocolate chip cookies, cookie sandwiches, sundaes, and milkshakes. **Known for:** great vegan options; ships ice cream all over the country; classic and offbeat flavors. [$] *Average main: $6* ✉ *119 S. 13th St., Midtown Village & The Gayborhood* 🌐 *vanleeuwenicecream.com.*

## Hotels

**Canopy by Hilton Philadelphia Center City**
$$$ | **HOTEL** | Taking over the historic Stephen Girard Building, Canopy's hotel melds the city's R&B culture with local history—think luxury department store-style that was present in the neighborhood at the start of the early 20th century. **Pros:** complimentary bikes to explore the city; filtered water stations on every floor; close to the city's must-see sights. **Cons:**; on-site parking is expensive; breakfast is not included. [$] *Rooms from: $259* ✉ *1180 Ludlow St., Midtown Village & The Gayborhood* ☎ *215/258–9400* 🌐 *canopy3.hilton.com* 🛏 *236 rooms* 🍴 *No Meals.*

**Doubletree By Hilton Philadelphia Center City**
$$ | **HOTEL** | The hotel's sawtooth design ensures that each room has a peaked bay window with an eye-popping 180-degree view. **Pros:** great location for the theatergoer; good views; sunny and unique lobby. **Cons:** lots of groups can make for a hectic lobby; expensive parking; Broad Street is noisy. [$] *Rooms from: $239* ✉ *237 S. Broad St., Midtown Village & The Gayborhood* ☎ *215/893–1600, 800/222–8733* 🌐 *www.philadelphia.doubletree.com* 🛏 *481 rooms* 🍴 *No Meals.*

★ **Guild House Hotel**
$$$ | **HOTEL** | Inside this National Historic Landmark building that once was the headquarters of the New Century Guild, a pro-women's rights organization that formed in 1906, the Guild House Hotel is full of thoughtful, historic details and spacious suites that feature an eclectic mix of vintage and modern decor that speaks to the women who once roamed these halls. **Pros:** celebrates the legacy of one of the nation's leading women's empowerment organizations; easily walkable to most Center City landmarks; stocked kitchenettes and comfy living rooms in some suites. **Cons:** no elevator, if mobility is an issue; no on-site dining; no traditional hotel amenities like pool, gym, or on-site concierge. [$] *Rooms from: $300* ✉ *1307 Locust St., Midtown Village & The Gayborhood* ☎ *855/484–5333* 🌐 *guildhousehotel.com* 🛏 *12 suites* 🍴 *No Meals.*

**Holiday Inn Express Midtown**
$$ | **HOTEL** | What this hotel lacks in frills it more than makes up for with its central location; on-site, 24-hour fitness center; and complimentary breakfast bar. **Pros:** free Wi-Fi; big rooms; outdoor seasonal

pool. **Cons:** small lobby can get cramped with groups; funky smells in common areas; lots of congested traffic during daylight hours. $ Rooms from: $189 ⊠ 1305 Walnut St., Midtown Village & The Gayborhood ☎ 215/735–9300, 800/564–3869 ⊕ www.himidtown.com ⬐ 168 rooms ⦿ Free Breakfast.

### Loews Philadelphia Hotel

$ | HOTEL | FAMILY | Topped by the red neon letters PSFS (for the former tenant, Pennsylvania Savings Fund Society), this 1930s building was the country's first skyscraper in the ultramodern international style. **Pros:** architectural gem; cool style throughout; amazing views; special amenities for kids. **Cons:** some guests have complained about the smell of smoke in rooms; you might need a cab to get to nightlife destinations; pricey parking. $ Rooms from: $169 ⊠ 1200 Market St., Midtown Village & The Gayborhood ☎ 215/627–1200, 800/235–6397 ⊕ www.loewshotels.com ⬐ 593 rooms ⦿ No Meals.

### Roost East Market

$$$ | HOTEL | The furnished accommodations at this "apartment hotel," part of the locally based Roost brand, are well equipped for weekly and even monthly stays, offering full-size kitchens (groceries can be delivered), in-room washer and dryer, and light-filled living and work spaces enlivened with house plants. **Pros:** full kitchens ideal for longer stays; sophisticated design and decor; 24-hour front desk and maintenance teams. **Cons:** no daily housekeeping; no on-site dining; area of town can be noisy. $ Rooms from: $269 ⊠ 1199 Ludlow St., Midtown Village & The Gayborhood ☎ 267/737–9000 ⊕ www.myroost.com ⬐ 60 rooms ⦿ No Meals.

# ⓨ Nightlife

## BARS AND LOUNGES

### The Bike Stop

BARS | A multifloored space, down a side alley, the Bike Stop caters specifically to those seeking leather-clad adventures. ⊠ 206 S. Quince St., Midtown Village & The Gayborhood ☎ 215/627–1662 ⊕ www.thebikestop.com.

### Dirty Frank's

BARS | Its outside walls decorated with famous Franks throughout history (Frankenstein's monster, FDR, Sinatra, Zappa, etc.), Dirty Frank's is a Philadelphia classic. A glorious mixture of students, artists, journalists, and resident characters crowds around the horseshoe-shaped bar and engages in friendly, beer-soaked mayhem. ⊠ 347 S. 13th St., Midtown Village & The Gayborhood ☎ 215/732–5010 ⊕ www.facebook.com/dirtyfranksbar.

### Franky Bradley's

BARS | A former supper club that attracted movers and shakers of yesteryear, the updated Franky's is now under the watch of Mark Bee, architect of North 3rd and Silk City. A kitschy dining room decorated with Bee's Technicolor flea market finds gives way to an upstairs performance space used by DJs and live acts. They serve food until 1 am every night except Friday and Saturday, when the kitchen closes at midnight. ⊠ 1320 Chancellor St., Midtown Village & The Gayborhood ☎ 215/735–0735 ⊕ www.frankybradleys.com.

### McGillin's Olde Ale House

BARS | For longevity alone, McGillin's stands proud. Open since 1860, it's the oldest continually operating pub in the city, as well as one of the oldest in the country. But though there are nostalgic touches, it's a modern watering hole, featuring a bevy of TVs for sports and hugely popular karaoke nights. The beer list, featuring 30 choices on draft, tends toward the local, including a series of signature house ales brewed by Adamstown,

Pennsylvania's Stoudts. ✉ *1310 Drury St., Midtown Village & The Gayborhood* ☎ *215/735–5562* ⊕ *www.mcgillins.com.*

### Tavern on Camac

**BARS** | Three venues in one, Tavern features a popular piano bar, a top-floor dance club called Ascend, and a late-night restaurant, which serves rib-sticking comfort food until midnight on weekdays and 1 am Friday and Saturday. Specialties include grilled cheese, a beefy Tavern burger, and beer can barbecue chicken; they make creative cocktails, too. ✉ *243 S. Camac St., Midtown Village & The Gayborhood* ☎ *215/545–1102* ⊕ *www.tavernphilly.com.*

### Woody's

**BARS** | Philadelphia's most popular gay nightlife destination is spread over two levels, offering several bars—with monitors playing music videos and campy moments from TV shows and movies—and a large dance floor upstairs. Themed nights include Latin music on Thursdays and house, EDM, and hip-hop on Fridays. ✉ *202 S. 13th St., Midtown Village & The Gayborhood* ☎ *215/545–1893* ⊕ *www.woodysbar.com.*

## DANCE CLUBS

### Voyeur

**DANCE CLUBS** | This gay-friendly after-hours joint offers late-night thrills, courtesy of diverse DJ booking and a potent light-and-sound system. Two massive dance floors are filled with gyrating bodies, and a third-level catwalk gives those wanting a rest (or further libations) an excellent vantage point. ✉ *1221 St. James St., Midtown Village & The Gayborhood* ☎ *215/735–5772* ⊕ *www.voyeurnightclub.com.*

## MUSIC CLUBS

### Time

**LIVE MUSIC** | A rocking big-city club from the same owners of the nearby Vintage Wine Bar, Time features three concepts in one—a whiskey-heavy cocktail bar; a dining room with a bar and live music seven nights a week; and an upstairs lounge and music venue. Downstairs acts tend toward the jazz persuasion, while DJs tend to dominate up top. ✉ *1315 Sansom St., Midtown Village & The Gayborhood* ☎ *215/985–4800* ⊕ *www.timerestaurant.net.*

## 🎭 Performing Arts

### Forrest Theatre

**THEATER** | The Forrest is the place to catch Broadway blockbusters in Philadelphia. Eight to 10 high-profile shows are presented each season—think hits like *The Book of Mormon, Bullets Over Broadway, Pippin,* and *The Sound of Music.* ✉ *1114 Walnut St., Midtown Village & The Gayborhood* ☎ *215/923–1515* ⊕ *www.forrest-theatre.com.*

### Wilma Theater

**THEATER** | Under founding artistic directors Blanka and Jiri Zizka, Czech natives who joined the Wilma Project feminist collective as its artists-in-residence in the late 1970s, this experimental theater has grown in size and renown, gaining favorable critical notices for innovative presentations of American and European drama. (Blanka remains at the helm; Jiri passed away in 2012.) Its season runs from September to June. ✉ *265 S. Broad St., at Spruce St., Midtown Village & The Gayborhood* ☎ *215/546–7824* ⊕ *www.wilmatheater.org.*

# Chinatown

Centered on 10th and Race Streets two blocks north of Market Street, Chinatown serves as the residential and commercial hub of the city's Chinese community. Chinatown has grocery stores, souvenir and gift shops, martial arts studios, a fortune cookie store, bilingual street signs, and more than 50 restaurants. Over the past 20 years Chinatown's population has become more diverse, reflecting the increase in immigration from Vietnam,

Originally settled in the mid-19th century, Philadelphia's Chinatown is home to Chinese, Korean, Thai, Malaysian, Burmese, and Vietnamese restaurants and stores.

Cambodia, Thailand, and Myanmar. One striking Chinatown sight is the Chinese Friendship Gate, straddling 10th Street at Arch Street. This intricate and colorful 40-foot-tall arch—the largest authentic Chinese gate outside China—was created by Chinese artisans, who brought their own tools and construction materials. The citizens of Tianjin, Philadelphia's sister city in China, donated the building materials, including the ornamental tile.

## Sights

### Chinatown Friendship Arch

**PUBLIC ART** | Conceptualized by the late Sabrina Soong, a Chinese-American architect/artist and Philadelphia resident, the 40-foot-tall, 88-ton "China Gate" has welcomed visitors to historic Chinatown since its introduction in 1984. Designed in a manner reminiscent of China's Qing dynasty, it features materials and cultural flourishes fabricated by artisans from Philadelphia's sister city of Tianjin, China. The Chinese characters emblazoned on the "Friendship Arch" translate simply to "Philadelphia Chinatown," a paean to the neighborhood's historic importance and resilience. ✉ *1000 Arch St., Chinatown* 🌐 *www.associationforpublicart.org/artwork/the-china-gate.*

## Restaurants

### ★ Dim Sum Garden

**$ | CHINESE** | Lines sometimes snake out the door as diners line up for the chance to slurp Dim Sum Garden's handmade soup dumplings; while you wait, peek through the window in the middle of the dining room to see the restaurant's staff fold the delicate wrappings around the porky fillings. The family-owned restaurant also does a brisk business in hand-stretched noodles, steamed chicken dumplings, and pan-fried beef dumplings. **Known for:** groups welcome; handmade soup dumplings; hand-stretched noodles. [$] *Average main: $12* ✉ *1020 Race St., Chinatown* ☎ *215/873–0258* 🌐 *www.dimsumgardenphilly.com.*

# Chinatown

**A** **B** **C** **D** **E**

1

Wood St.

N. 11th St.

Vine Street Expressway

Vine St.

2

Winter St.

Vine St.

7 3

Spring St.

6 4

Spring St.

N. 8th St.

Race St.

3

1

Chinatown

1

Race St.

3

2

Cherry St.

N. 11th St.

Appletree St.

5

N. 10th St.

4

N. 12th St.

1

Arch St.

2

N. 8th St.

N. 8th St.

Cuthbert St.

8

5

Filbert St.

N. 11th St.

N. 10th St.

Market St.

N. 8th St.

N. 8th St.

6

| 0 | 400 ft |
| 0 | 100 m |

Chestnut St.

Ranstead St.

7

**KEY**

1 Sights

1 Restaurants

1 Quick Bites

### ★ EMei

$$ | **SICHUAN** | Since 2011, Emei has been serving the city's best Sichuan food, all sizzling and hot with the region's signature peppercorn. Chef Yongcheng Zhao guides the kitchen crew each night, satisfying the city's need for wok-seared green beans, rich *mapo* (spicy sauce) tofu, and addictively salty, fried *chong-qing* (dried red chilies) chicken. **Known for:** good space for groups; sesame noodles; serving some of the city's best Sichuan food. [$] *Average main: $18* ✉ *915 Arch St., Chinatown* ☎ *215/627–2500* 🌐 *www.emeiphilly.com.*

### Lee How Fook Tea House

$ | **CHINESE** | Literally translated as "good food for the mouth," this unprepossessing BYOB spot is now being run by a second generation of restaurateurs. They do an excellent job with the most straightforward fare, like General Tso's chicken, hot-and-sour soup, and steamed pork dumplings, but they are best known for their salt-baked seafood and their hot pots. **Known for:** salt-baked seafood; hot pots; dumplings. [$] *Average main: $15* ✉ *219 N. 11th St., Chinatown* ☎ *215/925–7266* 🌐 *www.newleehowfook.com.*

### Ocean City

$ | **CHINESE** | It's largely locals eating at this smallish banquet space on the edge of Chinatown, and things can get a bit hectic with big-screen TVs hanging from every corner, spangly chandeliers overhead, and dim sum carts racing through the aisles. Snag a seat next to the kitchen to flag down the carts as they emerge—the dim sum is excellent and well priced. **Known for:** excellent dim sum; seafood dishes; accommodating to large groups. [$] *Average main: $14* ✉ *234 N. 9th St., Chinatown* ☎ *215/829–0688.*

### ★ Penang

$ | **MALAYSIAN** | The juxtaposition of bamboo and exposed pipes is indicative of the surprising mix of flavors in this perennially busy Malaysian restaurant. A taste of India creeps into a scintillating appetizer of *roti canai,* handkerchief-thin crepes served with a small dipping dish of spicy chicken curry, and the wide variety of soups are tasty and filling; *satay,* Singapore rice noodles, and *chow kueh teow* (Malaysian stir-fried flat rice noodles) are among the other popular dishes. **Known for:** Malaysian cuisine; roti canai (an Indian flatbread dish); Southeast Asian noodles. [$] *Average main: $13* ✉ *117 N. 10th St., Chinatown* ☎ *215/413–2531* 🌐 *penangphilly.com* 💳 *No credit cards.*

### Sang Kee Peking Duck House

$ | **CHINESE** | Open since 1980, this Chinatown barbecue stalwart hasn't missed a beat dishing up delicious plates based around its famously flavorful duck. Egg or rice noodles come in different styles and are simmered with duck, pork, or beef brisket; if you wish, you can customize your soup with both noodles, plus fat, tender wontons. **Known for:** Peking duck; noodle soups; dumplings. [$] *Average main: $16* ✉ *238 N. 9th St., Chinatown* ☎ *215/925–7532* 🌐 *www.sangkeechinatown.com.*

### ★ Vietnam

$ | **VIETNAMESE** | Owner Benny Lai took this humble noodle shop founded by his immigrant parents and built it into a chic restaurant with an upstairs lounge serving small plates and wacky cocktails like the Bachelor's Downfall and the Flaming Volcano (two straws included). In the dining room the best bets are the crispy spring rolls, salted squid, barbecue platter, and soups with rice noodles. **TIP→ Don't get this restaurant confused with the competing Vietnam Palace across the street.** **Known for:** strong cocktails; spring rolls; noodle soups. [$] *Average main: $10* ✉ *221 N. 11th St., Chinatown* ☎ *215/592–1163* 🌐 *www.eatatvietnam.com.*

### Xi'an Sizzling Woks

$ | **CHINESE** | **FAMILY** | This small restaurant serves freshly made versions of food from Xi'an (a city in central China), including thick and chewy hand-cut noodles, the slippery and refreshing *Liang pi* (cold noodles served with chili oil), and *rougamo* (a burger-like dish of leavened bread stuffed with your choice of meat). If it's your first time, the menu's photos are instructive, while those with knowledge of Xi'an's culinary traditions will be impressed by these well-made versions. **Known for:** another location in University City; Chinese hamburgers; hand-cut noodles. [$] *Average main: $12* ✉ *902 Arch St., Chinatown* ☎ *215/925–1688* 🌐 *www.xiansizzlingwoksphilly.com* 🕓 *Closed Tues.*

## Coffee and Quick Bites

### Hong Kong Bakery

$ | **BAKERY** | For a savory or sweet Chinese snack, stop at the Hong Kong Bakery to sample the steam buns, moon cakes, or a sweet egg-custard tart. Most items are cheap (usually under $1), and you might just find a new favorite snack, but remember to bring cash (no credit cards). **Known for:** Chinese pastry; egg tarts; bubble tea. [$] *Average main: $5* ✉ *917 Race St., Chinatown* ☎ *215/925–1288* 💳 *No credit cards.*

### Ray's Cafe and Tea House

$ | **CHINESE** | Pouring specialty coffee decades before it was cool, Ray's is renowned for its special syphon brewing system, a complex (and photogenic) technique that relies on the vacuum pressure to produce transcendent java. But this charming family-run café cooks up simple eats, too, like steamed or panfried dumplings, noodle soups, and rotating specials. **Known for:** high-end coffees; syphon brewing; homemade Chinese snacks. [$] *Average main: $12* ✉ *141 N. 9th St., Chinatown* ☎ *215/922–3299* 🌐 *www.rayscafe.com* 🕓 *Closed Sun.*

### Tea Do

$ | **CAFÉ** | A bustling bubble tea parlor with a young, cool clientele, Tea Do offers a wide-spanning selection of boba-laden beverages, including milk bubble tea, black- and green tea–based drinks, and blended fruit smoothies. There are also light Pan-Asian snacks, like *onigiri*, edamame, and *shumai*. **Known for:** bubble tea; smoothies; light snacks. [$] *Average main: $5* ✉ *132 N. 10th St., Chinatown* ☎ *215/925–8889* 🌐 *www.tea-do.com.*

## Nightlife

### Hop Sing Laundromat

**BARS** | Run by the mononym'd owner Lê, a one-of-a-kind personality, Hop Sing is a spirituous haven for bargoers who prefer their cocktails clandestine. Hopeful patrons wait in front of a nondescript door in Chinatown, adhering to a strict no-phones policy to gain admission. Once inside, the high-end spirits and creative cocktails flow in a moody, mismatched, haunted-library-esque room unlike any other in the city. ✉ *1029 Race St., Chinatown* 🌐 *www.hopsinglaundromat.com.*

Chapter 6

# CENTER CITY WEST AND RITTENHOUSE SQUARE

Updated by
Maddy Sweitzer-Lamme

 Sights
★★★★★

 Restaurants
★★★★★

 Hotels
★★★★★

 Shopping
★★★★★

 Nightlife
★★★★★

# NEIGHBORHOOD SNAPSHOT

## TOP EXPERIENCES

■ **Academy of Music and the Kimmel Center:** Opera, ballet, music, theater—it can all be found within the walls of these great cultural centers.

■ **Delancey Place:** Stroll the 2000 block to check out some of the city's most elegant town houses.

■ **Rittenhouse Square:** This lush park offers a lovely retreat in the heart of the city.

■ **Comcast Technology Center:** The city's new tallest building has restaurants, a coffee shop, bars, a soaring hotel, and sweeping city views.

## GETTING HERE

The heart of Center City is an easy 10- to 15-minute stroll from the Historic Area, or about a 20- to 25-minute walk from Penn's Landing. To orient yourself, Broad Street serves as a delineation for Center City East and Center City West, while City Hall, located at Broad and Market Streets, is the dividing line for north–south addresses on the numbered streets. You also can use SEPTA bus lines on Market or Walnut Streets, or the underground Market-Frankford line, to reach points west of the Historic Area, or take the seasonal PHLASH. The City Hall SEPTA station is a major hub that includes connections for the north–south Broad Street line, as well as the east–west Market-Frankford line and trolley lines.

## PLANNING YOUR TIME

You could walk through Center City West in 45 minutes, but reserve about half a day, with an hour each at the Masonic Temple, City Hall Tower, and the Pennsylvania Academy of the Fine Arts. If you get an early start, you can finish with lunch at the Reading Terminal Market.

Rittenhouse Square is one of the loveliest neighborhoods for strolling. Two hours allows enough time to wander through the area and visit the Rosenbach Museum and Library. Add at least another hour for a stroll along South Broad Street and a pop into the Ritz-Carlton.

## QUICK BITES

■ **The Concourse at Comcast Center.** Below the bustling Comcast Center hides the best grab-a-bite scenario this side of Reading Terminal Market. There's sandwiches and salads from Di Bruno Bros., nigiri by Tokyo Sushi, and cannoli by Termini Brothers. ⊠ *1701 John F. Kennedy Blvd., Center City West* ⊕ *comcastcentercampus.com/concourse* 🚇 *City Hall, Suburban Station*

■ **Di Bruno Bros.** This uptown outpost of the original Italian Market location is a one-stop gourmet shop with eat-in and take-out options. ⊠ *1730 Chestnut St., Rittenhouse Square*

■ **Federal Donuts.** Come for breakfast, lunch, or coffee to try inventive donut flavors like marble coffee cake and strawberry lavender, in addition to fried chicken, breakfast sandwiches, and fried-chicken sandwiches. ⊠ *1632 Sansom St., Rittenhouse Square* ⊕ *www.federaldonuts.com* 🚇 *Broad Street Line, Walnut-Locust St.*

## GOOD TO KNOW

■ The Masonic Temple is closed on Sunday and Monday.

Philadelphia's evolution into a must-visit city began in Rittenhouse Square and Center City West with the fine-dining establishments, cocktail bars, boutiques, high-end hotels, and palpable energy that still fill the neighborhoods today. The city's business district lives here, along with some of the best restaurants, shops, and public spaces in the area.

Always busy and always exciting, Rittenhouse Square and Center City West offer an experience for all, with bars slinging drinks until 2 am, museums showcasing Philadelphia history, trendy restaurants that transport guests across the world, happy hours that draw the after-work crowd, and shopping that rivals any other big city. The neighborhood is known for large festivals throughout the year that draw crowds of thousands for everything from arts celebrations in the centrally located Rittenhouse Square park to a multiblock food and drink festival on Rittenhouse's bustling Walnut Street.

For a grand introduction to the heart of downtown, climb the steps to the plaza in front of the Municipal Services Building at 15th Street and John F. Kennedy Boulevard. The structures that surround you—City Hall, the Philadelphia Saving Fund Society Building, the Art Museum, the skyscrapers at Liberty Place, Oldenburg's *Clothespin*, and more—shape Philadelphia's architectural landscape.

## Center City West

Stretching from the eastern banks of the Schuylkill River to Broad Street, Center City West is Philly's entertainment and business hub. Oriented around leafy Rittenhouse Square (the name of the park as well as the posh surrounding neighborhood), this side of Center City is where you can expect to do the bulk of shopping and dining. You'll find big brands and luxury labels along Walnut Street and Chestnut Street, with independent boutiques on the little side streets that fan out to the south, and restaurants that follow suit. This is also where most hotels set up shop in Philly.

Four blocks east of the square is the Avenue of the Arts, also known as Broad Street. "Let us entertain you" could be the theme of the ambitious cultural development project that has transformed North and South Broad Street from a commercial thoroughfare to a performing arts district. Dramatic performance spaces have been built, old landmarks have been refurbished, and South Broad Street has been spruced up with landscaping, cast-iron lighting fixtures, special architectural lighting of key buildings, and decorative sidewalk paving.

**TIP→ For Center City West, we have used the boundaries of the Schuylkill River to the West side of Broad Street, from South Street to Market Street.**

 **Sights**

### ★ Academy of Music

**NOTABLE BUILDING | FAMILY |** The only surviving European-style opera house in America is the current home of the Opera Philadelphia and the Pennsylvania Ballet; for the past century, it was home to the Philadelphia Orchestra. Designed by Napoleon Le Brun and Gustav Runge, the 1857 building has a modest exterior; the builders ran out of money and couldn't put marble facing on the brick, as they had intended. The lavish interior, modeled after Milan's La Scala, has elaborate carvings, murals on the ceiling, and a huge Victorian crystal chandelier. ⊠ *Broad and Locust Sts., Center City West* ☎ *215/893–1999 box office* ⊕ *www.academyofmusic.org* ⊠ *Free.*

### The Bellevue Hotel

**HOTEL |** Though its name has been changed many times, this building will always be "the Bellevue" to Philadelphians. The hotel has had an important role in city life, much like the heroine of a long-running soap opera. The epitome of the opulent hotels characteristic of the early 1900s, the Bellevue Stratford was the city's leading hotel for decades. It closed in 1976 after the first outbreak of Legionnaires' disease, which spread through the building's air-conditioning system during an American Legion convention. The hotel has reopened several times since then, and is currently undergoing a renovation to modernize the rooms while staying true to the hotel's historic character. ⊠ *200 S. Broad St., at Walnut St., Center City West* ☎ *215/893–1234* ⊕ *www.bellevuephiladelphia.com.*

### Clothespin

**PUBLIC ART |** Claes Oldenburg's 45-foot-high, 10-ton steel sculpture stands in front of the Center Square Building, above one of the entrances to SEPTA's City Hall subway station. Lauded by some and scorned by others, this pop-art piece contrasts with the traditional statuary so common in Philadelphia. ⊠ *1500 Market St., at 15th St., Center City West.*

### ★ The Comcast Center

**NOTABLE BUILDING |** Now Philadelphia's second-tallest building, the 975-foot Comcast Center is also one of its most eco-friendly: the 58-story design by Robert A.M. Stern Architects uses 40% less water than a traditional office building and also deploys its glass-curtain-wall facade to reduce energy costs significantly. Not to be missed is *The Comcast Experience,* a 2,000-square-foot high-definition video "wall" in the building's lobby, which also features "Humanity in Motion," an installation of 12 life-size figures by Jonathan Borofsky that appear to be striding along girders 110 feet above. The building is also the site of an upscale food court and a seasonal outdoor café. ⊠ *1701 John F. Kennedy Blvd., Center City West.*

### Comcast Technology Center

**BUSINESS DISTRICT |** With a height of 1,121 feet—that's 60 floors—Philadelphia's new tallest building is home to restaurants like Vernick Fish and Jean-Georges Philadelphia, a coffee shop, bars, the soaring Four Seasons Hotel Philadelphia, and sweeping views of the entire city. ⊠ *1800 Arch St., Center City West* ⊕ *corporate.comcast.com.*

### Dilworth Park

**CITY PARK |** This welcoming outdoor space has a café and a spacious Great Lawn for relaxing. There's a fountain for cooling off in the summer, and the space transforms into the Rothman Orthopaedics Ice Rink in the winter. It's also home to free events throughout the year including the Made in Philadelphia Holiday Market. ⊠ *1*

The Academy of Music—the country's oldest known opera house continuously in use—is home to Opera Philadelphia and the Pennsylvania Ballet.

*S. 15th St., Center City West ✛ West side of City Hall ⊕ centercityphila.org/ parks/dilworth-park.*

### ★ Kimmel Center for the Performing Arts

**PERFORMANCE VENUE** | **FAMILY** | Intended to make a contemporary design statement, the Kimmel Center for the Performing Arts has some architectural oomph with its dramatic vaulted glass roof. The 450,000-square-foot venue by architect Rafael Viñoly includes the 2,500-seat Verizon Hall, the more intimate 650-seat Perelman Theater, Jose Garces's restaurant Volvér, central plaza, and a rooftop terrace bar. Making their home at the Kimmel are the Philadelphia Orchestra, Philadanco, Philadelphia Chamber Music Society, Chamber Orchestra of Philadelphia, and the Philly Pops. Free performances are given before some performances and on many weekends in the center's Commonwealth Plaza. ⊠ *300 S. Broad St., Center City West* ☎ *215/790–5800, 215/893–1999 call center/tickets, 215/790–5886 tour info* ⊕ *www.kimmelcenter.org* ✉ *Free.*

### Liberty Place One and Two

**NOTABLE BUILDING** | **FAMILY** | **One Liberty Place** is the 945-foot office building designed by Helmut Jahn that propelled Philadelphia into the "ultrahigh" skyscraper era. Built in 1987, it became the city's tallest structure; however, that distinction now belongs to the 975-foot Comcast Center. Vaguely reminiscent of a modern version of New York's Chrysler Building, One Liberty Place is visible from almost everywhere in the city. The building is now mostly home to apartments and offices, while downstairs are dozens of stores and a food court. In 1990 the adjacent tower, **Two Liberty Place,** opened. Zeidler Roberts designed this second building with Murphy & Jahn, which now holds the Westin Philadelphia, luxury condominiums, and a restaurant on the 37th floor. ⊠ *One Liberty Pl., 1650 Market St., Center City West* ☎ *215/561– 3325* ⊕ *onelibertyplace.com* ✉ *One Liberty Observation Deck $15.*

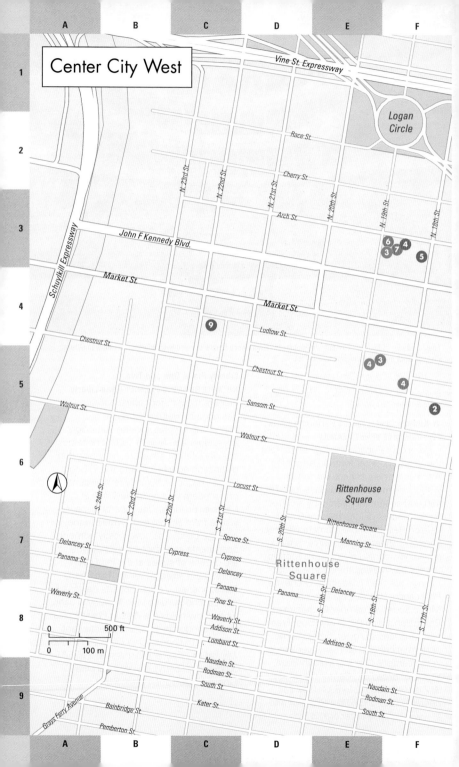

## Sights ▼

1 Academy of Music ............... **H7**
2 The Bellevue Hotel ............... **H7**
3 *Clothespin* ......................... **H5**
4 The Comcast Center............. **G3**
5 Comcast Technology Center ...... **F3**
6 Dilworth Park...................... **H5**
7 Kimmel Center for the
  Performing Arts................... **H8**
8 Liberty Place One and Two....... **G5**
9 Mütter Museum ................... **C4**

## Restaurants ▼

1 Aqimero ........................... **I5**
2 Butcher & Singer ................. **H7**
3 Condesa ........................... **E5**
4 Continental Mid-town ............ **F5**
5 Harp & Crown..................... **H6**
6 JG Skyhigh ........................ **F3**
7 Vernick Fish ....................... **F3**

## Quick Bites ▼

1 The Concourse at
  Comcast Center .................. **G4**
2 Gran Caffe L'Aquila................ **F5**
3 La Colombe
  Coffee Roasters .................. **H5**
4 Vernick Coffee Bar ............... **F3**

## Hotels ▼

1 The Bellevue Philadelphia ....... **H7**
2 Club Quarters Hotel in
  Philadelphia ...................... **G5**
3 Four Seasons Hotel
  Philadelphia at the
  Comcast Technology Center ...... **F3**
4 Motto By Hilton Philadelphia
  Rittenhouse Square ............... **E5**
5 Ritz-Carlton Philadelphia .......... **I5**
6 ROOST Apartment Hotel ......... **H6**
7 Westin Philadelphia............... **G5**
8 W Philadelphia.................... **H5**

**Mütter Museum**

**SCIENCE MUSEUM** | Skulls, antique microscopes, and a cancerous tumor removed from President Grover Cleveland's mouth in 1893 form just part of the unusual medical collection in the Mütter Museum, at the College of Physicians of Philadelphia. The museum has hundreds of anatomical and pathological specimens, medical instruments, and organs removed from patients, including a piece of John Wilkes Booth's neck tissue. The collection contains 139 skulls; items that belonged to Marie Curie, Louis Pasteur, and Joseph Lister; and a 7-foot, 6-inch skeleton, the tallest on public exhibition in the United States. ✉ *19 S. 22nd St., Center City West* ☎ *215/560–8564* 🌐 *muttermuseum.org* 🎫 *$20.*

## 🍴 Restaurants

**Aqimero**

**$$$ | LATIN AMERICAN** | Far below the Ritz-Carlton's 140-foot-tall rotunda sits this Latin-inspired grill by chef Richard Sandoval who creates meals that match the grandeur and excitement of the historic building. Many visit Aqimero for its wood-fired meats and fish, as well as its endless Champagne weekend brunch. **Known for:** wood-fired meats and fish; endless Champagne weekend brunch; swanky setting. [$] *Average main: $28* ✉ *10 Avenue of the Arts, Center City West* ☎ *215/523–8200* 🌐 *www.aqimero.com.*

**Butcher & Singer**

**$$$$ | STEAKHOUSE** | One of restaurateur Stephen Starr's many ventures is housed in an old wood-paneled and marbled brokerage (from which it borrows its name). Here the dishes are traditional rather than fancy (wedge salad, filet Oscar), portions are hefty, and the sides classic (green beans amandine, creamed spinach). **Known for:** juicy steaks; weekday lunch options; baked Alaska. [$] *Average main: $38* ✉ *1500 Walnut St., Center City West* ☎ *215/732–4444* 🌐 *www.butcherandsinger.com* 🕒 *No lunch weekends.*

**★ Condesa**

**$$ | MODERN MEXICAN** | In a neighborhood full of beautifully designed restaurants with exciting food to boot, it's hard to pick favorites, but Condesa certainly holds its own. Inspired by the flavors and style of Mexico City, the restaurant expands over an outdoor space, indoor dining room, lounge, and a bar, seating 140 people. **Known for:** margaritas; housemade corn tortillas; well-designed interior. [$] *Average main: $20* ✉ *1830 Ludlow St., Center City West* ☎ *267/930–5600* 🌐 *www.condesaphilly.com* 🕒 *No lunch weekends.*

**Continental Mid-town**

**$ | ECLECTIC | FAMILY** | You're not sure what decade you're in once you enter the vast, retro playground that shares a name with the Old City martini lounge, also from blockbuster restaurateur Stephen Starr. The cognoscenti have moved on, but others still line up for a spot on the popular rooftop lounge or sit inside, in a swinging wicker basket chair, a sunken banquette, or a baby-blue vinyl booth. **Known for:** large portions; solid martinis; rooftop bar. [$] *Average main: $15* ✉ *1801 Chestnut St., Center City West* ☎ *215/567–1800* 🌐 *www.continentalmidtown.com.*

**Harp & Crown**

**$$ | AMERICAN** | Dimly lit with exceptionally designed interiors, this Sansom Street haunt is a frequent stop for those looking for a cool space to enjoy new American–style bites. In this case, that means doughy pizzas, inspired veggie dishes, hearty meat-based meals, artisanal toasts, and a selection of raw dishes, in addition to a hefty drink list. **Known for:** happy hour with $5 drinks and $3–$5 snacks; pizzas; downstairs bowling. [$] *Average main: $20* ✉ *1525 Sansom St., Center City West* ☎ *215/330–2800* 🌐 *harpcrown.com* 🕒 *No lunch weekdays.*

**★ JG Skyhigh**

**$$$$ | FRENCH FUSION** | Of the Four Seasons Philadelphia's three restaurants, JG Skyhigh is the most approachable; it's the place to go for a drink while you take in the stunning city views from the 60th floor. The dinner menu includes modernized versions of hotel restaurant standards like a good burger, black truffle–topped pizza, and pumpkin-seed crusted salmon as well as a selection of high-end caviar. **Known for:** amazing city views; egg toast with caviar; seasonal tasting menu. [$] *Average main: $80* ✉ *1 N. 19th St., Center City West* ☎ *215/419–5000* 🌐 *www.jgskyhigh.com.*

**★ Vernick Fish**

**$$$ | SEAFOOD** | The formidable chef Greg Vernick used his Jersey Shore vacations as inspiration for Vernick Fish, an oyster bar reminiscent of the restaurants that dot the Jersey Shore—albeit with an elevated vibe. Located on the first floor of the soaring Comcast Technology Center, the seafood-focused restaurant serves lunch and dinner daily with a special focus on raw fish and fish-forward tartares. **Known for:** tartares; scallops; bar seating. [$] *Average main: $30* ✉ *1876 Arch St., Center City West* ☎ *215/419–5055* 🌐 *www.vernickfish.com.*

## Coffee and Quick Bites

**The Concourse at Comcast Center**

**$ | ECLECTIC | FAMILY** | A go-to spot for many who work in Center City, the Concourse on the bottom floor of the Comcast Center is a dining hall made up of Philadelphia favorites in addition to nationwide food brands. From sushi to Italian pastries, there are plenty of options for a quick meal or snack beneath the towering Comcast Center. **Known for:** affordable meals; grab-and-go lunch; diverse food options. [$] *Average main: $9* ✉ *1701 John F. Kennedy Blvd., Center City West* ☎ *215/496–1810* ⏲ *Closed Sun.*

**Gran Caffe L'Aquila**

**$$ | ITALIAN** | Open all day, Gran Coffee L'Aquila is the perfect spot for grabbing an on-the-go cup of house-roasted espresso first thing in the morning or sitting down for a nightcap and dessert at the end of the day. They also serve panini, which can be eaten at one of their sidewalk tables or taken to go, as well as a full dinner menu and award-winning gelato in flavors like *torrone* (nougat), citrus-vanilla, and cannoli. **Known for:** house-roasted espresso; housemade pasta; award-winning gelato. [$] *Average main: $20* ✉ *1716 Chestnut St., Center City West* ☎ *215/568–5600* 🌐 *grancaffelaquila.com.*

**★ La Colombe Coffee Roasters**

**$ | CAFÉ** | Adjacent to City Hall, the 9-to-5-ers flock to locally based La Colombe Coffee Roasters for their morning, afternoon, and evening cup of coffee among the hustle and bustle of Center City. The shop is small, but the staff is efficient, which keeps the line moving no matter how busy it may look from the outside. **Known for:** draft cold brew; impressive selection of pastries; oat milk latte. [$] *Average main: $4* ✉ *1414 S. Penn Sq., Center City West* ☎ *215/977–7770* 🌐 *www.lacolombe.com.*

**★ Vernick Coffee Bar**

**$ | CAFÉ** | Chef Greg Vernick has two spots within the Comcast Technology Center, including Vernick Coffee Bar, a high-end café with some of the best baked goods in the city. Located up the escalator in the second-floor lobby of the skyscraper, the coffee shop offers a space for to-go beverages, baked goods, and salads, in addition to a 40-seat café for a sit-down breakfast or lunch. **Known for:** baked goods; toasts; open-air seating. [$] *Average main: $9* ✉ *1800 Arch St., Center City West* ☎ *215/419–5052* 🌐 *vernickcoffeebar.com* ⏲ *Closed weekends. No dinner.*

# Hotels

### The Bellevue Philadelphia

$$$ | **HOTEL** | **FAMILY** | A Philadelphia institution for almost a century, The Bellevue offers elegant lodging and spacious rooms at the very heart of the city within walking distance of most attractions. **Pros:** centrally located; shopping downstairs; old-school elegance; amazing gym. **Cons:** rooms and hallways could use an upgrade; noise from Broad Street; lackluster room service. [$] *Rooms from: $300* ✉ *200 S. Broad St., Center City West* ☎ *215/893–1234, 800/233–1234* 🌐 *www.bellevuephiladelphia.com* 🛏 *185 rooms* 🍴 *No Meals.*

### Club Quarters Hotel in Philadelphia

$$ | **HOTEL** | Hoping to capture the look and feel of an old Scotch-and-cigar parlor, Philadelphia's Club Quarters, sometimes branded as "CQ Hotel," has a little more style than the typical business-minded lodge. **Pros:** excellent location; accommodations for both typical pleasure travelers and extended business travelers; "Sleep Better Kit" available to guests. **Cons:** studio kitchens only have a microwave; no on-site parking. [$] *Rooms from: $165* ✉ *1628 Chestnut St., Center City West* ☎ *215/282–5000* 🌐 *clubquartershotels.com/philadelphia/rittenhouse-square* 🛏 *275 rooms* 🍴 *No Meals.*

### ★ Four Seasons Hotel Philadelphia at the Comcast Technology Center

$$$$ | **HOTEL** | Sweeping views of Philadelphia, a world-class spa, luxurious accommodations, and multiple spaces for eating and drinking make up the Four Seasons Hotel atop the Comcast Technology Center. **Pros:** views of Philadelphia; comfortable beds; high-quality restaurants. **Cons:** expensive room rates; pricey parking. [$] *Rooms from: $570* ✉ *1 N. 19th St., Center City West* ☎ *215/419–5000* 🌐 *www.fourseasons.com* 🛏 *219 rooms* 🍴 *No Meals.*

### ★ Motto By Hilton Philadelphia Rittenhouse Square

$ | **HOTEL** | This seriously cool hotel focuses on sparse rooms with a small footprint—rooms range from 150 to 300 square feet, allowing for two people in the smaller rooms and three to four people in the larger—in a great location; rooms have more space than one would expect. **Pros:** modern design; excellent dining options within hotel; central location. **Cons:** small rooms; long waits at hotel restaurant; no room service. [$] *Rooms from: $130* ✉ *31 S. 19th St., Center City West* ☎ *267/494–0440* 🌐 *www.hilton.com* 🛏 *252 rooms* 🍴 *No Meals.*

### ★ Ritz-Carlton Philadelphia

$$$$ | **HOTEL** | **FAMILY** | You'll feel like you're checking into the Pantheon when you enter this neoclassical hotel set in a century-old bank building—more than 60,000 square feet of Georgian white marble makes up the dramatic lobby; a 2015 renovation modernized both the lobby (textures reminiscent of currency, in a nod to the building's banking past) and guest rooms (work and play spaces, set in a contemporary neutral palette with metallic touches). **Pros:** stunning architecture (the lobby bar is unparalleled); attentive and friendly service; modern in-room amenities. **Cons:** Wi-Fi available for a fee; elevators can be slow; rooms are smaller than some luxury competitors. [$] *Rooms from: $400* ✉ *10 S. Broad St., Center City West* ☎ *215/523–8000, 800/241–3333* 🌐 *www.ritzcarlton.com* 🛏 *299 rooms* 🍴 *No Meals.*

### ROOST Apartment Hotel

$ | **HOTEL** | Nestling thoughtful hyper-modern amenities in the bones of the venerable Packard Building, ROOST is an extended-stay establishment designed with the modern traveler in mind. **Pros:** stylish, thoughtfully curated design; excellent location for Center City; apartment-style rooms. **Cons:** not always the best fit for shorter stays; parking

Within walking distance of City Hall and the Pennsylvania Convention Center, the Ritz-Carlton resides in the former home of The Girard Trust Company.

can be far from the hotel; can be loud on weekend nights. $ *Rooms from: $155* ⊠ *111 S. 15th St., Center City West* ☎ *267/737–9000* ⊕ *www.myroost.com* ⇨ *27 suites* ⦿ *No Meals.*

### ★ Westin Philadelphia

$$$ | **HOTEL** | **FAMILY** | If comfortable accommodations and plenty of shopping are your top priorities, you're not going to beat the Westin. **Pros:** close to best shopping areas; excellent beds; comfortable furniture; quiet. **Cons:** pricey parking; common spaces could use updating; busy valet parking area. $ *Rooms from: $300* ⊠ *99 S. 17th St., at Liberty Pl., Center City West* ☎ *215/563–1600, 800/937–8461* ⊕ *www.westin.com/philadelphia* ⇨ *294 rooms* ⦿ *No Meals.*

### W Philadelphia

$$$ | **HOTEL** | Opened in 2021 to great excitement from visitors and locals alike, this sexy space focuses on creating a distinctively Philly feel with modern rooms and popular cocktail spots. **Pros:** nightlife vibes; good bar; excellent spa. **Cons:** busy lobby; dark rooms; families with younger

kids might not feel comfortable with the sexy vibe. $ *Rooms from: $300* ⊠ *1439 Chestnut St., Center City West* ⊕ *www.marriott.com* ⇨ *295 rooms* ⦿ *No Meals.*

 **Nightlife**

## BARS AND LOUNGES

### Continental Mid-town

**COCKTAIL LOUNGES** | A more elaborate offshoot of Stephen Starr's Old City martini lounge, the Continental Mid-town spreads the cocktail and global small-plates concept across three whimsically appointed floors, including an indoor-outdoor rooftop space. The items on the comprehensive food menu run the gamut from cheesesteak egg rolls to lobster macaroni and cheese. ⊠ *1801 Chestnut St., Center City West* ☎ *215/567–1800* ⊕ *www.continentalmidtown.com.*

### XIX (Nineteen)

**COCKTAIL LOUNGES** | Perched on the 19th floor of the Hyatt at the Bellevue, this high-end lounge bestows beautiful vistas of the city, solid cocktails, a seafood-centric menu, a roaring fireplace, and elegant decorative accents. It's certainly pricey, but the views make up for it. ⊠ *200 S. Broad St., Center City West* ☎ *215/790–1919* ⊕ *nineteenrestaurant. com.*

## MUSIC CLUBS
### Chris' Jazz Café
**LIVE MUSIC** | An intimate hangout off the Avenue of the Arts (aka Broad Street), Chris' showcases top talent Tuesday through Saturday. The jazz club stays accessible by doing the simple things right—friendly service, fair prices, great performers. The lunch and dinner menus feature some light New Orleans–style touches. ⊠ *1421 Sansom St., Center City West* ☎ *215/568–3131* ⊕ *www.chrisjazz-cafe.com.*

 # Performing Arts

## CLASSICAL MUSIC
### Chamber Orchestra of Philadelphia
**MUSIC** | Directed by Dirk Brossé, this prestigious group performs chamber music from September to May at the Perelman Theater at the Kimmel Center for the Performing Arts. ⊠ *300 S. Broad St., Center City West* ☎ *215/893–1999 box office, 215/545–5451 administrative office* ⊕ *www.chamberorchestra.org.*

### Philadelphia Chamber Music Society
**CONCERTS** | From October to May, the society presents numerous concerts featuring nationally and internationally known musicians. The schedule is packed with pianists, vocalists, and chamber music series, a jazz series, and string recitals. Performances are held in the Perelman Theater at the Kimmel Center for the Performing Arts, at the Philadelphia Museum of Art, and at other locations in the city. ⊠ *Center City West* ☎ *215/569–8587 information, 215/569–8080 box office* ⊕ *www.pcmsconcerts. org.*

### Philadelphia Orchestra
**CONCERTS** | Considered one of the world's best symphony orchestras, the Philadelphia Orchestra is overseen by the effervescent Yannick Nézet-Séguin. The orchestra's present home is the cello-shaped Verizon Hall at the Kimmel Center for the Performing Arts. The 2,500-seat hall is the centerpiece of the performing-arts center at Broad and Spruce Streets—a dynamic complex housed under a glass-vaulted roof. Orchestra concerts during the September–May season are still among the city's premier social events. In summer the orchestra performs at the Mann Center for the Performing Arts. ⊠ *300 S. Broad St., Center City West* ☎ *215/893–1999 box office, 215/893–1900 info* ⊕ *www. philorch.org.*

### The Philly Pops
**CONCERTS** | **FAMILY** | Music director David Charles Abell leads an orchestra of local musicians in programs that swing from Broadway to big band, or from ragtime to rock and roll, with ease. They perform mainly at the Kimmel Center in the fall, winter, and spring. ⊠ *300 S. Broad St., Center City West* ☎ *215/893–1900* ⊕ *www.phillypops.com.*

## DANCE
### ★ Philadelphia Ballet
**BALLET** | **FAMILY** | Artistic director Angel Corella leads the company through a season of classic favorites and new works; they dance on the stage of the Academy of Music and at the Merriam Theater at the University of the Arts. Their annual production of George Balanchine's *The Nutcracker* is a holiday favorite. ⊠ *Broad and Locust Sts., Center City West* ☎ *215/551–7000* ⊕ *philadelphiaballet.org.*

### Philadelphia Dance Company
**MODERN DANCE** | This modern troupe, also known as PHILADANCO, is recognized for its innovative performances that weld contemporary and classical forms and the traditions of other cultures, with a particular emphasis on African American

dance heritage. ✉ *Broad and Spruce Sts., Center City West* ☎ *215/387–8200* ⊕ *www.philadanco.org.*

## OPERA

### ★ Opera Philadelphia

**OPERA** | Opera Philadelphia's season begins with Festival O annually in September, a week-plus-long extravaganza featuring free and more affordably priced shows. Following the festival, the group stages four or five productions a year between October and May at the Academy of Music; some operas have international stars. All performances are in the original language with English supertitles above the stage. ✉ *240 S. Broad St., Center City West* ☎ *215/732–8400* ⊕ *www.operaphila.org.*

## THEATER

### Merriam Theater

**THEATER** | Built in 1918 as the Shubert, the ornate 1,688-seat theater has had many stage greats, including Al Jolson, Helen Hayes, Katharine Hepburn, Sammy Davis Jr., Angela Lansbury, and Sir Laurence Olivier. Named after a local benefactor, the lavishly decorated Merriam hosts a full schedule of national tours of Broadway shows, modern dance companies, and solo performers, from the magicians Penn & Teller to tap dancer Savion Glover. ✉ *250 S. Broad St., Center City West* ☎ *215/893–1999* ⊕ *www.kimmelcenter. org.*

### Philadelphia Film Center

**FILM** | Formerly the Prince Music Theater, the theater has evolved into a regular venue for movie screenings and the society's fall film festival, though it also hosts concerts, cabaret, opera, comedy, and more. ✉ *1412 Chestnut St., Center City West* ☎ *267/239–2941* ⊕ *filmadelphia.org.*

### Philadelphia Theatre Company

**THEATER** | Philadelphia and world premieres of works by contemporary American playwrights are performed here. In 2007 the Philadelphia Theatre Company moved to their new permanent home, the 365-seat Suzanne Roberts Theatre on the Avenue of the Arts. ✉ *480 S. Broad St., between Lombard and Pine Sts., Center City West* ☎ *215/985–0420* ⊕ *www.philadelphiatheatrecompany.org.*

##  Shopping

## MALLS

### Shops at Liberty Place

**NEIGHBORHOODS** | At 16th and Chestnut Streets is the Shops at Liberty Place. The complex features a food court and popular stores, including a Loft Outlet, Jos. A Bank, and Bloomingdales Outlet. More than 20 stores and restaurants are arranged in two circular levels within a strikingly handsome 90-foot glass-roof atrium. ✉ *1625 Chestnut St., Center City West* ☎ *215/851–9055* ⊕ *www.shopsat-liberty.com.*

# Rittenhouse Square

Rittenhouse Square has long been one of the city's swankiest addresses. The square's entrances, plaza, pool, and fountains were designed in 1913 by Paul Cret, one of the people responsible for the Benjamin Franklin Parkway. The square was named in honor of one of the city's 18th-century stars: David Rittenhouse, president of the American Philosophical Society. The first house facing the square was erected in 1840, soon to be followed by other grand mansions. Almost all the private homes are now gone, replaced by hotels, apartments, cultural institutions, and elegant restaurants and stylish cafés. The area south and west of the square is still largely residential and lovely, with cupolas and balconies, hitching posts, and stained-glass windows. Peek in the streets behind these homes or through their wrought-iron gates and into well-tended gardens.

There is more local flavor off the beaten path, down numbered streets and smaller streets around Rittenhouse Square. Parking is tough in this area and you'll pay a pretty penny for a meter or a lot. You'll have more fun and see much more if you walk these lively streets and let yourself get a little lost.

**TIP→** For this book, we have used the boundaries of 16th Street west to 23rd Street and Chestnut Street south to Lombard Street to determine what properties are in Rittenhouse Square. It is important to keep in mind that Rittenhouse Square is part of the larger Center City West neighborhood as well.

 **Sights**

### Curtis Institute of Music
**NOTABLE BUILDING** | Graduates of this tuition-free school for outstanding students include Leonard Bernstein, Samuel Barber, Ned Rorem, and Anna Moffo. The school occupies four former private homes and Lenfest Hall for student housing and practice rooms; the main building is in the mansion that belonged to banker George W. Childs Drexel. Built in 1893 by the distinguished Boston firm of Peabody and Stearns, it's notable for Romanesque and Renaissance architectural details. Free student and faculty concerts are given from October through May, usually on Monday, Wednesday, and Friday evenings. ⊠ *1726 Locust St., Rittenhouse Square* ☎ *215/893–5261 recital hotline, 215/893–7902 ticket office* ⊕ *www.curtis.edu* Ⓜ *Walnut/Locust stop; Broad Street Line.*

### Delancey Place
**STREET** | Cypress Street, north of Delancey Place, and Panama Street (especially the 1900 block, one block south of Delancey) are two of the many intimate streets lined with trees and town houses characteristic of the area. At No. 2010 is the Rosenbach Museum and Library. ⊠ *Rittenhouse Square.*

### ★ Rittenhouse Row
**BUSINESS DISTRICT | FAMILY** | Shop-'til-you-droppers make a beeline for Rittenhouse Row, the area between Broad and 21st Streets and Spruce and Market Streets. Lately chains like J.Crew, H&M, and Lululemon have been taking over Walnut Street between Rittenhouse Square and Broad Street, but this is still the greatest concentration of swanky stores, tony boutiques, and jewelers you'll find in the city. ⊠ *Rittenhouse Square* ⊕ *www.rittenhouserow.org.*

### ★ Rittenhouse Square
**PLAZA/SQUARE** | Once grazing ground for cows and sheep, Philadelphia's most elegant square is reminiscent of a Parisian park. One of William Penn's original five city squares, the park was named in 1825 to honor David Rittenhouse, 18th-century astronomer, clock maker, and the first director of the United States Mint. Many of Philadelphia's celebrities have lived here. Extra paths were made for Dr. William White, a leader in beautifying the square, so he could walk directly from his home to the exclusive Rittenhouse Club across the square and lunch with author Henry James. Until 1950 town houses bordered the square, but they have now been replaced on three sides by swank apartment buildings and hotels. Some great houses remain, including the former residence of Henry P. McIlhenny on the southwest corner. If you want to join the office workers who have lunch-hour picnics in the park, you can find many eateries along Walnut, Sansom, and Chestnut Streets east of the square. Or you can dine alfresco at one of several upscale open-air cafés across from the square on 18th Street between Locust and Walnut. The term "Rittenhouse Row" describes the greater Rittenhouse Square area, bordered by Pine, Market, 21st, and Broad Streets. ⊠ *Walnut St. between 18th and 19th Sts., Rittenhouse Square.*

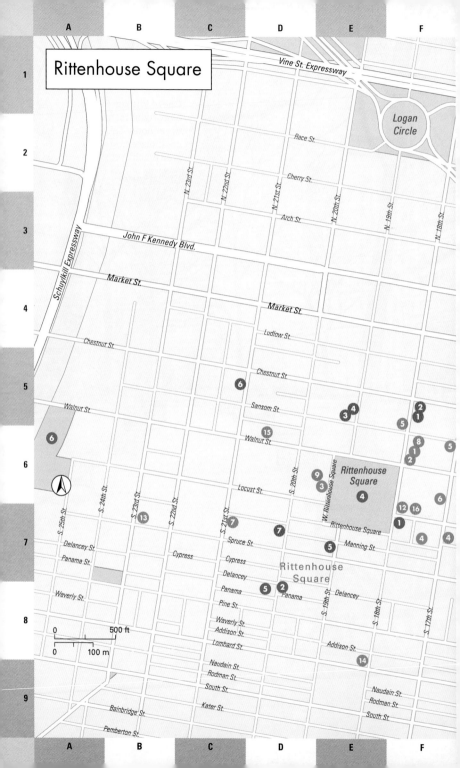

## Sights ▼
1 Curtis Institute of Music ........... **F7**
2 Delancey Place .................... **D8**
3 Rittenhouse Row.................. **G6**
4 Rittenhouse Square ............... **E6**
5 Rosenbach Museum and Library.............................. **D8**
6 Schuylkill River Park .............. **A6**

## Restaurants ▼
1 Abe Fisher .......................... **G6**
2 a.kitchen ............................ **F6**
3 Amma's South Indian Cuisine .... **H5**
4 Black Sheep......................... **F7**
5 The Dandelion....................... **F5**
6 Dizengoff ............................ **G6**
7 Friday Saturday Sunday ..........**C7**
8 Her Place Supper Club............**F6**
9 Lacroix Restaurant at the Rittenhouse........................**E6**
10 Mission Taqueria .................. **H6**
11 Monk's Cafe ........................ **G7**
12 PARC ................................. **F7**
13 Sally ................................. **B7**
14 SouthGate .......................... **E8**
15 Vernick Food & Drink............. **D6**
16 Via Locusta ........................ **F7**

## Quick Bites ▼
1 Alimentari at Di Bruno Bros. ...... **F5**
2 Di Bruno Bros. ..................... **F5**
3 Federal Donuts..................... **E5**
4 K'Far Cafe........................... **E5**
5 Metropolitan Bakery .............. **E7**
6 Rione ................................. **C5**
7 Spread Bagelry .................... **D7**

## Hotels ▼
1 AKA Rittenhouse Square .......... **F6**
2 Kimpton Hotel Palomar Philadelphia ....................... **G6**
3 The Rittenhouse ................... **E6**
4 Rittenhouse 1715................... **F7**
5 Sofitel Philadelphia at Rittenhouse Square ............... **F6**
6 Warwick Hotel Rittenhouse Square ............... **F6**

KEY
- Sights
- Restaurants
- Quick Bites
- Hotels

### Rosenbach Museum and Library

**ART MUSEUM** | This 1863 three-floor town house and an adjoining building are filled with Persian rugs and 18th-century British, French, and American antiques (plus an entire living room that once belonged to poet Marianne Moore), but the real treasures are the artworks, books, and manuscripts here. Amassed by Philadelphia collectors Philip H. and A. S. W. Rosenbach, the collection includes paintings by Canaletto, Sully, and Lawrence; drawings by Daumier, Fragonard, and Blake; book illustrations ranging from medieval illuminations to the works of Maurice Sendak, author of *Where the Wild Things Are*; the only known copy of the first issue of Benjamin Franklin's *Poor Richard's Almanack*; and the library's most famous treasure, the original manuscript of James Joyce's *Ulysses.* The Rosenbach celebrates "Bloomsday" on June 16 with readings from *Ulysses* by notable Philadelphians. The library has more than 130,000 manuscripts and 30,000 rare books. ✉ *2008–10 Delancey Pl., Rittenhouse Square* ☎ *215/732–1600* 🌐 *www.rosenbach.org* 🎫 *$10.*

### Schuylkill River Park

**CITY PARK** | **FAMILY** | A waterfront park that connects Center City with the Schuylkill River and offers city dwellers an expansive space for running, walking, playing, and dog walking. ✉ *300 S. 25th St., Rittenhouse Square* ☎ *215/309–5523* 🌐 *www.fsrp.org.*

## 🍴 Restaurants

### Abe Fisher

**$$** | **EASTERN EUROPEAN** | Having successfully turned the country into Israeli-food addicts, Michael Solomonov and Steve Cook have now turned their attention to the cuisines of the Ashkenazi Jews in Eastern Europe. The kitchen team creates incognito thrillers like matzo ball tamale, smoked salmon tartare, and veal schnitzel tacos. **Known for:** Montreal-style smoked short ribs; happy hour; retro-inspired digs. [$] *Average main: $18* ✉ *1623 Sansom St., Rittenhouse Square* ☎ *215/867–0088* 🌐 *www.abefisherphilly.com* 🕒 *No lunch.*

### ★ a.kitchen

**$$$** | **MODERN AMERICAN** | Smoke, coal, fire, and ash create a through line for the menu at a.kitchen, on the ground floor of the AKA Hotel. Attired in blond wood and Carrara marble, it looks like a spa in the Italian Alps, and its Rittenhouse address guarantees a scene, but the Chef Eli Collins has transformed it into a "serious restaurant" with an ace sommelier and a steak tartare that cannot be missed. **Known for:** seasonal small plates; fresh oysters; sleek interior. [$] *Average main: $25* ✉ *135 S. 18th St., Rittenhouse Square* ☎ *215/825–7030* 🌐 *www.akitchenandbar.com.*

### Amma's South Indian Cuisine

**$** | **INDIAN** | **FAMILY** | The menu at this popular Center City location includes a huge selection of crisp dosas as well as other regional specialties like mutton (prepared several different ways), chicken kurma (a curried chicken dish), biryani (rice dish), and plenty of vegetarian options. Tiffin specials, which include a couple of dishes, plus a drink and dessert, make for a good lunch, and the chai and filter coffee are both excellent pick-me-ups. **Known for:** excellent coffee and chai; takeout menu; southern Indian dishes. [$] *Average main: $13* ✉ *1518 Chestnut St., Rittenhouse Square* ☎ *808/762–6627* 🌐 *www.philadelphia.ammasrestaurants.com.*

### Black Sheep

**$$** | **IRISH** | Converted from a private club with blacked-out windows, this Dublin-style pub has been packing them in for rivers of Irish draft and kitchen specialties. Guinness-battered fish-and-chips could have been produced on the "auld sod," and the malt vinegar to sprinkle over it all does little to dampen the crisp crust. **Known for:** traditional pub fare; casual atmosphere; vast beer selection. [$] *Average main: $17* ✉ *247 S. 17th St.,*

*Rittenhouse Square* ☎ *215/545–9473* 🌐 *www.theblacksheeppub.com.*

**The Dandelion**

$$ | **BRITISH** | This Stephen Starr–helmed pub is as close to an English pub as you'll get stateside—there's a snarling bear head mounted on one wall; an assortment of mismatched divans and armchairs; and toasties, fish-and-chips, and puddings on the menu. While the entrées are solid, the apps and desserts shine brightest at this sprawling, cozy venue. **Known for:** happy hour; weekend brunch; Sunday roast. [$] *Average main: $18* ✉ *124 S. 18th St., Rittenhouse Square* ☎ *215/558–2500* 🌐 *thedandelion-pub.com.*

**Dizengoff**

$ | **ISRAELI** | Think of Dizengoff as Zahav lite. This graffiti-tagged spin-off of the nationally acclaimed Israeli restaurant is modeled after the hummus stalls of Tel Aviv, specializing in the dreamy chickpea puree crowned with an array of creative, seasonal toppings. **Known for:** rotating hummus toppings; fluffy pita; frozen lemonanna. [$] *Average main: $9* ✉ *1625 Sansom St., Rittenhouse Square* ☎ *215/867–8181* 🌐 *www.dizengoffphilly.com.*

**★ Friday Saturday Sunday**

$$ | **AMERICAN** | What was once a Rittenhouse institution is now a Rittenhouse darling after the restaurant was sold to husband-and-wife team Chad and Hanna Williams and revitalized as a cozy yet elevated space with boundary-pushing but still familiar food and drinks. The new American fare ranges from a curated raw bar, featuring the likes of oysters and caviar, to delicate pastas coated in punchy sauces with proteins like lobster and pork cheek. **Known for:** delicate pastas; cozy corner setting; raw bar. [$] *Average main: $24* ✉ *261 S. 21st St., Rittenhouse Square* ☎ *215/546–4232* 🌐 *www.fridaysaturdaysunday.com* 🕒 *Closed Mon. No lunch.*

**★ Her Place Supper Club**

$$$$ | **FRENCH FUSION** | Amanda Shulman's intimate dinner party–style restaurant has quickly become one of the hottest tickets in town. Reservations go live two weeks in advance for a fixed menu of French- and Italian-inspired, seasonal dishes served family style at each table. **Known for:** tasting menu; luxury ingredients; party atmosphere. [$] *Average main: $75* ✉ *1740 Sansom St., Rittenhouse Square* 🌐 *www.herplacephilly.com.*

**★ Lacroix Restaurant at the Rittenhouse**

$$$$ | **ECLECTIC** | Located inside the posh Rittenhouse Hotel, this elegant dining space has a view overlooking the iconic Rittenhouse Square Park. Afternoon tea is available in the Mary Cassatt Tea Room, and there's an à la carte menu that features dishes like aged duck, Berkshire pork, and King crab, but if you really want to indulge, try the Carte Blanche, a full-tasting menu (wine pairings possible) that includes dishes like risotto of new potatoes with caviar, smoked king salmon, and bluefin tuna carpaccio. **Known for:** full tasting menu and afternoon tea; Sunday brunch and breakfast seven days a week; expansive wine list. [$] *Average main: $45* ✉ *210 W. Rittenhouse Sq., Rittenhouse Square* ☎ *215/790–2533* 🌐 *www.lacroixrestaurant.com* 🕒 *No lunch Mon., Tues., and Sat. No dinner Mon. and Tues.*

**★ Mission Taqueria**

$ | **MEXICAN** | Within the highbrow Rittenhouse neighborhood, Mission Taqueria is the cool kid in town. Its neon signs, colorful digs, and collaborative games draw the crowds, while the fresh tacos, delectable dips, and margaritas in a multitude of flavors keep them full and happy. **Known for:** happy hour including $3 beer, $2 tacos, and $6 margaritas; cheap drinks and snacks; colorful digs. [$] *Average main: $14* ✉ *1516 Sansom St., 2nd fl., above Oyster House, Rittenhouse Square* ☎ *215/383–1200* 🌐 *www.mission-taqueria.com.*

**Monk's Cafe**

$ | **BELGIAN** | If the rumors are true, and Philadelphians do drink more Belgian beer than Belgians do, then it's because of the owners of Monk's, the seminal café with a pipeline of sours, dubbels, and saisons straight from the motherland. Whether steamed in classic style with white wine and shallots or with cream, mussels are a high point at Monk's and the fries that accompany them draw raves from the regulars who crowd the place. **Known for:** Monk's Café Flemish Sour Ale; mussels; burgers. [$] *Average main: $15* ✉ *264 S. 16th St., Rittenhouse Square* ☎ *215/545–7005* 🌐 *www.monkscafe.com.*

★ **PARC**

$$$ | **FRENCH** | Brass rails, silvered mirrors, claret-hued banquettes, and oak wainscoting reclaimed from now-shuttered Parisian restaurants, imbue patina—while small touches like newspapers on wooden poles, create extra realism—in the meticulous stage set placed on Philadelphia's most desirable corner by restaurateur Stephen Starr. Similarly, standard menu items (roasted chicken, trout amandine) hold their own, but the little things—desserts and salads, fresh-baked goods (including house-made macaroons), and excellent onion soup—stand out. **Known for:** onion soup; seafood tower; outdoor dining. [$] *Average main: $25* ✉ *227 S. 18th St., Rittenhouse Square* ☎ *215/545–2262* 🌐 *parc-restaurant.com.*

**Sally**

$$ | **PIZZA** | Naturally leavened, sourdough pizza is the star of the show at Sally, where crisp crusts carry an ever-changing selection of toppings, from classic cheese to bacon and sunchoke. Start your meal with a couple of vegetable-forward starters, a platter of oysters, and a glass of natural wine; if you find a wine you like, visit the wine store to take a bottle home with you. **Known for:** large natural wine list that's also available at the on-site shop; creative pizza toppings; seasonal vegetables. [$] *Average main: $17* ✉ *2229 Spruce St., Rittenhouse Square* ☎ *267/773–7178* 🌐 *www.sallyphl.com* 🕒 *Closed Tues. No lunch.*

**SouthGate**

$ | **KOREAN** | If you're looking for a more relaxed scene, head a couple of blocks south of Rittenhouse Square to find local beers and approachable cocktails paired with Korean-inspired bar food like a Seoul hot chicken sandwich, dolsot bibimbap, and crispy Brussels sprouts. Friday and Saturday nights are busy, so it's best to call ahead or make a reservation and, if possible, take advantage of the outdoor seating in nice weather. **Known for:** local beer; bar food; fried chicken sandwich. [$] *Average main: $13* ✉ *1801 Lombard St., Rittenhouse Square* ☎ *215/560–8443* 🌐 *www.southgatephilly.com* 🕒 *Closed Mon.*

★ **Vernick Food & Drink**

$$$$ | **MODERN AMERICAN** | South Jersey native and James Beard–award winning chef, Greg Vernick spent the bulk of his career opening restaurants around the world for Jean-Georges Vongerichten. When he and his wife, Julie, wanted to do their own place, they came back to the Delaware Valley and made waves with their bustling (but intimate) modern American restaurant whose ever-changing menu features delicious things on toast (avocado, foie gras, Maryland crab), Asian influences, and large-format proteins (whole chicken or rack of lamb) cooked in a wood-burning oven. **Known for:** thoughtful toasts like pumpkin, apple, and brown butter or sea scallop and black truffle butter; roasted meats; raw bar. [$] *Average main: $28* ✉ *2031 Walnut St., Rittenhouse Square* ☎ *267/639–6644* 🌐 *www.vernickphilly.com* 🕒 *Closed Mon. No lunch.*

**Via Locusta**

$$$$ | **ITALIAN** | **FAMILY** | Popular restaurateur Michael Schulson helms this romantic, Italian-inspired gem just off Rittenhouse Square. The menu features

With numerous locations around the city, Federal Donuts is a great snack stop. Try the "fancy" menu—daily and seasonal specials—or the hot menu, i.e. made while you watch.

seasonally focused dishes, with a particular emphasis on handmade pasta like the signature doppio ravioli (two conjoined ravioli, one side filled with fig and the other with Gorgonzola). **Known for:** from-scratch cocktail list; housemade pasta; focaccia with whipped honey butter. $ *Average main: $40* ✉ *1723 Locust St., Rittenhouse Square* ☎ *215/642–0020* ⊕ *www.vialocusta.com* ⊗ *No lunch weekdays.*

## ☕ Coffee and Quick Bites

### ★ Alimentari at Di Bruno Bros.
$ | ITALIAN | Above the Di Bruno Bros. Rittenhouse location lives Alimentari, a casual Italian restaurant with plenty of seating and enough space for large groups. **Known for:** mozzarella bar; charcuterie; Italian wine selection. $ *Average main: $14* ✉ *1730 Chestnut St., 2nd fl., Rittenhouse Square* ☎ *267/764–5143* ⊕ *dibruno.com/alimentari.*

### Di Bruno Bros.
$ | CAFÉ | This two-level gourmet shop has a dazzling array of prepared foods, mouthwatering pastries, and creamy gelato. Sampling the wares can make for a good snack, but if you require something more substantial, head to the recently redone café upstairs. **Known for:** grab-and-go lunch options; pastries; cheese selection. $ *Average main: $10* ✉ *1730 Chestnut St., Rittenhouse Square* ☎ *215/665–9220* ⊕ *www.dibruno.com.*

### ★ Federal Donuts
$ | CAFÉ | FAMILY | Cakey doughnuts are the star at this local-to-Philadelphia chain run by chefs Michael Solomonov and Steven Cook of the celebrated CookNSolo restaurants. The menu includes both a "fancy" doughnut menu, which includes daily and seasonal specials, along with a hot doughnut menu, which includes staples that are available throughout the year. **Known for:** inventive doughnut flavors; fried chicken and fried-chicken sandwich; breakfast sandwich. $ *Average main: $5* ✉ *1632 Sansom St.,*

*Rittenhouse Square* ☎ *215/665–1101* 🌐 *www.federaldonuts.com.*

### ★ K'Far Cafe

$ | **ISRAELI** | One of the latest ventures by James Beard Award–winning chef Michael Solomonov's CookNSolo group, K'Far is an ode to the all-day bakeries that populate Israeli mornings with traditional baked goods, coffee, and Jerusalem bagel sandwiches; lunch also features grain bowls and salads. There are so many options, you could easily visit multiple times a day to try them all. **Known for:** Jerusalem bagel sandwiches; full bar; fresh baked goods. [$] *Average main: $15* ✉ *110 S. 19th St., Rittenhouse Square* ☎ *267/800–7200* 🌐 *www.kfarcafe.com* 🕒 *Closed Mon. and Tues. No dinner.*

### Metropolitan Bakery

$ | **CAFÉ** | **FAMILY** | This Philadelphia institution was founded on the principle of artisanal baking, which explains why its loaves have such an intense flavor and crackly crust. Stop here for a round of cracked wheat or multigrain or for a small treat such as a chocolatey cookie or lemon bar. **Known for:** fresh breads; pizzas; sandwiches. [$] *Average main: $5* ✉ *262 S. 19th St., Rittenhouse Square* ☎ *215/545–6655 bakery, 267/990–8055* 🌐 *www.metropolitanbakery.com.*

### Rione

$ | **PIZZA** | **FAMILY** | Roman-style *pizza al taglio* (pizza by the "cut" or slice) is the main event at this pizza spot run by Francesco Crovetti, a Roman transplant. Perfect for a quick lunch or snack, browse the options of thick-bottomed, rectangular pies lined up in the bakery case, make your choice, and then pay by the weight. **Known for:** pizza al taglio (pizza by the slice); takeout; quick service. [$] *Average main: $7* ✉ *100½ S. 21st St., Rittenhouse Square* ☎ *215/575–9075* 🌐 *www.rionepizza.com.*

### ★ Spread Bagelry

$ | **CAFÉ** | **FAMILY** | This Montreal-style bagel shop operates its self-proclaimed "Spreadquarters" with views of the Schuylkill River and bagels and beer to boot; the Walnut Street shop partnered with Workhorse Brewing Company, a brewery based in King of Prussia, Pennsylvania. The café offers a menu of fresh Spread bagels and bagel sandwiches. **Known for:** bagels; beer; river views. [$] *Average main: $8* ✉ *2401 Walnut St., Rittenhouse Square* ☎ *267/692–2435* 🌐 *www.spreadbagelry.com.*

## 🛏 Hotels

### AKA Rittenhouse Square

$$$ | **HOTEL** | Though steps away from the popular park and surrounding shopping, this former apartment building operates in a below-the-radar fashion favored by visiting actors and athletes; the property offers homey studios and one- and two-bedroom suites that have lots of closet space and full kitchens with dishes, glassware, and large, stainless-steel refrigerators. **Pros:** large rooms; homey amenities and atmosphere; nice restaurant and bar. **Cons:** no parking; no room service; some of the lower rooms have views of a brick wall; gym lacks ample equipment. [$] *Rooms from: $305* ✉ *135 S. 18th St., Rittenhouse Square* ☎ *215/825–7000, 888/252–0180* 🌐 *www.hotelaka.com* 🛏 *78 rooms* 🍴 *No Meals.*

### ★ Kimpton Hotel Palomar Philadelphia

$$ | **HOTEL** | **FAMILY** | The Palomar marks the apex of Philadelphia's recent surge of hip hotels; three brightly colored busts of Ben Franklin greet you in this Kimpton property's chic lobby alongside a comfy fireside living room. **Pros:** superhip yet comfortable; eco-friendly and LEED Gold certified; good location near Rittenhouse Square restaurants. **Cons:** allows pets, including barking dogs; standard rooms are cleverly designed but a bit small; main entrance is along a busy street.

[$] *Rooms from: $185* ✉ *117 S. 17th St., Rittenhouse Square* ☎ *215/563–5006, 888/725–1778* ⊕ *www.hotelpalomar-philadelphia.com* ⇱ *247 rooms* ⦿ *No Meals.*

### The Rittenhouse

**$$$ | HOTEL | FAMILY |** From providing personal items that travelers commonly forget to dressing the pillows of weekend guests with chocolate-covered strawberries, the staff is among the most accommodating in the city. **Pros:** great service without the stuffiness; 24-hour room service; complimentary Wi-Fi; among the largest rooms for luxury hotels; quiet. **Cons:** furniture can seem a bit dated; pricey; valet area can be busy. [$] *Rooms from: $315* ✉ *210 W. Rittenhouse Sq., Rittenhouse Square* ☎ *215/546–9000, 800/635–1042* ⊕ *www.rittenhousehotel. com* ⇱ *98 rooms* ⦿ *No Meals.*

### ★ Rittenhouse 1715

**$$$ | HOTEL |** On a small street near Rittenhouse Square, this refined, European-style mansion offers the luxury of a large hotel in an intimate space. **Pros:** quiet option for downtown; romantic; unique, boutique-style rooms. **Cons:** no parking service; no laundry service; extra beds are an additional fee. [$] *Rooms from: $300* ✉ *1715 Rittenhouse Sq., Rittenhouse Square* ☎ *215/546–6500, 877/791–6500* ⊕ *www.rittenhouse1715. com* ⇱ *23 rooms* ⦿ *Free Breakfast.*

### Sofitel Philadelphia at Rittenhouse Square

**$$$$ | HOTEL | FAMILY |** In the middle of the city's French Quarter, this luxury hotel has more of a hip feeling than some of its stuffier Federal-style neighbors. **Pros:** luxury with a hipper feel; excellent location; great service. **Cons:** its central location can make driving in and out of the hotel a pain; can be loud; some travelers complain that the front-desk staff is unfriendly. [$] *Rooms from: $399* ✉ *120 S. 17th St., Rittenhouse Square* ☎ *215/569–8300, 800/763–4835* ⊕ *www. sofitel-philadelphia.com* ⇱ *373 rooms* ⦿ *No Meals.*

### Warwick Hotel Rittenhouse Square

**$ | HOTEL |** After a recent rebrand and remodel, the Warwick Hotel wlecomes guests into a sleek lobby featuring bulbous pendant lights, fireplaces, pop-art rugs and wall decor, and sofas upholstered with bold fabrics. **Pros:** historic hotel with modern amenities; great location; great service. **Cons:** smallish bathrooms; noise from busy street; expensive parking. [$] *Rooms from: $129* ✉ *220 S. 17th St., Rittenhouse Square* ☎ *215/735–6000, 800/333–3333* ⊕ *www. radisson.com/philadelphiapa* ⇱ *305 rooms* ⦿ *No Meals.*

 ## Nightlife

### BARS AND LOUNGES
#### a.bar

**BARS |** Attached to the AKA hotel and its restaurant, a.kitchen, a.bar boasts one of the most enviable views in the city, looking right out onto Rittenhouse Square. The food and drink, with its emphases on fresh seafood and cutting-edge cocktails, will encourage return visits. ✉ *AKA Rittenhouse Square, 1737 Walnut St., Rittenhouse Square* ☎ *215/825–7035* ⊕ *www.akitchenandbar.com.*

### Black Sheep

**PUBS |** This handsome pub is just off Rittenhouse Square, in a refurbished town house with a fireplace on the main floor and a quiet dining space on the upper level. Beer lovers can choose from a solid selection of draft, bottled, and canned beers; the food, including U.K.-style entrées like shepherd's pie and bangers and mash, is straightforward and satisfying. ✉ *247 S. 17th St., Rittenhouse Square* ☎ *215/545–9473* ⊕ *www. theblacksheeppub.com.*

### The Franklin Mortgage & Investment Co.

**BARS |** One of the city's premier bars for cocktail lovers, the sexy Franklin is named after a cover business established by infamous Philly gangster Max "Boo Boo" Hoff. Bartenders whip up potent and elaborate cocktails in a narrow parlor that often requires a wait; make a reservation to bypass that issue. The location is a little tough to find, but the payoff is worth it. ✉ *1715 Latimer St., Rittenhouse Square* ☎ *267/467–3277* ⊕ *www.thefranklinbar.com.*

### Good Dog Bar

**BREWPUBS** | Locals and visitors alike flock to Good Dog Bar for a friendly environment, tons of local beers, and a surprisingly elevated food menu. Check out their signature burger, try a vegan cheesesteak, or share a plate of wings and macaroni and cheese while you work your way through the draft and cocktail list. ✉ *224 S. 15th St., Rittenhouse Square* ☎ *215/985–9600* ⊕ *gooddogbar.com.*

### The Library Bar

**BARS** | Inside the Rittenhouse Hotel, this cozy bar has views of Rittenhouse Square and an impressive selection of cocktails (and a great whiskey collection) that makes it easy to lose track of time. Drinks range from classic to innovative, and the dimly lit interior makes this a great spot for after-dinner drinks. ✉ *210 W Rittenhouse Sq., Rittenhouse Square* ☎ *215/546–9000 hotel* ⊕ *www.rittenhousehotel.com/dining/librarybar.*

### Vango Lounge & Skybar

**COCKTAIL LOUNGES** | Upstairs from sister joint Byblos, this lively club and restaurant conjures up a Tokyo vibe, from its largely Japanese-themed menu to its emphasis on mod design. The real star, however, is the third-floor Skybar, offering panoramic views of the city. ✉ *116 S. 18th St., Rittenhouse Square* ☎ *215/568–1020* ⊕ *www.vangoloungeandskybar.com.*

## COMEDY CLUBS

### Comedy Sportz

**COMEDY CLUBS** | Anything goes during Comedy Sportz's nights of improvisational comedy, formatted as a high-energy competitive sport. The troupe hosts two shows every Saturday at the Adrienne Theater, while a minor-league troupe performs on Sunday. Audience participation is essential to the experience. ✉ *2030 Sansom St., Rittenhouse Square* ☎ *484/450–8089* ⊕ *www.comedysportz-philly.com.*

### Helium Comedy Club

**COMEDY CLUBS** | Everyone from major comedians to comedy's up-and-comers stops at Rittenhouse Square's Helium Comedy Club, a cozy space where every seat in the house is a good one. In addition to shows featuring big names, the club also hosts open-mic nights, stand-up workshops, and more. ✉ *2031 Sansom St., Rittenhouse Square* ☎ *215/496–9001* ⊕ *philadelphia.heliumcomedy.com.*

## 🎭 Performing Arts

### AVA Opera Theatre

**MUSIC** | The resident artists at the Academy of Vocal Arts, a four-year, tuition-free vocal training program, present four or five fully staged opera productions during their September to May season. They are accompanied by the Chamber Orchestra of Philadelphia and perform at various venues in and around the city. ✉ *1920 Spruce St., Rittenhouse Square* ☎ *215/735–1685* ⊕ *www.avaopera.org.*

### Curtis Institute of Music

**MUSIC** | The gifted students at this world-renowned music conservatory give free recitals several times a week from October through May. All of its students are on full scholarships; its alumni include such luminaries as Leonard Bernstein, Samuel Barber, and Anna Moffo. The school also has an opera and symphony orchestra series. ✉ *1726 Locust St., Rittenhouse Square* ☎ *215/893–5252 hotline, 215/893–7902 ticket office* ⊕ *www.curtis.edu.*

# Chapter 7

# PARKWAY MUSEUM DISTRICT AND FAIRMOUNT PARK

7

Updated by
Linda Cabasin

 **Sights**
★★★★★

 **Restaurants**
★★★☆☆

 **Hotels**
★★☆☆☆

 **Shopping**
★☆☆☆☆

 **Nightlife**
★★☆☆☆

# PHILADELPHIA: AMERICA'S GARDEN CAPITAL

The 18th Century Garden on Walnut Street

With more than 35 public gardens within 30 miles of the city, Philadelphia lays claim to being "America's Garden Capital." From arboretums to sprawling former estates, there's a garden for everyone.

This horticultural legacy began with Philadelphia's founding, and today garden treasures exist even within the city. William Penn's 1682 plan for a "greene countrie towne" included open green squares, many of which survive. The early Quaker settlers had an interest in nature, and this helped propel the young city as a horticultural center. Another Philadelphia tradition has been the conversion of private gardens to public ones.

## WHEN TO GO

Gardens are often loveliest in spring and summer; note that Shofuso closes in winter. Morris Arboretum and Laurel Hill have vivid colors in fall, and Morris Arboretum runs a miniature holiday garden railway. April brings the city's popular Subaru Cherry Blossom Festival (⊕ *japan-philly.org*); Shofuso and Fairmount Park's Horticulture Center are prime sites. Wyck's roses bloom mid-May through mid-June.

## HOW TO SEE THE GARDENS

For an overview of area gardens, from wildflower preserves to grand former du Pont estates, see ⊕ *americasgarden-capital.org*; there's also a paper (or downloadable) passport/guide to record your visits. Some, like Bartram's Garden, Wyck, and Laurel Hill Cemetery, are free; tours and events may have a charge, though. There's no overall money-saving pass, but if you are a member of a garden, check for any reciprocal garden memberships.

# THE CITY'S BEST GARDENS

**Bartram's Garden:** Quaker John Bartram, who founded the country's oldest surviving botanical garden in 1728, and his son William gathered and studied native plants at this nearly 50-acre National Historic Landmark in southwest Philadelphia. John established a thriving transatlantic trade in plants; today the garden and his home continue to inspire the public. ⊕ *bartramsgarden.org*

**Wyck:** Relax and smell the roses at this house in Germantown, where nine generations of one family lived, beginning with Quaker owners in 1690. The 1820s rose garden, with its original layout, contains rare, fragrant varieties and fascinating historic plants. There's also a fruit and vegetable farm on-site, as there was for centuries. ⊕ *wyck.org*

**Shofuso Japanese House and Garden:** A horticultural gem in itself, Fairmount Park holds many surprises, not least of which are outstanding traditional Japanese gardens and a re-creation of a 17th-century house. A waterfall, koi pond, teahouse, and Japanese trees and shrubs enhance the serene setting. ⊕ *japanphilly.org*

**Laurel Hill Cemetery:** From its 1836 founding by Quaker John Jay Smith and his partners on a bluff above the Schuylkill, Laurel Hill has been a site

Views of historic Laurel Hill Cemetery, which is north of East Fairmount Park.

The beautiful Shofuso Japanese House and Garden is located in Fairmount Park.

for contemplation of nature as well as a final resting place. This Level II arboretum north of East Fairmount Park has river views and winding paths lined by more than 6,000 shrubs and trees. ⊕ *thelaurelhillcemetery.org*

**Morris Arboretum:** In leafy Chestnut Hill, the 175-acre former estate showcases trees and plants from around the globe, cottage and rose gardens, and a Victorian fernery. Now Pennsylvania's official arboretum and part of the University of Pennsylvania, it began in 1887 as the summer home of Quaker brother and sister John and Lydia Morris. ⊕ *morris-arboretum.org*

## PHILADELPHIA FLOWER SHOW

This nine-day winter wonder (late February–early March) fills acres of space in the Pennsylvania Convention Center with dramatic displays, gardening demonstrations, and floral competitions galore. The Pennsylvania Horticultural Society (⊕ *phsonline.org*) has sponsored the show (⊕ *theflowershow.com*), the world's longest-running and largest of its type, since 1829. The first show introduced the poinsettia, now a Christmas favorite, to the American public. PHS also supports many community gardens and green initiatives.

# NEIGHBORHOOD SNAPSHOT

## TOP EXPERIENCES

■ **Barnes Foundation:** This impressive collection of impressionist, postimpressionist, and early modern art is a unique Philadelphia treasure.

■ **Eastern State Penitentiary Historic Site:** Gangster Al Capone lived in this enormous former prison.

■ **Fairmount Park:** Boathouse Row and Shofuso Japanese House and Garden are some of this vast park's pleasures.

■ **The Franklin Institute:** Learn about science and technology at this interactive museum.

■ **Philadelphia Museum of Art:** Modeled after a Greek temple, the building holds one of the country's greatest art collections.

■ **Philadelphia Zoo:** The nation's oldest zoo has lions and tigers and bears—oh, my!—as well as all kinds of wildlife.

## GETTING HERE

The Parkway is easily walkable from Rittenhouse Square, but it's a 30-minute walk from the far eastern sections of the Historic Area. SEPTA or the seasonal PHLASH are good options. Drivers can find parking on metered spaces along the Parkway or on Pennsylvania Avenue; the Art Museum has a garage.

Boathouse Row on Kelly Drive and portions of Martin Luther King, Jr. Drive are easily reached on foot from the Art Museum. To reach the Philadelphia Zoo or the Please Touch Museum, drive or take SEPTA or the seasonal PHLASH. The zoo and Please Touch are less than 15-minutes' drive from Center City West. For other Fairmount Park attractions, it's best to drive.

## PLANNING YOUR TIME

The Parkway's trees and flowers are at their most colorful spring through fall. Plan to spend a day here seeing some museums and part of Fairmount Park. On Friday, the Philadelphia Museum of Art is open until 8:45 pm.

## QUICK BITES

■ **Capriccio Café and Bar at Cret Park.** At the eastern end of the Parkway, the café is a convenient stop before or after exploring the area for coffee and tea, pastries and sandwiches, and even cocktails. ⊠ *110 N. 16th St., Parkway Museum District* ⊕ *www.capriccio-cafe.com*

■ **Cosmic Cafe.** This handy, casual spot has indoor and outdoor seating and serves all-day breakfasts plus sandwiches, wraps, and snacks prepared fresh on-site. Burgers are good, including a vegetable burger. ⊠ *1 Boathouse Row, at Lloyd Hall, Fairmount Park* ⊕ *cosmicfoods.com*

■ **Musette.** Pastries, local Rival Bros coffee, and fresh seasonal tartines and salads are served in an airy, white-painted space on a residential street in Fairmount. ⊠ *2441 Aspen St., Parkway Museum District* ⊕ *musettephiladelphia.com*

■ **OCF Coffee House.** Across from Eastern State Penitentiary, pop in for coffee and tea, breakfast, snack, and lunch choices (including vegetarian and vegan options). ⊠ *2100 Fairmount Ave., Parkway Museum District* ⊕ *www.ocfrealty.com/coffee-house*

Alive with flowers, flags, and fountains, the Benjamin Franklin Parkway stretches northwest from John F. Kennedy Plaza to the Kelly (East) and MLK Jr. (West) River drives. The Philadelphia Museum of Art and other cultural institutions crown the 250-foot-wide boulevard. To its north is the residential Fairmount neighborhood; to its northwest lies Fairmount Park.

The mile-long Parkway district adjoins the Fairmount neighborhood, named for the hill that is the site of the Philadelphia Museum of Art. The boulevard continues to expand its cultural footprint: at this writing, work has begun for the late-2024 opening of Calder Gardens (⊕ *calder-gardens.org*), a building and gardens designed by architectural firm Herzog & de Meuron and landscape designer Piet Oudolf, opposite the Barnes Foundation between 21st and 22nd Streets. Calder Gardens will hold rotating displays of works by sculptor and artist Alexander Calder, who was the third generation of Calders whose creations can be seen in Philadelphia. In addition, in the long term (no date announced), the African American Museum in Philadelphia will move to the Parkway.

Nearby, 2,050-acre Fairmount Park encompasses natural areas on both sides of the Schuylkill River—woodlands, meadows, hills, and two scenic waterways. It also contains tennis courts, ball fields, playgrounds, trails, several celebrated cultural institutions, and some historic Early American country houses that are operated by various cultural institutions and open to visitors. Philadelphia

is known for its large collection of outdoor art, and sculptures—including statues by Frederic Remington, Jacques Lipchitz, and William Rush—that are scattered throughout Fairmount Park. Some sections of the park that border underserved neighborhoods can be somewhat neglected; it's better maintained along the Schuylkill.

## Parkway Museum District

Modeled after the Champs-Élysées in Paris, the Benjamin Franklin Parkway (or simply, the Parkway, as locals call it) is Philadelphia's grand boulevard. French architects Jacques Gréber and Paul Cret—the latter taught at the University of Pennsylvania—designed the Parkway in the 1920s. Stretching a mile from City Hall to Logan Circle to the Art Museum on a diagonal and lined with international flags, the Parkway is where you'll find many of the city's major museums and institutions (as well as apartment buildings and a few hotels), including the Franklin Institute, the Barnes Foundation, and the Parkway Central Library. Near the library, at Vine and 17th Streets, the granite, neoclassical Philadelphia Pennsylvania Temple of the Church of Jesus Christ of Latter-Day Saints (closed to non-members) rises dramatically, with a statue of the angel Moroni atop the highest spire. In summer, the 8-acre area inside the Eakins Oval (a traffic circle near the Art Museum) gets festive with a Ferris wheel and beer garden. On a beautiful day, the Parkway is the most majestic stroll in town. Or you can rent a bike and ride the Parkway past the Art Museum into Fairmount Park. Just watch out for the *Rocky* runners.

Located north of the Parkway, Fairmount is a residential district popular with young families and the eds-and-meds crowd. It shares a name with nearby Fairmount Park but lies east of it. Mature trees, 19th-century row houses, and some new housing line the sleepy, strollable streets behind the main commercial strip, Fairmount Avenue. The neighborhood is also home to the hulking Eastern State Penitentiary, now a historic site and a popular visitor attraction. East of Fairmount, the developing Spring Garden and North Broad neighborhoods have a number of cultural attractions as well as restaurants.

#  Sights

### Academy of Natural Sciences of Drexel University

**OTHER MUSEUM | FAMILY |** One of this natural history museum's most popular attractions is Dinosaur Hall, with reconstructed skeletons of a *Tyrannosaurus rex* and some 30 others of its ilk, but interactive stations with docents and exhibits on topics including current environmental issues also help visitors engage with science and nature. Other areas are the Big Dig (open weekends at this writing), where you can hunt for real fossils, and Outside In, a hands-on experience where kids can climb into an eagle's nest, visit

with animals, and more. State-of-the-art changing exhibitions are another highlight. The more than 35 dioramas of animals from around the world displayed in their natural habitats still have appeal and are gradually being renovated. Founded in 1812, the academy is considered the oldest natural history institution in the western hemisphere and a world leader in the fields of natural-science research and education; the present building dates from 1876. ■**TIP→ Plan your visit ahead using the website's floor plan and program list. Weekdays and late afternoons are generally less busy times to visit.** ⊠ *1900 Benjamin Franklin Pkwy., at 19th St., Parkway Museum District* ☎ *215/299–1000* ⊕ *ansp.org* ✉ *$25 (tickets are cheaper online)* ☉ *Closed Mon. and Tues.*

### ★ Barnes Foundation

**ART MUSEUM |** One man's collection and now a Parkway treasure, the Barnes Foundation displays some of the most fabled paintings of impressionist, postimpressionist, and modern art—179 Renoirs, 69 Cézannes, 59 Matisses, 46 Picassos, 7 van Goghs, 6 Seurats, and plenty more—in a soaring, modern limestone-and-glass museum. Highlights include Cézanne's *The Card Players,* Georges Seurat's *Models,* van Gogh's *The Postman (Joseph-Etienne Roulin),* Monet's *Studio Boat,* Matisse's *La Danse II* triptych mural, Renoir's *The Artist's Family,* and Picasso's *Acrobat and Young Harlequin.* The collection was amassed after 1912 in Merion, Pennsylvania, by Dr. Albert C. Barnes (1872–1951), who made his fortune as co-inventor of an antiseptic; he conceived the foundation as an educational institution.

Barnes wanted to help people "see as an artist saw," and to do this he created each gallery wall as an "ensemble" that reflected visual relationships: a Picasso could hang side by side with an African sculpture, and below an Old Master sketch and an iron door hinge. Barnes's will decreed that nothing in

Set on four-and-a-half acres on the Ben Franklin Parkway, the Barnes Foundation features plenty of places to sit and reflect, including two outdoor water features.

the displays could be changed, so when the collection moved—lock, stock, and Modigliani—to the Parkway in 2012, the building's rooms and arrangements were re-created within a spacious modern structure that contains special exhibition galleries and a high-ceilinged court with a café. The pretty, more expensive Garden Restaurant, with indoor and outdoor (in season) seating, serves delicious modern American fare. ⊠ *2025 Benjamin Franklin Pkwy., Parkway Museum District* ☏ *215/278–7000* ⊕ *www.barnesfoundation.org* ⊠ *$30 (good for 2 days)* ⊗ *Closed Tues. and Wed.*

### Cathedral Basilica of Saints Peter and Paul

**CHURCH** | The basilica of the archdiocese of Philadelphia is the spiritual center for the Philadelphia area's 1.3 million Roman Catholics. Topped by a huge, distinctive copper dome, the large brownstone building was built between 1846 and 1864 in the Italian Renaissance style. Many of the interior decorations are by Constantino Brumidi, who painted the dome of the U.S. Capitol. Several Philadelphia bishops and archbishops are buried beneath the altar. Pick up a brochure for a self-guided tour by the entrance or gift shop, or see the website. ⊠ *1723 Race St., at 18th St. and Benjamin Franklin Pkwy., Parkway Museum District* ☏ *215/561–1313* ⊕ *cathedralphila. org* ⊠ *Free.*

### Eastern State Penitentiary Historic Site

**JAIL/PRISON** | Designed by John Haviland and built in 1829, Eastern State was at the time the most expensive building in America; this massive, now-crumbling structure, a very popular site for visitors, influenced international penal design and was the model for some 300 prisons from China to South America. Its system of solitary confinement (to encourage reflection and penitence) and firm discipline was ultimately recognized as flawed. Before it closed in 1971, the atmospheric prison was home to Al Capone, Willie Sutton, and Pep the Dog, who allegedly killed the cat that belonged to a governor's wife. The excellent audio tour of the prison features narration by

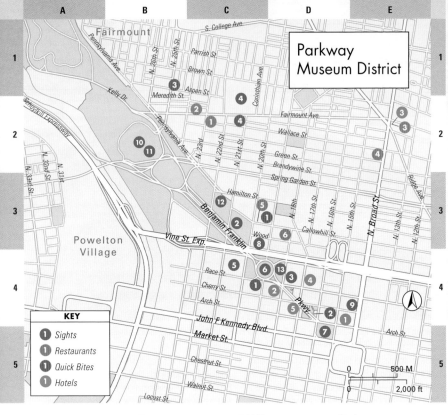

Parkway
Museum District

KEY

🔵 Sights
🔵 Restaurants
🔵 Quick Bites
🔵 Hotels

actor Steve Buscemi, and thoughtful permanent and changing exhibits examine issues relating to criminal justice reform. Guided tours are available; check online in advance. The penitentiary, a half mile north of the Rodin Museum, hosts changing art installations; Night Tours: Summer Twilight, with a beer garden; and Halloween Nights, a crowd-favorite selection of haunted house experiences, around Halloween. ■ TIP→ **Most areas you visit are unheated, so bundle up well in winter.** ✉ *2027 Fairmount Ave., at 22nd St., Fairmount* ☎ *215/236–3300* ⊕ *www. easternstate.org* ✉ *$17 (check for online discount); seasonal Halloween Nights attraction (separate admission; reserve in advance) $34–$79.*

### ★ The Franklin Institute

**SCIENCE MUSEUM** | **FAMILY** | Founded in 1824 to honor Benjamin Franklin, this large science museum is as clever as its namesake, thanks to many dazzling hands-on exhibits. To optimize your time, study the daily schedule of science demonstrations and events online before visiting, and check special exhibitions. Weekday afternoons are less busy. You can sit in the cockpit of a T-33 jet trainer and walk through an enormous artificial heart (15,000 times life-size). Popular exhibits include Electricity, which focuses on sustainable energy and displays Franklin's famous lightning rod; and Changing Earth. Don't miss the 30-ton white-marble statue of Franklin; you can see the likeness (and an accompanying 3½-minute multimedia presentation) without paying admission.

The Franklin Air Show celebrates powered flight with the Wright Model B Flyer and has virtual reality flight simulator experiences. Visitors to the interactive Tech Studio can engage with tech design processes. The Sports Zone conveys the physics, physiology, and material science behind your favorite sport by simulating surfing, testing your reaction time, and more. Shows in the Fels Planetarium

## Did You Know?

Famed sculptor Alexander Calder was the third generation of a famed Philadelphia family of artists. "Ghost," one of the mobiles Alexander Calder is famous for, hangs in the Philadelphia Museum of Art's Great Stair Hall, and his father, Alexander Stirling Calder, designed the Swann Memorial Fountain in Logan Circle. But the man who started it all, Alexander Milne Calder—Calder's grandfather—designed the statue of William Penn that tops City Hall.

(one show included in general admission) focus on the stars, space exploration, comets, and other phenomena. Open seasonally, the outdoor Science Park has play equipment and picnic tables. ✉ *222 N. 20th St., at Benjamin Franklin Pkwy., Parkway Museum District* ☎ *215/448–1200* ⊕ *www.fi.edu* ✉ *$23; special exhibitions require additional fees.*

### Logan Circle

**PLAZA/SQUARE** | The focal point of Logan Circle, one of the city's gems, is the Swann Memorial Fountain of 1920, designed by Alexander Stirling Calder, son of Alexander Milne Calder, who created the William Penn statue atop City Hall. You can find works by a third generation of the family, modern sculptor Alexander Calder (1898–1976), the mobile- and stabile-maker, in the nearby Philadelphia Museum of Art. The main figures in the fountain, three Native American figures in the form of river gods, symbolize Philadelphia's leading waterways: the Delaware and Schuylkill rivers and Wissahickon Creek. Around Logan Circle are examples of Philadelphia's magnificent collection of outdoor art, including *General Galusha Pennypacker,* the Shakespeare Memorial (*Hamlet and the Fool,* by Alexander Stirling

Calder), and *Jesus Breaking Bread*. One of William Penn's five squares, Logan Circle was originally a graveyard and execution grounds. In 1825 the square was named for James Logan, Penn's secretary; in the 20th century it became a circle. ⊠ *Benjamin Franklin Pkwy., at 19th St., Parkway Museum District.*

### LOVE Park

**PLAZA/SQUARE** | Also known as John F. Kennedy Plaza, LOVE Park at the start of the Parkway is the place to get your photo with *LOVE,* Robert Indiana's iconic red sculpture, although you may need to stand in line awhile to do so. The 6-foot sculpture, standing atop a 7-foot base, was placed in this area for the City of Brotherly Love's Bicentennial celebrations in 1976. (Another iteration of the sculpture is on the University of Pennsylvania campus.) Today the plaza has two fountains, views of City Hall and the Parkway, and an *I "HEART" Philly* sculpture. It serves as the site of civic happenings like the popular Christmas Village Market, too. The southwest corner has a flying saucer–like building (a former visitor center from the mid-20th century) with large glass windows. At this writing it's due to become a restaurant sometime in 2023. ⊠ *1501 John F. Kennedy Blvd., between 15th and 16th Sts., between Arch St. and John F. Kennedy Blvd., Parkway Museum District.*

### Parkway Central Library

**LIBRARY** | Philadelphia calls its public-library system, founded in 1891, the Fabulous Freebie, and the central library embraces the present in ways that go beyond its more than 1 million volumes. A grand entrance hall, marble staircase, and enormous reading rooms make this Greek Revival building look the way libraries should, but it also holds an area for community gatherings and a Culinary Literacy Center with a kitchen. With more than 22,000 circulating orchestral performance sets (a full score and other parts), the Edwin S. Fleisher collection

(appointment required) is the largest of its kind in the world. The rare-book department is a beautiful suite of rooms with first editions of Dickens, ancient Sumerian clay tablets, and medieval and other manuscripts, including the only known handwritten copy of Poe's "The Raven." (Also here is a taxidermied Grip, Dickens's pet raven.) The children's department houses the city's largest collection of children's books in a made-for-kids setting, and there's a special area for teens.

**TIP** ➔ **Check the website for events such as author readings, timely special exhibits, and tours of parts of the library.** ⊠ *1901 Vine St., between 19th St. and Benjamin Franklin Pkwy., Parkway Museum District* ☎ *215/686–5322* ⊕ *freelibrary.org* ☑ *Free* ⊘ *Closed weekends.*

### ★ Pennsylvania Academy of the Fine Arts

**ART MUSEUM** | The nation's first art school and museum (founded in 1805) displays a notable collection of American art that ranges from the Peale family and Gilbert Stuart to Andrew Wyeth and Faith Ringgold. *Fox Hunt* by Winslow Homer and *The Artist in His Museum* by Charles Willson Peale are two famous works. The academy's most prized work, *The Gross Clinic* by Eakins, depicts Samuel D. Gross, a celebrated 19th-century surgeon, presiding over an operation; the masterwork is co-owned with the Philadelphia Museum of Art and is displayed for six months at a time at each institution. A work of art in itself, the Gothic revival building was designed in 1876 by Philadelphia architects Frank Furness and George Hewitt with a multicolor stone-and-brick exterior and an interior in rich hues of red, yellow, and blue. Changing exhibitions of sculptures, paintings, and mixed-media artwork are presented in the adjacent modern Samuel M. V. Hamilton Building, an 11-story facility that holds classrooms and studios for more than 300 students. The 1400 block of Cherry Street, which runs between the

One of the city's iconic sights, Robert Indiana's *LOVE* sculpture can be found in John F. Kennedy Plaza (a.k.a LOVE Park), which is northwest of City Hall.

two buildings, is a pedestrian plaza featuring *Paint Torch,* a 51-foot-tall sculpture of a paintbrush by Claes Oldenburg. The Barnes Foundation and the Philadelphia Museum of Art may get more attention from visitors, but art lovers will appreciate this special place. ⊠ *118–128 N. Broad St., at Cherry St., Parkway Museum District* ☎ *215/972–7600* ⊕ *www. pafa.org* 💲 *$18* ⊙ *Closed Mon.–Wed.*

### ★ Philadelphia Museum of Art

**ART MUSEUM** | Set on a hill in a majestic 1928 building modeled after Greek temples, the city's premier cultural attraction is one of the country's leading art museums, with permanent collections focused on European, American, and Asian art. The museum's east entrance is the site of the "Rocky steps," with people running up the 72 steps immortalized in the movie *Rocky* and lining up at street level for photos with A. Thomas Schomberg's *Rocky* statue. In 2021, the museum completed much of a massive reorganization based on a plan by Frank Gehry; additional expansion will be done underground.

The reopened north entrance, at street level, and a revamped west entrance with easier access to the east entrance make navigating the 200-gallery museum more pleasant. Expanded first-floor galleries are dedicated to a more inclusive narrative of early American art and to contemporary art. A rehang of the European art (1850–1900) collection makes the most of the strong impressionist holdings, and other European collections contain modernist works by artists such as Brancusi, Braque, Matisse, and Picasso. Famous paintings include Van Eyck's *St. Francis Receiving the Stigmata*, van Gogh's *Sunflowers,* and Cézanne's *The Large Bathers*. The museum also has the world's most extensive collection of works by Marcel Duchamp (*Nude Descending a Staircase*) and fine works by 19th-century Philadelphia artist Thomas Eakins. The restructured Asian art galleries present some spectacular structures moved from around the world, such as a 17th-century Chinese palace hall and a Japanese teahouse. Children like the arms and armor collection, and the 1-acre outdoor sculpture garden has contemporary works. Museum visitors can eat lunch in the Gehry-designed restaurant or café. The intimate, upscale Stir restaurant (reserve ahead) provides a serene break from gallery-going and focuses on seasonal and regional fare. Friday evenings in the museum feature live music and food. ⊠ *2600 Benjamin Franklin Pkwy., Parkway Museum District* ☎ *215/763–8100* ⊕ *www.philamuseum. org* ⊠ *$25 for 2 consecutive operating days; includes the Rodin Museum and (when open) the Perelman Building and 2 historic houses; 1st Sun. of each month and every Fri. after 5 pm, pay what you wish* ☉ *Closed Tues. and Wed.*

### The Rocky Statue and the "Rocky Steps"

**PUBLIC ART** | Created by artist A. Thomas Schomberg for the 1982 film *Rocky III,* the life-size statue was donated by the film's director and star, Sylvester Stallone, to the City of Philadelphia after filming. The statue has moved around, but since 2006 it has stood at the bottom of the Philadelphia Museum of Art's steps. It continues to be one of the city's most popular destinations, with visitors lining up patiently to get their selfie with the bronze version of the "Italian Stallion." ⊠ *2600 Benjamin Franklin Pkwy., Parkway Museum District.*

### ★ Rodin Museum

**ART GALLERY** | This small jewel of a museum holds the biggest collection outside France—almost 150 bronzes, plasters, and marbles—of the work of sculptor Auguste Rodin (1840–1917). Movie theater owner Jules Mastbaum acquired the works to found the museum, which opened in 1929. The building and grounds, designed by architects Paul Cret and Jacques Gréber, honor Cret's original idea that inside and out offer a "unified setting" for the presentation of sculpture. Entering the museum, you pass through a peaceful, landscaped courtyard to reach Rodin's *The Gates of Hell*—a 21-foot-high sculpture with more

# Mural Arts

Almost everywhere you look in Philadelphia you're sure to spot one of the murals sponsored by the Mural Arts project (⊕ *www. muralarts.org*). Started in Philadelphia in 1984 to help eliminate graffiti, today the city boasts more than 4,000 public murals, which run the gamut from dull and faux-uplifting to innovative and fantastic. One of the best ways to learn about and see the murals is on one of the numerous walking and trolley tours offered thru Mural Arts; self-guided tours are also available on the Mural Arts website.

than 100 human and animal figures. The museum rotates works in thematic shows every two years but may include major works like *The Kiss, The Burghers of Calais, Balzac,* and *Eternal Springtime.* ⊠ *2151 Benjamin Franklin Pkwy., between 21st and 22nd Sts., Parkway Museum District* ☎ *215/763–8100* ⊕ *www.rodinmuseum.org* ⊠ *$12 suggested donation; $25 includes entrance to Philadelphia Museum of Art (for two days)* ☉ *Closed Tues.–Thurs.*

### Sister Cities Park

**CITY PARK** | **FAMILY** | Marking the city's connections with Florence, Italy; Tel Aviv, Israel; and eight other "sister cities," this small, family-focused park has a prime location near Logan Circle, the Logan Philadelphia hotel, and the Cathedral Basilica of Saints Peter and Paul. A play area for kids inspired by the local Wissahickon watershed features a rocky area to explore and a toy-boat and wading pond; there's a 10-spout fountain kids can play in late April through October. Sister Cities is also home to Robert Indiana's *AMOR* (Spanish and Latin for "love") sculpture, a companion to nearby LOVE Park's famous *LOVE.* The seasonal café

The Parkway Museum District is home to many of the city's museums and institutions including the Philadelphia Museum of Art, the Franklin Institute, and the Barnes Foundation.

(closed mid-December–early March), in a modern building with floor-to-ceiling windows, has some kid-friendly fare. ✉ *210 N. 18th St., Parkway Museum District* ☎ *215/440–5500* 🌐 *centercityphila.org/parks/sister-cities-park* 🎟 *Free.*

## 🍴 Restaurants

Think of the Benjamin Franklin Parkway as Philadelphia's Museum Row. Around the dignified boulevard are quick-stop cafés and restaurants catering to the crowds of museumgoers, but just north of the parkway you'll find lively neighborhood joints and charming BYOBs in residential Fairmount. East of Fairmount, the North Broad area has an established dining scene with fine dining and other options.

### A Mano

**$$$** | **ITALIAN** | The name of this neighborhood-favorite BYOB from Townsend Wentz (of Townsend and Oloroso) means "by hand," and the sophisticated, well-crafted Italian dishes reflect careful attention to seasonal ingredients. Settle into the cozy, serene dining room with its banquettes, white walls, and wooden tables and chairs; then put together your prix-fixe meal from the flavorful choices: antipasti, superb handmade pastas, mains including fish and meat choices, and satisfying desserts. **Known for:** three- or four-course prix-fixe options; multiregion Italian fare; worthy antipasti board (extra charge). [$] *Average main: $29* ✉ *2244 Fairmount Ave., Fairmount* ☎ *215/236–1114* 🌐 *www.amanophl.com* ⏲ *Closed Mon. No lunch.*

### Cantina "Calaca" Feliz

**$$** | **MEXICAN** | **FAMILY** | A colorful mural of freewheeling Day of the Dead skeletons gives this cheerful Fairmount cantina its name, but the polished *antojitos* (snacks), tacos, and enchiladas from Jose Garces veteran Tim Spinner are what will really make you happy. A deep tequila library informs the bar and cocktail list; choose from a list of margaritas in flavors like chili, adding a guacamole sampler on the side. **Known for:** worthy happy hours;

# Benjamin Franklin in Philadelphia

Unlike the bronze statue of William Penn perched atop City Hall, a marble likeness of Benjamin Franklin, the Benjamin Franklin National Memorial, is within **The Franklin Institute.** Perhaps that's as it should be: noble-born Penn above the people and common-born Franklin sitting more democratically among them.

Franklin (1706–90) was anything but a common man, though. In fact, biographer Walter Isaacson called him "the most accomplished American of his age." Franklin's insatiable curiosity, combined with his ability to solve problems in his own life, inspired his invention of bifocals, an odometer to measure postal routes, a "long arm" to reach books high on his shelves, and a flexible urinary catheter for his brother who was suffering with kidney stones. His great intellect inspired his launching of the American Philosophical Society, the oldest learned society in America. He was the only Founding Father who shaped and signed all of the nation's founding documents, including the Declaration of Independence, the Constitution, and treaties with France and England. He was a citizen of the world—a representative in the Pennsylvania General Assembly, a minister to France.

It's fortunate for Philadelphians that Franklin spent so many of his 84 years here. That might have been an act of fate or early recognition that "time is money," as he wrote in *Advice to a Young Tradesman* in 1748. Born in Boston in 1706, Franklin ran away from home and the oppression of his job as a printer's apprentice at his brother's shop. When he couldn't find work in New York, he didn't waste time; he moved on to Philadelphia. Within 10 years Franklin had opened his own printing office. His *Pennsylvania Gazette* was the most successful newspaper in the colonies; his humor propelled his *Poor Richard's Almanack* to best-seller status. Learn more about Franklin's legacy at the engaging **Benjamin Franklin Museum** in the **Franklin Court** complex, site of Ben's first permanent home in Philadelphia, and check out Franklin's Printing Office. At the nearby **B. Free Franklin Post Office & Museum**, you can get a letter hand-stamped with a "B. Free Franklin" cancellation.

Franklin had time and passion for civic duties. As postmaster, he set up the city's postal system. He founded the city's first volunteer fire company and the **Library Company of Philadelphia**, its first subscription library. After his famous kite experiment, he opened the first fire-insurance company, the **Philadelphia Contributionship for the Insurance of Houses from Loss by Fire.** He proposed the idea for the **University of Pennsylvania** and personally raised money to finance **Pennsylvania Hospital**, one of the nation's oldest hospitals.

Franklin was laid to rest in the **Christ Church Burial Ground** alongside his wife, Deborah, who died in 1774; the couple lived apart for many years because of Franklin's diplomatic role as a representative in Europe. Also here is the grave of one of his sons, Francis.

good variety of vegetarian, fish, and meat choices; patio dining in season. $ *Average main: $17* ✉ *2321 Fairmount Ave., Fairmount* ☎ *215/787–9930* 🌐 *cantinafeliz.com* ⏲ *No lunch weekdays.*

**★ Cicala at the Divine Lorraine**

**$$$$ | ITALIAN** | Located in the Mint House at the Divine Lorraine Hotel on the developing North Broad Street corridor, this elegant special-occasion restaurant from husband and wife Joe and Angela Cicala celebrates the food and drink of Southern Italy. The changing seasonal menu features a superbly executed and well-presented selection of antipasti, fresh pastas in small, first-course portions, roasted meats and fish, and a not-to-be-missed Italian pastry program spearheaded by Angela. **Known for:** excellent, expensive list of Italian wines; house-made gelato; lovely bar area. $ *Average main: $45* ✉ *699 N. Broad St., North Broad* ☎ *267/886–9334* 🌐 *www.cicalarestaurant.com* ⏲ *Closed Mon. No lunch.*

**Osteria**

**$$$ | ITALIAN** | Under the careful direction of chef-owner Jeff Michaud, Osteria has flourished, with a seasonally changing menu that offers everything from amazing brick-oven pizzas (try the Lombarda, with sausage and a soft-cooked egg) to delicate house-made pastas to a Black Angus strip steak. With its red concrete floors, rustic wooden tables, and soaring ceilings that blend loft and countryside, industry and art, this place helped establish the restaurant scene in the redeveloping North Broad neighborhood. **Known for:** glass-enclosed patio; pizzas for less expensive dining; 300-bottle largely Italian wine list. $ *Average main: $32* ✉ *640 N. Broad St., North Broad* ☎ *215/763–0920* 🌐 *www.osteriaphilly.com* ⏲ *No lunch.*

**Pizzeria Vetri**

**$ | PIZZA | FAMILY** | Started by noted Philly chef Marc Vetri (but no longer associated with him), this small, casual spot catercorner to the Barnes Foundation takes wood-fired pizza seriously, creating personal and larger-size pies both deliciously traditional (margherita, mushroom and pepperoni) and more creative (spicy sausage and others). Antipasti and salad bowls are secondary but round out the menu, along with cocktails, wine, and beer: enjoy it at the small bar or one of the communal wooden tables at this often-busy eatery. **Known for:** rotolo (pizza dough wrapped around mortadella and ricotta); pizza fired in a 650-degree oven; nutella pizza for dessert. $ *Average main: $16* ✉ *1939 Callowhill St., Fairmount* ☎ *215/600–2629* 🌐 *pizzeriavetri.com.*

**Sabrina's Cafe–Art Museum**

**$ | AMERICAN | FAMILY** | Orange-painted walls, classic diner-style booths, and tables add a cheerful, casual vibe to this comfort-food local favorite near the Parkway museums, one of five locations around the Philadelphia area. The food rises above standard diner fare in lunch options such as creative burgers and a veggie Philly cheesesteak, and breakfast and brunch shine with stuffed challah French toast, huevos rancheros, and all kinds of omelets. **Known for:** come hungry, as portions are large; good options for vegetarians; wait can get long on weekends. $ *Average main: $15* ✉ *1804 Callowhill St., Fairmount* ☎ *215/636–9061* 🌐 *sabrinascafe.com* ⏲ *No dinner.*

## ☕ Coffee and Quick Bites

**Buena Onda**

**$ | MEXICAN | FAMILY** | Philadelphia chef-darling Jose Garces's beachy, fast-casual spot in the City of Brotherly love serves Baja Peninsula–inspired fare ordered at the counter and eaten in or taken away. Tacos, burritos, and margaritas rule the menu, but buena bowls such as the adobo chicken and red chile short rib are good choices, too, as are the happy–hour specials. **Known for:** grilled fish tacos; good-value frozen margaritas; convenient location near the museums, including the Barnes. $ *Average main: $12* ✉ *1901 Callowhill St., Fairmount* ☎ *215/302–3530* ⊕ *www.buenaondata-cos.com.*

### Capriccio Café and Bar at Cret Park

$ | **CAFÉ** | At the far eastern end of the Parkway sits this small café, a glass-enclosed pavilion that offers good views of City Hall. On the menu are rather pricey hot and cold coffee-based drinks, along with breakfast items, pastries, and familiar sandwiches and salads; you can also have a cocktail, beer, or wine at the little bar or at your table. **Known for:** alfresco dining or sipping in season; convenient spot at beginning or end of Parkway exploration; can get very busy, and service may not be the best. $ *Average main: $10* ✉ *110 N. 16th St., in Cret Park, Parkway Museum District* ☎ *215/735–9797* ⊕ *www.capricciocafe.com* ⊗ *No dinner.*

### Musette

$ | **CAFÉ** | Opened in 2021 on a residential street in Fairmount, this bright, charming café with white-painted walls and large windows makes a good stop for coffee drinks and a tempting selection of pastries, or for tartines, sandwiches, and salads that rise a notch above the usual. European cafés inspired the owners, but Musette also has a pleasantly local, neighborhood vibe; it can get busy. **Known for:** locally roasted Rival Bros coffee; seasonal menu; supportive of cycling community. $ *Average main: $12* ✉ *2441 Aspen St., Fairmount* ☎ *215/315–8340* ⊕ *musettephiladelphia.com* ⊗ *No dinner.*

### OCF Coffee House

$ | **CAFÉ** | **FAMILY** | At this large café opposite Eastern State Penitentiary, the tall windows, high ceilings with exposed ductwork, and dozens of wooden tables create an airy, casual space for trying delicious La Colombe coffee with breakfast, lunch, or a snack. The students and families who flock here appreciate the number of gluten-free and vegetarian options, as well as the fresh-tasting, build-your-own egg sandwiches, melts and other sandwiches, and salads. **Known for:** good list of coffee drinks; gluten-free bagels; nice smoothie options. $ *Average main: $12* ✉ *2100 Fairmount Ave., Fairmount* ☎ *267/773–8081* ⊕ *www.ocfrealty.com/coffee-house* ⊗ *No dinner.*

##  Hotels

### Le Méridien Philadelphia

$$$$ | **HOTEL** | Offering a welcome boutique alternative to more standard chain hotels near the convention center, the 10-story Le Méridien occupies an old YMCA built in 1908 that has maintained some architectural character. **Pros:** hipper alternative (for a Marriott) near convention center; 24-hour gym; coffee and cocktails in the lobby gathering space. **Cons:** rooms could use some extra seating; immediate neighborhood can be a bit empty at night; can take a while to get your car on busy check-out mornings. $ *Rooms from: $360* ✉ *1421 Arch St., Parkway Museum District* ☎ *215/422–8200* ⊕ *le-meridien.marriott.com* ⏎ *202 rooms* ⦿| *No Meals.*

### The Logan Philadelphia, Curio Collection by Hilton

$$$$ | **HOTEL** | The Logan, part of Hilton's independent Curio Collection, provides a relaxing retreat with gracious, contemporary public areas and guest rooms that blend modern style with natural materials and local touches, such as impressive installations of Philly-inspired art in common areas. **Pros:** convenient to Parkway museums, Fairmount Park, and convention center; secluded ambience in a busy area; indoor pool and health club. **Cons:** steak-house restaurant may not suit all tastes; spa has worthy but expensive treatments; nice rooftop bar gets crowded. $ *Rooms from: $403* ✉ *1 Logan Sq., Parkway Museum District* ☎ *215/963–1500, 844/634–3605 reservations* ⊕ *www.theloganhotel.com* ⏎ *391 rooms* ⦿| *No Meals.*

### Mint House at The Divine Lorraine Hotel – Philadelphia

$$ | **HOTEL** | **FAMILY** | Mixing Philly history and high-tech modernity, this extensively renovated Mint House property in the developing North Broad area has one- and two-bedroom apartments in a grand 10-story building from 1893 (the Lorraine Hotel) that became America's first racially integrated hotel after spiritual leader Father Divine purchased it. **Pros:** spacious and modern living area, kitchen, and bedroom; supermarket within walking distance, or preorder groceries through the hotel through Mint; excellent Cicala restaurant on-site, with others nearby. **Cons:** minimalist design may not appeal to all tastes; a bit farther from city sights than other options; parking is off-site. $ *Rooms from: $250* ⊠ *699 N. Broad St., North Broad* ☎ *855/972–9090* ⊕ *minthouse.com* ⮑ *101 apartments* ⦿ *No Meals.*

### Sheraton Philadelphia Downtown

$$$ | **HOTEL** | A convenient convention hotel, this modern Sheraton catering to both business and leisure travelers completed an overhaul in 2020 that added airy, common gathering spaces and redecorated guest rooms in tan, pale gray, and light blue. **Pros:** good location between Parkway museums and convention center; fitness center open 24/7; great city or Parkway views from some rooms. **Cons:** large convention crowds; in-house dining not the best; not good choice for those who don't like chains. $ *Rooms from: $260* ⊠ *201 N. 17th St., Parkway Museum District* ☎ *215/448–2000* ⊕ *marriott.com* ⮑ *759 rooms* ⦿ *No Meals.*

### The Windsor Suites

$$ | **HOTEL** | **FAMILY** | This 24-story all-suites hotel close to the Parkway museums and Center City's restaurants, shopping, and nightlife caters to corporate business travelers (some on extended stays) as well as vacationing families, and features both studio and one-bedroom spaces. **Pros:** small seasonal rooftop infinity pool and terrace; some good city views from rooms; fitness studio. **Cons:** located at busy intersection, so you may hear street noise; guests share building with full-time apartment tenants; not all rooms have balconies. $ *Rooms from: $230* ⊠ *1700 Benjamin Franklin Pkwy., Parkway Museum District* ☎ *215/981–5678* ⊕ *thewindsorsuites.com* ⮑ *199 suites* ⦿ *No Meals.*

##  Nightlife

### South Restaurant and Jazz Club

**LIVE MUSIC** | Besides an evening of jazz, purchasing a ticket for a performance in the club's intimate 75-seat, modern-industrial space reserves a table so you can order drinks and good upscale Southern fare (separate cost) before and during the show. It's a nice setting for hearing different jazz styles from local, regional, and global artists; the dress code is dressy casual. The club shares a menu with South Restaurant, a separate space in the same building. ⊠ *600 N. Broad St., Fairmount* ☎ *215/600–0220* ⊕ *southjazzkitchen.com.*

## Performing Arts

### The Met Philadelphia

**CONCERTS** | The Met began life in 1908 as the lavish Metropolitan Opera House, and today the 3,500-seat venue presents concerts and other programming, such as speakers like Michelle Obama and Bill Maher, in an elegantly detailed space. The look may be old-style, but the sound is good and the artists varied, including Alicia Keys, Jeezy, and Brett Young. The Met is in the redeveloping North Broad neighborhood. ⊠ *858 N. Broad St., North Broad* ☎ *215/309–0112 box office (open only on show days)* ⊕ *themetphilly.com.*

## MUSIC FESTIVALS
### Wawa Welcome America Festival

**FESTIVALS | FAMILY |** In the days leading up to Independence Day (July 4), Welcome America highlights Philly's history with patriotic, family-friendly happenings downtown and around the city, from a massive block party on the Benjamin Franklin Parkway to concerts to free museum access. In 2021, the festival introduced annual programming to commemorate and raise awareness of Juneteenth. It all culminates with a free July 4th Welcome America Concert and Fireworks extravaganza on the Parkway; past performers have included Jason Derulo, Ava Max, and Tori Kelly. ⊠ *20–24th Sts. and Benjamin Franklin Pkwy., Parkway Museum District* ⊕ *www. welcomeamerica.com* 🎟 *Free.*

##  Shopping

Museum gift shops, including excellent ones at the Philadelphia Museum of Art and the Barnes Foundation, anchor the shopping scene around the Parkway. Along Fairmount Avenue and nestled in the residential streets behind it, you'll find some independent stores.

### The Barnes Shop

**SOUVENIRS |** You don't need an admission ticket to the Barnes Foundation to shop at this well-curated space that show-cases distinctive artisan-made items for the home, jewelry, and accessories in a range of prices, as well as books and artsy souvenirs related to works in the museum. The store is open during the museum's open hours. ⊠ *2025 Benjamin Franklin Pkwy., Parkway Museum District* ☎ *215/278–7000* ⊕ *barnesfoundation.org.*

# Fairmount Park

Stretching north from the edge of down-town for 4 miles, Fairmount Park is Phila-delphia's largest park and a city treasure. Its development began in the late 19th century when the city purchased land by the river to create a place for outdoor activities and to guard Philadelphia's water supply. Today, whether by foot, bike, or car, exploring a bit of Fairmount Park is an essential part of a Philadelphia visit. The 2,050-acre park winds along the banks of the Schuylkill River—which divides it into west and east sections—and through different city neighborhoods. Historic houses and buildings, more than 40 outdoor sculptures, the Please Touch Museum for kids, a Japanese garden, a performing arts center, trails, and more enhance the park's natural areas. On weekends Kelly Drive is crowded with joggers, bicycling moms and dads with children strapped into kiddie seats atop the back wheel, hand-holding couples of all ages out for some fresh air, colle-giate crew teams sculling on the river, and budding artists trying to capture the area's sylvan magic just as Thomas Eakins once did.

As in any city, visitors should use com-mon sense. It's best to stay within sight of other park visitors and, in general, avoid the park after dark. Those driving should keep all items in their trunk, and parked cars should be locked.

## VISITOR INFORMATION

The nonprofit Fairmount Park Conserv-ancy works with Philadelphia Parks & Recreation to support the city's parks, and its website has useful information about exploring Fairmount and other parks. In December, some of Fairmount Park's historic houses are decorated for Christmas and have special events; check ⊕ *parkcharms.org* for information about this city tradition.

The view of Boathouse Row from the west side of the Schuylkill River is marvelous—especially at night, when the buildings are outlined with hundreds of small lights.

**CONTACT Fairmount Park Conservancy.**
☎ *215/988–9334* ⊕ *myphillypark.org.*

 Sights

### Belmont Plateau
**VIEWPOINT** | Belmont Plateau has a view from 243 feet above river level, which will literally be the high point of a tour of Fairmount Park. In front of you are recreation areas, sweeping park vistas, and, 4 miles away, the Philadelphia skyline. The large Palladian house on the plateau, Belmont Mansion, is home to the Underground Railroad Museum (⊕ *belmont-mansion.org*), which is open a few days a week; it's also an event space. ✉ *2000 Belmont Mansion Dr., Fairmount Park.*

### ★ Boathouse Row
**HISTORIC SIGHT** | These architecturally varied, quaint-looking 19th-century buildings—a National Historic Landmark and riverside city icons built in Victorian Gothic, Gothic Revival, and Italianate styles—are home to the rowing clubs that make up the Schuylkill Navy, an association of boating clubs organized in 1858. The clubs host various races, including the Dad Vail Regatta (held in New Jersey in 2023 due to dredging of the Schuylkill River) and the Head of the Schuylkill Regatta. The view of the 15 buildings from the west side of the Schuylkill is splendid, especially at night when they're outlined with hundreds of small lights. Lloyd Hall (✉ *1 Boathouse Row*), is a public recreation center with a gymnasium, bicycle rentals in season, a café, and restrooms. ✉ *Kelly Dr., near Sedgeley Dr., Fairmount Park* ⊕ *www.visitphilly.com/things-to-do/attractions/boathouse-row.*

### Ellen Phillips Samuel Memorial
**PUBLIC ART** | Seventeen bronze and granite sculptures stand in a series of tableaux and groupings that were completed in 1961 on three separate riverside terraces. Portraying American themes and traits, the memorial includes *The Quaker,* by Harry Rosen; *Birth of a Nation,* by Henry Kreis; and *Spirit of Enterprise,* by Jacques Lipchitz. The

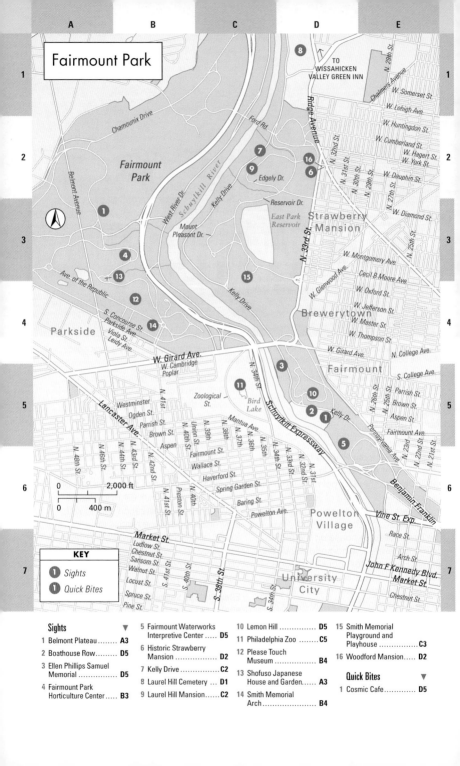

# Fairmount Park

**Fairmount Park**

Chamounix Drive

Belmont Avenue

Ave. of the Republic

Parkside

S. Concourse St.
Parkside Ave.
Viola St.
Leidy Ave.

Lancaster Ave.

West River Dr.

Schuylkill River

Kelly Drive

Mount
Pleasant Dr.

Edgely Dr.

Reservoir Dr.

East Park
Reservoir

Ford Rd.

Ridge Avenue

TO
WISSAHICKEN
VALLEY GREEN INN

Chalmers Avenue

W. Somerset St.

W. Lehigh Ave.

W. Huntingdon St.

W. Cumberland St.

N. 32nd St.

N. 31st St.

N. 30th St.

W. Hagert St.
W. York St.

W. Dauphin St.

W. Diamond St.

N. 29th St.

N. 28th St.

N. 27th St.

N. 25th St.

Strawberry
Mansion

W. Montgomery Ave.

Cecil B Moore Ave.

W. Oxford St.

W. Jefferson St.

Brewerytown

W. Master St.

W. Thompson St.

W. Girard Ave.

N. 33rd St.

W. Glenwood Ave.

Fairmount

N. College Ave.

S. College Ave.

W. Girard Ave.

W. Cambridge
Poplar

Zoological
St.

Bird
Lake

Schuylkill Expressway

N. 34th St.

Westminster
Ogden St.

Parrish St.

Brown St.

Aspen

Mantua Ave.

Union St.

Fairmount St.

Wallace St.

Haverford St.

Spring Garden St.

Baring St.

Powelton Ave.

N. 48th St.
N. 46th St.
N. 44th St.
N. 43rd St.
N. 42nd St.
N. 41st St.
N. 40th St.
N. 39th St.
N. 38th St.
N. 37th St.
N. 36th St.
N. 35th St.
N. 34th St.
N. 33rd St.
N. 32nd St.
N. 31st St.

Preston St.
N. 41st St.
N. 40th St.

Parrish St.

Brown St.

Aspen St.

Fairmount Ave.

Kelly Dr.

N. 26th St.
N. 25th St.
N. 23rd St.
N. 22nd St.
N. 21st St.

Pennsylvania Ave.

Benjamin Franklin

Powelton
Village

Vine St. Exp.

Race St.

Arch St.

John F Kennedy Blvd.
Market St.

Market St.
Ludlow St.
Chestnut St.
Sansom St.
Walnut St.
Locust St.
Spruce St.
Pine St.

University
City

Chestnut St.

S. 38th St.
S. 34th St.

0        2,000 ft
0    400 m

## KEY

**1** Sights

**1** Quick Bites

## Sights ▼

1  Belmont Plateau ........ **A3**
2  Boathouse Row ......... **D5**
3  Ellen Phillips Samuel
   Memorial ................ **D5**
4  Fairmount Park
   Horticulture Center ..... **B3**

5  Fairmount Waterworks
   Interpretive Center ..... **D5**
6  Historic Strawberry
   Mansion ................. **D2**
7  Kelly Drive .............. **C2**
8  Laurel Hill Cemetery ... **D1**
9  Laurel Hill Mansion ...... **C2**

10  Lemon Hill .............. **D5**
11  Philadelphia Zoo ........ **C5**
12  Please Touch
    Museum ................ **B4**
13  Shofuso Japanese
    House and Garden ... **A3**
14  Smith Memorial
    Arch .................... **B4**

15  Smith Memorial
    Playground and
    Playhouse .............. **C3**
16  Woodford Mansion ..... **D2**

### Quick Bites ▼

1  Cosmic Cafe ............. **D5**

memorial focuses mostly on European immigrants, providing a narrower view of America's history. ⊠ *Kelly Dr., Fairmount Park* ✛ *South of the Girard Ave. Bridge* ⊕ *associationforpublicart.org.*

### Fairmount Park Horticulture Center

GARDEN | On the Horticulture Center's 27 wooded acres are an arboretum, a greenhouse and exhibition hall (used for weddings and events), a reflecting pool, and the Pavilion in the Trees (by artist Martin Puryear) for bird-watching. The Shofuso Japanese House and Garden (fee) is nearby as well. See ⊕ *associationforpublicart.org* for information about sculptures in this area. The center is on the site of the 1876 Centennial Exposition's Horticultural Hall. ⊠ *100 N. Horticultural Dr., Fairmount Park* ☎ *215/685–0096* ⊕ *www.phila.gov/departments/philadelphia-parks-recreation* 🖃 *Free* ⊗ *Greenhouse closed Fri.–Sun. and during events.*

### Fairmount Water Works Interpretive Center

NOTABLE BUILDING | FAMILY | Designed by Frederick Graff, this National Historic Landmark completed in 1815 was the first steam-pumping station of its kind in the country, and the notable assemblage of Greek Revival buildings is one of the city's most beautiful sights. The waterworks, just behind the Philadelphia Museum of Art, include a small interpretive center with historical features on display and some kid-friendly exhibits about the region's water and the site's history. A short film, a seasonal mussel hatchery, and changing exhibits are other attractions. Nearby paths provide good views of the waterworks and the Art Museum. ⊠ *640 Waterworks Dr., Off Kelly Dr., Fairmount Park* ☎ *215/685–0723* ⊕ *www.fairmountwaterworks.org* 🖃 *Free* ⊗ *Closed Sun. and Mon.*

### Historic Strawberry Mansion

HISTORIC HOME | Seen on a guided tour focused on the mansion's history and its furnishings, the largest of Fairmount Park's historic houses has antiques, art, and furniture from the Federal and Empire period. On display is rare Tucker and Hemphill porcelain, and the house also showcases a large collection of antique dolls and toys. Rooms have been decorated by different groups, some in Colonial Revival style, which can be intriguing or somewhat distracting. The house was originally built around 1783–93 by Judge William Lewis, an abolitionist lawyer. ⊠ *2450 Strawberry Mansion Dr., near 33rd and Dauphin Sts., Fairmount Park* ☎ *215/228–8364* ⊕ *www.historicstrawberrymansion. org* 🖃 *$8 includes guided hour (on the hour)* ⊗ *Closed Jan. and Feb. (except by appointment) and Mon.–Wed. Mar.–Dec.*

### ★ Kelly Drive

SCENIC DRIVE | One of the city's most scenic byways, woodsy Kelly Drive has a popular walking, running, and biking path that parallels the road as it stretches more than 4 miles along the eastern side of the Schuylkill River from behind the Philadelphia Museum of Art to City Avenue. You can make an almost 9-mile loop on bike or foot by crossing Falls Bridge and returning on the path parallel to the west side's Martin Luther King, Jr. Drive (MLK Drive closes to cars on weekends April–October and has great Boathouse Row views). Notable sights, as well as river views, can distract you as you head north from the museum: Boathouse Row (rent a bike at Wheel Fun Rentals); the Ellen Phillips Samuel Memorial Sculpture Garden (and other artworks; see ⊕ *associationforpublicart.org/tours*), and nearby Laurel Hill Cemetery. Kelly Drive is named for John B. Kelly Jr., a city councilman and Olympic rower who was the brother of actress Grace Kelly. ⊠ *Kelly Dr., Fairmount Park.*

### Laurel Hill Cemetery

CEMETERY | John Notman, architect of the Athenaeum and other noted local buildings, designed Laurel Hill's eastern section in 1836; it is an important example of an early rural burial ground and

Built in 1896–1897 for the trolley, Strawberry Mansion Bridge, as seen from Kelly Drive, crosses the Schuylkill River. Today it can be crossed by foot or car.

the first cemetery in America designed by an architect. Its hills overlooking the Schuylkill River, its rare trees, and its monuments and mausoleums sculpted by Alexander Milne Calder, Alexander Stirling Calder, William Strickland, Thomas U. Walter, and others made the cemetery a popular picnic spot in the 19th century. Today the 78-acre eastern necropolis is a tranquil place to stroll or bike, take a guided tour (fee), or download an app for a self-guided tour. Among the notables buried here or in the 200-acre western section (opened in 1869 across the river) in suburban Bala Cynwood are General George Meade and 39 other Civil War–era generals. ■TIP➔ Burials still take place here, so visit respectfully. ⊠ 3822 Ridge Ave., Fairmount Park ✢ North of Fairmount Park; pedestrian entrance at Kelly Dr. at Hunting Park Dr. ☎ 215/228–8200 Laurel Hill East, 610/668–9900 Laurel Hill West ⊕ www.laurelhillphl.com ☎ Free; tours $15 Ⓜ SEPTA bus 61 from Center City.

## Laurel Hill Mansion

**HISTORIC HOME** | Built around 1767, this Georgian house on a laurel-covered hill overlooking the Schuylkill River once belonged to Dr. Philip Syng Physick, who was also owner of Society Hill's Hill-Physick House. Admission includes a history-focused guided tour; the house furnishings are from a variety of periods. Women for Greater Philadelphia sponsors summer candlelight chamber music concerts here; there are other events, too. Call before visiting. ⊠ 3487 Edgley Dr., Fairmount Park ☎ 215/235–1776 ⊕ www.laurelhillmansion.org ☎ $8 ⊘ Closed Mon.–Wed. and Jan.–late Apr.

## Lemon Hill

**HISTORIC HOME** | An impressive example of a Federal-style country house, Lemon Hill was built in 1800 on a 350-acre farm and has distinctive oval parlors with concave doors and an entrance hall with a checkerboard floor of Valley Forge marble. It was purchased by the city in 1844 and became part of Fairmount Park. The renovated house is not furnished, but docents provide historical information; its location at the start of Kelly Drive makes it a convenient way to sample the park houses. ✉ *1 Lemon Hill Dr., off Sedgeley Dr., Fairmount Park* ☏ *215/232–4337* ⊕ *parkcharms.org* ✉ *$8* ⊘ *Closed Mon.– Wed.; also Jan.–Mar.*

### Philadelphia Zoo

**ZOO | FAMILY** | Opened in 1874, the 42 acres of America's first zoo are home to more than 1,700 animals representing six continents. It's small and well landscaped enough to feel pleasantly intimate, and the naturalistic habitats allow you to get close enough to hear the animals breathe. Some animals travel around the grounds via see-through trails called Zoo360. The Reptile and Amphibian House houses species from 15-foot-long snakes to frogs the size of a dime. The 2½-acre Primate Reserve is home to species from around the world, such as gorillas and orangutans. Other notable attractions include Big Cat Falls, with leopards, jaguars, tigers, and lions; the McNeil Avian Center, a state-of-the-art nest for birds; and African Plains, stomping ground of giraffes, rhinoceroses, and zebras. The children's zoo, KidZooU, has indoor and outdoor learning areas as well as opportunities to get closer to animals. WildWorks (extra charge) is a seasonal ropes course for kids and adults. ◼ **TIP→ Advance timed reservations are required at the time of this writing. It takes two or three hours to explore the exhibits.** ✉ *3400 W. Girard Ave., Fairmount Park* ☏ *215/243–1100* ⊕ *philadelphiazoo.org* ✉ *$24 in summer; $16 in winter; some attractions require additional fees/tickets; $17 parking* ⊘ *Closed Jan.; also Mon. and Tues. Labor Day–mid-Mar.*

### ★ Please Touch Museum

**CHILDREN'S MUSEUM | FAMILY** | Philadelphia's deservedly popular interactive children's museum, aimed at children ages eight and younger, instills a sense of wonder and fun from the get-go with an 80-foot-high entrance hall that has

## Philly's Cherry Blossom Festival

In 1926, Philadelphia was gifted 1,600 flowering trees from the people of Japan in honor of the 150th anniversary of American Independence; another 1,000 cherry trees were planted between 1998 and 2007. Every spring, the Subaru Cherry Blossom Festival in Fairmount Park celebrates Japanese and American culture with events like taiko drumming, hip-hop, funk, jazz, and reggae performers. Visit the Japan America Society of Greater Philadelphia's website (⊕ *japanphilly.org*) for more information.

a 40-foot-tall sculpture of the torch of the Statue of Liberty as its centerpiece. The museum occupies a majestic beaux arts–style building constructed for the 1876 Centennial Exhibition, one of just two public buildings still standing from the event. On two floors, Please Touch fills 65,000 square feet with more than 15 themed exhibits, including areas designed for toddlers, where kids can learn through hands-on play. Some popular areas are Food and Family, a mock supermarket; River Adventures, a water area; Wonderland, themed to Alice's adventures; a Makerspace and a Creative Arts Studio for inventing and creating; a Rocket Room for space adventures; and a theater with interactive performances. Another highlight is a circa-1908 Dentzel Carousel ride with 52 colorful horses, pigs, cats, and rabbits. The café serves lunch items and snacks. ◼ **TIP→ All visitors require advance reservations. Allow about three hours for a visit; weekdays are less crowded. Note that there is some free parking in the park.** ✉ *Memorial Hall, 4231 Ave. of the Republic, Fairmount Park*

☎ 215/581–3181 ⊕ www.pleasetouchmu-seum.org ✉ $19 Mon., Wed., and Thurs.; $22 Fri.–Sun; $5 unlimited carousel rides; $16 parking (must be prepaid) ⊘ Closed Tues. Ⓜ SEPTA bus 38 stops at Memorial Hall; buses 40, 43, and 64 stop nearby; PHLASH.

## ★ Shofuso Japanese House and Garden

NOTABLE BUILDING | Designed by Japa-nese architect Yoshimura Junzo, this exquisite replica of a traditional 17th-cen-tury house, reassembled here in 1958 after being exhibited at the Museum of Modern Art in New York City, is set in 1.2 acres of gardens with a teahouse, tiered waterfall, Japanese trees, and a koi pond. It was created as an example of buildings that influenced mid-20th-cen-tury architecture. Shofu-So means "pine breeze villa," and the house's roof is made of the bark of the hinoki, a cypress that grows only in Japan. Twenty murals by acclaimed Japanese contemporary artist Hiroshi Senju decorate the main room and help visitors appreciate the serene spirit of the compact house and gardens. Staff is on hand to answer ques-tions. Check the website for periodic tea ceremonies (reservations required) and events like the spring Shofuso Cherry Blossom Festival. Note: Shofuso is not wheelchair accessible, and visitors must remove their shoes to enter the house. ■TIP→ Timed tickets are required, so reserve ahead. A visit takes 30 minutes to an hour, more if you linger and soak in this escape from the urban bustle. ✉ N. Horticultural Dr. and Lansdowne Dr., Fairmount Park ☎ 215/878–5097 ⊕ www.japanphilly.org ✉ $14 ⊘ Closed mid-Dec.–late Mar.; Mon. and Tues. late Mar.–Oct; and weekdays Nov.–mid-Dec. Ⓜ SEPTA 38 bus or PHLASH park loop, Please Touch Museum stop.

## Smith Memorial Arch

MONUMENT | Built between 1897 and 1912 with funds donated by wealthy foundry owner Richard Smith, the memorial honors Pennsylvania heroes of the Civil War. Among those immortalized in bronze are Generals George Meade and Winfield Scott Hancock (both on horseback), and Smith himself. At the base of each tower is a curved wall with a bench. If you sit at one end and listen to a person whispering at the other end, you can understand why they're called the Whispering Benches. For information about the 14 statues and busts on the memorial, see ⊕ associationforpublicart. org. ✉ Ave. of the Republic, Fairmount Park.

## Smith Memorial Playground and Playhouse

OTHER ATTRACTION | FAMILY | Founded in 1899, this beloved facility dedicated to the belief that unstructured play is essen-tial has state-of-the-art, age-specific equipment for children 12 and younger. A favorite on the 6½-acre site is the Ann Newman Giant Wooden Slide, measur-ing 39 feet long, 12 feet wide, and 10 feet tall. The park, run by a nonprofit organization, includes the renovated 16,000-square-foot Playhouse, which reopened in 2022 and includes areas such as Smithville (a miniature town) and TinkerTown (kids can play with tools). ✉ 3500 Reservoir Dr., Near 33rd and Oxford Sts., Fairmount Park ☎ 215/765–4325 ⊕ www.smithplayground.org ✉ Free ⊘ Closed Mon. Ⓜ SEPTA bus 3 to 33rd St. and Cecil B. Moore Ave.

## Woodford Mansion

HISTORIC HOME | A good choice for those who love the decorative arts, the Naomi Wood collection of antique household goods, including Colonial furniture, unu-sual clocks, and English delftware, and "Colonial household gear" designated in her will, can be seen on guided tours (required) in this Georgian mansion, a National Historic Landmark built about 1756 as a summer retreat from the city. ✉ 3400 W. Dauphin St., Fairmount Park ☎ 215/229–6115 ⊕ www.woodfordman-sion.org ✉ $8 ⊘ Closed Mon. and Tues.

# A Drive Around Fairmount Park

**Timing:** You could do the drive in an hour or so with some brief time to explore, or you could check the open hours of different sights and spend a day exploring with your car.

**The Drive:** Begin your tour at East Fairmount Park's Boathouse Row on Kelly Drive heading west. Follow Kelly Drive to the end of Boathouse Row; turn right up the hill to a Federal-style country house, Lemon Hill. Head back to Kelly Drive, turn right, pass through the rock archway, and turn right again at the equestrian statue of Ulysses S. Grant. The first left takes you to Mount Pleasant (closed at this writing), a Georgian house. Continue along the road that runs to the right of the house (as you face it) past Rockland, a Federal house in private use. At the road's end, turn left onto Reservoir Drive. You'll pass the redbrick Georgian-style Ormiston (open for rare special events). Take the next left, Randolph Drive, to another Georgian house, **Laurel Hill Mansion**; the street becomes Dauphin Street. Just about 10 feet before reaching 33rd Street, turn left on Greenland Drive and you're at **Woodford Mansion,** which has an interesting collection of household goods. A quarter-mile northwest of Woodford stands the house that gave its name to the nearby section of Philadelphia, **Historic Strawberry Mansion**. It has furniture from three periods of its history.

Visit Laurel Hill Cemetery before you cross the river to West Fairmount Park. To get there, drive back down the driveway of Strawberry Mansion, turn left at the stop sign, and follow the narrow road as it winds right to the light. Turn left onto Ridge Avenue and follow it to the cemetery's entrance gate, which sits between eight Greek columns.

To skip the cemetery and continue your tour, proceed down the Strawberry Mansion driveway to the stop sign, turn left, and follow the road as it loops down and around to the Strawberry Mansion Bridge. Cross the river and follow the road; when it splits, stay left. You'll come to Chamounix Drive. Turn left and then left again on Belmont Mansion Drive for a fine view from **Belmont Plateau.** Follow Belmont Mansion Drive down the hill. Where it forks, stay to the left, cross Montgomery Drive, and bear left to reach the **Fairmount Park Horticulture Center** with its greenhouse and garden. Loop all the way around the Horticulture Center to visit the serene **Shofoso Japanese House and Garden** (closed in winter).

Drive back around the Horticulture Center and continue through the gates to Montgomery Drive. Turn left and then left again at the first light (Belmont Avenue). Turn left again on Avenue of the Republic. On your left is the **Please Touch Museum.** The two towers ahead are part of the **Smith Memorial Arch.** Turn left just past them to see Cedar Grove (closed at this writing), a stone Colonial house. Head to Lansdowne Drive. Follow signs to the **Philadelphia Zoo** or head back toward the Art Museum and the Parkway.

## Coffee and Quick Bites

**Cosmic Cafe**

$ | **CAFÉ** | "Good food, good drink, good karma" is the slogan of this well-worn, no-frills café in Fairmount Park that focuses on fresh local food produced sustainably and prepared on-site, and it delivers. Outdoor and indoor seating make this a convenient choice for coffee and fare such as breakfast burritos and egg sandwiches; wraps and burgers including a good veggie burger; soups; and cookies, desserts, and snacks. **Known for:** park views inside and out; all-day breakfast options; seasonal hard cider and other drinks outside. [$] *Average main: $13* ✉ *Lloyd Hall, 1 Boathouse Row, Fairmount Park* ☎ *215/978–0900* 🌐 *cosmicfoods.com* 🕓 *Closed Mon. and Tues. in winter. No dinner in winter.*

## Performing Arts

★ **Mann Center for the Performing Arts**

**ARTS CENTERS** | Symphonic music, jazz, rock, contemporary music (hip-hop, R&B, pop, and more), Broadway theater, opera, dance, and movies are presented in the open-air TD Pavilion and the standing-room-only (bring a blanket or chair) Skyline Stage in Fairmount Park from May through September. In summer, the Philadelphia Orchestra has some performances at the Mann. **TIP→ The site has great skyline views.** ✉ *5201 Parkside Ave., Fairmount Park* ☎ *800/982–2787 ticketing* 🌐 *www.manncenter.org.*

### MUSIC FESTIVALS

**Roots Picnic**

**MUSIC FESTIVALS** | A one- or two-day summer festival now held at the Mann in Fairmount Park, the Roots Picnic is hosted by Philly's own hip-hop legends The Roots and includes a slew of hip-hop, indie, R&B, rap, and DJ performances, including previous performers Pharrell, Public Enemy, and Nas. **TIP→ Buy tickets well in advance.** ✉ *Mann Center for the Performing Arts, 5201 Parkside Ave., Fairmount Park* 🌐 *rootspicnic.com/philly.*

## Activities

There are all kinds of outdoor activities throughout Fairmount Park. The park's paths are especially popular for walking, jogging, and biking. You can rent a bike at Indego stations (🌐 *rideindego.com*) around the city or near Boathouse Row.

### BIKING

**Wheel Fun Rentals**

**BIKING** | **FAMILY** | From its space next to Lloyd Hall and the Cosmic Cafe (and the path near Kelly Drive), Wheel Fun rents bicycles from kids' bikes to cruisers to tandems, as well as e-bikes. Surreys and double surreys, which hold adults and a couple of children, are another option. Rental season is mid-March through early November. ✉ *1 Boathouse Row, Fairmount Park* ☎ *215/232–7778* 🌐 *wheelfunrentals.com* 🎟 *From $10 an hour, $25 half day, $32 full day.*

### ZIPLINE

**Treetop Quest**

**ZIP LINING** | **FAMILY** | Explore more than 60 obstacles and ziplines in the trees at this aerial adventure park. Each participant is outfitted with a harness—helmets are available—and given a briefing on how things work. You can stay up to 2½ hours. **TIP→ Kids can be as young as four years old to participate, but more activities are available for ages seven and up. Reservations are required in advance.** ✉ *51 Chamounix Dr., Fairmount Park* ☎ *267/901–4145* 🌐 *www.treetopquest.com* 🎟 *$55 (book online)* 🕓 *Closed mid-Nov.–mid-Mar., weekdays mid-Mar.–mid-June and mid-Aug.–mid-Nov.*

# Chapter 8

# EAST PASSYUNK, QUEEN VILLAGE, BELLA VISTA, AND SOUTH PHILADELPHIA

8

Updated by
Maddy Sweitzer-Lamme

 **Sights**
★★★★☆

 **Restaurants**
★★★★★

 **Hotels**
★★★☆☆

 **Shopping**
★★★★☆

 **Nightlife**
★★★☆☆

# NEIGHBORHOOD SNAPSHOT

## TOP EXPERIENCES

■ **Italian Market:** Bring your appetite with you while you tour America's oldest continuously operating open-air market.

■ **Fleisher Art Memorial:** Take a brief eating break and fit in some culture at this historic community art space.

■ **Mummers Museum:** Get the real story behind the one New Year's Day tradition that's uniquely and gloriously Philly.

■ **Pat's and Geno's:** Scarf down cheesesteaks from both famed purveyors to declare which grill reigns supreme.

■ **Sports Complex:** Mingle with Philly's (in)famous sports fans on South Broad Street, home to the city's big four professional teams.

■ **Bella Vista and Queen Village:** Explore the best bars, restaurants, shops, and boutiques throughout these charming old neighborhoods.

## GETTING HERE

You can reach the Italian Market and its South Philadelphia surrounds on foot from Center City, or you may take SEPTA bus route 47, which runs south on 8th Street and makes a return loop north on 7th Street. There is both free and metered parking available in the neighborhood, at the official Italian Market lot on Carpenter Street between 9th and 10th Streets and in lots just off Washington Avenue between 8th and 9th Streets and 9th and 10th Streets.

## PLANNING YOUR TIME

It's best to visit the Italian Market Tuesday through Saturday, since many businesses close early on Sunday and take Monday off. Start early—vendors and shoppers tend to wind down by later afternoon—and allow three to four hours.

## QUICK BITES

■ **East Passyunk Avenue.** For generations, East Passyunk was the primary commercial corridor for South Philly's Italian-Americans; it's more recently blossomed into an exciting and ever-changing shopping, dining, and nightlife district. ⊠ *1904 E. Passyunk Ave., East Passyunk* ⊕ *www.visiteastpassyunk.com*

■ **Italian Market.** Stroll up 9th Street to take in the tastes of South Philly as it once was—walk-up counters, cafés, and sit-down restaurants join cheese shops, fishmongers, produce peddlers, and old-school Italian groceries along the stretch. ⊠ *919 S. 9th St., Bella Vista*

■ **Wing Phat Plaza.** A central gathering place for South Philly's "Little Saigon" community, this busy shopping center features a well-stocked Asian grocery store, plus Vietnamese, Indonesian, and Chinese restaurants. ⊠ *1122-38 Washington Ave., East Passyunk*

South Philadelphia is home to some of the city's most dynamic pockets: Queen Village, Bella Vista, and the neighborhoods around East Passyunk Avenue. Though they don't enjoy as much historical cachet as Old City or Society Hill, each played an invaluable role in the early rise of Philadelphia, nurturing industries and immigrant communities that define this great city. A contemporary influx of young professionals and the creative class has attracted interesting bars, restaurants, and shops to these traditionally residential areas.

Queen Village, stretching from Front to 6th Street and from South Street to Washington Avenue, was a hub of commercial activity in its earliest days, home to expert tradespeople, especially the shipbuilders active on the nearby Delaware River. Directly to the west, Bella Vista is a traditionally Italian hub, exemplified by the open-air market along 9th Street, still buzzing with charismatic produce hawkers and old-school butcher shops. Presidential candidates are fond of visiting the market on their swings through South Philly; it's a great photo op for them—and for you.

Further south, beyond Washington Avenue, you'll find an interesting mix of old- and new-school energy along East Passyunk Avenue, which cuts diagonally across the gridded streets. These are the neighborhoods that gave us Italian-American entertainers like Mario Lanza, Bobby Rydell, Frankie Avalon, and Fabian, but two other names in these parts might have even more renown—Pat's and Geno's. At the corner of 9th Street and East Passyunk Avenue, Pat's and Geno's are world-famous for their cheesesteaks, though locals tend to patronize smaller, lesser-known shops. Below Snyder Avenue stretches the rest of South Philadelphia to the south, east, and west, home to a diverse population, the city's flashy pro sports complexes, and myriad other gems.

# Philly Cheesesteaks

Philly's best-known culinary creation is simple in theory but complex in the details of its execution. Begin with the basic roll, which should be slightly crusty with a good amount of chew—Amoroso's is a popular choice. Add to that thin-sliced strips of top round or rib eye, griddled until well browned, next to a simmering bed of chopped onions. If you want the full effect, order your sandwich "wiz wit," meaning with a ladle of Cheez Whiz and fried onions; if you want only Whiz, it's simply "wiz witout."

American and provolone are other commonly requested cheeses. As befitting a cultural touchstone, there are many other homages on Philly menus, including chicken dumplings, cheesesteak egg rolls, and vegetarian versions. Even high-end restaurants pay their respects—including a famous $120 Wagyu rib eye/foie gras/truffled Whiz version at Stephen Starr's Barclay Prime in Rittenhouse Square (a half bottle of champagne is included in the price).

# East Passyunk

South of Bella Vista, East Passyunk technically comprises two neighborhoods: Passyunk Square and East Passyunk Crossing. Together, they stretch between Washington and Snyder Avenues, Broad Street and 8th Street. The Italian presence is also felt around Passyunk (pronounced pash-unk), but in recent years, an influx of new home buyers has changed the cultural complexion of the area, not unlike Bella Vista. Among the century-old pizza parlors and cheese shops are wine bars, artisanal butcher shops, hip baby boutiques, and restaurants helmed by *Top Chef* winners. Passyunk Square is also where you'll find Little Saigon, one of the city's largest Vietnamese neighborhoods.

No trip to South Philly would be complete without a stop at the site of the city's best-known cheesesteak rivalry, Pat's King of Steaks and adjacent competitor Geno's Steaks. Both can be found at the intersection of 9th Street and Passyunk Avenue and are open 24 hours a day. Each has its loyal fans for what's essentially the same sandwich: thinly sliced

rib-eye steak, grilled onions, cheese—provolone, American, or Cheez Whiz—all piled on a fresh-baked Italian roll.

## Restaurants

Over the past few years, East Passyunk Avenue (the main thoroughfare of the neighborhood of the same name) has emerged as one of the city's eminent dining strips; it seems there are more critically acclaimed restaurants along its central stretch than anywhere else in town.

### Bing Bing Dim Sum

$$ | ASIAN FUSION | Funky, unorthodox dim sum gets all the cool kids in the door at Bing Bing, which proudly bills itself as inauthentic. But beyond the high-low appeal of cheesesteak bao buns and corned beef ribs with beet barbecue sauce, there's real finesse from chef Ben Puchowitz's kitchen here. **Known for:** creative dim sum variations; shareable cocktails; young lively crowd. $ *Average main: $18 ⊠ 1648 E. Passyunk Ave., East Passyunk* 📞 *215/279–7702* ⊕ *www.bingbingdimsum.com* ⏱ *No lunch Mon.–Thurs.*

"HOW TO ORDER A STEAK" By I. M. Hungry

STEP 1.
SPECIFY IF YOU WANT YOUR STEAK WITH ( WIT ) OR WITHOUT ( WIT-OUT ) ONIONS.
(IF YOU'RE NOT A ROOKIE THIS SHOULD COME NATURALLY)

STEP 2.
SPECIFY PLAIN - CHEEZ WHIZ - PROVOLONE - AMERICAN CHEESE OR A PIZZA STEAK.

STEP 3.
HAVE YOUR MONEY READY. *(DO ALL OF YOUR BORROWING IN LINE)*

STEP 4.
PRACTICE ALL OF THE ABOVE WHILE WAITING IN LINE.
(IF YOU MAKE A MISTAKE, DON'T PANIC, JUST GO TO THE BACK OF THE LINE AND START OVER)

Intimidated by ordering your first cheesesteak? Follow these simple instructions posted at Pat's King of Steaks.

### ★ Gabriella's Vietnam

**$$$** | **VIETNAMESE** | Vietnamese food is very popular in Philadelphia and many people have a local pho spot that they frequent multiple times a week. Gabriella's, though, showcases regional dishes with light, flavorful, and addictive menu items like steamed water fern dumplings, savory crepes wrapped in herbs and lettuce, and stir-fried soft shell crab. **Known for:** regional Vietnamese cooking; group dining; shaken beef. $ *Average main: $30* ⊠ *1837 E. Passyunk Ave., East Passyunk* ☎ *272/888–3298* ⊕ *gabriellasvietnam.com* ☾ *Closed Mon. No lunch.*

### Geno's Steaks

**$** | **AMERICAN** | Geno's, open since 1966, is a fresh-faced upstart compared to neighboring rival Pat's, which has been slinging steaks since 1930. That gulf manifests itself visually in the contrast between Pat's understated aesthetic and Geno's over-the-top use of neon, which burns so brightly astronauts can probably see it from space, and the fact that Geno's meat is sliced, not chopped. **Known for:** 24-hour service; classic cheesesteaks; late-night scene. $ *Average main: $11* ⊠ *1219 S. 9th St., East Passyunk* ☎ *215/389–0659* ⊕ *www.genosteaks. com* ⊟ *No credit cards.*

### Le Virtù

**$$$** | **ITALIAN** | Sublime charcuterie, ethereal pastas, and interesting wines by the glass are just a few of the details that make Le Virtù one of the best Italian restaurants in town. The sun-washed space began with a fierce dedication to the underappreciated region of Abruzzo, where the owners run culinary tours; that focus has been sharpened for years. **Known for:** rare Abruzzese cuisine; excellent pastas; charming atmosphere. $ *Average main: $30* ⊠ *1927 E. Passyunk Ave., East Passyunk* ☎ *215/271–5626* ⊕ *www.levirtu.com* ☾ *No lunch.*

### Nam Phuong

**$** | **VIETNAMESE** | Competition is fierce in South Philly's "Little Saigon," but Nam Phuong has managed to keep fans of Vietnamese cuisine happy for years, with its wide-spanning menu. Far more

# East Passyunk, Bella Vista, and Queen Village

## Sights ▼

| | | |
|---|---|---|
| 1 | Fabric Row | G3 |
| 2 | Fleisher Art Memorial | E3 |
| 3 | Gloria Dei Old Swedes' Episcopal Church | H5 |
| 4 | Italian Market | D4 |
| 5 | Mummers Museum | G5 |
| 6 | Philadelphia's Magic Gardens | D2 |
| 7 | South Street | G2 |

## Restaurants ▼

| | | |
|---|---|---|
| 1 | Bing Bing Dim Sum | C7 |
| 2 | Bistrot La Minette | F2 |
| 3 | Blue Corn | D4 |
| 4 | Comfort & Floyd | C5 |
| 5 | Cry Baby Pasta | G3 |
| 6 | Dante & Luigi's | D3 |
| 7 | Fiore Fine Foods | H3 |
| 8 | Fitz on 4th | G3 |
| 9 | Gabriella's Vietnam | B7 |
| 10 | Geno's Steaks | D5 |
| 11 | The Good King Tavern | E2 |
| 12 | Jim's Steaks | G2 |
| 13 | Le Virtù | B8 |
| 14 | Little Fish | F3 |
| 15 | Nam Phuong | C4 |
| 16 | Pat's King of Steaks | D5 |
| 17 | Perla | C6 |
| 18 | Ralph's Italian Restaurant | D3 |
| 19 | River Twice | C6 |
| 20 | South Philly Barbacoa | D4 |
| 21 | South Street Souvlaki | F2 |

## Quick Bites ▼

| | | |
|---|---|---|
| 1 | Anthony's Italian Coffee House | E3 |
| 2 | D'Emilio's Old World Ice Treats | B8 |
| 3 | Essen Bakery | C6 |
| 4 | Federal Donuts | G6 |
| 5 | Termini Brothers Bakery | E6 |
| 6 | Wing Phat Plaza | C4 |

## Hotels ▼

| | | |
|---|---|---|
| 1 | Sonder The Queen | F2 |

**KEY**

- 1 *Exploring Sights*
- 1 *Restaurants*
- 1 *Quick Bites*
- 1 *Hotels*

spacious than some of the spartan pho parlors around the neighborhood, the dining room is equipped with round tables that can fit the whole crew—and all your food, too. **Known for:** lengthy Vietnamese menu; room for big groups; ample family dinner options. [$] *Average main: $14* ✉ *1100–1120 Washington Ave., East Passyunk* ☎ *215/468–0410* 🌐 *www.namphuongphilly.com.*

**Pat's King of Steaks**

$ | **AMERICAN** | New cheesesteak restaurants come and go, but two of the oldest—Pat's and Geno's, at 9th and Passyunk—have a long-standing feud worth weighing in on. It comes down to a matter of taste, as both serve equally generous portions of rib-eye steak, grilled onions, and melted provolone, American, or Cheez Whiz on freshly baked Italian rolls. **Known for:** 24-hour service; classic cheesesteak; late-night scene. [$] *Average main: $11* ✉ *1237 E. Passyunk Ave., East Passyunk* ☎ *215/468–1546* 🌐 *patskingofsteaks.com* 💳 *No credit cards.*

**Perla**

$$$ | **FILIPINO** | Chef-owner Lou Boquila brings his modern interpretations of Philippine cuisine to South Philly with this romantic BYOB. Thursday to Saturday, Boquila creates the popular *kamayan* dinner (Filipino style of communal eating without plates or utensils) which features loads of delicious food presented to the table on banana-leaf placemats. **Known for:** creative Filipino food; intimate dining room; communal kamayan dinners. [$] *Average main: $27* ✉ *1535 S. 11th St., East Passyunk* ☎ *267/273–0008* 🌐 *www.perlaphilly.com* 🕒 *Closed Mon. and Tues. No lunch.*

**River Twice**

$$$$ | **MODERN AMERICAN** | Chef Randy Rucker does seasonal, elevated food inspired by many things, including his southern heritage, love of Philadelphia, and interest in Japanese cooking. Go here for modern dishes like swordfish with housemade *yuzu kosho* (a Japanese condiment made from fresh chiles), carrot tartare with black truffles, very fresh oysters, and the Mother Rucker, a burger that's available as an add-on to the tasting menu. **Known for:** modern cuisine; luxurious ingredients; tasting menu. [$] *Average main: $95* ✉ *1601 E. Passyunk Ave., East Passyunk* ☎ *267/457–3698* 🌐 *www.rivertwicerestaurant.com* 🕒 *Closed Tues. and Wed. No lunch.*

★ **South Philly Barbacoa**

$ | **MEXICAN** | Chef Cristina Martinez specializes in *barbacoa,* the succulent, slow-cooked lamb of Martinez's Mexican homeland. The staff chop the meat with cleavers and pile it on fluffy corn tortillas, which you top at the salsa station with strips of fried cactus paddle, onion-laced pickled jalapeño escabeche, chopped cilantro, and fresh lime; go early, as they usually sell out at this weekend-only operation. **Known for:** lamb tacos; aguas frescas; early hours. [$] *Average main: $12* ✉ *1140 S. 9th St., East Passyunk* ☎ *215/694–3797* 🌐 *www.facebook.com/chefmtz* 💳 *No credit cards* 🕒 *Closed weekdays. No dinner.*

## ☕ Coffee and Quick Bites

**D'Emilio's Old World Ice Treats**

$ | **AMERICAN** | **FAMILY** | After a few years of selling his ices from a freezer sidecar on his motorcycle, owner Chris D'Emilio opened a brick-and-mortar shop selling ice cream, sorbetto, and water ice (a Philly specialty). Using his grandmother's recipe, D'Emilio sells his "ice treats" aka water ice, in original flavors like blueberry pomegranate and cherry lemonade. **Known for:** ice cream–filled pretzel; selling ices from a freezer sidecar on his motorcycle; huge sundaes. [$] *Average main: $10* ✉ *1928 E. Passyunk Ave., East Passyunk* ☎ *215/514–3930* 🌐 *www.facebook.com/oldworldicetreats* 🕒 *Closed Mon. and mid-Dec.–Feb. No lunch.*

**Essen Bakery**
$ | **BAKERY** | Babka, bagels, rugelach, and challah are but a few of the specialties at Tova du Plessis's "little Jewish bakery," where everything's handmade in small batches. In addition to these tasty artisanal items, Essen doles out traditional neighborhood bakery options like cookies, croissants, coffee, and simple sandwiches. **Known for:** homemade bagels; Jewish baked goods; quaint atmosphere. [$] *Average main: $7* ✉ *1437 E. Passyunk Ave., East Passyunk* ☎ *215/271–2299* 🌐 *www.essenbakery.com* 🕒 *No dinner.*

**Termini Brothers Bakery**
$ | **BAKERY** | Churning out Italian pastries since 1921, this famed bakery is best known for its filled-to-order cannoli, but its counters are also packed with pizzelles (Italian waffle cookies), biscotti, cakes, and other traditional Italian sweet treats. It's the perfect spot to stop for some traditional edible souvenirs to bring home—think cookie trays and gift boxes—or ship to your favorite cousin in California. **Known for:** filled-to-order cannoli; ships gift boxes everywhere; additional locations in Reading Terminal Market and the Market and Shops at Comcast Center. [$] *Average main: $10* ✉ *1523 S. 8th St., East Passyunk* ☎ *215/334–1816* 🌐 *www.termini.com.*

**Wing Phat Plaza**
$ | **ASIAN** | A central gathering place for South Philly's "Little Saigon" community, this busy shopping center features a well-stocked Asian grocery store, plus Vietnamese, Indonesian, and Chinese restaurants including the popular Nam Phuong. **Known for:** well-stocked Asian grocery store; home to Nam Phuong; great lunch spot. [$] *Average main: $7* ✉ *1122–38 Washington Ave., East Passyunk* ☎ *215/271–5866* 💳 *No credit cards.*

## Nightlife

Farther south, below Bella Vista and Queen Village, is the burgeoning nightlife draw of the bars, cafés, and restaurants of East Passyunk.

**The Pub on Passyunk East**
**PUBS** | Less concerned with the papacy than fine craft beer, the P.O.P.E., as it's called by locals, is a comfy neighborhood joint smack-dab in the middle of the drinking and dining enclave of East Passyunk Avenue. A bona fide neighborhood hangout that gets slammed on the weekends, the bar offers 14 beers on tap and loads more in bottles; the kitchen prepares straightforward fare, including burgers, nachos, and vegetarian options. ✉ *1501 E. Passyunk Ave., East Passyunk* ☎ *215/755–5125* 🌐 *www.pubonpassyunkeast.com.*

**Triangle Tavern**
**BARS** | An old-school grandpa bar rejiggered by the owners of Khyber Pass Pub, Royal Tavern, and Cantina Los Caballitos, the Triangle is at once new and old. While the smart craft beer and spirit selections nod to nouveau drinkers, the bar's nostalgic menu, featuring pastas, roast pork sandwiches, and other hearty specialties, is as South Philly as it gets. ✉ *1338 S. 10th St., East Passyunk* ☎ *215/800–1992* 🌐 *www.triangletavernphilly.com.*

## Shopping

**Occasionette**
**SOUVENIRS** | Sara Villari got her start screen-printing tea towels and totes, but her business eventually grew enough to open a bricks-and-mortar shop on East Passyunk. The store is a cheerful menagerie of thoughtful gifts and trinkets like indie greeting cards, eco-friendly water bottles, alluring candles, books, and cocktail mixers. Check the website for special events and deals. ✉ *1825 E. Passyunk Ave., East Passyunk* ☎ *215/465–1704* 🌐 *www.occasionette.com.*

# Bella Vista

Bella Vista nuzzles against Queen Village, running from 6th Street to Broad Street, though the exact boundary is a favorite topic of debate among locals. It's the historic heart of Italian-American Philadelphia, and its centerpiece is the outdoor Italian Market along 9th Street, packed with vendors, shops, and restaurants. In more recent years, Mexican immigrants have made spaces in the Market their own, so the drag is now also the place to pick up warm-from-the-press tortillas, dozens of different dried chilies, and even festive piñatas.

##  Sights

### Fleisher Art Memorial

**ART MUSEUM** | The realization of founder Samuel S. Fleisher's open invitation "to come and learn art," this school and gallery has offered classes, some tuition-free, since 1898. Fleisher presents regular exhibits of contemporary art as well as works by faculty and students. The Memorial consists of several connected buildings, including the Sanctuary, a Romanesque Revival Episcopal church designed by the architectural firm of Frank Furness and featuring European art from the 13th to the 15th century. A satellite building at 705 Christian Street is dedicated to works on paper. ⊠ *719 Catharine St., Bella Vista* ☏ *215/922–3456* ⊕ *www.fleisher.org* ⊒ *Free.*

### Italian Market

**MARKET** | If you want local color, nothing compares with South Philadelphia's Italian Market. On both sides of 9th Street from Fitzwater Street to Wharton Street and spilling out onto the surrounding blocks, outdoor stalls and indoor stores sell spices, cheeses, pastas, fruits, vegetables, and freshly slaughtered poultry and beef, not to mention household items, clothing, shoes, and other goods.

It's crowded and filled with the aromas of everything from fresh garlic to imported salami. Food shops include Grassia's Italian Market Spice Co., Di Bruno Bros. House of Cheese, Claudio's, and Talluto's Authentic Italian Food. Fante's is well known for cookware. The market's general hours are Tuesday–Saturday 9–5:30; some vendors open earlier and others close around 3:30. Some shops are open Sundays and even Mondays; it's wise to call ahead to specific shops and check. ⊠ *9th St., between Fitzwater and Wharton Sts., and the surrounding blocks, Bella Vista.*

### South Street

**STREET** | "Where do all the hippies (or "hippiest" depending on your source) meet? South Street." So goes a 1963 song by Philadelphia R&B group the Orlons, helping this west-to-east strip of pavement develop a reputation as a gathering place for counterculture types. In its day, the immediate street was populated by artists and musicians and their left-of-center bars, galleries, and stores. Nowadays, this bohemian energy is far less palpable, but the section between Broad and Front Streets still hosts many gems amid duller holdings like chain pharmacies and cell phone stores. Peruse the various antiques and vintage stores, clothing boutiques, bookstores, and record sellers between people-watching. There's a vast range of culinary options, too, from classic cheesesteak shops (Jim's and Ishkabibble's) to Peruvian chicken at Braza's and vegan-friendly eats at Tattooed Moms. ⊠ *1400 South St., Bella Vista* ☏ *215/413–3713* ⊕ *www.southstreet.com.*

## 🍴 Restaurants

In Bella Vista, a plethora of new restaurants have joined existing old-world pasta houses and bars.

One of the city's most famous streets, South Street has chain pharmacies, vintage shops, clothing boutiques, and food options like cheesesteaks at Jim's Steaks.

### Bistrot La Minette

**$$$** | **FRENCH** | The cheery atmosphere inside this long, narrow bistro exudes warmth and attention to detail, from the flea-market knickknacks picked out by chef Peter Woolsey and his Burgundian wife, Peggy, to the ceramic pitchers of house wine delivered to your table. Woolsey studied at the Cordon Bleu, fell in love with French food culture (and Peggy), and came back to his native Philadelphia to share the experience with his city; regulars swear by the mustard-braised rabbit with housemade pasta; pork cheeks braised in Malbec; and the exemplary desserts that speak to Woolsey's extensive training as a pastry chef. **Known for:** romantic atmosphere; classic French bistro menu; authentic ingredients. $ *Average main: $27* ✉ *623 S. 6th St., Bella Vista* ☎ *215/925–8000* ⊕ *www.bistrotlaminette.com* ⊗ *No lunch weekdays.*

### ★ Blue Corn

**$$** | **MEXICAN** | The sheer volume of Mexican restaurants on South 9th Street can be daunting—many are excellent, but how do you pick? The family-run Blue Corn consistently delivers, serving Pueblan cuisine with personality like tacos *al pastor* (taco made with spit-grilled pork) and *queso fundido* (hot melted cheese with spicy chorizo) alongside harder-to-find specialties like *huaraches* (crispy masa–pinto bean flatbreads) or whole fish stuffed with the corn truffle *huitlacoche*. Warm service and killer cocktails round out the experience. **Known for:** authentic Pueblan cooking; tequila and mezcal cocktails; friendly service. $ *Average main: $20* ✉ *940 S. 9th St., Bella Vista* ☎ *215/925–1010* ⊕ *www. facebook.com/bluecornrestaurant* ▭ *No credit cards.*

### Comfort & Floyd

$ | **AMERICAN** | **FAMILY** | Spend a morning tucked into pancakes, breakfast sandwiches, and bottomless coffee at this little neighborhood spot and you'll find yourself ready to move to South Philly. Those in the know grab a seat at the bar and wait for an outside table, but the wait is worth it for the hot, buttery pancakes, fluffy eggs, and the Pennsylvania delicacy known as scrapple (somewhere between a breakfast sausage and a hash) that help nurse your hangover or feed your kids. **Known for:** cozy vibes; pancakes, pancakes, pancakes; tuna melt. $ *Average main: $12* ✉ *1301 South 11th St., Bella Vista* ☎ *215/465–2917* ⊕ *comfortandfloyd.com* ⊘ *Closed Tues.–Wed. No dinner.*

### Dante & Luigi's

$$ | **ITALIAN** | Established in 1899 in the heart of Philly's Italian Market, Dante & Luigi's is located in two gorgeously appointed converted town houses. The menu features old-world Italian cuisine like red-sauce pasta, lasagna (some say its the best in Philly), and osso buco. **Known for:** old-world Italian cuisine; lasagna; reservations by phone only. $ *Average main: $18* ✉ *762 S. 10th St., Bella Vista* ☎ *215/922–9501* ⊕ *www.danteandluigis.com* ⊘ *Closed Mon. No lunch weekends.*

### The Good King Tavern

$$ | **FRENCH** | Specializing in French country cooking and expertly selected wines, the Good King offers casual Gallic flair at accessible neighborhood prices. Pair a *socca* (chickpea pancake) platter or steak frites with a glass or pitcher of house red or white, helpfully classified "Good," "Better," and "Best." The bar also makes up a mean cocktail, with daily changing specials. **Known for:** creative wine program; simple French cuisine; upstairs wine bar. $ *Average main: $20* ✉ *614 S. 7th St., Bella Vista* ☎ *215/625–3700* ⊕ *www.thegoodkingtavern.com* ⊘ *Closed Sun. No lunch.*

### ★ Little Fish

$$$$ | **SEAFOOD** | Philadelphia native Alex Yoon is the chef and owner of the tiny but beloved BYOB where creativity and inspiration run the show. The menu changes all the time, but the scallop toast, where raw scallops are shingled across a thick slice of sesame sourdough and topped with chopped herbs, is a favorite that diners return for over and over. **Known for:** seafood dishes like seared scallops and roasted halibut; scallop toast; friendly service. $ *Average main: $35* ✉ *746 S. 6th St., Bella Vista* ☎ *267/455–0172* ⊕ *www.littlefishbyob.com* ⊘ *Closed weekends. No lunch.*

### Ralph's Italian Restaurant

$$ | **ITALIAN** | Owned and operated by the fourth and fifth generation of the Dispigno/Rubino family, you can expect old-world favorites like sausage and peppers, osso bucco, and braciole, as well as house specialties like lasagne and fettuccini alfredo. **Known for:** traditional Italian comfort dishes; warm vibes; South Philly staple. $ *Average main: $18* ✉ *760 S. 9th St., Bella Vista* ☎ *215/627–6011* ⊕ *www.ralphsrestaurant.com.*

## 🍵 Coffee and Quick Bites

### Anthony's Italian Coffee House

$ | **CAFÉ** | When you're ready for an atmospheric break, stop by Anthony's Italian Coffee House in the heart of the Italian Market. Here, to the strains of Frank Sinatra, you can sample a fresh panino with prosciutto and mozzarella or indulge in homemade cannoli or gelato imported from Italy. **Known for:** Italian espresso drinks; Italian desserts; outdoor seating. $ *Average main: $8* ✉ *903 S. 9th St., Bella Vista* ☎ *215/627–2586* ⊕ *www.italiancoffeehouse.com.*

Nightlife

## 12 Steps Down

**BARS** | Regulars abound at 12 Steps Down, where people shoot pool, sing karaoke every Tuesday, and belly up to the bar for local and domestic beers, pours of bourbon, and plenty of classic bar snacks. ⊠ *831 Christian St., Bella Vista* ⊕ *www.12stepsdown.com.*

 Shopping

### FOOD

**Cardenas Oil & Vinegar Taproom**

**MARKET** | You've seen shops like Cardenas Oil & Vinegar Taproom in small-town downtowns all across the country. At this Italian Market shop, they've got the requisite refillable oils and vinegars (in flavors that include blood orange and coconut) but distinguish themselves with a serious lineup of rare, unadulterated elixirs sourced from Italy, Spain, even South Africa. The team is generous with samples. ⊠ *942 S. 9th St., Bella Vista* ☎ *267/928–3690* ⊕ *www.cardenastaproom.com.*

### Di Bruno Bros.

**FOOD** | The first location of the famed specialty cheese shop, this Di Bruno's looks laughably tiny compared to the enormous branches in Center City and the suburbs. Slight in size though it may be—it's long, narrow, and cavelike, with salamis hanging from the ceiling like stalactites—it's absolutely jam-packed with all the specialties you expect from *la famiglia.* Peruse all the cheeses, oils, antipasti, and charcuterie you want, comforted by the assurance that the gregarious employees behind the counter will always break you off samples. ⊠ *930 S. 9th St., Bella Vista* ☎ *215/922–2876* ⊕ *www.dibruno.com.*

### HOME DECOR

**Fante's Kitchen Shop**

**HOUSEWARES** | One of the nation's oldest gourmet supply stores offers amateur and pro cooks alike an impressive selection of kitchen tools and equipment. Family-owned since 1906, Fante's is famous for oddball kitchen gadgets such as truffle shavers and pineapple peelers; restaurants and bakeries all over the country and overseas order from the store. It's in the Italian Market, so you can conveniently combine a visit here with shopping for ingredients. ⊠ *1006 S. 9th St., Bella Vista* ☎ *215/922–5557, 800/443–2683* ⊕ *www.fantes.com* Ⓜ *Broad and Ellsworth.*

### JEWELRY

**Bario-Neal Jewelry**

**JEWELRY & WATCHES** | Stunningly simple earrings, bracelets, and necklaces are designed and handcrafted locally at this store-workshop by two women (Anna Bario and Page Neal) who create environmentally friendly jewelry. All materials are reclaimed, ethically sourced, or retrieved using low-impact practices. Even the packaging—reclaimed glass bottles with cork stoppers—is green. ⊠ *700 S. 6th St., Bella Vista* ☎ *215/454–2164* ☞ *Appointments preferred.*

# Queen Village

North of South Street is Society Hill. South of South, Queen Village. Though there was a time when the former looked down its nose at its southern neighbor, Queen Village has been a mighty nice place to live for the last 20 years, home to some of the city's priciest historic homes. Queen Village is dense, residential, and prettiest on the streets closer to the Delaware River. Cafés and restaurants dot the corners, while Fabric Row on 4th Street is where budding designers go shopping for materials at decades-old cotton and silk houses.

## Sights

### Fabric Row

**STREET** | In the early 1900s, 4th Street, today's Fabric Row, was teeming with pushcarts selling calico, notions, and trimming. It was known as "der Ferder," or "the Fourth" in Yiddish. Today, several century-old fabric stores still stand, like stalwarts Maxie's Daughter and Fleishman Fabrics and Supplies, but many of the storefronts are home to locals selling wares from European-label shoes to fair-trade coffee. ✉ *400 Monroe St., Queen Village* ✣ *S. 4th St. between Monroe and Catharine Sts.* 🌐 *www.fabricrow.com.*

### Gloria Dei Old Swedes' Episcopal Church

**CHURCH** | One of the few remaining relics from the Swedes who settled Pennsylvania before William Penn, Gloria Dei, also known as Old Swedes' Church, has been active since 1700. It's the oldest church in Pennsylvania and second oldest in the entire country. Models of the ships that transported the first Swedish settlers hang from the ceiling in the center of the church; the baptismal font dates all the way back to 1731, while religious carvings on display are even older. Grouped around the house of worship are the parish hall, the sexton's house, the rectory, and the church offices. Sitting in the center of a graveyard, Old Swedes' is calming in its tranquility. ✉ *916 S. Swanson St., Queen Village* ☎ *215/389–1513* 🌐 *www.old-swedes.com* 🎟 *Free.*

### Mummers Museum

**HISTORY MUSEUM** | **FAMILY** | Even if you aren't in Philadelphia on January 1, you can still get a feel for one of the city's unique traditions by stopping by this museum. Famous for their extravagant sequin-and-feather costumes and boisterous behavior, the Mummers spend all year practicing for their New Year's Day parade down Broad Street, a tradition since 1901. With roots in old European folk performance traditions, today's Mummers clubs fall into several different categories, including satirical Comics, musical String Bands, and theatrical Fancies. All this and more is covered at the museum, which features family-friendly exhibits on Mummers culture; there are outdoor concerts in the summer. ✉ *1100 S. 2nd St., at Washington Ave., Queen Village* ☎ *215/336–3050* 🌐 *www.mummersmuseum.com* 🎟 *$5* 🕒 *Closed Sun.–Tues.*

### Philadelphia's Magic Gardens

**OTHER ATTRACTION** | Stroll around South Street and it won't be long before you come across the work of mosaic muralist Isaiah Zagar, recognizable by its intricate, irreverent mix of found materials and folk motifs. The Magic Gardens is home base for Zagar's eye-catching art, which he's been creating around here since he and wife, Julia, a fellow artist, moved there in the 1960s. Consisting of two indoor galleries and an outdoor sculpture garden, it's an impressive and immersive visual feat. It's a popular spot with tourists and groups, so it's best to purchase tickets in advance; they go on sale online for visits one month in advance. ✉ *1020 South St., Queen Village* ☎ *215/733–0390* 🌐 *www.phillymagicgardens.org* 🎟 *$10* 🕒 *Closed Tues.*

## Restaurants

### Cry Baby Pasta

**$$** | **ITALIAN** | Queen Villagers shed tears of joy when longtime neighborhood restaurateur Bridget Foy introduced this easy-to-love restaurant, specializing in handmade pastas and wine priced to glug. You'll spot plenty of young families with kids in tow in the early dinner hours, while the crowd gets a little more grown-up later in the evening. **Known for:** house-made pasta; family friendly; accessible wine list. [$] *Average main: $21* ✉ *627 S. 3rd St., Queen Village* ☎ *267/534–3076* 🌐 *crybabypasta.com* 🕒 *Closed Mon. No lunch.*

Philadelphia's Magic Gardens is home base for mosaic muralist Isaiah Zagar, whose eye-catching art can also be seen all around South Street.

**Fiore Fine Foods**

$$$ | **ITALIAN** | Fiore is many things for many people: at dinnertime, regional Italian pastas like stuffed *culurgiones* (a Sardinian ravioli-like stuffed pasta) and cacio e pepe are served alongside fire-kissed proteins, creative vegetable dishes, and a tight but well-curated wine and cocktail list. Inventive pastries pair with well-made coffee, rich breakfast sandwiches, and the crispiest hash brown in town, and on the weekends, the sunny dining room is host to one of the best brunches in the city. **Known for:** pastries; handmade pasta; breakfast sandwiches. [$] *Average main: $30* ✉ *757 S. Front St., Queen Village* ☎ *215/339–0509* 🌐 *www.fiore-finefoods.com* 🕓 *Closed Mon. and Tues. No dinner Sun.*

**Fitz on 4th**

$ | **VEGETARIAN** | The creative mother-and-son team of Alison Fitzpatrick and Alex Soto own this upscale vegan restaurant that features a stylish and lively ambience and a menu of delectable homemade specialties. A popular corner spot with big windows, Fitz on 4th serves up many delicious delights that vegans and non-vegans will appreciate like sesame delicata squash, empanadas, and "crab" cakes. **Known for:** upscale vegan; creative cocktails; lively and fun ambience. [$] *Average main: $15* ✉ *743 S. 4th St., Queen Village* ☎ *215/315–8989* 🌐 *www.fitzon4th.com* 🕓 *Closed Mon. and Tues. No lunch Wed. and Thurs.*

**Jim's Steaks**

$ | **AMERICAN** | **FAMILY** | You'll know you're nearing Jim's when the scent of frying onions overwhelms your senses—or when you see people lined up around the corner. Big, juicy cheesesteaks—shaved beef piled high on long crusty rolls—come off the grill with amazing speed when the counter workers hit their stride, whether it's lunchtime or late-night. **Known for:** cheesesteaks; long and lively lines; nostalgic environment. [$] *Average main: $9* ✉ *400 South St., Queen Village* ☎ *215/928–1911* 🌐 *www.jimssouthstreet.com* 💳 *No credit cards.*

# Philly's Music History

Philly holds a special place in pop music history. *American Bandstand*, hosted by Dick Clark, began here as a local dance show. When it went national in 1957, it gave a boost to many hometown boys, including teen heartthrob Fabian, Bobby Rydell, Frankie Avalon, and Chubby Checker, of "Twist" fame. Sun Ra, the legendary jazz pianist, was from Philly, in keeping with the city's rich tradition of jazz luminaries such as saxophonists Grover Washington Jr., Stan Getz, and John Coltrane, drummer Philly Joe Jones, and vocalist Billie Holiday.

In the 1970s, the Philadelphia Sound—a polished blend of disco, pop, and R&B—came alive through producers Kenny Gamble and Leon Huff at the famed Philadelphia International Records studios for artists like The Ojays, Lou Rawls, Teddy Pendergrass, and Three Degrees, whose megahit "Love Train" helped to define the '70s

era. That lush sound was kept alive by chart toppers such as Hall and Oates, Patti LaBelle, Boyz II Men, Will Smith, Jill Scott, The Roots (now the house band for *Late Night With Jimmy Fallon*, among other accomplishments), neo-soul stylist Musiq Soulchild, pop queen Pink, and R&B sensation Jazmine Sullivan. Meek Mill, Lil Uzi Vert, PnB Rock, and Tierra Whack are just a few of the Philadelphia hip-hop artists to find a national, and in some cases international, audience in recent years.

Contemporary rock acts from Philly that have gained national renown include Dr. Dog, Kurt Vile, Man Man, Hop Along, Circa Survive, and The War on Drugs. The local DJ scene is also potent, with stalwart spinners like King Britt, Rich Medina, and The Roots' Questlove paving the way for a new generation of party starters.

### South Street Souvlaki

$ | **GREEK** | **FAMILY** | The first thing you'll see is the large rotisserie, trumpeting the ubiquitous gyro—tasty slices of meat are stuffed inside a large fresh pita, with tangy yogurt and some exemplary fresh veggies. Other Greek specialties, such as stuffed grape leaves, moussaka, and, of course, souvlaki, round out the menu. **Known for:** simple and authentic Greek fare; group dining; value-driven menu. $ *Average main: $13* ⊠ *509 South St., Queen Village* ☎ *215/925–3026* ⊕ *www. southstreetsouvlaki.com* ⊙ *Closed Mon.*

## ☕ Coffee and Quick Bites

### Federal Donuts

$ | **CAFÉ** | **FAMILY** | In 2011, the owners of the acclaimed Zahav partnered with a team of Philly food entrepreneurs to open the first Federal Donuts, and Philly quickly fell in love with the whimsical doughnut-and–fried chicken concept. The minichain now runs many shops throughout the city, but this tiny flagship, on an unassuming corner in quiet Pennsport, is still going strong. **Known for:** unconventional doughnut flavors; creative fried-chicken styles; good coffee. $ *Average main: $10* ⊠ *1219 S. 2nd St., Queen Village* ☎ *267/687–8258* ⊕ *www. federaldonuts.com* ⊙ *No dinner.*

## Hotels

**Sonder The Queen**

$ | **APARTMENT** | Sonder's offering is somewhere in between hotel and Airbnb as they offer serviced apartments that are well stocked for longer stays or guests who would like to cook some meals, with local touches and a few amenities like room cleaning and great locations. **Pros:** good location; more spacious than a hotel; great option for longer stays. **Cons:** lacks the amenities (gym, pool, etc.) of a traditional hotel; no concierge. [$] *Rooms from: $144* ✉ *628 S. 5th St., Queen Village* 🌐 *www.sonder.com* 🛏 *30 units* 🍴 *No Meals.*

## Nightlife

**For Pete's Sake**

**BARS** | Pete's, in Queen Village, could easily be mistaken for just another neighborhood watering hole, but the menu is eclectic, featuring a regularly changing lineup of creative food alongside the requisite wings and burgers. ✉ *900 S. Front St., Queen Village* ☎ *215/462–2230* 🌐 *www.forpetessakepub.com.*

**Le Caveau**

**WINE BARS** | The snug wine bar above the Good King Tavern in Queen Village is the closest you'll get to France while still in Philadelphia. Owner Chloe Grigri painstakingly selects wine to offer by the glass and by the bottle. Her French background affords her access to hard-to-find bottles, which she and her staff pour at very fair prices. The snack selection is also good, especially the French hot dog stuffed into a baguette. ✉ *614 S. 7th St., Queen Village* 🌐 *lecaveaubar.com.*

**New Wave Café**

**BARS** | To its devoted Queen Village clientele, the New Wave is more than just the place to wait for a table at a nearby restaurant. The regulars come to this welcoming neighborhood bar to unwind with a local craft brew, play a game of darts, watch the game, or enjoy the oft-changing gastropub menu. ✉ *784 S. 3rd St., Queen Village* ☎ *215/922–8484* 🌐 *newwavecafe.com.*

## Performing Arts

**Theatre of Living Arts**

**MUSIC** | A former playhouse, mainstream movie theater, and art-house cinema, the TLA is a South Street institution that helped launch the careers of many indie filmmakers; it was known for hosting screenings of cult hits like *The Rocky Horror Picture Show*. Nowadays, it's a midsized live-music venue, hosting a range of rock, blues, hip-hop, and alternative acts. ✉ *334 South St., Queen Village* ☎ *215/922–1011* 🌐 *venue.tlaphilly.com.*

## Shopping

### BOOKS

**Brickbat Books**

**BOOKS** | The charming, worn-in feel of this store lined with wooden shelves befits the merchandise for sale: the focus is on rare, small-press used and new books, although it's not unheard-of to find a $4 Hardy Boys paperback next to a first-edition Edward Gorey. The store also acts as a venue for fringe musicians from near and far. Follow Brickbat on Instagram (@brickbatphilly) to stay abreast of the latest arrivals. ✉ *709 S. 4th St., Queen Village* ☎ *215/592–1207* 🌐 *www.brickbatbooks.com.*

**Garland of Letters**

**BOOKS** | Open since 1972, this is the original New Age bookstore, hailing from the days when hippies arrived on South Street and established its reputation as an artsy enclave. Follow the aroma of incense and step inside to find books on astrology, tarot, shamanism, and world religions and cultures, plus a selection of jewelry, crystals, and candles. ✉ *527 South St., Queen Village* ☎ *215/923–5946* 🌐 *www.southstreet.com/business/garland-of-letters.*

## Head House Books

**BOOKS** | Sunlight streams into the front windows of this well-curated indie bookshop. It's the kind of place that attracts regulars who sit sipping tea and reading for hours with a dog curled at their feet. This inviting shop has become a meeting place for the local literary community—both the readers and the writers. ✉ *619 S. 2nd St., Queen Village* ☎ *215/923–9525* ⊕ *www.headhousebooks.com.*

### GIFTS AND SOUVENIRS
#### Eye's Gallery

**SOUVENIRS** | This long-running shop, in a new location across the street from its original home, has the feel of a folk art museum, its shelves stocked with vibrant handmade textiles and garments, Day of the Dead art, instruments, carvings, masks, jewelry, and decorative pieces sourced from all over Mexico and South America. Across the street, the former space now home to the expanded space of Jim's Steaks, is adorned with the mosaic murals of Philadelphia artist Isaiah Zagar; he and his wife, Julia Zagar, a fellow artist, founded Eye's in 1968, directly shaping the artsy, bohemian reputation that's long been associated with South Street. ✉ *327 South St., Queen Village* ☎ *215/925–0193* ⊕ *www.eyesgallery.com.*

# South Philadelphia

Outside Bella Vista, Queen Village, and East Passyunk, dozens of mini-neighborhoods comprise the bulk of South Philadelphia, like historically Irish-American Pennsport, where 2nd Street is called "Two Sweet" and lined with Mummers clubhouses. Residential Newbold, a subsection of Point Breeze, is home to popular craft-beer bars like South Philadelphia Tap Room. Down by the Sports Complex, where fans catch the Phillies, Eagles, Sixers, and Flyers, the decommissioned Navy Yard has become an urban oasis of rolling lawns and slinky canals, home to more than 150 companies and organizations. There's also the area around the airport, where you'll find the hidden gems of Fort Mifflin and the John Heinz National Wildlife Refuge at Tinicum.

 **Sights**

### American Swedish Historical Museum

**HISTORY MUSEUM** | This neoclassical building in FDR Park celebrates Swedish contributions to American history. The Swedes settled the Delaware Valley in the mid-1600s, and it was a pair of Swedish brothers who sold William Penn the land that became Philadelphia. Modeled after a 17th-century Swedish manor house, it features galleries and rooms that concentrate on specific eras and industrious characters. The John Ericsson Room honors the designer of the Civil War ship the USS *Monitor*; the Jenny Lind Room contains memorabilia from the P.T. Barnum–led American tour the soprano known as the "Swedish Nightingale" embarked upon in 1850. Other rooms display handmade dolls, crafts, paintings, and drawings, all in addition to rotating cultural exhibitions. It's not the most riveting place on paper, but the unconventional location, combined with its examination of overlooked history, make for an interesting visit. ✉ *1900 Pattison Ave., South Philadelphia* ⊕ *Take the Orange Line subway south to its final stop (NRG Station); cross Broad Street and walk 5 blocks west through the park to the museum* ☎ *215/389–1776* ⊕ *www.americanswedish.org* 🎫 *$10.*

### Bartram's Garden

**GARDEN** | Established in 1728 by pioneering botanist John Bartram, this is America's oldest surviving botanical garden. Bartram, with his son William, collected and identified thousands of indigenous North American (and beyond) plants, showcasing them for both scientific and commercial purposes. Today, the 45-acre National Historic Landmark on the west bank of the Schuylkill River boasts a diversity of flora to wander leisurely about—from flowering shrubs and trees (azalea, rhododendron, magnolia) to rare specimens like the Franklinia, a tree that died out in its native Georgia, surviving today only because Bartram cultivated it. The best months to come are April–June, when the gardens are fragrant and filled with the lively chatter of birds, but summer and fall also have their charms. The original 18th-century farmhouse still stands, and you can tour its rooms and various exhibits, including Native American artifacts from the property dating back 3,000 years.

■ TIP→ **Drive or take a cab, as the grounds are tucked down a driveway in an out-of-the-way part of Southwest Philadelphia.** ⊠ *5400 Lindbergh Blvd., at 54th St., Southwest Philadelphia* ☎ *215/729–5281* ⊕ *www.bartramsgarden.org* ✉ *Garden free to the public daily, dusk to dawn; house tour $12 available Apr. 1–Dec. 3, Thurs.–Sun.* Ⓜ *SEPTA Rte. 36 Trolley.*

### Citizens Bank Park

**SPORTS VENUE** | Since 2004, the Philadelphia Phillies have played in Citizens Bank Park, a 42,792-seat stadium that has a 13,000-square-foot interactive kids' baseball experience called The Yard. Ticketed tours are available all year long and feature stops in the Phillies' dugout, the Diamond Club, the Hall of Fame Club, the broadcast booth, and the media room. ⊠ *1 Citizens Bank Way, South Philadelphia* ☎ *215/463–1000* ⊕ *www.mlb.com/phillies* ✉ *Tours $20.*

### Franklin Delano Roosevelt Park

**CITY PARK** | Frederick Law Olmsted is best known as the designer of New York's Central Park, and his sons followed in their father's footsteps in founding the Olmsted Brothers firm, which created this high-profile park in deep South Philly. Originally called League Island Park, when it was designed in the decade leading up to the 1926 Sesquicentennial Exposition, it's now colloquially known as "The Lakes" for its network of channels

and lagoons. The park contains numerous historical structures, including a soaring granite gazebo ringed in Doric columns, the dramatically arched boathouse, and the castlelike American Swedish Historical Museum. ⊠ *1500 Pattison Ave., South Philadelphia* ☎ *215/685–0060* ⊕ *www.fdrparkphilly.org.*

### ★ Fort Mifflin

**MILITARY SIGHT** | There are number of strange, forgotten sights in Philadelphia that in any other city would be a major, if not *the* major tourist attraction. Fort Mifflin may be the best of these sights in Southwest Philadelphia. The fort is enormous and nearly always empty. Within its walls, spread out on a huge lawn, are cannons and carriages, officers' quarters, soldiers' barracks, an artillery shed, a blacksmith shop, a bomb shelter, and a museum. The exhibits are dated, but the stories are fascinating, from the 40-day battle in 1777 to hold off British ships coming up the Delaware to the use of the site as a prison during the Civil War. The fort was almost totally destroyed during the Revolution, but was rebuilt in 1798 from plans by French architect Pierre L'Enfant, who also designed Washington, D.C. If you wander off beyond the fort and into the other parts of the 49-acre National Historic Landmark, you will find a long embankment of overgrown and unexcavated battlements from the 1800s. From Penn's Landing it's an easy jaunt on I–95. ⊠ *6400 Hog Island Rd., at Island Rd., Southwest Philadelphia* ✛ *on Delaware River near Philadelphia International Airport* ☎ *215/685–4167* ⊕ *www.fortmifflin.us* ✉ *$10* ◷ *Closed mid-Dec.–Feb.* ☞ *You can call to arrange an appointment or private tour during the off-season.*

### ★ John Heinz National Wildlife Refuge at Tinicum

**WILDLIFE REFUGE | FAMILY** | Part of the appeal of this refuge is its truly strange location for a nature preserve: it's between the airport and an oil refinery,

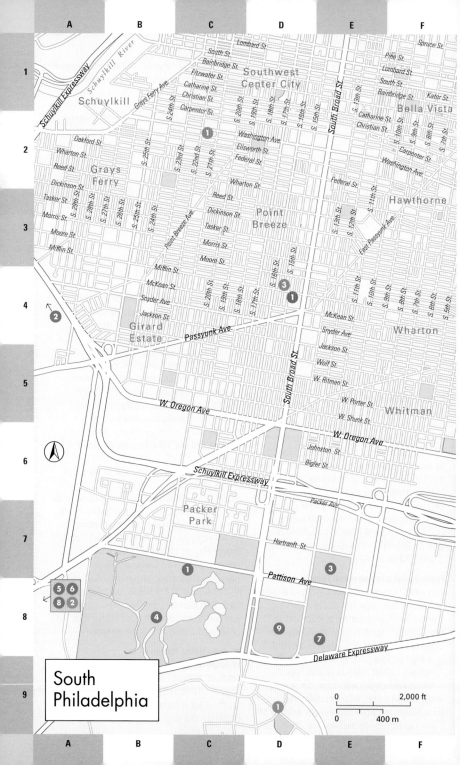

## Sights ▼

1 American Swedish
  Historical Museum ......**C7**
2 Bartram's Garden.......**A4**
3 Citizens Bank Park.......**E7**
4 Franklin Delano
  Roosevelt Park ..........**B8**
5 Fort Mifflin ...............**A8**
6 John Heinz National
  Wildlife Refuge
  at Tinicum................**A8**
7 Lincoln Financial
  Field ......................**E8**
8 Simeone Foundation
  Automotive Museum ... **A8**
9 Wells Fargo Center .....**D8**

## Restaurants ▼

1 Dock Street South .......**C2**
2 John's Roast Pork ......**H5**
3 South Philadelphia
  Tap Room ................**D4**
4 Tony Luke's ..............**G6**

## Quick Bites ▼

1 Ultimo Coffee............**D4**

## Hotels ▼

1 Courtyard Philadelphia
  South at
  The Navy Yard...........**D9**
2 Fairfield Inn
  Philadelphia Airport .... **A8**

# City 6 Basketball

There are many storied rivalries in college sports, but none quite like Philadelphia's Big 5—a round-robin tournament featuring basketball teams from La Salle, UPENN, St. Joseph's, Temple, and Villanova. Established in 1955, this in-season, intracity round-robin tournament supersedes formalities like school size, national polls, or conference affiliation. The unique mix of public, Ivy League, and Catholic institutions produced fierce annual competition, and Philly basketball bragging rights were the coveted prize.

Starting with the 2023–2024 season, the Big 5 will become the City 6 with the inclusion of Drexel. Formerly hosted at Penn's nearly century-old Palestra, the games are slated to take place at the Wells Fargo Center.

and visitors seem to really enjoy the oddity of it. More than 280 species of hawks, swallows, herons, egrets, geese, gallinules, eagles, orioles, ducks, and other birds have been spotted at this 1,200-acre preserve, the largest remaining freshwater tidal marsh in Pennsylvania. There are 10 miles of foot trails, an observation deck, and boardwalks through the wet areas. The refuge is also home to fox, deer, muskrat, turtles, and frogs, and you'll likely see large carp and catfish flopping about the lilies. An environmental education center has some explanatory exhibits on wetlands and regional wildlife. There are many guided tours. You can even canoe, kayak, and mountain bike, but there are no rentals here. Binoculars and fishing rods are available for loan, free of charge. The refuge is convenient to I–95, which you can pick up from Penn's Landing. ⊠ *8601 Lindbergh Blvd., Southwest Philadelphia* ☎ *215/365–3118* ⊕ *www.fws.gov/refuge/john_heinz* ⊠ *Free* ⊙ *Closed Sun.–Tues.*

### Lincoln Financial Field

**SPORTS VENUE** | The Linc, as it's called by locals, is a state-of-the-art facility with a grass playing field. It holds nearly 68,000 passionate Philadelphia Eagles fans, as well as supporters of the Temple Owls football team; the stadium also plays host to other sports, plus large-scale events and concerts. Tours are available. ⊠ *1 Lincoln Financial Field Way, South Philadelphia* ☎ *267/570–4000* ⊕ *www.lincolnfinancialfield.com* ⊠ *Tours $15.*

### Simeone Foundation Automotive Museum

**TRANSPORTATION** | A nondescript hangar five minutes from the Philadelphia International Airport is home to what's been dubbed the most impressive racing car collection on the planet. Dr. Fred Simeone spent half a century amassing a fleet of more than 75 vehicles that tell the sweeping story of racing history. You can see them in action during regular "demo days," which happen twice a month on Saturdays when staffers fire up a selection of the antique roadsters and take them out for some air. ⊠ *6825 Norwitch Dr., Southwest Philadelphia* ☎ *215/365–7233* ⊕ *www.simeonemuseum.org* ⊠ *$15* ⊙ *Closed Mon.*

### Wells Fargo Center

**SPORTS VENUE** | The Wells Fargo Center is the home to the Flyers (NHL), 76ers (NBA), and Wings (NLL, pro lacrosse), and regularly hosts Villanova basketball (and other collegiate sports), big-name concerts, and high-profile arena entertainment of all kinds. Behind-the-scenes tours last 60 to 90 minutes and include a commemorative photo and frame for each guest. ⊠ *3601 S. Broad St., South*

*Philadelphia* ☎ *215/336–3600* 🌐 *www.wellsfargocenterphilly.com* 🎫 *Tours $10.*

## 🍴 Restaurants

### Dock Street South

$ | **AMERICAN** | **FAMILY** | Housed in a former warehouse, this local brewery is a welcoming all-day destination for South Philadelphians; it's an ideal stop for large groups, and it's kid-friendly. The menu items, which all pair well with the dozen beers on tap, range from wood-fired pizzas and sandwiches (try the roast Italian pork or the double smashburger) to sharable plates like honey whipped ricotta served with crostini and fresh naan, fried mozzarella, or chicken wings. **Known for:** Saturday brewery tours ($10); outdoor dining in the spring, summer, and fall; wood-fired pizzas. [$] *Average main: $13* ✉ *2118 Washington Ave., South Philadelphia* ☎ *215/337–3103* 🌐 *www.dockstreetbeer.com* 🕘 *Closed Mon.*

### ★ John's Roast Pork

$ | **ITALIAN** | **FAMILY** | Housed in humble digs next to a defunct railroad crossing, John's doesn't wow with curb appeal, but wise eaters know the close-to-centenarian grill spot turns out some of Philly's best sandwiches. Newbies and lifers alike line up in a zigzag along the counter, grabbing outdoor picnic tables after paying for their roast pork, roast beef, or cheesesteak. **Known for:** Italian roast pork sandwiches; highly praised cheesesteaks; friendly South Philly staff. [$] *Average main: $9* ✉ *14 E. Snyder Ave., South Philadelphia* ☎ *215/463–1951* 🌐 *www.johnsroastpork.com* 🕘 *Closed Sun. and Mon. No dinner.*

### ★ South Philadelphia Tap Room

$$ | **MODERN AMERICAN** | **FAMILY** | Championing craft beer well before it was cool, this laid-back Newbold tavern set the bar for Philly's gastropub boom way back in 2003. SPTR's ever-rotating 14 tap selections, plus cask ales and a nice bottle selection, hit local, national, and international notes that nicely accompany a menu that reaches well beyond the expected pub grub with creative snacks, sandwiches, and seasonal specials conceived to celebrate local and organic products and produce. **Known for:** smart craft-beer program; local and seasonal menu items; relaxed atmosphere. [$] *Average main: $20* ✉ *1509 Mifflin St., South Philadelphia* ☎ *215/271–7787* 🌐 *www.southphiladelphiataproom.com.*

### Tony Luke's

$ | **AMERICAN** | The first Tony Luke's—way down in deep South Philly, basically under I–95—earned such a reputation from truckers who'd pull off for hefty cheesesteaks and Italian pork sandwiches that word spread across the city, allowing charismatic namesake Tony Lucidonio Jr. to expand the brand to multiple states. Little more than a walk-up window and a scattering of seats, this original location is still humming, and its generous early-morning and weekend late-night hours accommodate early birds, night owls, and the hungry people who fall somewhere in between. **Known for:** cheesesteaks, cheesesteaks, cheesesteaks; Italian roast pork sandwiches; accommodating breakfast and late-night hours. [$] *Average main: $9* ✉ *39 E. Oregon Ave., South Philadelphia* ☎ *215/551–5725* 🌐 *www.tonylukes.com.*

## ☕ Coffee and Quick Bites

### Ultimo Coffee

$ | **CAFÉ** | Aaron and Elizabeth Ultimo launched a specialty coffee chain in 2009, offering expert espresso, pour-over brewing, and single-origin beans well before these were staples. The couple has since added three more shops, a bakery, and a roastery to the roster, while their relaxed Newbold flagship keeps on keeping on perhaps because of the comfortable space and friendly staff. **Known for:** specialty coffee; outdoor seating; craft beer bottle shop. ⓢ *Average main: $5 ⊠ 1900 S. 15th St., South Philadelphia ☎ 215/339–5177 ⊕ www.ultimocoffee.com.*

##  Hotels

### Courtyard Philadelphia South at The Navy Yard

**$$ | HOTEL |** A welcome alternative to cookie-cutter accommodations down by Philadelphia International Airport, this LEED-certified Courtyard takes up residence in the Navy Yard, a 1,200-acre business campus in deep South Philly that is home to companies like GlaxoSmithKline and Urban Outfitters. **Pros:** close proximity to Sports Complex; quick ride to/from PHL Airport; better design than hotels in vicinity. **Cons:** far away from Center City; few walkable dining options outside hotel; isolated Navy Yard feels more like a college campus than a city. ⓢ *Rooms from: $199 ⊠ 1001 Intrepid Ave., South Philadelphia ☎ 215/644–9200 ⊕ www.marriott.com/phlcs ➷ 212 rooms ⦿l No Meals.*

### Fairfield Inn Philadelphia Airport

**$$$ | HOTEL |** As far as airport hotels are concerned, this Fairfield Inn is standard, but its staff has a reputation for being quite accommodating. **Pros:** accommodating staff; 24-hour shuttle service to airport; 24-hour fitness center. **Cons:** isolated from Center City; limited dining options outside hotel; surroundings can be noisy. ⓢ *Rooms from: $264 ⊠ 8800 Bartram Ave., Southwest Philadelphia ☎ 215/365–2254 ⊕ www.marriott.com/hotels/travel/phlfa-fairfield-inn-philadelphia-airport ➷ 97 rooms ⦿l Free Breakfast.*

##  Nightlife

Once known primarily for the Italian Market and cheesesteak icons Pat's and Geno's, South Philly has rapidly developed into the place for low-key hang-out spots with great drinks.

### Dolphin Tavern

**DANCE CLUBS |** An constant stream of DJs rolls through the Dolphin every month, with something for everyone, from throwback nights featuring only vinyl to house music or soul. The drinks are dive bar standards: beer, simple cocktails, and plenty of them. ⊠ *1539 S. Broad St., South Philadelphia ☎ 215/278–7950 ⊕ www.dolphinphilly.com.*

### Sidecar Bar & Grille

**BARS |** An anchor establishment south of Center City, the Sidecar delivers an approachable mix of craft beer on tap, creative but satisfying pub food, and positive vibes. The narrow but cozy street-level bar is complemented by a roomier second-floor hangout that can host events and get-togethers in addition to everyday hangs. Specialties of the kitchen include handmade pastas and charcuterie, hearty sandwiches, and Detroit-style pizzas. ⊠ *2201 Christian St., South Philadelphia ☎ 215/732–3429 ⊕ www.thesidecarbar.com.*

Chapter 9

# UNIVERSITY CITY AND WEST PHILADELPHIA

Updated by
Joshua McIlvain

 Sights
★★★☆☆

 Restaurants
★★★☆☆

 Hotels
★★★☆☆

 Shopping
★★★☆☆

 Nightlife
★★☆☆☆

# NEIGHBORHOOD SNAPSHOT

## TOP EXPERIENCES

- **Penn Museum:** A world-class treasury of global antiquities.

- **Institute of Contemporary Art:** Andy Warhol, Robert Mapplethorpe, and Laurie Anderson have all shown their work at this exhibition space.

- **University of Pennsylvania:** This Ivy League school's leafy campus offers a bucolic respite, as well as libraries, an art gallery, and a performance venue that hosts national and international acts.

- **World Cafe Live:** A concert venue and the broadcast home of FM radio station WXPN hosts live performances from an array of artists, including XPN's "Free at Noon" daytime concert series.

## GETTING HERE

The blocks seem longer in West Philly. Unless you're a big walker or have access to a bike, you can take either a SEPTA bus or the Blue or Green Subway Line to University City. Otherwise, call an Uber.

If you're driving, street parking is easier to find here than in Center City, although it can be tight near the Penn and Drexel campuses when school's in session.

## PLANNING YOUR TIME

When school is in session, the students rushing to classes give the area its frenetic flavor. Allow half an hour each in the Arthur Ross Gallery and the Institute of Contemporary Art, two hours in the Penn Museum. Keep an eye out for concerts at World Cafe and performances at Penn Live Arts. A more vibrant nightlife is found on Baltimore Avenue between 47th and 50th Streets.

## QUICK BITES

- **Franklin's Table.** A food hall with a variety of grab-and-go options from some of the city's better eateries. ⊠ *3401 Walnut St., University City*

- **Honeysuckle Provisions.** Fresh-from-the-farm goods, tasty bites both healthy or indulgent, and great coffee. ⊠ *310 S. 48th St., West Philadelphia* ⊕ *www.honeysuckleprovisions.com*

- **Wah-Gi-Wah.** This no-frills Pakistani eatery specializes in *lahore chargha*, a fiery fried-chicken dish. ⊠ *4447 Chestnut St., West Philadelphia* ⊕ *www.wahgiwah.com*

## DID YOU KNOW?

- Citywide, West Philadelphia has a progressive reputation, given its historical importance to the American civil rights movement, artistic leanings, and embrace of global influences, in the form of both the international student population and its many established immigrant enclaves. African, Caribbean, South Asian, and West Indian influences are palpable throughout the area, present in everything from the many languages spoken on the street to the diversity of authentic restaurants offering authentic cuisine.

On the side of the Schuylkill River opposite Center City, West Philadelphia is rich in heritage and personality. Here you'll find University City, the academic heart of the region given the confluence of college campuses, as well as a collection of charming neighborhoods characterized by Victorian architecture and ample green space.

University City is the portion of West Philadelphia that includes the campuses of the University of Pennsylvania, Drexel University, the University of the Sciences, and several other institutions. It also has the University City Science Center, the Annenberg Center for the Performing Arts, an impressive collection of Victorian houses, and a variety of moderately priced restaurants, stores, and lively bars. The neighborhood stretches from the Schuylkill River west to 50th Street, and from Woodland Avenue north to Powelton Avenue and Market Street.

This area was once the city proper's western suburbs, where wealthy Philadelphians built estates and established summer villages. It officially became part of the city in 1854. In the 1870s, the University of Pennsylvania moved its main campus here from Center City. Though closely associated with academia, University City is also a fast-growing professional and residential hub, its diverse population working and living throughout distinct pockets like Cedar Park, Powelton Village, and Spruce Hill.

 Sights

### Arthur Ross Gallery

ART GALLERY | Penn's official art gallery contains treasures from the university's collections—especially prints and drawings—and traveling exhibitions. The gallery shares its historical-landmark building, designed by Frank Furness, with the Fisher Fine Arts Library. ✉ *220 S. 34th St., between Walnut and Spruce Sts., University City* ☏ *215/898–2083* ⊕ *www.arthurrossgallery.org* 🎟 *Free* ☉ *Closed Mon. and holidays.*

### Fisher Fine Arts Library

NOTABLE BUILDING | The University of Penn campus is worth a stroll around, and this is one of the few places the public is welcome (admittance is 9–6 weekdays for non-Penn visitors). One of the finest examples of the work of Frank Furness, this was the most iconoclastic library building in America when it opened in 1891. The acclaimed Philadelphia architect adorned the enormous reading room with Romanesque archways and skylights, and separated the soaring stairwell from study areas and stacks to minimize distractions. The unusual aesthetic extends to the exterior, with its

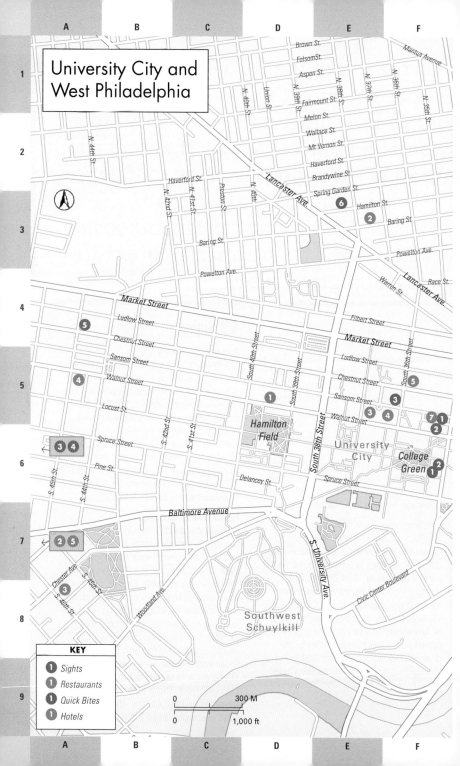

## Sights ▼

## Restaurants ▼

## Quick Bites ▼

## Hotels ▼

terra-cotta panels, short heavy columns, and gargoyles on the north end. The mottoes inscribed on many of the original leaded-glass windows were chosen by Horace Howard Furness, Frank's older brother and a Shakespeare scholar on Penn's faculty. Energetic visitors can make the long climb up the main staircase to see the upper half of the tower. ⊠ *220 S. 34th St., University City* ☏ *215/898–8325* ⊕ *www.library.upenn. edu/finearts* ⊠ *Free (must have a photo ID)* ⊗ *Closed weekends; may be closed or restricted to the public during exams, school holidays, and campus events* Ⓜ *34th and Market Sts. (SEPTA Market-Frankford Blue Line); 33rd and Market Sts. and 36th and Sansom Sts. (SEPTA subway-surface Green Lines, Rtes. 11, 13, 34, 36).*

### Institute of Contemporary Art

**ART MUSEUM** | This museum, part of the University of Pennsylvania, has established a reputation for identifying promising contemporary artists and championing them at critical points in their careers. Among the creators who have had exhibitions at ICA and later gone on to international prominence are Andy Warhol (his first-ever solo museum show, in 1965), Laurie Anderson, and Robert Mapplethorpe. Its modest size is a refreshing break, and ICA is dedicated to the one or two exhibitions they show at a time. Closing between exhibitions is not uncommon, so check what's up before you go. ⊠ *118 S. 36th St., at Sansom St., University City* ☏ *215/898–7108* ⊕ *www. icaphila.org* ⊠ *Free* ⊗ *Closed Mon. and Tues.* Ⓜ *SEPTA Green Line Trolley stop at 36th St. (University of Pennsylvania).*

### ★ Penn Museum

**HISTORY MUSEUM** | This is considered one of the world's finest archaeological and anthropological museums and research institutes. The vast collection includes a large Egyptian sphinx, numerous mummies, a crystal ball once owned by China's dowager empress, some of the oldest writing known to humanity—Sumerian cuneiform clay tablets—and 4,600-year-old golden jewels from the royal tombs of Ur (modern-day Iraq). Other collections focus on artifacts from Africa, Asia, Central and North America, ancient Europe, and more. Much revamped in the past 10 years, today the museum mixes in contemporary culture as well to connect the past to the present, such as with Native American tribes, who helped reimagine the North American galleries. Two of the main Egyptian galleries will be closed until about 2027, but many of the Egyptian highlights remain on view in other rooms. The museum specializes in tours like Ancient Alcohol or Global Guides, where guides are native to the area they are speaking about. You can download self-guiding tours like Amazing Artifacts from the museum's website, where you can also check out what events might be happening during your visit. The koi pond and gardens out front are free to enter and a great hideaway to bring your lunch or just have a little respite in the sun. ⊠ *3260 South St., University City* ⊕ *Parking is around the corner on Convention Ave.* ☏ *215/898–4000* ⊕ *www.penn.museum* ⊠ *$18; active military and teachers free* ⊗ *Closed Mon.* Ⓜ *Market-Frankford Subway Line, 34th and Market Sts.; Blue and Green Line Trolley Rtes. 11, 13, 34, 36.*

### Penn Park

**CITY PARK** | Unveiled in 2011, this 24-acre park stretches along the western side of the Schuylkill River and serves as a green-space conduit connecting Center City and the University of Pennsylvania campus. The park offers natural grass and turf playing fields, 12 tennis courts for public use, and bike and walking trails; its most striking feature is an elevated walk offering pedestrians panoramic views of the Philadelphia skyline. A friendly culture of pickup soccer exists here on the weekends, with small nets to accommodate games. ⊠ *3000 Walnut St., University City* ☏ *215/898–5986* ⊕ *www.*

Penn Museum's vast collection includes priceless artifacts from Africa, Asia, Central and North America, and ancient Europe.

*facilities.upenn.edu/maps/locations/penn-park* ✉ *Free.*

### The Tiberino Museum

**ART MUSEUM** | A truly unique experience, the creative legacy of the Tiberinos, a dynamic family of artists sometimes referred to as "the West Philly Wyeths," is celebrated at this indoor-outdoor museum built out of the family's Powelton Village home. Though Ellen Powell and Joseph Tiberino, the matriarch and patriarch of this artistic clan, have passed away, their paintings, murals, and sculptures are preserved for future generations by their children, who incorporate their own original work, along with contributions from dozens of other artists, into the mix. ✉ *3819 Hamilton St., University City* 🕿 *215/386–3784* ⊕ *tiberinomuseum. com* ✉ *$10 suggested donation* ◷ *Visits by appointment only.*

### ★ World Cafe Live

**PERFORMANCE VENUE** | While the venue gets its name from the well-known WXPN-FM program, and WXPN is housed in the same building, World Cafe Live is in fact a separate entity, even though aesthetically it hews to the XPN sound of acoustic, independent, and world-beat contemporary music. There are two restaurants and two live concert spaces, the larger of which, Downstairs Live, can pack in up to 650 concertgoers. If you can land gratis tickets via online pre-registration, XPN's "Free at Noon" is a wholly unique concert experience—notable artists break the routine, performing stripped-down lunchtime sets for an intimate crowd. Adele, John Legend, Kacey Musgraves, Pixies, and the Pretenders are just a few of the big names who have graced the daytime stage. The upstairs venue is more of a drop-in place to listen to quality, mostly local bands. ✉ *3025 Walnut St., University City* 🕿 *215/222–1400* ⊕ *www. worldcafelive.com.*

## 🍴 Restaurants

In University City you can enjoy the many affordable, funky eateries geared toward Penn and Drexel students. West Philly features some of the city's best ethnic dining along Baltimore Avenue, from Ethiopian to Lebanese.

### City Tap House

**$$ | AMERICAN |** A popular hangout with the Penn crowd, this large, contemporary bar and grill pours a staggering six dozen draft options, with a heavy focus on local and regional craft beer. The gastropub menu offers a little of everything, from burgers and brick-oven pizzas to mussels and prime steaks, which are best enjoyed out on the terrace around one of five stone fire pits overlooking Walnut Street. **Known for:** craft beer on tap; outdoor terrace; young and lively crowd. $ *Average main: $20* ⊠ *The Radian, 3925 Walnut St., University City* ☎ *215/662–0105* ⊕ *www.citytaphouseucity.com.*

### Dahlak

**$ | ETHIOPIAN |** A Baltimore Avenue institution, Dahlak is often credited with introducing the cuisines of Ethiopia and Eritrea to a wider Philadelphian audience. Family owned and operated, it serves signatures like *doro wat* (chicken stew spiced with zingy berbere) and *beg tibs* (stir-fried lamb with peppers and onions), accompanied by ample *injera,* the spongy bread traditionally used as a utensil. **Known for:** Ethiopian/Eritrean cuisine; vegetarian friendly; DJ nights. $ *Average main: $15* ⊠ *4708 Baltimore Ave., University City* ☎ *215/726–6464* ⊕ *www. dahlakrestaurant.com* ☾ *No lunch.*

### Kpod

**$$ | JAPANESE |** Formerly the futuristic Pod, Kpod sports a brightly colored look that's both modern and retro (i.e. made to look like a time that never was) complimented by a lot of wood details that make it comfortably familiar, like a very stylish family restaurant. Diners can opt for the snacky, fun route with wings, *mandu* (dumplings), and cocktails, or really dig into the heftier stews, meats, and noodle soups. **Known for:** lively atmosphere; Korean specialties; good for sharing. $ *Average main: $24* ⊠ *3636*

*Sansom St., University City* ☎ *215/387–1803* ⊕ *www.kpodrestaurant.com* ☾ *No lunch weekends.*

### ★ Manakeesh Cafe

**$ | LEBANESE | FAMILY |** A Spruce Hill staple, Manakeesh specializes in the Lebanese flatbreads of the same name. Served warm from the oven, the puffy, round loaves come with both traditional toppings (za'atar, kafta) and nontraditional ones (turkey bacon–egg–cheese, cheesesteak), which speak to the diverse crowd that fills the café-style space. **Known for:** Lebanese/Middle Eastern cuisine; housebaked Middle Eastern pastries; coffee and fruit smoothies. $ *Average main: $7* ⊠ *4420 Walnut St., University City* ☎ *215/921–2135* ⊕ *www.manakeeshcafe.com* ☾ *Closed 1–2 pm Fri. for prayer.*

### Vientiane Cafe

**$$ | LAO |** The Phanthavong family has long served the soulful cuisine of its native Laos to the West Philly community, starting with a spartan street tent that blossomed into this homey, friendly BYOB restaurant. Don't miss the truly heartwarming Lao soups—the King's soup being a winner—or the house-made pork sausages and yellow curry fried rice. **Known for:** Lao cuisine; adventurous dishes; BYOB and cash-only. $ *Average main: $20* ⊠ *4728 Baltimore Ave., University City* ☎ *215/726–1095* ⊕ *www. vientiane-cafe.com* ▭ *No credit cards* ☾ *Closed Sun.*

### Walnut Street Café

**$$$ | AMERICAN |** Taking up the ground floor of the FMC Tower, home to the AKA University City, the Walnut Street Café serves refined new American cuisine in a light-flooded, art deco-inspired space. Open for breakfast, lunch, and dinner, plus weekend brunch, the restaurant's edible highlights include house-baked bread and pastries, elegant raw seafood platters, and rotating handmade pasta. **Known for:** something for everyone; innovative wine list; open most of the day. $ *Average main: $28* ⊠ *Cira Centre*

*South, 2929 Walnut St., University City* ☎ *215/867–8067* 🌐 *www.walnutstreetcafe.com* 🕒 *No dinner Sun.–Tues.*

**White Dog Cafe**

$$$ | **AMERICAN** | White Dog did farm-to-table long before the concept rose to national prominence, and the Sansom Street stalwart continues to remain fresh, lively, and unpretentious. The menu specializes in sustainable foods ethically sourced from the region—think simple cooking that highlights the beauty of Kennett Square mushrooms, Lancaster beef, or Chester County goat cheese. **Known for:** farm-to-table cooking; local and seasonal ingredients; casual-chic decor. [$] *Average main: $27* ✉ *3420 Sansom St., University City* ☎ *215/386–9224* 🌐 *www.whitedog.com.*

## ☕ Coffee and Quick Bites

**Avril 50**

$ | **CAFÉ** | They don't make shops like this University City mainstay anymore. An international newsstand, stuffed with foreign periodicals, newspapers, postcards, and hip art publications, they also run a café of sorts, offering coffee, tea, and chocolate, and an old-school smoke shop selling specialty tobacco products. **Known for:** a coffee (or tea) stop while exploring; all sorts of magazines; no internet. [$] *Average main: $3* ✉ *3406 Sansom St., University City* ☎ *215/222–6108* 🌐 *www.avril50.com* 🕒 *No dinner.*

**Franklin's Table**

$ | **CONTEMPORARY** | At 8,000 square feet, with 175 indoor seats and even more room on an alfresco patio, this multi-concept food hall across from Penn's campus dishes out diverse quick-serve options for hungry students (these kids don't know how good they've got it!) and faculty. Choose between Japanese (DK Sushi), Israeli falafel (Goldie), specialty sandwiches (High Street Provisions, KQ Burger), and artisanal pizza (Pitruco). **Known for:** lunch scene (eateries close between 3 and 8 pm); a food court with known restaurant outlets; grab-and-go options. [$] *Average main: $10* ✉ *3401 Walnut St., University City* ☎ *215/746–0123* 🌐 *www.shopsatpenn.com/franklins-table* 🕒 *Closed Sun.*

**Honeysuckle Provisions**

$ | **AFRICAN** | This popular café and market, with offerings sourced from the owners' own farm as well as other predominantly local Black farmers and producers, is a great stop either for coffee and pastries (try the pop tarts) or eggs, grits, and fresh pork sausage. You can be healthy with their salads and "BLACKEYED-PEAscrapple" (a vegetarian version of the Pennsylvania breakfast meat that you don't ask the origins of), or indulgent with The Haitian sandwich, a cheesy fried pork shoulder mix. **Known for:** refined touch on basics; goods from their farm; African American and Haitian cooking. [$] *Average main: $10* ✉ *310 S. 48th St., University City* ☎ *215/307–3316* 🌐 *www.honeysuckleprovisions.com* 🕒 *Closed Mon.–Wed.*

**ReAnimator Coffee**

$ | **CAFÉ** | ReAnimator stands out in the Philadelphia coffee scene thanks to its dedicated sourcing of single-origin beans, dynamic roasting techniques, and smartly designed cafés—at five and counting placed throughout the city. Tucked away in the tiny Garden Court area, removed from the University City hubbub, this West Philadelphia outpost is a calming caffeinated oasis, a clean minimalist shop with a laid-back vibe. **Known for:** single-origin coffees; espresso drinks; relaxed atmosphere. [$] *Average main: $5* ✉ *4705 Pine St., University City* ☎ *215/921–5953* 🌐 *www.reanimatorcoffee.com.*

**Wah-Gi-Wah**

$ | **PAKISTANI** | This no-frills Pakistani eatery specializes in lahore chargha, a fiery fried-chicken dish. But that's not the only dish worth seeking out here—they cook up a wide variety of flavorful halal meat skewers in the tandoor, along with hot-from-the-oven naan and roti breads, and vegetarian-friendly offerings. **Known for:** Pakistani fried chicken; fresh naan and roti; vegetarian options. [$] *Average main: $13* ✉ *4447 Chestnut St., University City* ☎ *215/921–5597* 🌐 *www.wahgiwah.com.*

## Hotels

**AKA University City**
$$$$ | **HOTEL** | This property, with apartment-style rooms, undoubtedly has the best 360-degree views of the city. **Pros:** sizable rooms; close to 30th Street Station, World Cafe Live, and UPenn; indoor pool has excellent views. **Cons:** office building aesthetic; not on a particularly interesting block; not for the boutique-minded. [$] *Rooms from: $395* ✉ *Cira Centre South, 2929 Walnut St., University City* ☎ *215/372–9000* 🌐 *www.stayaka.com* 🛏 *130 rooms* 🍴 *Free Breakfast.*

**Akwaaba Philadelphia**
$$ | **B&B/INN** | Akwaaba is a collective of five mid-Atlantic bed-and-breakfasts founded by Monique Greenwood, the former editor-in-chief of *Essence*, and her husband, Glenn Pogue; Philadelphia's outpost occupies a circa-1880s porched residence on a leafy residential block just north of the main University City drag. **Pros:** charming historic setting; hotel-style concierge service in a B&B; complimentary afternoon wine and refreshments. **Cons:** somewhat removed from sights; street parking; not for children under 12. [$] *Rooms from: $230* ✉ *3709 Baring St., University City* ☎ *866/466–3855* 🌐 *www.akwaaba.com/akwaaba-philadelphia* 🛏 *6 rooms* 🍴 *Free Breakfast.*

**The Gables**
$$ | **B&B/INN** | Built in 1889 by architect Willis Hale and first occupied by a prominent doctor and his family, this ornate mansion is a wonderful place for a B&B—the ground-floor parlor and entryway feature natural cherry and chestnut wood, and the guest rooms have oak floors with elaborate inlays of mahogany, ash, and cherry. **Pros:** off the beaten path; a dream for lovers of Victorian; free parking. **Cons:** removed from central areas, attractions; Victorian style can be overwhelming for some; No children under 10. [$] *Rooms from: $250* ✉ *4520 Chester Ave., University City* ☎ *215/662–1918* 🌐 *www.gablesbb.com* 🛏 *10 rooms* 🍴 *Free Breakfast.*

**The Inn at Penn, a Hilton Hotel**
$$$ | **HOTEL** | With a grand lobby staircase and a beautiful wood-paneled living room complete with a working fireplace (and cocktails), this hotel near the University of Pennsylvania offers a warm, collegiate atmosphere in the thick of the action. **Pros:** collegiate feel near major campuses; amenities such as in-room iPads; handsome and comfortable communal areas. **Cons:** rates can fluctuate around collegiate events and gatherings; away from Center City; rooms have a ho-hum style. [$] *Rooms from: $259* ✉ *3600 Sansom St., University City* ☎ *215/222–0200, 800/445–8667* 🌐 *www.theinnatpenn.com* 🛏 *249 rooms* 🍴 *No Meals.*

**Sheraton Philadelphia University City**
$$ | **HOTEL** | With plush beds and 52-inch flat-screen televisions, spacious work areas, and complimentary Internet access, this hotel offers a nice balance of luxury and practicality. **Pros:** convenient location; good views; pet friendly options. **Cons:** check-in during big weekends can be slow; rates vary widely with university events; style is a little dated. [$] *Rooms from: $250* ✉ *3549 Chestnut St., University City* ☎ *215/387–8000, 877/459–1146* 🌐 *www.sheraton.com/universitycity* 🛏 *332 rooms* 🍴 *No Meals.*

University City is home to radio station WXPN-FM, which does the popular NPR music program "World Cafe." If you like acoustic, independent, and world-beat music, try for tickets when you're in town.

##  Nightlife

### Carbon Copy

**BREWPUBS** | Picking up where the last brewpub (Dock Street) at this location—an old fire station—left off, Carbon Copy provides an excellent selection of in-house brews accompanied by tasty wood-fired pizzas. The owners/beermakers have come from creating beer in numerous celebrated craft breweries from San Diego (Modern Times) to the Philly area (Tired Hands), and their beers are often defined by richness and depth of flavor. ✉ *701 S. 50th St., University City* ⊕ *www.carboncopyphilly.com.*

## Performing Arts

### Penn Live Arts

**ARTS CENTERS** | Best described as artsy but accessible, Penn Live Arts presents national and international works of dance, music, circus, theater, and multidisciplinary groups at the Annenberg Center of Performing Arts. The performing arts complex on the UPenn campus features the 115-seat Bruce Montgomery Theatre and the 936-seat Zellerbach. This is a good bet to find high-quality performances. ✉ *Annenberg Center, 3680 Walnut St., University City* ☎ *215/898–3900* ⊕ *pennlivearts.org.*

## Shopping

Most of the action in University City revolves around the universities, specifically the University of Pennsylvania and Drexel University. An active retail scene has sprouted around the UPenn campus to serve that huge population of students. A pocket of interesting, eclectic shops and restaurants also exists farther west along Baltimore Avenue from about 47th Street to 50th Street.

### ART GALLERIES

#### VIX Emporium

**OTHER SPECIALTY STORE** | Owned by married couple Sean and Emily Dorn—he's a graphic designer, she's a jewelry maker—this boutique stocks a curated array of one-of-a-kind items, many of them crafted by Philadelphia artists. At VIX (Roman numerals for the "5009" address), you'll also find locally made soaps, prints, greeting cards, candles, shirts, home wares, and more. The quaint shop still features the original cabinetry and beveled-glass windowpanes from its former life as a millinery, nearly a century ago. ⊠ *5009 Baltimore Ave., University City* ☎ *215/471–7700* ⊕ *www.vixemporium.com.*

## BOOKSTORES
### House of Our Own

BOOKS | Located in an old brownstone, this is a book lover's bookstore, albeit flanked by University of Pennsylvania fraternity residences. Two floors of rambling rooms are stacked with shelves reaching up to the ceilings, boasting an enormous mix of literature, course texts for students, and used books alike. You can spend an hour getting lost in the world of books, and the promise of wisdom. ⊠ *3920 Spruce St., University City* ☎ *215/222–1576* ⊕ *www.shopsatpenn.com/house-our-own-books.*

### Penn Bookstore

BOOKS | At more than 50,000 square feet, this shop, operated by Barnes & Noble, is one of the largest academic bookstores in the United States. Renovated in 2018, it offers best sellers and tomes from the University of Pennsylvania faculty, loads of insignia clothing and memorabilia, a multimedia section, and space for regular author events. ⊠ *3601 Walnut St., University City* ☎ *215/898–7595* ⊕ *www.upenn.edu/bookstore.*

## HOME DECOR
### Hello World

OTHER SPECIALTY STORE | A tastefully curated destination for unique gifts, this bright lifestyle boutique sells artisan-crafted jewelry, whimsical housewares, colorful handbags, and children's toys, as well as customizable mid-century modern furniture. ⊠ *3610 Sansom St., University City* ☎ *215/382–5207* ⊕ *www.shophelloworld.com.*

## MARKETS
### Clark Park Farmers Market

FOOD | Coming to Saturday's farmers' market, open 10 am–2 pm, is reason enough to stroll about Clark Park with a coffee, fresh bread, and a hunk of cheese. The market grows in size in relation to the fairness of the weather and the park, especially from May into September when there are often events on weekends, including the Clark Park Music Fest, Shakespeare in Clark Park, and craft fairs. This 9-acre city park is an inviting introduction to the all-are-welcome, multicultural energy so closely associated with West Philadelphia. ⊠ *Clark Park, 4300 Baltimore Ave., University City* ☎ *215/552–8186* ⊕ *www.friendsofclarkpark.org.*

# Chapter 10

# NORTHERN LIBERTIES AND FISHTOWN

Updated by
Maddy Sweitzer-Lamme

⦿ Sights
★★★★★

🍴 Restaurants
★★★★★

🏨 Hotels
★★★☆☆

🛍 Shopping
★★★★★

🍸 Nightlife
★★★★★

# NEIGHBORHOOD SNAPSHOT

## TOP EXPERIENCES

■ **Food scene:** Fishtown and Northern Liberties are home to a diverse array of cuisines and some of Philadelphia's best restaurants.

■ **Breweries:** With major players like Yards, Philadelphia Brewing, Goose Island, and Evil Genius, beer fans have plenty of spots to enjoy a pint.

■ **Nightlife:** On any given night, but especially on weekends, the bars along 2nd Street, Frankford Avenue, and Girard Avenue welcome troves of people looking to party until last call.

■ **Shopping:** There are cool indie shops in both neighborhoods.

■ **People watching:** Fishtown and NoLibs are very young neighborhoods with lots of people out and about.

## GETTING HERE

SEPTA's Market-Frankford subway line makes stops in the heart of Fishtown via the Girard stop and a few blocks from the hustle and bustle of Northern Liberties at the Spring Garden stop. It's a quick, 10-minute subway ride from City Hall to both stops, which are just one stop apart from each other. As far as driving, street parking is available throughout both neighborhoods, along with a number of paid parking lots and a free parking lot at the Piazza.

## PLANNING YOUR TIME

Depending on your interests, the time you visit these neighborhoods will vary. Night owls can enjoy plenty of late-night food and drink options, along with concerts and dance parties. Those who enjoy daytime strolls can visit the neighborhoods for shopping, brunch, and festivals at set points throughout the year.

## QUICK BITES

■ **Joe's Steaks and Soda Shop.** Open until 3 am on the weekends—and for lunch and dinner before that—Joe's is a go-to spot for all-day and all-night cheesesteaks, burgers, loaded fries, milkshakes, and sodas at the corner of Girard and Frankford Avenues. ⊠ *1 W. Girard Ave., Fishtown* ⊕ *www.joessteaks.com* ⚇ *Girard Station, Market-Frankford Line*

■ **One Shot Coffee.** Set away from the hustle and bustle of 2nd Street, this two-level café serves Stumptown coffee beverages, sweet lattes, herbal teas, and an assortment of brunch-ready food items. ⊠ *217 W. George St., Northern Liberties* ⊕ *oneshotcoffeecafe.com* ⚇ *Girard Station, Market-Frankford Line*

■ **Middle Child Clubhouse.** The Fishtown outpost of this Center City favorite serves breakfast in the morning and sandwiches during the day, making it a good spot to rest up for an afternoon of exploring. ⊠ *1232 N. Front St., Fishtown* ⊕ *middlechildphilly.com*

As Philly has grown as a city in the metaphorical sense, so have the borders of Center City. Nowadays, it's a regular part of daily life for locals (and visitors) to spend time (sometimes most of their time) in outlying neighborhoods like Northern Liberties and Fishtown, that, among other things, offer a bevy of culinary distractions.

An influx of new residents and businesses has brought Northern Liberties and the nearby neighborhoods of Fishtown, Kensington, and Port Richmond into the zeitgeist. Specifically Northern Liberties and Fishtown have evolved into some of Philly's coolest neighborhoods, with restaurants by award-winning chefs, picture-ready bars, and concert venues that host some of the biggest musicians in the world. While they are beginning to expand, Kensington and Port Richmond are still largely residential and have a working-class feel, though much of the area's old industry—including printing, textiles, and metalworking—is long gone.

## Northern Liberties

Once a postindustrial graveyard, Northern Liberties has been transformed over the last decade into a haven whose hipster edge has faded into a family-friendly neighborhood. At the northern end of the district, the The Piazza, redevelopment of the former Schmidt's Brewery draws a young professional crowd.

## ◉ Sights

**Edgar Allan Poe National Historic Site**
HISTORIC HOME | One of America's most original writers, Edgar Allan Poe (1809–49), lived here from 1843 to 1844; it's the only one of his Philadelphia residences still standing. During that time some of his best-known short stories were published: "The Telltale Heart," "The Black Cat," and "The Gold Bug." You can tour the three-story brick house; to evoke the spirit of Poe, the National Park Service displays first-edition manuscripts and other rare books and offers interactive exhibits as well. An adjoining house has exhibits on Poe and his family, his work habits, and his literary contemporaries; there's also an eight-minute film and a small Poe library and reading room. A statue of a raven helps set the mood. The site is five blocks north of Market Street and just a stone's throw away from Spring Garden Street. SEPTA bus 47 travels on 7th Street to Green Street, where you should disembark. ✉ 532 N. 7th St., Northern Liberties ☎ 215/597–8780 ⊕ www.nps.gov/edal 🖼 Free ⊘ Closed Mon.–Thurs.

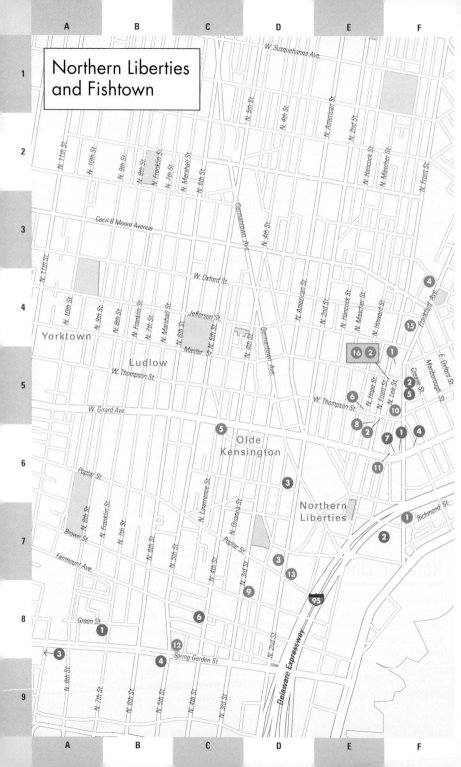

# Northern Liberties and Fishtown

10

## Sights ▼

1 Edgar Allan Poe
   National Historic Site............. **B8**
2 Philadelphia Distilling ............. **F7**
3 The Rail Park ...................... **A8**
4 Yards Brewing Company......... **B9**

## Restaurants ▼

1 Elwood ............................. **F7**
2 Front Street Cafe.................. **E5**
3 Heritage............................ **D7**
4 Kalaya Thai Kitchen ............... **F4**
5 Las Cazuelas ...................... **C6**
6 Laser Wolf.......................... **E5**
7 Martha ............................. **H1**
8 Middle Child Clubhouse............ **I2**
9 North Third ........................ **D8**
10 Pizzeria Beddia .................... **F5**
11 Sancho Pistola's ................... **F6**
12 Silk City
    Diner, Bar and Lounge ............ **C8**
13 Standard Tap....................... **D7**
14 Sulimay's Restaurant.............. **H5**
15 Suraya ............................. **F4**
16 Wm. Mulherin's Sons ............. **F5**

## Quick Bites ▼

1 Joe's Steaks +
   Soda Shop Fishtown .............. **F6**
2 La Colombe......................... **F5**
3 One Shot Coffee ................... **D6**
4 Pizza Shackamaxon............... **F6**
5 REAP Mini Mart.................... **F5**
6 Suya Suya ......................... **C8**
7 Weckerly's Ice Cream............. **F6**

## Hotels ▼

1 Lokal Hotel Fishtown .............. **F5**
2 Wm. Mulherin's Sons ............. **F5**

0        1,000 ft

0     200 m

**KEY**

1 *Sights*
1 *Restaurants*
1 *Quick Bites*
1 *Hotels*

Fishtown

95

Delaware River

### The Rail Park

**PROMENADE** | **FAMILY** | The first phase of The Rail Park is a quarter-mile trail that turned an abandoned, elevated train line into a public park lined with greenery and offering stunning views of the city. The project is envisioned to eventually span 3 miles from near the Art Museum into Northern Liberties. While the open part of the park is small, it's a lovely way to understand the future of the city's unused spaces. There are swings for children, bike racks, and lots of native plants. ⊠ *1300 Noble St., Northern Liberties* ⊕ *www.therailpark.org* ⊠ *Free.*

### Yards Brewing Company

**BREWERY** | Yards is the oldest continuously operating craft brewer in the city, and runs a sprawling brewery and taproom. Guided tours ($10, 40 minutes) are offered daily for those 21 and over and include a beer sample, a full "walk-about" beer, and a souvenir. The bar features 20 taps of their signature beers—Loyal Lager, Philadelphia Pale Ale, Love Stout, to name a few—as well as limited releases only available in the taproom. The kitchen includes classic pub fare as well as Philly favorites like the Yards IPA Pretzel and a Roast Pork sandwich. ⊠ *500 Spring Garden St., Northern Liberties* ☎ *215/525–0175* ⊕ *yardsbrewing.com.*

## 🍴 Restaurants

When it comes to dining options, Northern Liberties is the more established of Center City's outlying neighborhoods, with 20-year-old gastropubs and comfort-driven converted diners.

### Heritage

**$$** | **MODERN AMERICAN** | A spacious neighborhood hangout on bustling 2nd Street, Heritage is an industrial-style restaurant where you'll find live music on the dining-room stage, live herbs creeping over the reclaimed ceiling beams, and lively cooking from chef Mackenzie Hilton. Regulars gravitate toward the hearty sandwiches served with crisp fries, the signature cocktails, which are largely named after classic songs, or one of the 30-plus draft-beer options. **Known for:** live music; seasonally focused menu; extensive draft-beer list. $ *Average main: $20* ⊠ *914 N. 2nd St., Northern Liberties* ☎ *215/627–7500* ⊕ *heritage.life* ⊗ *No lunch weekdays.*

### Las Cazuelas

**$$** | **MEXICAN** | **FAMILY** | This laid-back, family-run place is an anomaly in sceney Northern Liberties. The colors, both inside and out, are warm and bright and the food is simple and rather gently spiced, apropos of the family's roots in the town of Puebla. **Known for:** hearty weekend brunch; BYOB margaritas; convenience for large groups. $ *Average main: $18* ⊠ *426–28 W. Girard Ave., Northern Liberties* ☎ *215/351–9144* ⊕ *www.lascazuelastogo.com* ⊗ *Closed Mon.*

### North Third

**$** | **AMERICAN** | North Third was one of the first restaurants to settle in Northern Liberties at the infancy of the neighborhood's transformation. The menu hasn't changed much, mostly because locals love hits like the thick burger, crisp fried chicken, and house-made pierogies. **Known for:** late-night food; exciting craft-beer list; sought-after buffalo wings. $ *Average main: $16* ⊠ *801 N. 3rd St., Northern Liberties* ☎ *215/413–3666* ⊕ *www.norththird.com* ⊗ *No lunch weekdays.*

### Silk City Diner, Bar, and Lounge

**$** | **AMERICAN** | Mark Bee, the local restaurateur behind favorite gastropub North Third, bought the Silk City Diner in 2006, polished off its grease-coated, 1950s-era pink Formica counter, and started serving updated comfort food. Menu items include a fierce plate of buttermilk fried chicken, deep-fried veggie wings, the city's best bowl of mac and cheese (baked with a garlic-bread crust),

A National Historic Site, American author Edgar Allan Poe lived here from 1843 to 1844; it's the only one of his Philadelphia residences still standing.

and some lighter fare (salads and roasted veggies) should you want to go next door to the bar and lounge and dance 'til dawn beneath the disco ball. **Known for:** brunch every day; brightly colored outdoor dining space; late-night dancing. $ *Average main: $16* ⊠ *435 Spring Garden St., Northern Liberties* ☎ *215/592–8838* ⊕ *www.silkcityphilly.com.*

### Standard Tap

$ | **AMERICAN** | This neighborhood gastro-pub is a Northern Liberties fixture, popular with the young professionals who populate this particular neighborhood, and for good reason. The frequently changing menu, presented unpretentiously on a chalkboard, is much more ambitious—and much tastier—than you'd expect from average bar food, and since you're in a bar, you can wash down the shellfish, terrines, local-veggie-forward salads, and wild game with one of the local microbrews on tap. **Known for:** local draft beers; multiple areas for hanging out throughout the multifloor, indoor-out-door space; local produce. $ *Average main: $12* ⊠ *901 N. 2nd St., Northern Liberties* ☎ *215/238–0630* ⊕ *www.standardtap.com* ⊗ *No lunch weekdays.*

## ☕ Coffee and Quick Bites

### One Shot Coffee

$ | **CAFÉ** | Serving Stumptown coffee in a bi-level space, One Shot Coffee is a hidden spot for solid beverages and snacks, set a few blocks back from the hustle and bustle of the Piazza. The menu features café staples like cold brew, drip coffee, flavored lattes, hot tea, and more, in addition to brunch-focused fare like breakfast burritos, egg sandwiches, and croissants. **Known for:** seasonal lattes; upstairs library; vegetarian-friendly menu. $ *Average main: $5* ⊠ *217 W. George St., Northern Liberties* ☎ *215/627–1620* ⊕ *oneshotcoffeecafe.com* ⊗ *No dinner.*

### Suya Suya

$ | **AFRICAN** | Suya Suya's owner-chef Dera Nd-Ezuma was raised in Nigeria before moving to South Jersey as a teenager. His restaurant highlights Nigerian and

West African dishes like its namesake *suya* (a spiced and grilled beef) and *jollof* rice (rice, tomatoes, onions, and spices) in a fast-casual environment—similar setup to a Chipotle or Sweetgreen—where guests can build their own bowls or enjoy suya and other proteins folded into tacos. **Known for:** BYOB; Nigerian street food like jollof rice (rice, tomatoes, onions, and spices) and suya (a spiced and grilled beef); build-your-own suya bowl. ⓢ *Average main: $15* ✉ *400 Fairmount Ave., Northern Liberties* ☎ *267/704–9033* ⊕ *www.suyasuya.co* ⏲ *Closed Sun.*

#  Nightlife

## BARS AND LOUNGES

### The Abbaye

**BARS** | NoLibs' reliable corner bar takes a Belgian approach, serving the appropriate beers (Chimay, Duvel) along with local crafts, in bottle and on draft. The hearty pub menu skews Euro, too, with some twists (vegan versions of wings and meatballs). ✉ *637 N. 3rd St., Northern Liberties* ☎ *215/627–6711* ⊕ *theabbaye. net/index.php.*

### North Bowl

**BARS** | Cleverly located in the thick of Northern Liberties' 2nd Street scene, this boozing-friendly bowling alley delivers in the tenpin department. The large, colorful space serves a snacky menu, featuring a big selection of wackily topped tater tots. ✉ *909 N. 2nd St., Northern Liberties* ☎ *215/238–2695* ⊕ *www.northbowlphilly. com.*

## MUSIC CLUBS

### Franklin Music Hall

**LIVE MUSIC** | Hip-hop artists, singer-songwriters, rock bands, and more regularly perform at the Franklin Music Hall, formerly known as the Electric Factory. With room for 3,000 guests, the venue offers a not-too-big, not-too-small viewing experience within a historic venue to boot. ✉ *421 N. 7th St., Northern Liberties* ☎ *215/627–1332* ⊕ *franklinmusichall.com.*

### Ortlieb's Lounge

**LIVE MUSIC** | This out-of-the-way, yet fan-favorite, venue in NoLibs has expanded its musical scope well beyond traditional jazz. The vintage barroom, named after a defunct Philly brewery, now books indie rock, hip-hop, funk, and pop music DJs. Hit up the bar for the cheap tacos, pretty close to the perfect drinking snacks. ✉ *847 N. 3rd St., Northern Liberties* ☎ *267/324–3348* ⊕ *ortliebsphilly.com.*

### Union Transfer

**LIVE MUSIC** | A former train station and restaurant converted into a haven for live music, Union Transfer might be Philly's best pound-for-pound place to catch a show. The spacious layout, impressive booking, and incredible sound make for an easygoing, one-of-a-kind concert experience. ✉ *1026 Spring Garden St., Northern Liberties* ☎ *215/232–2100* ⊕ *utphilly.com.*

#  Shopping

Northern Liberties is a taxi or bus ride from Old City, but it's worth checking out, especially if you combine an afternoon there with a dinner reservation at one of the area's best dining rooms, and live music at one of the area's bars or concert halls that host acts of all sizes.

## ART GALLERIES

### Dane Fine Art

**ART GALLERIES** | The specialty here is contemporary paintings and prints by such artists as Salvador Dalí, Peter Max, Marc Chagall, Louis Icart, Erté, Andy Warhol, Pablo Picasso, and Roy Lichtenstein. ✉ *606 Spring Garden St., Northern Liberties* ☎ *267/687–8378* ⊕ *www. danefineart.com.*

### Fleisher/Ollman Gallery

**ART GALLERIES** | Active since 1952, this gallery focuses on the creations of self-taught American artists with alternative and avant-garde origins, such as Sister Gertrude Morgan, Martín Ramírez, and Joseph Yoakum. ✉ *915 Spring Garden*

*Street, Suite 215, Northern Liberties* ☎ *215/545–7562* 🌐 *www.fleisher-ollman-gallery.com.*

# Fishtown

One of Philly's hottest neighborhoods, Fishtown spent the better part of the last century as a working-class enclave for Irish- and Polish-Americans. Longtime residents still live in Fishtown, proud flags fluttering from their tidy row homes, but the area has gotten way more diverse as the creative class took refuge in the affordable real estate, and families and speculators followed. Great independent restaurants and funky boutiques make it a great place to spend a day.

## Sights

### ★ Philadelphia Distilling

**DISTILLERY** | A move to a former warehouse in central Fishtown helped elevate Philadelphia Distilling's popularity and grow the following of its high-quality spirits. Today, its tasting room, shop, distillery—which is open for tours—and private-event space are all housed on East Allen Street mere steps away from the Fillmore and Punchline Philly. The bar is the focal point, with cocktails expertly made by experienced bartenders using Philadelphia Distilling's own Bluecoat American Dry Gin, Penn 1681 Vodka, Bluecoat Elderflower Gin, and more. The drink menu features cocktails rooted in ingredients like bitters and citrus, and elderflower and lavender. The food complements the inspired drink list with options like cheese boards, brisket grilled cheese, and snackable veggies. ✉ *25 E. Allen St., Fishtown* ☎ *215/671–0346* 🌐 *philadelphiadistilling.com* 🕓 *Closed Mon.–Wed.*

## Restaurants

Fishtown is home to the HQ of local roaster La Colombe and the pizza one glossy food magazine calls the best in America.

### Elwood

**$$$$** | **AMERICAN** | At Elwood, chef Adam Diltz's fine-dining homage to Philadelphia cuisine, the menu finds inspiration from the different eras of the city's history, showcased in locally sourced dishes like potato rolls, the Pennsylvania cheese plate, and Earl Keiser's guinea hen. Diners are presented with an amuse-bouche of venison scrapple, dotted with harissa ketchup and spiked onto deer antlers to start the dining experience. **Known for:** afternoon tea on weekends; family-style dining; BYOB. [$] *Average main: $50* ✉ *1007 Frankford Ave., Fishtown* ☎ *215/279–7427* 🌐 *elwoodrestaurant.com* 🕓 *Closed Mon. No lunch.*

### Front Street Cafe

**$** | **AMERICAN** | Beneath the Market-Frankford subway line lives this all-day dining destination suitable for guests seeking everything from smoothies to steak. The front door opens to the café section of the restaurant, which promises a menu of draft kombucha, hot teas, coffee, juices, and pastries, but beyond the café, the sit-down restaurant and outdoor dining area have health-focused menu items available along with breakfast, lunch, dinner, and drinks served daily. **Known for:** multiple areas for dining; healthy menu; weekend brunch. [$] *Average main: $14* ✉ *1253 N. Front St., Fishtown* ☎ *215/515–3073* 🌐 *frontstreetcafe.net.*

### ★ Kalaya Thai Kitchen

**$$$$** | **THAI** | Chef Nok Suntaranon shares a wealth of Thai family recipes at Kalaya, which began as a BYOB in South Philadelphia and has now been expanded into a large, modern space with a full bar in Fishtown. Addressing Philadelphia's dearth of authentic Thai restaurants, she offers curries, soups, and noodle dishes that don't skimp one bit on real-deal fiery, fishy flavor. **Known for:** authentic Thai cooking; fiery flavors; warm service. [$] *Average main: $35* ✉ *4 W. Palmer St., Fishtown* ☎ *215/545–2535* 🌐 *kalayaphilly.com* 🕓 *No lunch.*

### ★ Laser Wolf

**$$$$** | **ISRAELI** | Like many of CookNSolo's places, Laser Wolf focuses on an aspect of Israeli cuisine, this time the grill or skewer house. Meals are prix-fixe so diners pick their protein to grill (beef, lamb, chicken) and the rest is taken care of. **Known for:** opened by James Beard Award winners Mike Solomonov and Steve Cook; a homemade ice cream sundae is included in the prix-fixe; Israeli grillhouse cuisine. [$] *Average main: $35* ✉ *1301 N. Howard St., at W. Thompson St., Fishtown* ☎ *267/499–4660* 🌐 *laserwolfphilly.com* 🕓 *No lunch.*

### ★ Martha

**$** | **AMERICAN** | Though technically right outside of Fishtown, Martha is the neighborhood bar that every neighborhood wants but only some are lucky enough to have. Large, with indoor and outdoor space, the bar-restaurant boasts one of the most impressive natural-wine programs in the city and some of the tastiest hoagies, too. **Known for:** hoagies; vegetarian-friendly options; charcuterie and cheeses. [$] *Average main: $12* ✉ *2113 E. York St., Fishtown* ☎ *215/867–8881* 🌐 *marthakensington.com* 🕓 *Closed Tues.*

### Middle Child Clubhouse

**$$** | **AMERICAN** | Part café, part restaurant, part bar, Middle Child Clubhouse opened and immediately became part of the essential fabric of Fishtown. Come by midday to sample one of the sandwiches that made the brand Philly-famous, make a reservation for dinner to sample modern American comfort food like a Caesar salad topped with Old Bay fried shrimp, okonomiyaki-style latkes, and a juicy burger, and stay for the restaurant's bar program, which leans heavily on lower-ABV ingredients like vermouth and sherry, as well as savory ingredients like the kombu. **Known for:** overstuffed sandwiches; cocktails like the restaurant's signature seawater margarita, which tastes like a margarita that studied abroad in Japan; kitchen is closed between 2 and 5 pm. [$] *Average main: $20* ✉ *1232 N. Front St., Fishtown* ☎ *267/858–4325* 🌐 *middlechildphilly.com* 🕓 *Closed Mon.*

### ★ Pizzeria Beddia

**$$** | **PIZZA** | The second iteration of Pizzeria, just blocks away from the original location, is a different world, with more than 100 seats, the ability to make reservations, and a larger menu that goes beyond pizza—think natural wines, flavorful salads, and creamier-than-you-can-ever-imagine soft serve. Pizza is still the focal point, though, with options like a classic red pie with pepperoni, a red-sauce-based anchovy pizza, and the white pie, made with local cream and topped with garlic and greens. **Known for:** red-sauce pizzas; natural wines; private hoagie room. [$] *Average main: $20* ✉ *1313 N. Lee St., Fishtown* ☎ *267/928–2256* 🌐 *pizzeriabeddia.com* 🕓 *No lunch.*

### Sancho Pistola's

**$** | **MEXICAN** | An offshoot of Jose Pistola's in Center City, brother Sancho brought a bigger kitchen for more varied and ambitious dishes. Staples of the menu include ultratraditional inky black bean soup seasoned with avocado leaf and zesty ceviche, while other plates (Korean rib tacos, spicy tuna guacamole) mash up Mexican heritage with a global hipster aesthetic. **Known for:** late-night food menu; fresh-fruit margaritas; weekend brunch. [$] *Average main: $12* ✉ *19 W. Girard Ave., Fishtown* ☎ *267/324–3530* 🌐 *www.pistolaslife.com.*

### Sulimay's Restaurant

**$** | **AMERICAN** | **FAMILY** | This old-school diner serves traditional breakfast and lunch fare that runs the gamut from overstuffed omelets to pancakes and French toast and burgers. Don't miss Sulimay's take on scrapple, the traditional Pennsylvania Dutch breakfast meat, which is showcased in the Eggs Bensington, a breakfast sandwich that features runny eggs, thick toast, scrapple, and cheddar cheese. **Known for:** large portions of breakfast faves; good for families; vintage, diner-style vibe. $ *Average main: $10* ⊠ *632 E. Girard Ave., Fishtown* ☎ *215/423–1773* ⊕ *www.facebook.com/sulimays* ☽ *No dinner.*

### ★ Suraya

**$$$ | LEBANESE |** Fishtown's official transformation into a foodie haven came in the form of Suraya, a Levant all-day café with an interior that sends design buffs spinning. The 12,000-square-foot expanse is composed of a coffee shop slinging Lebanese chai tea topped with crushed pistachios and rose petals, drip coffee, pastries, and more; a sit-down area for lunch, dinner, and brunch; a bar overlooking the buzzing kitchen; and a picturesque outdoor garden. **Known for:** creamy hummus; brunch pastry basket; arak (a spirit made from aniseed and grapes) cocktails. $ *Average main: $25* ⊠ *1528 Frankford Ave., Fishtown* ☎ *215/302–1900* ⊕ *surayaphilly.com.*

### Wm. Mulherin's Sons

**$$$ | ITALIAN |** Wood-fired pizzas topped with creamy cheeses, striking meats, or in-season vegetables are the major draw at Wm. Mulherin's Sons, an elevated Italian restaurant—that sounds Irish—nestled in the midst of Fishtown. Located inside of a 20th-century distillery, the interior has been updated to welcome a modern Italian restaurant while still respecting the old-world charm by way of beautiful brickwork and heavy wood accents. **Known for:** wood-fired pizza; weekend brunch; upstairs four-room hotel. $ *Average main: $25* ⊠ *1355 N. Front St., Fishtown* ☎ *215/291–1355* ⊕ *wmmulherinssons.com* ☽ *No lunch weekdays.*

## ☕ Coffee and Quick Bites

### Joe's Steaks + Soda Shop Fishtown

**$ | AMERICAN |** Open until 3 am on weekends—and for lunch and dinner before that—Joe's is a go-to spot for all-day and all-night cheesesteaks, burgers, loaded fries, milkshakes, and sodas at the corner of Girard and Frankford Avenues. Its central location means it's often packed with Frankford Avenue barhoppers who are in need of a late-night snack. **Known for:** cheesesteaks; late-night hours; burgers. $ *Average main: $9* ⊠ *1 W. Girard Ave., Fishtown* ☎ *215/423–5637* ⊕ *joessteaks.com.*

### ★ La Colombe

**$ | CAFÉ |** A photo-ready interior invites guests to La Colombe's world headquarters, a sprawling space covered in artsy graffiti and crusty brick walls, that offers food, drinks, and ample space for hanging out. Communal tables stream down the center of the space, so grab your spot before you order at the counter: savory scones, sandwiches on excellent baguettes, sweet pastries, and coffee, of course. **Known for:** draft lattes; enticing sandwiches; picturesque space. $ *Average main: $8* ⊠ *1335 Frankford Ave., Fishtown* ☎ *267/479–1600* ⊕ *www.lacolombe.com* ☽ *No dinner.*

### ★ Pizza Shackamaxon

**$ | PIZZA |** If good roots can make a pizza place, then Pizza Shackamaxon has it made. Housed in the original location of the much-loved Pizzeria Beddia, Shackamaxon slings pizza by the slice and by the pie. They pride themselves on being a slice-first pizza shop in order to serve the most people possible. **Known for:** slice-first pizza shop; tomato pie; standing-room only. $ *Average main: $10* ⊠ *115 E. Girard Ave., Fishtown* ⊕ *www.pizzashackamaxon.com.*

Suraya in Fishtown serves Middle Eastern cuisine all day long; it's also a great place to pop in for coffee and pastries.

### REAP Mini Mart

**$ | AMERICAN |** When the cheesesteaks and hoagies start to weigh you down, head to Reap Wellness for creative—and genuinely delicious—smoothies and salads. Former health journalist Adjua Fisher and her husband and chef Zach Rice, started REAP as a meal delivery service, but its popularity quickly turned into a storefront that's brought nutritious, creative meals to Fishtown. **Known for:** salads like the savory Seaweed Caesar; smoothies like the Sneaky Greens (spinach, purslane, mango, ginger and hemp); holistic approach to eating and living. $ *Average main: $15* ⊠ *1325 Frankford Ave., Fishtown* ☎ *724/924–6240* ⊕ *www. reapwellness.com* ⊙ *No dinner.*

### ★ Weckerly's Ice Cream

**$ | CAFÉ |** The bright and cheerful one-room ice-cream shop matches the happy feelings that accompany a cup, cone, or ice-cream sandwich from Weckerly's Ice Cream. Local dairy, fruit, herbs, and eggs are the base for the shop's creamy and decadent flavors, which change to match the season (with the exception of a few staples). **Known for:** handmade ice-cream sandwiches; creamy custards; dairy-free sorbet options. $ *Average main: $5* ⊠ *9 W. Girard Ave., Fishtown* ☎ *215/423–2000* ⊕ *www.weckerlys.com* ⊙ *Closed Mon.*

##  Hotels

### Lokal Hotel Fishtown

**$$ | HOTEL |** Touting itself as Philadelphia's first "invisible service" boutique hotel, Lokal Hotel Fishtown offers its namesake: a local experience for all guests. **Pros:** truly local experience; curated rooms; high-quality amenities, including Sonos speakers and Apple TV. **Cons:** no front desk; no on-site staff unless requested; sells out quickly. $ *Rooms from: $250* ⊠ *1421 N. Front St., Fishtown* ☎ *267/702–4345* ⊕ *staylokal.com* ⤴ *6 rooms* ⦿ *No Meals.*

## Wm. Mulherin's Sons

$$$ | **HOTEL** | Part restaurant, part boutique hotel, Wm. Mulherin's Sons is Fishtown's answer to an all-in-one space for visitors to the neighborhood. **Pros:** thoughtful design; proximity to Fishtown bars, restaurants, and attractions; local-inspired experience. **Cons:** no front desk; housekeeping for weeklong visitors only; can be loud. $ *Rooms from: $350* ✉ *1355 N. Front St., Fishtown* ☎ *215/291–1355* ⊕ *wmmulherinssons.com* ⇗ *4 rooms* ⦿ *No Meals.*

 # Nightlife

## BARS AND LOUNGES

### ★ Evil Genius Beer

**BREWPUBS** | The brews on the menu are as delicious as they are uniquely named. With options like Purple Monkey Dishwasher (a chocolate–peanut butter porter) and Ma! The Meatloaf (a Belgian white ale), the beers stick out, and for good reason. Within the Front Street brewpub, the beers are brewed and moved just a few steps to the often-busy bar. Guests can order flights, pints, and a selection of easy-to-eat food like grilled-cheese sandwiches, tacos, and dips. ✉ *1727 Front St., Fishtown* ☎ *215/425–6820* ⊕ *evilgeniusbeer.com.*

## Frankford Hall

**BEER GARDENS** | Stephen Starr's big, loud, and lively beer garden brings a bit of Bavaria to Fishtown's nightlife scene. You and your crew can sit outside at one of the large picnic tables, or hang indoors when it's too cold for the heat lamps. Draft beers, many of them German, come in half or full liters, accompanied by rib-sticking pretzels, wurst, and schnitzel. ✉ *1210 Frankford Ave., Fishtown* ☎ *215/634–3338* ⊕ *www.frankfordhall.com.*

## Johnny Brenda's

**BARS** | Fishtown's "cool kid" vibes are felt all throughout Johnny Brenda's, a neighborhood original that has grown with the neighborhood's evolution without losing its first-on-the-street edge. Part bar-restaurant, part music venue, the Frankford Avenue hangout offers visitors a space for drinking local beer and eating the better-than-regular-bar-food fare—think fresh oysters and solid burgers—as well as a space for playing billiards and listening to the diverse lineup of performers booked for the upstairs stage. ✉ *1201 N. Frankford Ave., Fishtown* ☎ *215/739–9684* ⊕ *www.johnnybrendas.com.*

## MUSIC CLUBS

### The Fillmore Philadelphia

**LIVE MUSIC** | Since its opening in 2015, the 25,000-square-foot Fillmore has seen sold-out shows featuring everyone from local musicians to top-40 singers. The venue is the first of its kind in Fishtown, introducing a rock club experience for the 21st century. Three raised balconies provide solid sight lines for as many as 2,500 concertgoers, with a secondary club, the Foundry, holding about 450 for smaller concerts and late-night dance parties. ✉ *29 E. Allen St., Fishtown* ☎ *215/309–0150* ⊕ *www.thefillmorephilly.com.*

## Kung Fu Necktie

**LIVE MUSIC** | Depending on the night, the music rocking Kung Fu Necktie ranges from local bands to national bands, to DJs spinning dance-party-ready sets. A block removed from the major intersection of Frankford and Girard, KFN welcomes music-loving fans to its small, moody barroom hidden underneath the elevated tracks of SEPTA's Market-Frankford line. ✉ *1250 N. Front St., Fishtown* ☎ *215/291–4919* ⊕ *kungfunecktie.com.*

#  Shopping

### Downerss

**WOMEN'S CLOTHING** | Shopping at Down-erss kind of feels like going shopping with your best friends, even if you're on your own. The super-friendly staff will help you sort through their selection of reasonably priced (lots of pieces are under $100), trendy women's clothing and accessories. They're happy to weigh in on fit or grab an extra size. Browsing the constantly changing selection is a great way to spend an afternoon in the neighborhood. ⊠ *2050 Frankford Ave., Fishtown* ⊕ *downerss.com.*

### ★ Harriett's Bookshop

**BOOKS** | Harriett's Bookshop is the first shop from owner Jeannine Cook, who opened the shop in 2020. The store, which is named for Harriet Tubman, was created with the mission of celebrating female authors, artists, and activists, and has become a hub for black culture in the city. Harriet's hosted the launch of Will Smith's book tour in 2021, and regularly hosts cultural events. Wander in for a curated selection of books, many by black authors, or schedule a visit during one of the events. ⊠ *258 E. Girard Ave., Fishtown* ☎ *267/241–2617* ⊕ *oursister-bookshops.com.*

### Jinxed Fishtown

**SECOND-HAND** | Jinxed has gained a large following on Instagram, where they regularly post about the used mid-century modern furniture pieces that come into their showrooms. Those pieces often sell quickly, but their Fishtown location is chock-full of curated items like vintage typewriters, rugs, couches, and beautifully bound old books. They also have locations in West and South Phila-delphia. ⊠ *1331 Frankford Ave., Fishtown* ☎ *215/800–1369* ⊕ *www.facebook.com/jinxedfishtown.*

# Chapter 11

# MANAYUNK, GERMANTOWN, AND CHESTNUT HILL

Updated by
Joshua McIlvain

👁 **Sights**
★★★☆☆

🍴 **Restaurants**
★★★☆☆

🛏 **Hotels**
★☆☆☆☆

🛍 **Shopping**
★★★☆☆

🍸 **Nightlife**
★★☆☆☆

# NEIGHBORHOOD SNAPSHOT

## TOP EXPERIENCES

■ **American history:** More than 70 buildings dating to the 1700s still stand in Germantown, including the Germantown White House.

■ **The Schmitter:** Head to Chestnut Hill's McNallly's Tavern for one of the all-time great bar sandwiches, the Schmitter—steak, cheese, and fried onions topped with fried salami and a special sauce, all on a kaiser roll.

■ **Mountain biking:** Believe it or not, serious mountain bike trails snake throughout the steep wooded hillsides near Valley Green, as well as the Schuylkill River Trail, which extends along the river for more than 30 miles.

■ **Main Street Manayunk:** Spend a pleasant afternoon ambling along the towpath, window-shopping, and refueling in bars along the way.

■ **Walking Chestnut Hill:** Perfect if you like strolling around neighborhoods, looking at people's homes, and deciding which ones you'd like to live in.

## GETTING HERE

Manayunk is a 10-minute drive from the Philadelphia Museum of Art, along Kelly Drive. Heading north along Germantown Avenue, Germantown becomes Mount Airy around Upsal Street and then becomes Chestnut Hill at Cresheim Valley Drive. Wissahickon Park (the section of Fairmount Park that runs from Lincoln Drive to Northwestern Avenue) divides Mount Airy and Chestnut Hill from the Roxborough, East Falls, and Manayunk neighborhoods.

A car is helpful to explore the area. Though Manayunk's backstreets can be intimidating (and steep!), parking lots are accessible from Main Street, with a very large city lot by Venice Island. Chestnut Hill, Mount Airy, and Germantown have abundant street-side parking; Chestnut Hill also has cheap parking lots.

An Uber or Lyft from downtown to the area usually costs $15–$25.

## QUICK BITES

■ **Market at the Fareway.** Great variety of lunch-stand choices from Vietnamese noodle soups and Korean tacos to rustic pizza.⊠ *8221 Germantown Ave., Chestnut Hill* ⊕ *www. marketatthefareway.com*

■ **Uncle Bobbie's Coffee and Books.** Their tagline pretty much says it all: Cool People, Dope Books, Great Coffee.⊠ *5445 Germantown Ave., Germantown* ⊕ *www. unclebobbies.com*

## PLANNING YOUR TIME

■ Northwest Philadelphia appeals to sporty people and strolling shoppers. Manayunk, Germantown, and Chestnut Hill can be visited on the same day; Manayunk is more of a late afternoon and evening destination.

■ Spring and fall are the best times to visit, but Chestnut Hill and Mount Airy, the city's leafiest sections, are noticeably cooler during the summer. In winter, most of the historical sites in Germantown are closed, but in October the Revolutionary Germantown Festival features a reenactment of the Battle of Germantown. If you've never driven on cobblestones before, now's your chance—Germantown Avenue is made of them.

Northwest Philadelphia includes several interlocking neighborhoods between the banks of the Schuylkill River, across the upper forested borders of Fairmount Park, and to the city's border. Each has a distinct personality reflected in its dining scene. Manayunk has a young-professional vibe and dining options to match. Mount Airy has family-friendly bar-restaurants, while its tony neighbor, Chestnut Hill, has chichi brunch spots, bakeries, and historic pubs.

Main Street in Manayunk is like a vacation village, with boutiques, bars, and restaurants. The main commercial corridor runs along the Schuylkill River, while the rest of the neighborhood rises steeply up the hill with houses crammed together up twisting streets.

Chestnut Hill is Philadelphia's most village-like neighborhood and one of its greenest. People gather here to eat and wander about the precious shops on Germantown Avenue. It's a great neighborhood for peering into people's homes as well. Mount Airy has seen an increase in dining, drinking, and shopping establishments. Although it has fewer options than Chestnut Hill, a number of hidden corners reveal charming cafés and local pubs.

In 1683, at the founding of Germantown by German settlers, the county encompassed present-day Germantown, Mount Airy, and Chestnut Hill. The area played

an important role in the nation's founding: during the American Revolution, it was the site of the Battle of Germantown, which marked the first attack by American armed forces on the British. Originally intended as a farming community, the land was too rocky for anything but subsistence farming. Instead the Germans turned to making textiles, milling, and printing—you can visit the remnants of this industry at Historic Rittenhouse Town in Wissahickon Park.

Mount Airy and Chestnut Hill came into their own in the 19th century as a location for summer homes for Philadelphia business owners drawn to Germantown's booming textile industry. Indeed, Philadelphia University (now part of Jefferson University) had been the Philadelphia College of Textiles from the late 1800s to 1999. Germantown township was incorporated into Philadelphia in 1854, when local trains were already

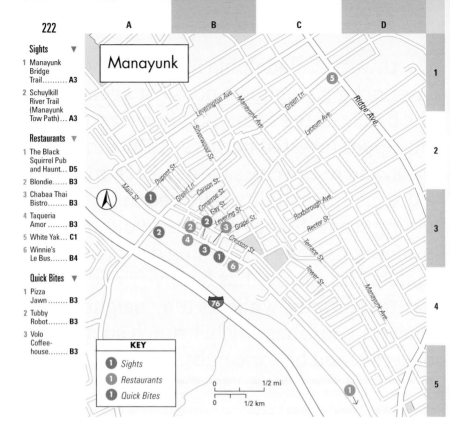

Manayunk

**KEY**

1 *Sights*

1 *Restaurants*

1 *Quick Bites*

0 ___ 1/2 mi

0 ___ 1/2 km

servicing the area, making rail travel to the city convenient to this day.

Aside from a number of B&Bs in the area, the only hotel is the Chestnut Hill Hotel, a pleasant option in a great location about halfway up the hill in Chestnut Hill. If you are keen on staying at a B&B or Airbnb in Chestnut Hill, make sure it's in easy walking distance of Germantown Avenue—the whole charm of the area is to be able to walk out on the avenue and leave your car behind.

# Manayunk

Manayunk has little of its industrial history on display, unless you follow the towpath up the Schuylkill to see the last remnants of decaying mills. This predominantly Polish and Irish neighborhood renovated its Main Street in the 1980s into a quaint avenue with restaurants, funky shops, and a few good bars, evoking a small-town tourist destination like New Hope. It's perfect for a pleasant afternoon. It's also something of way station for bicyclists, as it sits on the Schuylkill River Trail that runs from Center City to Valley Forge and beyond—and serves as a point of departure for trails into Wissihickon Park. Up from Main Street the hill rises steeply and houses are jammed together along narrow, twisted streets—fun to walk on, but almost completely residential. Don't expect to find hidden treasures. Though it is less pronounced these days, the blue-collar veneer of the rest of Manayunk, a mill town in the 1800s, still strikes a contrast to Main Street, and there's something old-world about the hill-town community.

### GETTING HERE AND AROUND

If you're driving from Center City, follow I–76 west (the Schuylkill Expressway) to the Belmont Avenue exit. Turn right across the bridge and right again onto Main Street and park. On weekends you can be strolling with hundreds of visitors—and fighting with them for parking spaces. There are parking lots off Main Street toward the river. Participating stores offer validation stickers for reduced rates. From 6 pm on, valet parking is available for diners and shoppers for $10, but it's an easy Uber or Lyft ride from Center City. You can also take the SEPTA Norristown train from Market East, Suburban Station, or 30th Street Station to the Manayunk Station (on Cresson Street) and walk two blocks downhill to Main Street.

### ESSENTIALS

**BIKE RENTALS Cadence.** ✉ *3740 Main St., Manayunk* 🌐 *www.cadencecycling.com.* **Trek Bicycle.** ✉ *4159 Main St., Manayunk* ☎ *215/487–7433* 🌐 *www.trekbikes.com.*

**VISITOR INFORMATION Manayunk Development Corporation.** ☎ *215/482–9565* 🌐 *www.manayunk.com.*

## 👁 Sights

### Manayunk Bridge Trail

**TRAIL** | An old train trestle was revamped into a pedestrian- and bike-only bridge, now with lighting for night walkers, with pleasant views of Manayunk and the Schuylkill River Valley. It connects to the Cynwyd Heritage trail, an easy 2-mile "rail trail" for biking, jogging, and walking that leads past Laurel Hill Cemetery West and ends at Cynwyd Station. ✉ *Manayunk Bridge Trail, Corner of Dupont and High Sts., Manayunk.*

### ★ Schuylkill River Trail (Manayunk Tow Path)

**TRAIL** | This very popular bike and pedestrian trail follows the river to Valley Forge National Park (and well beyond), or, in the other direction, to the Philadelphia Art Museum and beyond. It's easy biking, and while you can go for miles, you'll want a hybrid or mountain bike because not all of it is paved. ✉ *Manayunk Tow Path, Main St. and Gay St., Manayunk* ✥ *There are many access points, but here a small park leads to the path* 🌐 *schuylkillriver.org.*

## 🍴 Restaurants

### The Black Squirrel Pub and Haunt

$$ | **BRITISH** | Downriver one neighborhood from Manayunk, this East Falls spot is obsessive about creating the true English pub experience, albeit with excellent food. A delicious array of room-temperature English beer is on tap to complement the dark comfy interior where guests dine on fresh oysters and clams (thankfully not from England) and expertly prepared traditional dishes like short-rib cottage pie and Scottish salmon. **Known for:** popular terrace; afternoon drinks and bites; English pub fare. [$] *Average main: $24* ✉ *3749 Midvale Ave., Manayunk* ☎ *267/323–2611* 🌐 *www.blacksquirrelphilly.com* 🕒 *Closed Mon. and Tues.*

### Blondie

$$ | **AMERICAN** | This welcome addition to the Manayunk dining scene offers what may be best described as American pleasure food—shrimp and grits, short ribs, fried chicken and biscuits, and other bar food standards—all prepared with inventive flourishes. Rare for the area, big windows and high ceilings provide an expansiveness and style that is both throwback and modern. **Known for:** tasty classics; retro bistro setting; fun vibe. [$] *Average main: $22* ✉ *4417 Main St., Manayunk* ☎ *215/253–3833* 🌐 *www.blondiephilly.com* 🕒 *No lunch weekdays.*

### Chabaa Thai Bistro

$$ | **THAI** | Known for the varieties of pad Thai—from crispy duck to peanut-crusted scallop—and delicious soups, this Thai bistro is a nice, calming escape from the

The Schuylkill River Trail (a.k.a the Manayunk Tow Path) follows the river from the Philadelphia Art Museum to Valley Forge National Park.

noisy restaurant scene of Main Street. Enjoy authentic Thai flavors, including seasonal specialties, in your lime-infused Thai sausage, *po tek* (a spicy seafood hot pot with basil and lemongrass) portioned for two, or the various face-flushing curries. **Known for:** numerous versions of pad Thai; crazy noodles (stir-fried wide rice noodles with colorful veggies); pleasant atmosphere. $ *Average main: $18* ✉ *4371 Main St., Manayunk* ☎ *215/483–1979* ⊕ *www.chabaathai.com* ☸ *Closed Tues. No lunch.*

### Taqueria Amor

$ | **MEXICAN** | This jumping joint satisfies the margarita-and-nachos crowd as well as those seeking more authentic Mexican flavors. A lively spot with colorfully painted walls as well as sidewalk seating, it's most fun to share the smaller bites— braised brisket tacos, mushroom quesadilla, tortilla soup—but the enchiladas are also excellent. **Known for:** great sharing plates; sidewalk tables; fresh ingredients. $ *Average main: $14* ✉ *4410 Main St.,* *Manayunk* ☎ *267/331–5874* ⊕ *www.taqueriaamor.com.*

### White Yak

$$ | **TIBETAN** | If you're new to Tibetan food, go for the *momos*, Tibetan dumplings that hold a hearty dollop of minced goodness within and come with a dipping broth. While there are good vegetarian options, the emphasis—as befits a high altitude cuisine—is generally on the meat dishes, whether curries, savory pastries, or the hearty beef-broth-based soups. **Known for:** the momos!; homemade noodles; friendly atmosphere. $ *Average main: $18* ✉ *6118 Ridge Ave., Roxborough* ✛ *less than 1½ miles (by car) from Manayunk's Main St.* ☎ *215/483–0764* ⊕ *www.whiteyakrestaurant.com* ☸ *Closed Mon.*

### Winnie's Le Bus

$ | **AMERICAN** | **FAMILY** | Lively and upbeat, Le Bus is a solid choice for high-quality basics like burgers, tacos, and fish-and-chips. Winnie's also serves breakfast and baked goods. **Known for:** comfort foods; homemade chips; big open space.

$ *Average main: $15* ✉ *4266 Main St., Manayunk* ☎ *215/487–2663* ⊕ *www. lebusmanayunk.com* ⊘ *No dinner Sun.*

 ## Coffee and Quick Bites

### Pizza Jawn

**$$$** | **PIZZA** | One of the city's new crop of highly touted pizza joints, here you select one of three types of crust—round (Neapolitan/New York blend), "Grandma" (hearty with a nutty flavor), and the Detroit style (crust melds with sauce and cheese into an alchemic layer of sensory pleasure)—and then you pick your toppings, which range from meats and cheeses to veggies and vegan options. Hours are limited, and you must order online for a pie, but slices are often available for walk-ins. **Known for:** special guest chef specials; high demand; crusty goodness. $ *Average main: $28* ✉ *4330 Main St., Manayunk* ⊕ *www.pizzajawn. com* ⊘ *Closed Sun.–Tues. No lunch.*

### Tubby Robot

**$** | **AMERICAN** | Stop here for delicious ice cream served in small, pricey scoops—including many nondairy options. The fun part is playing video games displayed on two screens mounted on a wall across a narrow alley, while inside, four joysticks allow up to four players to go head-to-head. **Known for:** fun flavors that include nondairy options; old-school arcade games; trendy vibe. $ *Average main: $5* ✉ *4369 Main St., Manayunk* ☎ *267/423–4376* ⊕ *www.tubbyrobot.com* ⊘ *Closed Mon. and Tues.*

### Volo Coffeehouse

**$** | **CAFÉ** | A good place to camp out with a book or for a chat, this coffeehouse serves local La Colombe coffee, as well as tasty baked goods or simple sandwiches. **Known for:** a good cup of coffee; great location; no-fuss service. $ *Average main: $8* ✉ *4360 Main St., Manayunk* ☎ *215/483–4580* ⊘ *No dinner.*

 ## Nightlife

### BARS AND LOUNGES

#### The Goat's Beard

**PUBS** | Offering a bit more elegance than your average Main Street bar, the Goat's Beard specializes in hearty American bistro-style cooking, local beers, and smartly curated spirits (especially whiskey), with an emphasis on local offerings. ✉ *4201 Main St., Manayunk* ☎ *267/323–2495* ⊕ *www.thegoatsbeardphilly.com.*

#### Lucky's Last Chance

**BARS** | A down-to-earth pub, Lucky's is well known for (what some consider to be) the city's best burgers—we recommend the Pickle Monster. It's also a solid place to drink, with DJs, dance nights, and special events. ✉ *4421 Main St., Manayunk* ☎ *215/509–6005* ⊕ *www. luckyslastchance.com.*

### BREWERIES AND BEER GARDENS

#### Manayunk Brewery & Restaurant

**BREWPUBS** | A long-running destination on the banks of the Schuylkill Canal, this brewpub offers a well-rounded selection of ales and lagers brewed on the premises. Check out the patio in the spring and summer—best for snacking. ✉ *4120 Main St., Manayunk* ☎ *215/482–8220* ⊕ *www.manayunkbrewery.com.*

#### Wissahickon Brewing Company

**BREWPUBS** | In the adjacent neighborhood of East Falls, tucked partway down a hillside, you'll find this beer lovers' gem. They don't serve food, but often have food trucks—and yoga at 10 am on Saturdays (no joke). ✉ *3705 W. School House La., Manayunk* ☎ *215/483–8833* ⊕ *wissahickonbrew.com.*

### MUSIC CLUBS

#### Dawson's Street Pub

**LIVE MUSIC** | Manayunk's best live-music venue features many of the most talented local bands curated for their crowd-pleasing aesthetics and musicianship. Expect excellent sound in a cozy, laid-back, and corner bar setting that's tucked away in a residential area. ✉ *100 Dawson St., Manayunk* ☎ *215/482–5677* ⊕ *www.dawsonstreetpub.com.*

#  Shopping

Manayunk's Main Street is a mix of clothing boutiques, antiques shops, athletic-wear joints, furniture stores, and a variety of quirky gift shops. Many stores stay open until 9 on Friday and Saturday nights. On the last weekend in June the Manayunk Arts Festival lines Main Street with the region's largest outdoor arts and crafts show, and there tends to be one major neighborhood event per month to liven things up.

## BOOKS
### The Spiral Bookcase
**BOOKS** | This charming bookstore features a book-savvy staff, a rich collection of often lesser-known authors, a cozy setting of plush chairs and crystals, and an affinity for the occult. ✉ *4257 Main St., Manayunk* ☎ *215/482–0704* ⊕ *spiralbookcase.com.*

## CLOTHING
### LILA Philadelphia
**WOMEN'S CLOTHING** | This boutique specializes in fun, comfy, bright styles that are a nice contrast to normally dour and conservative fashion (or non-fashion) often available in Philadelphia outside of downtown. There is a sassy, confident attitude to the clothes and accessories that is also welcoming. ✉ *4339 Main St., Manayunk* ☎ *267/331–6995* ⊕ *lilaphiladelphia.com.*

## HOME DECOR
### UrbanBurb Furniture
**FURNITURE** | Featuring an array of modern furniture circa the 1950s, 1960s, and 1970s, this fun home-furnishings store has everything from bright yellow couches to old Coke machines, as well as funky lamps, random statuary, and giant slabs of wood. The store is full of kitschy charm, but the items are actually things you'd want to have; they also make

custom tables from giant slabs of wood. ✉ *4313 Main St., Manayunk* ☎ *215/298–9534* ⊕ *urbanburbfurniture.com.*

## JEWELRY
### Gary P. Mann Design
**JEWELRY & WATCHES** | Noted local goldsmith Gary Mann creates elegant custom jewelry. The store is also known for its estate jewelry, carved jade and emerald pieces, stack rings, and Judaica. ✉ *4349 Main St., Manayunk* ☎ *215/482–7051* ⊕ *www.garymannjewelers.com.*

# Germantown

Germantown, about 6 miles northwest of Center City, has maintained an integrated, progressive community since 13 German Quaker and Mennonite families moved here in 1683. They soon welcomed English, French, and other European settlers seeking religious freedom. The area has a tradition of free thinking—the first written protest against slavery in America came from its residents. It was also the seat of government for two summers during Washington's presidency, when yellow fever epidemics raged in the city. And the area became fashionable for wealthy Philadelphians wanting to escape the city's heat in the mid-1700s.

Today the area houses a wealth of exceptionally well-preserved architectural masterpieces including more than 70 homes dating from the 1700s and some of the country's oldest mills. The business section of Germantown is still evolving but offers some quirky eateries, a great coffee shop, and new shops.

## GETTING HERE AND AROUND
The best way to tour the area is by car. From Center City follow Kelly Drive to Midvale Avenue and turn right. Follow Midvale all the way to Germantown Avenue. To get to Mount Airy and Chestnut Hill from Germantown, follow Germantown Avenue north. SEPTA's Regional Rail Chestnut Hill West and Chestnut Hill

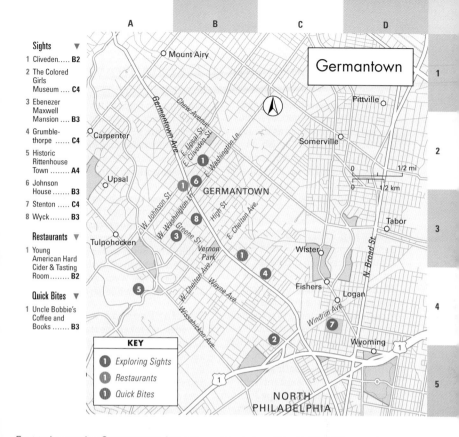

## Sights ▼

1 Cliveden..... **B2**
2 The Colored Girls Museum .... **C4**
3 Ebenezer Maxwell Mansion .... **B3**
4 Grumble-thorpe ...... **C4**
5 Historic Rittenhouse Town ........ **A4**
6 Johnson House ....... **B3**
7 Stenton ..... **C4**
8 Wyck........ **B3**

## Restaurants ▼

1 Young American Hard Cider & Tasting Room........ **B2**

## Quick Bites ▼

1 Uncle Bobbie's Coffee and Books ....... **B3**

**KEY**

🔵 Exploring Sights
🔴 Restaurants
🟤 Quick Bites

East trains service Germantown, but can be a 10- to 15-minute walk to the avenue depending where you go. The 23 bus runs along Germantown Avenue—useful between Germantown, Mt. Airy, and Chestnut Hill, but a very long ride if you pick it up downtown.

## 👁 Sights

### Cliveden

**HISTORIC HOME** | The grounds take up an entire block, and its unique history, impressive architecture, and the guides who spin a good yarn combine to make Cliveden perhaps the best visiting experience of the historic Germantown homes. The elaborate country house was built in 1767 by Benjamin Chew (1722–1810), a Quaker and chief justice of the colonies, and something of a fence-straddler during the Revolution. Cliveden was at the center of the Battle of Germantown, occupied by British troops, and the walls still bear the marks of American cannon fire. An elaborate reenactment of the Battle of Germantown is held here annually on the first Saturday in October. Cliveden excels at its programming, much of which explores the experiences of slaves, servants, and workers at Cliveden, and larger themes of Northern slavery and slaveholders, like the Chew family, who owned plantations in the South. The house, on 6 acres, can be seen on a 45-minute guided tour. Off-season tours can be arranged by calling. ✉ *6401 Germantown Ave., Germantown* ✛ *Entrance on E. Cliveden St.* ☎ *215/848–1777* ⊕ *www.cliveden.org* 💲 *$10* ⊘ *Closed Mon.–Wed. and Dec.–Apr.; tours on the hr, last tour at 3 pm.*

# Historic Highlights of Germantown

Germantown was settled the same year as Philadelphia, 1683, by—you guessed it—Germans, so as its history was not chronicled in English, its story of pre-Revolutionary America life is not widely known. A number of historical houses tell the history of the area's beginnings and on through the 19th century.

## Planning Your House Tours

Generally speaking, you won't want to take in more than three sites, as you will become house-weary, but immersing yourself into the area's history is worth the visit. The first thing to keep in mind is that the hours can be wonky at these sites and it's best to double-check the hours before you go; nearly all the houses are closed during the winter—heating is simply too expensive or nonexistent. With that said, Cliveden, Wyck, the Johnson House, Ebenezer Maxwell Mansion, and Stenton are the most consistent in their hours. The Germantown White House, Grumblethorpe, and the Historic Rittenhouse Town hours are almost absurdly fickle (though you can walk about Historic Ritten-house at any time). The Germantown Historical Society (⊠ 5501 German-town Ave.) has served in the past as a center to help guide visitors to the various houses, but Historic Germantown's Freedom's Backyard website (⊕ freedomsbackyard.com) has the most complete list of attrac-tions and works to bring the various sights under a single umbrella. The houses themselves, however, operate separately, and should be contacted directly. The upside is that you can often arrange a tour on off days by calling a couple of weeks in advance. The Germantown White House, Grumblethorpe, Wyck, and Stenton also have worthwhile gardens.

## Special Programming

Cliveden has taken the lead in offering lectures and conversations—led by authors, historians, educators, and archivists—on subjects like slavery and slaveholders in the North, the lives of those who worked (paid and forced labor) at Cliveden, and various unexplored stories of the American Revolution era. Programs at Wyck and Stenton are also worthwhile, but the theatrical productions at Ebenezer Maxwell Mansion are surprisingly good, as are the Victorian-themed events and the hosted teas, like Tea with Frederick Douglass.

### The Colored Girls Museum

OTHER MUSEUM | Looking for something other than colonial history? This museum was created to tell the *herstory* of Black girls through personal objects used and cherished in everyday life. Established in 2015, the unique museum embraces the value of intimate spaces and the experiences of Black girls and their home life, with the aim to also be a research facility, exhibition space, gathering place, and think tank. The space hosts special exhibitions, and weekend tours are avail-able via online reservations only. ⊠ 4613 Newhall St., Germantown ☎ 267/630–4438 ⊕ thecoloredgirlsmuseum.com 🎟 $20 ⊗ Closed weekdays.

### Ebenezer Maxwell Mansion

HISTORIC HOME | Philadelphia's only mid-19th-century house-museum is a Vic-torian Gothic extravaganza of elongated windows and arches that's used to illus-trate the way Victorian social mores were reflected through its decoration. The

Built in 1767 by the Chew family, Cliveden is perhaps the best visiting experience of the historic Germantown homes.

downstairs highlights the Rococo Revival (circa 1860), the upstairs is fashioned after the Renaissance Revival (1880s), and the difference is striking, especially the art deco–like wall details you may not associate with the time. Throughout the year there are a number of quality theater productions within the house—from Ibsen to Shakespeare to original work and lighter fare, as well special teas and holiday themed events. The house is two blocks from the Tulpehocken stop on SEPTA's Chestnut Hill West line. ⊠ *200 W. Tulpehocken St., at Greene St., Germantown* ☎ *215/438–1861* ⊕ *www. ebenezermaxwellmansion.org* ✉ *$8* ⊙ *Closed Sun.–Thurs.* ♿ *Reservations required.*

## Grumblethorpe

**HISTORIC HOME** | The blood of General James Agnew, who died after being struck by musket balls during the Battle of Germantown, stains the floor in the parlor of this Georgian house. Built by Philadelphia merchant and wine importer John Wister in 1744, Grumblethorpe is

one of Germantown's leading examples of early-18th-century Pennsylvania-German architecture. The Wister family lived here for 160 years, and during the Revolution a teenage Sally Wister kept a diary that has become an important historical source for what that time was like. On display are period furnishings and family mementos, but the best part of the house is the large garden. Wisteria, the flowering vine, is named after Charles Wister (John's grandson), who was an avid botanist and amateur scientist, and there is plenty of it in the garden. There are also an enormous hundred-year-old rosebush, a peony alley, a two-story arbor with climbing clematis and a grapevine working its way across its base, and tulips in season.

◼ **TIP→ Tours are offered May–October, on the second Saturday of the month; additional tours can be scheduled for Tuesday and Thursday.** ⊠ *5267 Germantown Ave., Germantown* ☎ *215/843–4820* ⊕ *www. philalandmarks.org* ✉ *$8 tours* ⊙ *Closed Nov.–Apr.*

## Historic RittenhouseTown

**HISTORIC DISTRICT** | North America's first paper mill was built here in 1690 by Mennonite minister William Rittenhouse. Over the next 150 years, 10 generations of his family lived on the site and operated the mill. His most famous offspring, born in 1732, was David Rittenhouse, astronomer, statesman, and first president of the U.S. Mint. You can stroll any time through this National Historic District that consists of 30 picturesque acres along the Wissahickon and seven outbuildings. Special events include papermaking workshops, cooking demonstrations, and an annual 5K race. Public tours (summer only) are offered intermittently—private tours can be arranged by phone. ⊠ *206 Lincoln Dr., Germantown* ⊹ *Accessible from lots on Lincoln Drive and trails in Wissahickon Park.* ☎ *215/438–5711* ⊕ *www.rittenhousetown.org* ⊴ *$10 (no credit cards).*

## Johnson House

**HISTORIC HOME** | After bringing visitors through the hidden back entrance of this 1768 home, guides retrace the experience of slaves who found a haven here when the Johnson House was a key station on the Underground Railroad. They weave the story of the Johnson family, Quakers who worked to abolish slavery, with that of Harriet Tubman, who was sheltered here with runaway slaves and later guided them to freedom. Visitors see hiding places, including the third-floor attic hatch that runaways used to hide on the roof when the sheriff came by, learn Underground Railroad code words, and view slavery artifacts, such as ankle shackles and collars. The home has contained the gamut of American history; in 1777 the house was in the line of fire during the Battle of Germantown; the shutters still show the impact of the musket rounds. In the early 1900s it was saved from demolition when it became a women's club. The house itself does not amaze, but hearing the stories of the home when you are standing within it is fascinating.

▨ **TIP➔ Friday and Saturday tours are offered year-round by appointment only and there are tours available in the spring and fall on Thursday.** ⊠ *6306 Germantown Ave., Germantown* ☎ *215/438–1768* ⊕ *www.johnsonhouse.org* ⊴ *$10* ⊘ *Closed Sun.–Wed.*

## Stenton

**HISTORIC HOME** | James Logan may not be a household name, but he was a seminal figure in pre-Revolutionary America. Equal parts visionary, opportunist, and rogue, he was secretary to William Penn and managed the daily affairs of the colony. Logan, who went on to hold almost every important public office in the colonies, designed the 1730 Georgian manor himself and named it for his father's birthplace in Scotland. He used it to entertain local luminaries and Native American tribal delegates. It was also where he kept one of the area's first libraries, at a time when books were looked upon with suspicion. British General Howe claimed Stenton for his headquarters during the Battle of Germantown. The Stenton mansion is filled with family and period pieces; the site also includes a kitchen wing, barn, and Colonial-style garden. With more regular hours than most of the other houses, the guided 45-minute tour interprets the life of three generations of the Logan family and the life of the region from the 1720s through the American Revolution. Stenton has one of the best interiors of any of the Germantown homes.

▨ **TIP➔ Tours are offered April to late December Tuesday–Saturday, noon–4.** ⊠ *4601 18th St., Germantown* ☎ *215/329–7312* ⊕ *www.stenton.org* ⊴ *$8* ⊘ *Closed Jan.–Mar.*

## Wyck

**HISTORIC HOME** | Between the 1690s and 1973, Wyck sheltered nine generations of the Wistar-Haines family. Their accumulated furnishings are on display, along with ceramics, children's needlework, dolls, and artifacts generally contemporary with the mid-1800s. On one side is the oldest rose garden in the United States, dating to the 1820s, which blooms in May, as well as a magnolia tree from that time. Out back are a large lawn, where you can picnic, and a vegetable garden—the land has been continuously farmed since 1690, and during the summer it hosts many kid-friendly garden-related events. Known as the oldest house in Germantown, Wyck was used as a British field hospital after the Battle of Germantown. Walk-in tours are offered April–November, Thursday–Saturday, noon–4 pm, and the grounds are open for wandering Friday afternoons. Off-season tours are available by appointment.

**TIP→ There's a farmers' market May to November on Friday.** ✉ *6026 Germantown Ave., Germantown* ☎ *215/848–1690* 🌐 *www.wyck.org* 🎟 *$5* 🕒 *Closed Dec.–Mar.*

## 🍴 Restaurants

**Young American Hard Cider & Tasting Room**
$ | **AMERICAN** | While the menu is limited to homemade hand pies, soups, and special entrées, the ingredients are fresh and local and the tasty results have made the Young American a popular dining spot. Food isn't the only draw, as hard cider and local craft brew fans have also flocked to this craft distillery housed within a handsomely restored turn-of-the-19th century building. **Known for:** Sunday brunch; everything local; craft hard cider. [$] *Average main: $15* ✉ *6350 Germantown Ave., Germantown* ☎ *215/406–5307* 🌐 *www.youngamericancider.com* 🕒 *Closed Mon.–Wed.*

## ☕ Coffee and Quick Bites

**Uncle Bobbie's Coffee and Books**
$ | **AMERICAN** | Besides its popularity for its great coffee and light fare, Uncle Bobbie's is the most literary salonlike coffee shop in the city, with numerous author and reading events. Focused squarely on African American literature and history, intellectual studies, as well as mainstream biographies and the like, the books, all new, are both for sale and displayed in a way that makes you wish you had a library so neat and shiny. **Known for:** friendly service; cultural hub; lively up front, quiet in the back. [$] *Average main: $6* ✉ *5445 Germantown Ave., Germantown* ☎ *215/403–7058* 🌐 *www.unclebobbies.com.*

## 🍸 Nightlife

**Attic Brewing Company**
**LIVE MUSIC** | Besides serving excellent beer, Attic Brewing hosts great music ranging from funk and soul to rock and roll. A sizable outdoor area also hosts special events and food trucks. ✉ *137 Berkley St., Germantown* ☎ *267/748–2495* 🌐 *www.atticbrewing.com.*

# Chestnut Hill and Mount Airy

Mount Airy and then Chestnut Hill are northwest of Germantown. Chestnut Hill is one of the farthest points you can get from Center City while still being within the city limits. The enclave looks the part with fairy-tale woods, winding drives, and moneyed addresses, but the walkable, family-oriented commercial district is true to its streetcar suburb history. Beyond cobblestone Germantown Avenue, lined with restaurants, galleries, and boutiques, you can find lovely examples of Colonial Revival and Queen Anne houses. Wissahickon Park runs adjacent to Chestnut Hill and Mount Airy.

Between Germantown and Chestnut Hill, Mount Airy got its start as a vacation village for wealthy Philadelphians in the 1800s. Today, the area is an ideal mix of its neighbors, a blend of Germantown's grit and Chestnut Hill's polish with the same staggeringly gorgeous stock of Victorian and Colonial Revival architecture.

Mount Airy is also recognized as one of the first racially integrated neighborhoods in the country, a point of pride among today's businesses and residents.

Chestnut Hill and Mount Airy are very pleasant, predominantly residential neighborhoods. Travel to downtown Philadelphia is easy by car or train. Restaurants and shops run all along a mile of Germantown Avenue in Chestnut Hill. Mount Airy is a little more sprawling, but there are a number of good restaurants and bars as well. Reservations are not typically needed in this area, except for Jansen.

### GETTING HERE AND AROUND
To get to Mount Airy or Chestnut Hill by car, follow Kelly Drive to Lincoln Drive and take that road to its end, making a right on Allens Lane and then a left on Germantown Avenue. SEPTA's Regional Rail Chestnut Hill West and Chestnut Hill East trains are good options as well.

 Sights

**Morris Arboretum**
GARDEN | FAMILY | This is one of the best arboretums in the country. It's a great place to reward yourself on a sunny day with an afternoon stroll, and you can let your kids run free. With 3,500 trees and shrubs from around the world, this 92-acre arboretum was based on Victorian-era garden and landscape design, with romantic winding paths, a hidden grotto, a fernery, a koi pond, and natural woodland. The highlights are the spectacular rose garden, the swan pond, and "Out on a Limb," a 50-foot-high canopy where you can commune with the birds—and gleeful children. Large modern sculptures, some of which are spectacular, are sprinkled throughout the property, with outdoor sculptural exhibits during the year such as October's Scarecrow Walk. Twice annually, the popular Garden Railway exhibit features an elaborate model railroad surrounded by miniature replicas of historic Philadelphia landmarks. You may

want to drive, as it's a good hike from the top of Chestnut Hill. ⊠ 100 E. Northwestern Ave., Chestnut Hill ☎ 215/247–5777 ⊕ www.morrisarboretum.org 🖾 $20.

★ **Wissahickon Park (Valley Green)**
CITY PARK | There are many great sections of Fairmount Park, but the 1,800 acres around Valley Green known as Wissahickon Park may be the most stunning. Miles and miles of trails running along and above the river lead to covered bridges, a statue of a Lenape chief (rife with inaccuracies but created with good intentions), caves used by a 17th-century free-love cult, large boulders that drip water, and mallards quacking for bread bits. Forbidden Drive, on which cars are forbidden, runs from Northwestern Avenue (the westernmost part of Chestnut Hill) all the way to Lincoln Drive, where it connects to a bike and walking path that leads to Manayunk and Kelly Drive, where additional bike paths can take you to the city or out along the Schuylkill to Valley Forge. There are also many miles of surprisingly difficult mountain-bike trails. The Valley Green Inn is a decent restaurant at Forbidden Drive and Valley Green Road, and the Cedar House is a coffee and smoothie café at the Northwestern Avenue entrance. ⊠ Valley Green Rd., Chestnut Hill ✦ Follow Valley Green Road down to the parking lots. There are many trails all over the area that also lead into the park ☎ 215/247–0417 ⊕ www.fow.org 🖾 Free.

**Woodmere Art Museum**
ART MUSEUM | On the far side of Chestnut Hill, on the slope leading toward the suburbs, this Philly artist–centric museum focuses on 19th- and 20th-century eastern Pennsylvania art. The permanent collection features mid-1900s woodcuts and a number of 19th-century Pennsylvania landscapes. Perhaps more worthwhile are the contemporary special exhibitions, which have grown increasingly more engaging, along with live jazz and movie nights. ⊠ 9201 Germantown Ave., Chestnut Hill ☎ 215/247–0476

Located in Chestnut Hill, the 92-acre Morris Arboretum has 3,500 trees and shrubs from around the world and a 50-foot-high canopy where you can commune with the birds.

⊕ *www.woodmereartmuseum.org* 🖼 *$10* ⊙ *Closed Mon. and Tues.*

## 🍴 Restaurants

Chestnut Hill has the largest selection of restaurants, with Mount Airy not far behind, though Mount Airy is more spread out. You may have to wait at times, but rarely do you need reservations.

### Cake

$ | **AMERICAN** | Housed inside a former greenhouse, Cake is a refined spot for breakfast and lunch, though the sweets and pastries are still a highlight at this former bakery. The menu includes creative twists on lunchtime classics: try the Philly cheesesteak marsala or the croque monsieur brushed with apricot mustard. **Known for:** garden atmosphere; refined breakfast and lunch; buttery scones. $ *Average main: $13* ⊠ *8501 Germantown Ave., Chestnut Hill* ☎ *215/247–6887* ⊕ *www.cakeofchestnuthill.com* ⊙ *Closed Mon. No dinner.*

### El Poquito

$ | **MEXICAN** | Authentic Mexican flavors are generally well prepared, especially the tacos, and the Brussels sprouts are a particularly inspired take on the usually ho-hum vegetable. But, the real draw here is the outdoor seating, which makes this lively and festive spot perfect for gatherings with friends and families, especially with some excellent margaritas. **Known for:** street-style tacos; margaritas; outdoor seating. $ *Average main: $15* ⊠ *7402 Germantown Ave., Chestnut Hill* ☎ *267/766–5372* ⊕ *www.elpoquito.com* ⊙ *Closed Mon. No lunch weekdays.*

### Hokka Hokka

$$ | **JAPANESE** | This high-quality sushi joint has friendly service and particularly good rolls, including fun ones like the Hollywood—a massive creation with tempura shrimp, avocado, salmon, and eel sauce. Near the bottom of Chestnut Hill, Hokka Hokka also serves a variety of tempura and other Japanese dishes for the non–sushi eater. **Known for:** creative sushi rolls; cozy fireplace; good service. $ *Average*

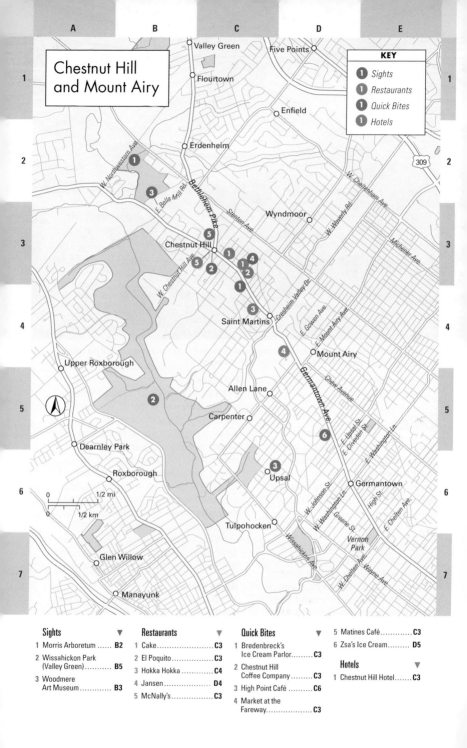

# Chestnut Hill and Mount Airy

**KEY**

- ① Sights
- ① Restaurants
- ① Quick Bites
- ① Hotels

Valley Green
Five Points
Flourtown
Enfield
Erdenheim
309
Wyndmoor
Chestnut Hill
Saint Martins
Mount Airy
Upper Roxborough
Allen Lane
Carpenter
Dearnley Park
Upsal
Roxborough
Germantown
Tulpohocken
Vernon Park
Glen Willow
Manayunk

*W. Northwestern Ave.*
*E. Bells Mill Rd.*
*Bethlehem Pike*
*Stenton Ave.*
*W. Cheltenham Ave.*
*W. Waverly Rd.*
*Michener Ave.*
*W. Chestnut Hill Ave.*
*Cresheim Valley Dr.*
*E. Gowen Ave.*
*E. Mount Airy Ave.*
*Germantown Ave.*
*Chew Avenue*
*E. Upsal St.*
*E. Cliveden St.*
*E. Washington Ln.*
*W. Johnson St.*
*W. Washington Ln.*
*High St.*
*Greene St.*
*E. Chelten Ave.*
*Wissahickon Ave.*
*W. Chelten Ave.*
*Wayne Ave.*

0    1/2 mi
0    1/2 km

main: $20 ✉ 7830 Germantown Ave., Chestnut Hill ☎ 215/242–4489 ⊕ www. restauranthokka.com ⊙ Closed Sun.

### Jansen

$$$ | AMERICAN | French cooking methods are married with refined takes on seasonal American comfort fare in the area's most classic fine-dining establishment. Set in an 18th-century "cottage" with a gorgeous back patio, the service is old-school in the care they take of diners, while a light touch—and seasonal ingredients—pervades their culinary concoctions. **Known for:** classic dishes expertly done; meticulous presentation; located in Cresheim Cottage, a building from the 1700s. $ Average main: $30 ✉ 7402 Germantown Ave., Mount Airy ☎ 267/335–5041 ⊕ www.jansenmtairy. com ⊙ Closed Sun.–Tues. No lunch.

### McNally's

$ | AMERICAN | FAMILY | People come to McNally's more for the food than the beer (families are welcome), and generally order one of the six featured sandwiches. The Schmitter, a cheesesteak on a kaiser roll with fried salami, fried onions, and a special sauce, is insanely delicious. **Known for:** The Schmitter; family vibe; no-nonsense service. $ Average main: $13 ✉ 8634 Germantown Ave., Chestnut Hill ☎ 215/247–9736 ⊕ www.mcnallys-tavern.com ⊙ Closed Mon. and Tues.

## ☕ Coffee and Quick Bites

### Bredenbreck's Ice Cream Parlor

$ | CAFÉ | It's all about the ice cream, hot fudge, and homemade whipped cream. They scoop Bassetts ice cream, make fabulous sundaes, and stay open late in the summer. **Known for:** generous sundaes; tipping usually gets you bigger scoops; friendly vibe. $ Average main: $5 ✉ 8126 Germantown Ave., Chestnut Hill ☎ 215/247–7374 ⊕ www.bredenbecks.com.

### Chestnut Hill Coffee Company

$ | CAFÉ | This trendy-for–Chestnut Hill spot roasts its own rich, delicious coffee, and fashions quite good mochas and frothy drinks with over-serious attention. The upstairs is a nice spot to chill for a while. **Known for:** its coffee-roasting pedigree; tasty mochas; hiring hip staff. $ Average main: $5 ✉ 8620 Germantown Ave., Chestnut Hill ☎ 215/242–8600 ⊕ chestnuthillcoffee.com ⊙ No dinner.

### High Point Café

$ | CAFÉ | Coffee shop, crêperie, purveyor of baked goods, and local gathering spot, the High Point offers a convivial picture of Mount Airy life. Daily pastry offerings are posted on their Facebook page. **Known for:** bustling atmosphere; sweet and savory crepes; orange-zest mocha. $ Average main: $8 ✉ 602 Carpenter La., Mount Airy ☎ 215/992–2077 ⊕ www. highpointcafe.us.com ⊙ No dinner.

### Market at the Fareway

$ | INTERNATIONAL | A mix of farmers' market, specialty-goods stands, and eateries with indoor and outdoor seating, this is an excellent lunch or late-afternoon meal destination. The best options include Chestnut Hill Brewing Company (beer and pizza), Chicko Tako (Korean tacos), and the Saigon Noodle Bar. **Known for:** something for everyone with options from 15 vendors; great lunch spot; modern farmer's market. $ Average main: $15 ✉ 8221 Germantown Ave., Chestnut Hill ☎ 215/242–5905 ⊕ www.marketat-thefareway.com ⊙ Closed Mon.–Tues. No dinner.

### Matines Café

$ | CAFÉ | This classic French café, run by a (real) French couple, has excellent pastries, baguette sandwiches, and soups. But, some might say most importantly, they know how to make a great cup of coffee. **Known for:** cozy spot; everything done just right; classic French café. $ Average main: $14 ✉ 89 Bethlehem Pike, Chestnut Hill ☎ 215/621–6667 ⊕ www. matinescafe.com ⊙ No dinner.

### Zsa's Ice Cream

$ | **AMERICAN** | Be prepared to get your mind blown by the creamy insanity of Zsa's ice cream. The salted caramel, Black Magic (chocolate cake and coffee ice cream), and a chocolate sorbet—so rich you won't believe it's sorbet—vie with other specialty flavors that continue to conquer the artisanal-ice-cream wars. **Known for:** inventive flavors; ice-cream sandwiches; ultimate dessert decadence. $ *Average main: $5* ✉ *6616 Germantown Ave., Mount Airy* ⊕ *zsasicecream.com* ◷ *Closed Mon. and Tues.*

##  Hotels

### Chestnut Hill Hotel

$ | **HOTEL** | This attractive midsize hotel is the place to rest if you want to station yourself in Northwest Philadelphia; it's not fancy inside, but it's well run and offers a perfectly pleasant stay at a great location. **Pros:** multiple lunch and dinner options next door; convenient to shops; standard but attractive rooms. **Cons:** not a bells-and-whistles hotel. $ *Rooms from: $149* ✉ *8229 Germantown Ave., Chestnut Hill* ☎ *215/242–5905* ⊕ *www.chestnuthillhotel.com* ⤵ *36 rooms* ⌾ *Free Breakfast.*

##  Nightlife

### BARS AND LOUNGES

#### McMenamins

**BREWPUBS** | This lively, family-friendly Mount Airy favorite has a fantastic choice of craft beer on tap, plus pretty good burgers, fish-and-chips, and dinner specials. ✉ *7170 Germantown Ave., Mount Airy* ☎ *215/247–9920.*

#### Mount Airy Tap Room

**BARS** | A spacious spot if you want to stretch out your legs, there's a nice patio as well as a wood-burning stove, a stellar draft list, and decent pub fare. ✉ *300 W. Mount Pleasant Ave., Mount Airy* ☎ *267/766–6668* ⊕ *mountairytaproom.com.*

### MUSIC CLUBS

#### Mermaid Inn

**LIVE MUSIC** | If you head to the Mermaid, know the vibe is a little provincial, but you can hear good live music (folk, blues, rock, jazz) Thursday through Saturday. Cover charges range from $5 to $10. ✉ *7673 Winston Rd., at Mermaid La., Chestnut Hill* ☎ *215/247–9797* ⊕ *www.themermaidinn.net.*

##  Performing Arts

### Quintessence Theatre Group

**THEATER** | Quintessence mounts quality, and at times innovative, productions of classic plays. ✉ *7137 Germantown Ave., Mount Airy* ☎ *215/987–4450* ⊕ *www.quintessencetheatre.org.*

##  Shopping

### Caleb Meyer Studio

**JEWELRY & WATCHES** | You'll find elegant and distinctive jewelry in gold and platinum at this well-known shop, where you can see new items being made behind the counter. It also sells an excellent collection of crafts in wood, glass, pottery, and silver. ✉ *8520 Germantown Ave., Chestnut Hill* ☎ *215/248–9250* ⊕ *www.calebmeyer.com.*

### Greene Street

**SECOND-HAND** | Don't be surprised by the great finds here—this is the consignment shop for people who like to say, "Look, I got this $300 designer dress in perfect condition for only $60!" ✉ *8524 Germantown Ave., Chestnut Hill* ☎ *215/331–6725* ⊕ *greenestreetstores.com/chestnuthill.*

Chapter 12

# SIDE TRIPS FROM PHILADELPHIA

Updated by
Linda Cabasin

 Sights
★★★★★

 Restaurants
★★★☆☆

 Hotels
★★★☆☆

 Shopping
★★★☆☆

 Nightlife
★★☆☆☆

# WELCOME TO
# SIDE TRIPS FROM PHILADELPHIA

## TOP REASONS TO GO

★ **Brandywine Museum of Art:** The work of iconic American artists Andrew Wyeth, N. C. Wyeth, and Jamie Wyeth are the focus.

★ **Longwood Gardens:** Internationally renowned gardens and conservatories are worth a visit any time of the year.

★ **American history lesson:** Valley Forge and Washington Crossing Historic Park are filled with structures and information recalling the American Revolution.

★ **Winterthur:** The collections of American furniture and objects offer a window on the nation's past through design. Its gardens are magnificent, too.

★ **Delaware River towns:** Historic riverfront towns like Bucks County's New Hope and Lambertville (across the river in New Jersey) attract day-trippers.

★ **Fun for kids:** Both LEGOLAND Discovery Center Philadelphia and Sesame Place are great spots for kids.

**1** **West Chester.** Restaurants, shops, and some interesting sights.

**2** **Chadds Ford.** The Brandywine Museum of Art is a top draw.

**3** **Centreville, Delaware.** This tiny village has a great location near Brandywine sights.

**4** **Kennett Square.** Strollable and filled with restaurants.

**5** **Wilmington, Delaware.** Beyond the city's downtown are sights such as Nemours Estate.

**6** **Valley Forge.** The historical park marking Washington's 1777–78 encampment and the King of Prussia mall.

**7** **Plymouth Meeting.** Kids can get creative at LEGOLAND Discovery Center Philadelphia.

**8** **Sesame Place.** Younger kids enjoy this Bucks County theme park.

**9** **Washington Crossing.** A park marks the site where Washington crossed the Delaware in 1776.

**10** **New Hope.** Delaware River views, indie shops, and lively restaurants.

**11** **Lambertville, New Jersey.** This quaint town lures canal-path strollers and antique shoppers.

12

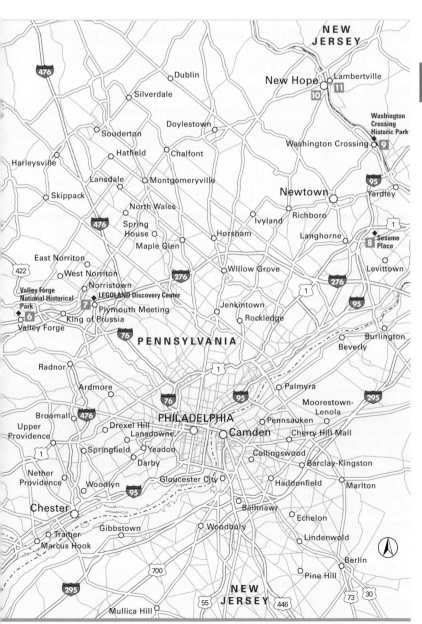

NEW JERSEY

476

Dublin

New Hope ○ Lambertville

Silverdale

10

11

Doylestown

Washington Crossing Historic Park

Souderton

Washington Crossing ○ 9

Hatfield ○ Chalfont

Harleysville

Lansdale ○ Montgomeryville

95

Newtown ○

Yardley

Skippack

North Wales

476

Spring House ○

Ivyland

Richboro

1

Maple Glen

Horsham

Langhorne ○

Sesame Place

8

East Norriton

422

West Norriton

276

Willow Grove

Levittown

Norristown

LEGOLAND Discovery Center

276

Valley Forge National Historical Park

7

Plymouth Meeting

Jenkintown

1

95

6

King of Prussia

Rockledge

Valley Forge

76

PENNSYLVANIA

Burlington

Beverly

Radnor ○

1

Ardmore

Palmyra

295

76

95

Moorestown-Lenola

Broomall

476

PHILADELPHIA

Pennsauken

Upper Providence

Drexel Hill

Cherry Hill Mall

1

Lansdowne

Camden

Springfield ○ Yeadon

Collingswood

Darby

Barclay-Kingston

Nether Providence

Woodlyn

95

Gloucester City ○

Haddonfield

Marlton

Chester ○

Bellmawr

Echelon

Trainer

Gibbstown

Woodbury

Lindenwold

Marcus Hook

Berlin

700

Pine Hill

295

NEW JERSEY

73

30

Mullica Hill ○

55

446

It's easy to expand your view of the Philadelphia area by taking one or more day trips to destinations that are within a 30-minute to one-hour drive of the city. Whether you head southwest or north, you can be immersed in a whole new world—or make that "worlds." An abundance of historic and artistic treasures, magnificent gardens, walkable towns, and fun shopping await you.

Southwest of the city are the verdant hills and ancient barns of the Brandywine Valley, home to three generations of Wyeths and other artists inspired by the rural landscapes outside their windows. Stop by the Brandywine Museum of Art to explore regional art, including works by N. C., Andrew, and Jamie Wyeth. Then you can visit the extravagant realm of du Pont country, including Pierre S. du Pont's resplendent Longwood Gardens in Kennett Square, whose summer fountain displays are world-renowned, and Winterthur, an important repository of American decorative furnishings, over the border near Wilmington, Delaware. Or you can explore the Revolutionary War battlefield of Brandywine at Chadds Ford, taste local wines, or stroll charming towns like Kennett Square and West Chester. These attractions are year-round favorites of Philadelphians, and area bed-and-breakfasts and inns (and plenty of chain hotels) make the Brandywine appealing as an overnight or weekend trip and as a day excursion.

The national historical park at Valley Forge, where Washington and his troops spent a difficult winter, adds another dimension to the revolutionary story that began in Independence Hall. Nearby, the John James Audubon Center at Mill Grove has a museum exploring the life and work of the famous naturalist and artist, whose first American home is here. Also not far from Valley Forge, the town called King of Prussia dates to that period but is now primarily synonymous with shopping thanks to its huge upscale mall. It's a half hour from Philadelphia and also accessible by public transportation. Families can enjoy expanding their creativity at LEGOLAND Discovery Center Philadelphia in Plymouth Meeting.

About an hour north of Philadelphia, Bucks County is known for quaint towns, art colonies, shopping, regional theater, and country inns. It's also home to Sesame Place, a water and theme park great for younger children. A park in Washington Crossing honors the site where Washington crossed the Delaware in 1776 and has historic buildings you can tour. Popular New Hope has historic sites as well as riverside walks, independent shops, and lively restaurants and bars. Pair a visit here with a stroll across the

Delaware River to Lambertville, New Jersey, with its canal path and plenty of antiques and home-furnishing shops, galleries, and restaurants.

## MAJOR REGIONS

With a strong legacy from two families, the artistic Wyeths and the industrialist du Ponts, the **Brandywine Valley,** an area southwest of Philadelphia, spans Pennsylvania and Delaware and offers many reasons to stay awhile, whether to take in vistas of the small river and tranquil landscapes, or explore top sights. **West Chester** and **Kennett Square** are both walkable towns with shops and restaurants; Kennett Square is near a major du Pont–related attraction, colorful Longwood Gardens. **Chadds Ford** has the excellent Brandywine Museum of Art, with works by the Wyeths and regional artists, and a Revolutionary War battlefield. In Delaware, tiny **Centreville** is near major sights like Winterthur's American decorative arts collection, and **Wilmington,** the state's capital, has good museums and another former du Pont home, Nemours Estate. Despite encroaching development, there are also still plenty of scenic back roads to explore around the Brandywine.

Several popular but very different attractions draw people to the area near suburban **Valley Forge,** northwest of the city. Serene **Valley Forge National Historical Park** commemorates and interprets the site of George Washington's 1777–78 winter encampment, a crucial point in the American Revolution. Nearby, sprawling King of Prussia mall has more than 450 shops and is a destination in itself. Twelve miles to the east, **LEGOLAND Discovery Center Philadelphia** provides engaging fun for kids who love the classic building toy.

About an hour north of Philadelphia by car, **Bucks County** was 622 square miles of sleepy, pretty countryside before being "discovered," first by artists and then by suburbanites and exurbanites. **Sesame Place,** in the more developed

southern part of the county, is a favorite theme and water park for younger kids. **Washington Crossing,** by the Delaware River, evokes the American Revolution with a historic park and buildings. To the north, the river town of **New Hope** has long been popular with artists, craftspeople, and shoppers, or anyone seeking a fun day out. **Lambertville,** across the Delaware in New Jersey, shares the same vibe and has a canal path, antiques and home furnishings shops, and restaurants.

# Planning

## Getting Here and Around

While some attractions can be reached by public transportation, the only practical way to tour Bucks County and much of the Brandywine Valley is by car.

### BUS

To get to Valley Forge, you can take SEPTA Bus 124 from 13th and Market Streets (it leaves about twice an hour starting at 4:30 am) for King of Prussia mall. Bus 125 also goes to the mall and continues on to Valley Forge National Historical Park; the service (about once an hour) is limited to times the park is open.

**CONTACTS SEPTA.** ☎ 215/580–7800 ⊕ www.septa.org.

### CAR

To reach the Brandywine Valley from Philadelphia, take I–95 south to U.S. 322 and then U.S. 1; it is about 25 miles away, and many attractions are on or near U.S. 1. To reach Wilmington, take I–95 south from Philadelphia; if you're on U.S. 1, pick up U.S. 202 south just past Concordville.

For Valley Forge, take the Schuylkill Expressway (I–76) west from Philadelphia to Exit 327 (Mall Boulevard). Make a right onto Mall Boulevard and a right onto North Gulph Road. Follow the road 1½ miles to Valley Forge National Historical

Park. Mall Boulevard also provides easy access to the King of Prussia shopping mall.

The most direct route to Bucks Country is I–95 north, which takes you near sights in the southern part of the county. Before you cross into New Jersey, take the exit and continue on Route 32, which runs along the Delaware past Washington Crossing Historic Park. New Hope is about 40 miles north of Philadelphia.

### TRAIN

Amtrak has frequent service from Philadelphia's 30th Street Station to Wilmington's station at 100 South French Street on the edge of downtown. It's a 20-minute ride. SEPTA's Wilmington/Newark commuter train has roughly hourly (less often on weekends) departures to Wilmington from Philadelphia's 30th Street, Suburban, and Jefferson train stations. The trip takes about 50 minutes.

**CONTACTS Amtrak.** ☎ 800/872–7245 ⊕ www.amtrak.com. **SEPTA.** ☎ 215/580–7800 ⊕ www.septa.org.

# When to Go

Each season provides plenty of reasons to visit the Brandywine, which is about 45 minutes' to an hour's drive from Center City Philadelphia, and Bucks County, about an hour north of the city. Spring and summer bring a Technicolor display of flowers at Longwood Gardens and verdant green to the Brandywine Valley countryside, Valley Forge National Historical Park, and Bucks County. The chance to witness spectacular fall foliage and crisper weather is a compelling case for an autumnal visit, although the spectacular indoor and outdoor holiday light show at Longwood and the chance to relax by a fireplace at a charming inn are reasons enough to come during the cold-weather months. Christmas season brings holiday festivals to Bucks County

as well, including the annual reenactment of Washington crossing the Delaware. You can easily make day trips to these regions from the city, but avoid traveling west on I–76, and to a lesser extent, north or south on I–95, during rush hour. Weekends, spring through fall, tend to be the busiest season for visitors; December brings crowds and traffic for Longwood's holiday light displays (timed tickets required).

# Hotels

Many of the more charming, even historic, accommodations in these areas may be considered bed-and-breakfasts because of their intimate atmosphere, but they're far from the typical B&B—which is usually a room or two in a private home—and are more accurately characterized as inns or small hotels. These days, though, chain hotels are plentiful around the region. Although they have less atmosphere than inns, they are a family-friendly, good-value alternative to B&Bs, which may not accept very young children.

# Restaurants

Many restaurants in both the Brandywine Valley and Bucks County serve American cuisine, with creative contemporary touches at the better establishments. International cuisines also have a growing presence. You'll find sophisticated restaurants and casual country spots. Most present local and regional specialties—fresh seafood from the Chesapeake Bay and dishes made with Kennett Square mushrooms. Restaurants here (as elsewhere these days) can have staffing issues, so it's best to make a reservation when possible and confirm opening days and hours.

## HOTEL AND RESTAURANT PRICES

⇨ *Hotel prices in the reviews are the lowest cost of a standard double room in high season. Restaurant prices in the reviews are the average cost of a main course at dinner, or if dinner is not served, at lunch. Restaurant and hotel reviews have been shortened. For full information, visit Fodors.com.*

## Visitor Information

Operated by the Chester County Conference and Visitors Bureau, the Brandywine Valley visitor center near the entrance to Longwood Gardens has helpful staff, a few exhibits, and brochures (on everything from sights to local wineries and breweries) and maps. The building, a former Quaker meeting house, played a role in the Underground Railroad.

Bucks County maintains a visitor center in Bensalem, but the county website has information on all the region's sights, restaurants, and lodgings.

The website for the Greater Wilmington Convention and Visitors Bureau (⇨ *see Wilmington, Delaware for more information*) has information about the seasonal (late May through early September) Brandywine Treasure Trail Passport, which entitles an individual or family to discounted admission at 12 attractions, including Longwood Gardens in Pennsylvania. If you're visiting a number of sights, it's a good value and can be purchased online or at the sights themselves.

**CONTACTS Brandywine Valley Tourism Information Center.** ⊠ *300 Greenwood Rd., Kennett Square* ☎ *484/770–8550* ⊕ *brandywinevalley.com.* **Bucks County Visitors Bureau.** ⊠ *3207 Street Rd., Bensalem* ☎ *215/639–0300 Bucks County Visitor Center* ⊕ *visitbuckscounty.com.*

# West Chester

*35 miles west of Philadelphia via I–95.*

The county seat since 1786, this historic mile-square city (population 19,000) holds distinctive 18th- and 19th-century architecture in Greek Revival and Victorian styles. It's also home to West Chester University, which adds a lively student vibe. A small but vital downtown has shopping possibilities as well as restaurants and bars serving everything from classic American fare to microbrews. Fine examples of classical architecture, including the Historic Chester County Courthouse (⊠ *2 N. High St.*), can be found near the intersection of High and Gay Streets.

## GETTING HERE AND AROUND

From Philadelphia, West Chester is a 50-minute drive via I–76 west and U.S. 202 south. The downtown area is highly walkable but you need a car to access nearby attractions.

## ESSENTIALS

**VISITOR INFORMATION West Chester Downtown.** ⊕ *downtownwestchester. com.*

##  Sights

### American Helicopter Museum & Education Center

**OTHER MUSEUM | FAMILY |** Ever since Philadelphian Harold Pitcairn made the first rotorcraft flight in 1928, the southeastern Pennsylvania area has been considered the birthplace of the helicopter industry, and the impressive aircraft filling this museum in a business park near Brandywine Regional Airport reflect this heritage. A number of leading manufacturers remain in the region. About three dozen vintage and modern aircraft, a room of models, and information boards and short videos reflect the copter's historic roles in war and rescue missions, in agriculture, and in police surveillance.

# Visiting the Brandywine Valley

The Brandywine Valley encompasses 350 square miles, incorporating parts of three counties in two states: Chester and Delaware counties in Pennsylvania and New Castle County in Delaware. Winding through this scenic region (about 25 miles southwest of Philadelphia), the Brandywine River flows lazily from West Chester, Pennsylvania, to Wilmington, Delaware. Although in spots it's more a creek than a river, it has nourished many of the valley's economic and artistic endeavors. Today the Philadelphia (and Wilmington) suburbs continue to encroach: new housing developments continue to crop up, and the main highways, U.S. 1 and U.S.

202, bring with them shopping malls and traffic snarls. Still, traveling down country roads, particularly those that intersect Route 52, makes you feel you have discovered a remote treasure. Just be careful driving those curving back roads at night.

If you start early enough, and limit your time at each stop, you can tour the valley's top three attractions—the Brandywine Museum of Art, Longwood Gardens, and Winterthur—in one day. If you have more time to spend in the valley, you can visit additional sites in Pennsylvania and then move on to those near Wilmington.

Docents provide helpful context, and visitors can climb aboard a few aircraft and try the (nonmoving) flight simulator to get a sense of the helicopter experience. The museum is serious and packed with information, but older children will appreciate it. Check the website for special exhibitions and events, including helicopter rides. ⊠ *1220 American Blvd., West Chester* ☎ *610/436–9600* ⊕ *www. americanhelicopter.museum* 🎫 *$10* 🕐 *Closed Mon.–Wed.*

### Chester County History Center

**HISTORY MUSEUM** | *Becoming Chester County,* the center's excellent permanent exhibition, uses its rich collections of historical objects and modern interactive displays to tell compelling stories of the challenges and opportunities Delaware Valley inhabitants faced from the late 1600s to today. Galleries address the Lenape people, the American Revolution, slavery, industrialization, women's suffrage, immigration, and other issues, often using the examples of local residents. The collections are gorgeous, including decorative furniture, quilts,

period clothing, tall-case clocks, and cross-stitch samplers. A hands-on history lab lets kids try some old-style tools and dress up in a hoop skirt, and the center's library has extensive records and photographs. The society's two-building complex includes a former horticultural hall that was the site of the first women's rights convention in Pennsylvania. ⊠ *225 N. High St., West Chester* ☎ *610/692– 4800* ⊕ *mycchc.org* 🎫 *$8* 🕐 *Closed Sun. and Mon.*

## 🍴 Restaurants

### Andiario

**$$$$** | **ITALIAN** | Only its name in fairly small lettering on the door announces Andiario, a 24-seat, prix-fixe restaurant that has attracted national attention for its brilliant use of Pennsylvania ingredients in weekly-changing four-course, Italian-inspired menus featuring fish and seafood, poultry, and meat. The setting for each night's sophisticated feast is simple: a gleaming open kitchen faces the small dining room with its clean

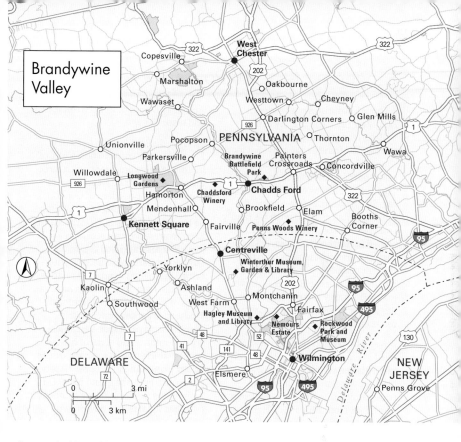

## Brandywine Valley

lines and tables with white tablecloths, and large windows overlook the street. **Known for:** good wine list includes some Pennsylvania bottles; superb handmade pasta; hard-to-score reservations. $ *Average main: $80* ⊠ *106 W. Gay St., West Chester* ☎ *484/887–0919* ⊕ *andiario.com* ⊗ *Closed Sun.–Tues. No lunch.*

### The Couch Tomato Café

$ | **AMERICAN** | **FAMILY** | College students, their parents, and locals gather at this casual eatery for tasty soups, pizzas, sandwiches, and salads that favor fresh, local, and organic ingredients. Step up to the counter to order from the menu or build your own sandwich or pizza from generous ingredient lists, then grab a seat in a space with exposed brick walls, tomato-colored (of course) banquettes, and simple, well-worn wooden tables. **Known for:** good vegan and gluten-free options; grilled cheese and tomato bisque soup combo; rooftop deck for alfresco dining. $ *Average main: $13* ⊠ *31 W. Gay St., West Chester* ☎ *484/887–0241* ⊕ *thecouchtomato.com.*

### Iron Hill Brewery & Restaurant

$$ | **AMERICAN** | **FAMILY** | An old Woolworth's building with tin ceilings and maple floors is now this large, bustling restaurant and brewpub in the heart of downtown, one of a number of Iron Hill outposts in the mid-Atlantic. The extensive menu lists everything from nachos and flatbreads to all kinds of burgers (meat and non-meat), steaks, and salads. **Known for:** seasonal beers on tap; two weekday happy hours (one early and one later at night); vegetarian, vegan, and gluten-free options. $ *Average main: $19* ⊠ *3 W. Gay St., West Chester* ☎ *610/738–9600* ⊕ *www. ironhillbrewery.com.*

# Kingdom of the du Ponts

Although paintings of the Wyeth family distilled the Brandywine Valley's tranquil landscapes, it was the du Pont family that provided more than a bit of its magnificence, adding grand gardens, mansions, and mills. Their kingdom was established by the family patriarch, Pierre-Samuel du Pont, who had escaped with his family from post-Revolutionary France and settled in northern Delaware. The earliest version of what is now the DuPont company was founded in 1802 by his son Éleuthère Irénée (E.I.), who made the family fortune in gunpowder and iron; later generations would focus on chemicals and textiles.

E.I. and five generations of du Ponts lived in Eleutherian Mills, the stately family home on the grounds of a black-powder mill that has been transformed into the Hagley Museum. The home, from which Mrs. Henry du Pont was driven after accidental blasts at the powder works, was closed in 1921. Louise du Pont Crowninshield, a great-granddaughter of E.I., restored the house fully before opening it to the public. Louise's relatives were busy, too. Henry Francis du Pont was filling his country estate, Winterthur (now a museum), with furniture by Duncan Phyfe, silver by Paul Revere, splendid decorative objects made or used in America, and entire interior woodwork fittings salvaged from American homes built between 1640 and 1860.

Pierre S. du Pont (cousin of Henry Francis) was devoted to horticulture, but he was also president and a director of E.I. du Pont de Nemours and Company and president of General Motors during his long career. In 1906, he bought 202 acres of an 18th-century farm to preserve its historic trees (now Peirce's Park) and created Longwood Gardens, where he entertained his many friends and relatives. Today the 1,100-acre gardens have 350 acres of meadows and meticulously landscaped gardens open to the public. Displays include Versailles-style fountains and acres of heated conservatories with tropical gardens, desert plants, and lush floral displays. Pierre also built the grand Hotel Du Pont in 1913, adjacent to the company's then-headquarters in downtown Wilmington. (The Du Pont company no longer owns the hotel.) No expense was spared; more than 18 French and Italian craftspeople labored for two years, carving, gilding, and painting. Alfred I. du Pont's country estate, Nemours, was named after the family's ancestral home in north-central France. It encompasses 200 acres of grounds with formal French gardens and a grand but somehow homey mansion in Louis XVI style.

## 🛍 Shopping

### Baldwin's Book Barn

**BOOKS** | In the countryside 2 miles south of downtown West Chester, this book lover's refuge in a converted, five-story 1822 barn has nooks and crannies filled with more than 300,000 used and rare books on almost every subject, along with historic maps and prints. ✉ *865 Lenape Rd. (Rte. 52), West Chester* ☎ *610/696–0816* ⊕ *bookbarn.com.*

### Malena's Vintage Boutique

**WOMEN'S CLOTHING** | Carefully curated, color-themed displays make this well-lighted vintage women's clothing and accessories shop downtown a delightful place to browse and buy. Nicely organized jewelry cases offer Bakelite, rhinestone, and other costume pieces. The moderately priced and higher-end clothing is mostly from around 1900 through the 1970s; for more options, make an appointment to see additional vintage, couture, and even antique items at the nearby showroom. ⊠ *101 W. Gay St., West Chester* ☎ *610/738–9952* ⊕ *malenasboutique.com.*

### Pine + Quill

**HOUSEWARES** | Stylish modern housewares, home decor, and furniture are attractively arranged at this locally owned shop, which also displays jewelry and crafts by area residents. It's a good option for reasonably priced gifts or a treat for your own home. ⊠ *23 N. Walnut St., West Chester* ☎ *302/383–9759* ⊕ *pineandquillshop.com.*

 Activities

### Northbrook Canoe Co.

**SELF-GUIDED TOURS** | **FAMILY** | May through October, you can explore the slow, gentle Brandywine River by kayak, canoe, or tube on a relaxing short or half-day self-guided trip with the family-run Northbrook Canoe Co. Check the website for periodic special trips, like a twilight canoe trip followed by dinner. Rentals run from $25 per tube to $50 per canoe or kayak. ⊠ *1810 Beagle Rd., West Chester* ☎ *610/793–2279, 800/898–2279* ⊕ *www.northbrookcanoe.com.*

# Chadds Ford

*8 miles south of West Chester, 30 miles southwest of Philadelphia via I–95 and U.S. 322.*

Immortalized in painter Andrew Wyeth's serene landscapes, Chadds Ford was less bucolic in the 18th century, when one of the bloodiest battles of the Revolutionary War was fought here along Brandywine Creek. A battlefield park and the excellent Brandywine Museum of Art, which celebrates American masters including Brandywine Valley residents, make this historic town appealing. Many businesses are spread out along U.S. 1, and developments make the town busier each year, but there are pretty side roads to explore as well.

### GETTING HERE AND AROUND

From Philadelphia, take I–95 south to U.S. 322 toward West Chester and follow signs to U.S. 1. The latter is the major thoroughfare to visit attractions in Chadds Ford and can get congested on weekends, so be prepared for some stop-and-go traffic.

 Sights

### Brandywine Battlefield Park

**MILITARY SIGHT** | The quiet park is near the site of the Battle of Brandywine, where British general William Howe and his troops defeated George Washington on September 11, 1777, after which the Continental Army fled to Chester, leaving Philadelphia vulnerable to British troops. The battle covered 10 square miles, involved almost 30,000 soldiers, and played an important role in the larger war. The small visitor center has a film and displays about the battle that are a good introduction to the area's history. On the site are two restored Quaker farmhouses, one of which once sheltered Washington and General Lafayette; guided tours of these are offered Friday and Saturday. The 50-acre park is a fine place for a picnic. Ask for info about driving to see key battlefield sights like the Birmingham Friends Meeting house, where soldiers lie in a common grave, or reserve ahead for a guided battlefield tour. ⊠ *1491 Baltimore Pike, Chadds Ford* ☎ *610/459–3342* ⊕ *www.brandywinebattlefield.org* 🎟 *Park and grounds free; house tours, museum, and film $8; guided battlefield tour $25 per person (reserve ahead)* ⊘ *Park closed*

The Gideon Gilpin House is one of two restored Quaker farmhouses on the Brandywine Battlefield Park site; the other was Washington's headquarters.

*Sun., Mon., and mid-Dec.–mid-Mar. Visitor center closed Sun.–Thurs.*

### ★ Brandywine Museum of Art

**ART MUSEUM** | In a beautifully converted Civil War–era gristmill, the museum contains the art of Chadds Ford native Andrew Wyeth (1917–2009), a major American realist painter, as well as works by his father, N. C. Wyeth, illustrator of many children's classics; and Jamie Wyeth, Andrew's son. The collection also emphasizes still lifes, landscape paintings, and American illustration, with works by such artists as Howard Pyle and Horace Pippin. A glass-wall lobby on each of the three floors overlooks the river and countryside that inspired artists. Seasonal tours (daily, but a limited number) of three other buildings enhance the museum experience; children under age seven are not permitted on these. The N. C. Wyeth House and Studio, set on a hill, holds many props N. C. used in creating his illustrations. His daughter, Carolyn, lived and painted here until 1994. Andrew Wyeth's Studio, where the artist produced many notable works, is on view, too. You can also tour the Kuerner Farm; Andrew used the landscape, buildings, and animals as the subjects of many of his best-known paintings. A shuttle takes you from the museum to the buildings for an hour-long guided tour. A fine gift shop and the Millstone Café, both acessible without paying admission, round out the offerings. ⊠ *1 Hoffman's Mill Rd., Chadds Ford* ✛ *At U.S. 1 and Rte. 100* ☎ *610/388–2700* ⊕ *brandywine. org/museum* ⊠ *$18 museum, free first Sun. of month Feb.–Nov.; $10 for studio and farm tours* ☉ *Closed Tues. Jan–late Nov. No house or studio tours Dec.–Mar.*

### Chaddsford Winery

**WINERY** | Pennsylvania's wine scene keeps growing: the Brandywine area has more than a dozen wineries, and at Chaddsford you can sample the vintages of one of the oldest (1982). Visitors can purchase flights and snacks for self-guided tastings, sampling dry and sweeter wines made with grapes grown in Pennsylvania, New York, and Maryland. One-hour reserve tastings

# Wyeth Country

You may experience a strong sense of déjà vu during a journey to the Brandywine Valley. While creating some of the most beloved works in 20th-century American art, Andrew Wyeth made the valley's vistas instantly recognizable. Using colors quintessentially Brandywine—the earthen brown of its hills, the slate gray of its stone farmhouses, and the dark green of its spruce trees—the famous American realist captured its unostentatiously beautiful landscape. Andrew's father, N. C. Wyeth, moved to then-rural Chadds Ford in 1908, and others have come to fall in love with its peaceful byways.

Although Andrew Wyeth is the most well-known local artist, the area's artistic tradition began long before, when artist-illustrator Howard Pyle started a school of illustration in Wilmington in 1900. He had more than 100 students, including the famous illustrator and artist N.C. Wyeth; Frank Schoonover; Jessie Willcox Smith; and Harvey Dunn. It was this tradition, as well as their famous father and grandfather, that inspired Andrew and his son Jamie.

In 1967 local residents formed the Brandywine Conservancy to prevent industrialization of the area and pollution of the river; their actions included significant land purchases. In 1971 the organization opened the Brandywine Museum of Art in a preserved 19th-century gristmill. It celebrates the Brandywine School of artists in a setting much in tune with their world. The work of the conservancy continues today, focusing on protection of land and water, and may be more critical than ever as development continues around the Brandywine Valley.

(reservations required) with cheeses are offered weekends in the barrel room. Visitors can also buy bottles, and the winery has a tent. There's no restaurant, but food trucks come on weekends. Chaddsford has concerts and special events (some require an extra fee) on its grounds, generally on weekends, and it can get busy. ⊠ *632 Baltimore Pike/U.S. 1, Chadds Ford* ☎ *610/388–6221* ⊕ *chaddsford.com* 🍷 *Self-guided 3- wine flights $12–$16; 1-hr guided reserve tastings (weekends) $35.*

### Penns Woods Winery
**WINERY** | A family-run business founded in 2001, this winery produces award-winning wines from Pennsylvania-grown grapes that range from sweet and floral Moscato to bold Bordeaux-style wines. The 30-acre property is a great place to picnic with the family (note that children can't go indoors), with about 100 tables on the grounds. An outdoor wine bar is open April through October. A short menu of cheeses, crackers, and charcuterie is offered. Check the website as there's live music, food and wine pairings, tours, and other events most weekends. ⊠ *124 Beaver Valley Rd., Chadds Ford* ☎ *610/459–0808* ⊕ *www.pennswoodswinery.com* 🍷 *Tasting $18 for 5 wines (reservations required for weekend tastings); tours $10 (Sat. June–Aug. by reservation)* ⊘ *Closed Mon. Jan.–Mar.*

## 🍴 Restaurants

### Antica Restaurant & Wine Bar
**$$** | **ITALIAN** | At this locally popular spot, some stone and brick walls, a bar area, and a pleasant patio (open for dining in season) establish a comfortable atmosphere for enjoying tasty handmade pastas and other Italian dishes. Wine choices aren't extensive, but the food

menus are lengthy, with lunch options such as a chicken parmigiana sandwich and sweet pea ravioli, and dinner choices that include veal saltimboca and fettuccine bolognese. **Known for:** pork cheeks and tagliatelle in a cream sauce; gemelli carbonara with pancetta; Italian favorites and some more adventurous dishes. ⓢ *Average main: $24 ⊠ 1623 Baltimore Pike, Chadds Ford ☎ 484/770–8631 ⊕ anticapa.com ⊘ Closed Mon.*

### Terrain Café

$$$ | AMERICAN | Part of the Terrain garden center and home furnishings store, this BYOB café and restaurant occupies a greenhouse space adorned with pieces of wood, party lights, and leafy plants. It's the perfect match for a brunch/lunch or dinner of sophisticated, seasonal regional fare such as artisanal cheeses, mushroom soup, vegetable-filled bowls, salads, and creative meat and fish options. **Known for:** bread served in a clay pot; list of teas, coffee drinks, and flavored spritzers; outdoor seating in season. ⓢ *Average main: $25 ⊠ 914 Baltimore Pike (U.S. 1), at Evergreen Dr., Glen Mills ✢ 7½ miles southwest of downtown West Chester ☎ 610/459–6030 ⊕ shopterrain.com.*

#  Hotels

### Brandywine River Hotel

$ | HOTEL | Near the Brandywine Museum of Art, this modern two-story hotel has traditional Queen Anne–style furnishings and some floral fabrics that create a somewhat more B&B feel than is found in the many nearby chain hotels. **Pros:** convenient to major attractions; fitness room; near some restaurants and a café-bakery. **Cons:** uninspired decor and facilities could use some updating; close to busy U.S. 1; small continental breakfast. ⓢ *Rooms from: $159 ⊠ 1609 Baltimore Pike (U.S. 1), Bldg. 300, Chadds Ford ☎ 610/388–1200 ⊕ brandywineriverhotelpa.com ⇆ 39 rooms ❖❖l Free Breakfast.*

### Fairville Inn

$$ | B&B/INN | Centrally located halfway between Longwood Gardens and Winterthur, this three-building B&B renovated in 2020 by new owners sets itself apart from others with bright, uncluttered rooms stylishly furnished for modern but still traditional tastes in white, cream, and light gray with mostly wood floors. **Pros:** gas fireplaces and decks in all rooms; electric car-charging station; delicious, creative breakfast. **Cons:** some street noise at times from busy Route 52; design may be too minimal for some; suites are expensive. ⓢ *Rooms from: $240 ⊠ 506 Kennett Pike (Rte. 52), Chadds Ford ☎ 610/388–5900 ⊕ www.fairvilleinn.com ⇆ 10 rooms ❖❖l Free Breakfast.*

### ★ The Inn at Grace Winery

$$ | B&B/INN | With a classic stone house at its center, this historic property with multiple buildings—part of William Penn's land grant to the Hemphill family—carves out a tranquil 35 acres of Brandywine Valley countryside, including a winery. **Pros:** elegant decor in rooms and public areas; tasting room and Manor House dining options on weekends; some cottage rooms are child- and pet-friendly. **Cons:** walking in the dark from cottage rooms to the main house; small free continental breakfast; somewhat farther from main Brandywine attractions. ⓢ *Rooms from: $210 ⊠ 50 Sweetwater Rd., Glen Mills ☎ 610/459–4711 ⊕ gracewinery.com ⇆ 18 rooms ❖❖l Free Breakfast.*

#  Shopping

### Terrain at Styer's

OTHER SPECIALTY STORE | The Philly-based folks behind Anthropologie also created Terrain, a lively store that integrates the outdoors (a garden center) with the indoors (stylish home furnishings). Though this branch is set amid shopping centers, its barn- and greenhouse-like buildings (some from Styer's, the nursery formerly in this location) create a small, enchanted world. Seasonal plants appear outdoors and inside, and terrariums, planters and pots, serving pieces and dishes, and soaps and lotions are all part of the mix; the holidays are particularly enchanting. Linger at the excellent café for lunch or dinner. ⊠ *914 Baltimore Pike (U.S. 1), Glen Mills* ✛ *7½ miles southwest of downtown West Chester* ☎ *610/459–2400* ⊕ *shopterrain.com.*

# Centreville, Delaware

*5 miles south of Chadds Ford via U.S. 1 and Rte. 52 (Kennett Pike).*

The village is aptly named: Centreville, Delaware, founded in 1750 and listed in the National Register of Historic Places, was a midway point between the farms of Kennett Square and the markets of Wilmington. The tiny village, with a historical tavern and some art and antiques shops, is in the middle of the Brandywine Valley's attractions. Longwood Gardens, Winterthur, and the Brandywine Museum of Art are all less than 5 miles away. Kennett Pike (Route 52) runs through the village; the surrounding two-lane roads take you through some of the still-bucolic parts of the valley.

## GETTING HERE AND AROUND
Traffic on Kennett Pike picks up during rush hours; U.S. 1 gets busy on weekends, too.

## ◉ Sights

### ★ Winterthur Museum, Garden & Library
**HISTORY MUSEUM** | Henry Francis du Pont (1880–1969) housed his nearly 90,000 objects of American decorative art in this 1,000-acre sprawling country estate; his collection, displayed in 175 rooms, is recognized as one of the nation's finest. Its objects, created or used in America between 1640 and 1860, include Chippendale furniture, silver tankards by Paul Revere, and Chinese porcelain made for George Washington. General admission includes a self-guided introductory tour and access to special exhibitions, the garden tram, and grounds. Themed guided tours (reserve in advance; extra fee) allow a deeper look the ceramics, textiles, furniture, and more. Children are welcome on introductory tours but must be eight years old for themed tours. Surrounding the estate are landscaped lawns and 60 acres of famous naturalistic gardens, including spectacular azaleas in spring, which you visit on a narrated tram ride (weather permitting) or on your own. There are also 25 miles of walking trails. The Enchanted Woods is a fantasy-theme 3-acre children's garden with an 8-foot-wide bird's nest, a faerie cottage with a thatch roof, and a troll bridge. A gift shop and cafeteria are on the grounds. ∎**TIP➔ Allow four hours minimum to explore the museum, gardens, and grounds.** ⊠ *5105 Kennett Pike, Winterthur* ✛ *5 miles south of U.S. 1* ☎ *302/888–4600, 800/448–3883* ⊕ *winterthur.org* ⊠ *$22 ($27 mid-Nov.–early Jan.) for self-guided introductory tour, special exhibition galleries, garden tram, and grounds; $10 extra for special guided tours (advance reservations required); admission valid for 2 consecutive days* ☉ *Closed early Jan.–Feb., and Mon. Mar.–late Nov. Library (open to researchers by appointment) closed Sat.–Mon.*

## ⓦ Restaurants

### Buckley's Tavern
**$$** | **AMERICAN** | **FAMILY** | This casual roadside tavern in a building dating back to 1817 serves typical burgers, classic comfort food, and salads, but the menu has some surprises such as shrimp and grits and crab Cobb salad, and the dessert and hors d'oeuvres menus are appealing. Pick from the wine list and dine on the sunny porch or patio, by the bar with its TV, or in a dining room with a fireplace. **Known for:** longtime spot popular with locals and travelers; rooftop bar and grill;

long list of U.S. and some international beers. $ *Average main: $19* ✉ *5812 Kennett Pike, Centreville* ☎ *302/656–9776* ⊕ *www.buckleystavern.com.*

### Krazy Kat's

**$$$$ | MODERN AMERICAN |** Oil paintings of regal felines and other cat-themed images watch over diners at this plushly but wittily furnished restaurant, complete with animal-print chairs, in a former blacksmith shop at the Inn at Montchanin Village. The unique setting and creative modern American menu draw regulars from Wilmington, Philadelphia, and beyond, who come for a frequently changing seasonal menu that includes ample seafood options as well as beef choices. **Known for:** romantic special-occasion vibe; crab bisque with lump crab; good weekend brunch menu. $ *Average main: $35* ✉ *Inn at Montchanin Village, 528 Montchanin Rd., Montchanin* ☎ *302/888–4200* ⊕ *krazykatsde.com* 🕑 *No lunch weekdays.*

 ## Hotels

### The Inn at Montchanin Village & Spa

**$$ | HOTEL |** This historical lodging, also home to Krazy Kat's restaurant, includes 28 guest rooms in 11 painstakingly restored 19th-century cottages that once housed workers from the nearby du Pont powder mills. **Pros:** mix of modern amenities and period charm in rooms and suites; long list of treatments at spa; beautiful gardens. **Cons:** steps and stairs around property may be an issue for some people; rooms vary widely in size and configuration; guests pay for weekend breakfast (free continental breakfast weekdays is picked up at front desk). $ *Rooms from: $209* ✉ *528 Montchanin Rd., Montchanin* ✛ *Near intersection of Rte. 100 and Kirk Rd.* ☎ *302/888–2133* ⊕ *montchanin.com* ⇘ *28 rooms* ⦿ *No Meals.*

# Kennett Square

*7 miles northwest of Centreville via Rte. 52 and U.S. 1.*

Just 3 miles west of popular Longwood Gardens, this small town (population 5,900) charms with its Victorian-era buildings, tree-lined streets, and shops, galleries, and good restaurants centered on East State Street between Broad and Union Streets. Coffee shops, breweries, and artisan markets are among the businesses that have refreshed downtown (⊕ *kennettcollaborative.org*). Kennett Square was active in the Underground Railroad because of the area's proximity to the Mason-Dixon Line; the Kennett Underground Railroad Center (⊕ *kennettundergroundrr.org*) offers a monthly bus tour of sites spring through fall. The longtime Mexican community adds diversity to the town.

Kennett Square is where mushroom cultivation began in the United States. By the mid-1920s, 90% of the nation's mushrooms were grown in southeastern Pennsylvania, and the area still produces more than 60% of the nation's mushrooms. The town celebrates its heritage with its annual Mushroom Festival in September, on the first weekend after Labor Day.

 ## Sights

### ★ Longwood Gardens

**GARDEN | FAMILY |** Today it has an international reputation for its immaculate, colorful gardens and conservatories full of flowers and themed displays, but the Longwood Gardens story began in 1906, when Pierre S. du Pont (1870–1945) bought part of a Quaker farm and turned it into the ultimate early-20th-century estate garden, with magnificent fountain displays. Seasonal attractions on the nearly 400 acres of the 1,100-acre property open to the public include magnolias and azaleas in spring; floral borders in summer; chrysanthemums in fall; and very popular nighttime light displays in summer and the winter holiday season. Spring through fall, fountain shows (some with fireworks) in the 1,719-jet main fountain garden are a highlight. Bad weather is no problem, as cacti, orchids, and floral displays fill heated conservatories. The Water Lily Court has undergone renovations, replacing the West Conservatory with a new conservatory and Cascade Garden, and adding a new restaurant. Besides children's gardens outside and in the conservatories, kids can explore three tree houses on the grounds. Concerts and other performances (some requiring separate tickets) take place year-round. The cafeteria and fancier 1906 restaurant (the latter is closed January and February) serve varied fare; the seasonal Beer Garden is a fun option. ✉ *1001 Longwood Rd., Kennett Square* ✛ *3 miles northeast of Kennett Square off U.S. 1* ☎ *610/388–1000* ⊕ *longwoodgardens.org* ✉ *$25 off-peak; $30 peak season, including winter holiday season; timed tickets required* ✪ *Closed Tues. in non-peak periods.*

## 🍴 Restaurants

### Hank's Place
**$ | AMERICAN | FAMILY |** Flooding in 2021 destroyed this Chadds Ford diner open since 1950, so while it waits to rebuild, Hank's has relocated to Kennett Square, where locals and visitors flock to the airy, homey, wood-paneled space for hearty breakfasts and lunches. Classic comfort cooking includes the omelet with roasted Kennett Square mushrooms, Hank's eggs Benedict, burgers, a triple decker club, and mac and cheese. **Known for:** some breakfast selections served all day; lines may be long on weekends but move fast; Andrew Wyeth was a patron back in the day. $ *Average main: $15* ✉ *201 Birch St., Kennett Square* ☎ *610/448–9988* ⊕ *hanksplacechaddsford.com* ✪ *No dinner.*

### Sovana Bistro
**$$$ | MODERN AMERICAN |** A fire caused a rebuilding of this longtime favorite in 2021, but chef Nicholas Farrell still transforms local and organic seasonal ingredients into satisfying meals in a rustic-chic space (think exposed brick, open kitchen, wood, a large aluminum-topped bar, and modern fixtures) 2 miles north of downtown Kennett Square in a shopping center. The cuisine mixes contemporary American choices with French, Italian, and Mediterranean fare, including sophisticated pastas, wood-fired pizzas, meat and seafood, and sandwiches and bowls at lunch (including vegetarian options). **Known for:** artisanal cheese plate and charcuterie board; wood-roasted local mushroom appetizer; plenty of vegetarian options. $ *Average main: $30* ✉ *Willowdale Town Center, 696 Unionville Rd., Kennett Square* ☎ *610/444–5600* ⊕ *www.sovanabistro.com* ✪ *Closed Sun. and Mon.*

### ★ Talula's Table
**$$$$ | AMERICAN |** The pricey eight-course prix-fixe dinner at this cozy, cult-favorite market and eat-in spot in the heart of Kennett Square requires advance planning, but fortunately Talula's has its own artisanal cheeses, house-cured meats, and handmade breads and pastas throughout the day, along with a coffee bar and prepared meals for takeout. Breakfast and lunch at the communal table feature seasonal soups, salads, and sandwiches using local ingredients. **Known for:** dinner reservations required a year in advance (but check website for cancellations); delicious baked goods and coffees; mini gourmet grocery. $ *Average main: $125* ✉ *102 W. State St., Kennett Square* ☎ *610/444–8255* ⊕ *www.talulastable.com.*

## Hotels

**Inn at Whitewing Farm**

$$$ | **B&B/INN** | Just 2 miles from Longwood Gardens, this family-run, countryside bed-and-breakfast on 13 acres of beautifully landscaped grounds and gardens offers more amenities than most and has plush, traditionally furnished rooms and suites in four buildings separate from the main house. **Pros:** landscaped patio with outdoor pool and whirlpool bath; tennis court and pond stocked for fishing; delectable three-course breakfasts. **Cons:** popular spot can get booked up; some walking as buildings are spread out; not all rooms have fireplaces. [$] *Rooms from: $255* ✉ *370 Valley Rd., West Chester* ☎ *610/388–2013* 🌐 *innatwhitewingfarm.com* 🛏 *11 rooms* 🍴 *Free Breakfast.*

## Shopping

**The Woodlands at Phillips Mushroom Farms**

**FOOD** | Kennett Square is famous for mushrooms that appear on many local menus, and this small shop in the old brick family farmhouse overflows with mushroom-theme items from aprons to guest towels; fresh, dried, and marinated mushrooms; and specialty mushroom products like soups and teas. Steps away, in the farm's informative mushroom-growing exhibit, you'll see and learn how mushrooms are grown indoors. It's 1½ miles south of downtown. (The Mushroom Cap downtown at ✉ *114 W. State St.* is another option for mushrooms and themed gift items.) ✉ *1020 Kaolin Rd., Kennett Square* ☎ *610/444–2192* 🌐 *thewoodlandsatphillips.com* 🕒 *Closed Sun.*

**worKS**

**OTHER SPECIALTY STORE** | More than two dozen regional artisans, makers, and curators present changing displays of their wares in this trendy concept shop. Jewelry, housewares, textiles, food such as honey and cookies, and even vintage fashions are on display. It's open Friday through Sunday. ✉ *432 S. Walnut St., Kennett Square* ☎ *484/732–8586* 🌐 *workskennettsquare.com.*

# Wilmington, Delaware

*15 miles southeast of Kennett Square via Rte. 52, 32 miles southwest of Philadelphia via I–95.*

Delaware's commercial hub and largest city (population 70,000) has some handsome architecture—with good examples of styles such as Federal, Greek Revival, Queen Anne, and Art Deco—and abundant cultural attractions. Wilmington began in 1638 as a Swedish settlement and later was populated by employees of various du Pont family businesses and nearby poultry ranches. In the mid-20th century, events such as the building of I–95 through the city led to population and business loss, but these days redevelopment is gradually reshaping parts of Wilmington.

The 10-block downtown area centered on Market Street, undergoing revitalization, has apartments, shops, and restaurants as well as the Grand Opera House (🌐 *thegrandwilmington.org*). The four-story theater, built by the Masonic Order in 1871, has a white cast-iron facade in French Second Empire style to mimic the old Paris Opera. The city also has a 1½-mile Riverwalk (✉ *801 Justison St.* 🌐 *riverfrontwilm.com*) on Riverfront Wilmington along the Christina River. It's near restaurants and sights such as a statue of Harriet Tubman and Thomas Garrett helping enslaved people as they fled to freedom along the Underground Railroad in the state. Outside Wilmington's compact city center are several outstanding museums, including some that are legacies of the du Ponts.

# Underground Railroad & Kennett Square

Geography made Kennett Square an important stop for people fleeing enslavement before the Civil War. Slavery was legal in Maryland and Delaware in the 19th century, but not in Pennsylvania, and the area was one of the closest to the Delaware border. A two-hour-long bus tour of surviving sites offered monthly by the **Kennett Underground Railroad Center** (✉ *120 N. Union St., Kennett Square* ☎ *484/544–5070* ⊕ *kennett-tundergroundrr.org* ⌖ *$35, bus tours Mar.–Oct.*) presents the stories of those who sought freedom and the Quakers, free African Americans, and other abolitionists who assisted them. The Underground Railroad, though not a physical railroad, used the language of trains to cover its secret activities: "passengers" were those escaping, "station masters" housed the freedom seekers, and "conductors" guided people along the routes. The center itself is a research room, though it has a timeline of the local and national Underground Railroad, and a map of Chester County; it's open weekends April through October, but check ahead.

The Longwood Progressive Friends Meetinghouse, built around 1855, was founded by Quakers dedicated to reforms such as abolition. Today it's the **Brandywine Valley Tourism Information Center** (✉ *300 Greenwood Rd., Kennett Square* ☎ *484/770–8550* ⊕ *brandywinevalley.com*), near Longwood Gardens, with brochures including one from the KURC giving information about eight Underground Railroad sites. It's also a stop on the **Harriet Tubman Underground Railroad Byway** (⊕ *harriettubman-byway.org*), which stretches from Maryland to Delaware to Pennsylvania, following the route of activist Harriet Tubman as she escaped to freedom in 1849. Those involved with the Underground Railroad in Kennett Square and around Chester County worked closely with station master Thomas Garrett in Wilmington, Delaware, who helped some 2,300 freedom seekers. A statue of Tubman and Garrett in **Tubman-Garrett Riverfront Park** (⊕ *nps.gov/places/tubman-garrett-riverfront-park.htm*) in Wilmington honors their friendship and work with people escaping enslavement between 1854 and 1860.

## GETTING HERE AND AROUND

The city of Wilmington is less than 45 minutes by car via I–95 south from Philadelphia and is easily accessible by Amtrak and commuter rail. But since you won't want to miss visiting Longwood Gardens, Winterthur, or some of the other stately mansions in the area, you'll want to have a car. Typically, those driving south from Philadelphia to Wilmington during rush hours will encounter some traffic but not gridlock, because the commute mostly runs the opposite way. Downtown Wilmington is compact and walkable, and despite the opening of new restaurants and bars, it is still somewhat quiet after business hours.

## ESSENTIALS

**VISITOR INFORMATION Greater Wilmington Convention and Visitors Bureau.** ✉ *Wilmington* ☎ *800/489–6664* ⊕ *visitwilmingtonde.com*.

#  Sights

### Delaware Art Museum

**ART MUSEUM** | In an 85,000-square-foot building, the museum presents several notable American and international collections in galleries freshly reinstalled and reimagined in 2021 to reflect more diverse, engaging stories about artists and the periods in which they worked. Its strong holdings of American illustration include paintings by Howard Pyle (1853–1911), a Wilmington native known as the "father of American illustration," and works by his students N. C. Wyeth, Frank Schoonover, and Maxfield Parrish. Some other American artists represented are Benjamin West, John Sloan, Winslow Homer, and Robert Motherwell. The museum is renowned for the largest American collection of 19th-century English pre-Raphaelite paintings and decorative arts, with works by Dante Gabriel Rossetti and Edward Burne-Jones, among others. Dale Chihuly's colorful *Persian Window* glass installation, the interactive Kids' Corner, and the Copeland Sculpture Garden are other highlights. ⊠ *2301 Kentmere Pkwy., Wilmington* ☎ *302/571–9590, 866/232–3714* ⊕ *www.delart.org* ✉ *$14, free all day Sun. and Apr.–Dec. Thurs. 4–8* ⊗ *Closed Mon. and Tues.*

### Hagley Museum and Library

**HISTORY MUSEUM | FAMILY** | A restored mid-19th-century mill community on 235 landscaped acres along the Brandywine River, the Hagley Museum and Library provides an enlightening look at the development of early industrial America and the du Pont family's role in it. This is the site of the first of the family's black-powder mills (founded 1802), family home, and gardens. A visitor center has displays about DuPont Company history and the exhibition "Nation of Inventors," an engaging, family-friendly experience that opened in 2022 and tells the stories of diverse American inventors over the centuries, using more than 120 patent models from various industries. Admission includes a narrated bus tour through the powder yards with stops at Eleutherian Mills, the 1803 Georgian-style home furnished by five generations of du Ponts (guided tour of house included); Workers' Hill, where costumed interpreters describe the life of a typical mill worker; and demonstrations in a machine shop and power yard that show the dangerous work of the early explosives industry. No food is sold, but you can bring a picnic.

■ TIP➡ **Be prepared for some walking (there is a shuttle bus, too) and allow a minimum of two hours for your visit, which can include tours and self-guided exploration.** ⊠ *200 Hagley Creek Rd., Wilmington* ✛ *Off Rte. 141 between Rte. 100 and U.S. 202* ☎ *302/658–2400* ⊕ *www.hagley.org* ✉ *$20.*

### Nemours Estate

**HISTORIC HOME** | For a look at how the very wealthy lived in the early 20th century, visit Nemours, a country estate on 200 acres with impressive gardens and a 47,000-square-foot mansion built for Alfred I. du Pont in 1910 by noted architectural firm Carrère and Hastings, which added the latest in technology. This modified Louis XVI château showcases more than 30 (of 77 in all) rooms of European and American furnishings, rare rugs, tapestries, and art from different eras. Despite its splendor, the mansion feels homey and personal, and it's fun to explore on your own and ask the pleasant interpretive staff questions. The formal French-style gardens, reminiscent of those at Versailles, are landscaped with fountains, pools, and statuary; garden tours are offered in summer. Vintage cars are on display in the Chauffeur's Garage. The visitor center has an excellent film and exhibits about the house, Alfred I. du Pont, and du Pont's three wives. ■ TIP➡ **There is no food on-site.** ⊠ *1600 Rockland Rd., on the campus of Nemours Children's Health (follow signs), Wilmington* ☎ *302/651–6912* ⊕ *nemours-estate.org* ✉ *$20* ⊗ *Closed Mon. and Jan.–Apr.*

Reproductions of Revolutionary War cannons are lined up at the Artillery Park at Valley Forge National Historical Park.

**Rockwood Park and Museum**
**HISTORIC HOME** | Rockwood, both a park and an elegant English-style country house that is a fine example of rural Gothic Revival architecture, stands in contrast to the opulent, French-inspired du Pont estates in the area. Built in 1851 by Joseph Shipley, a Quaker banker, and occupied by descendants of his extended family (the Bringhursts) until 1972, the house is now a museum with ornate Victorian furnishings and decorative items from later periods. Visitors can explore the house's first floor on their own or take a 90-minute guided tour (Friday and Saturday); there are also popular paranormal tours and other on-site programs. Besides the 6-acre heritage garden near the house, the 72-acre park features 2½ miles of paved, lighted trails. In July Rockwood hosts a play in the Delaware Shakespeare Festival. ✉ *4651 Washington St. Extension, south of Shipley Rd., Wilmington* ☎ *302/761–4340* 🌐 *newcastlede.gov* 🎟 *Park free; museum $10 self-guided or guided tour; museum free 1st Sun. of month* 🕑 *Museum closed Mon.–Wed.*

## 🍴 Restaurants

★ **Bardea Food & Drink**
**$$$** | **MODERN ITALIAN** | Italy-trained chef Antimo DiMeo's exciting, creative Italian fare using regional ingredients helped spark a culinary resurgence in Wilmington since 2018 and makes Bardea's 120 seats a tough reservation. Service is professional and warm, and the industrial-look space, with high ceilings, tile, and wooden floors and tables, is attractive, but the food steals the show: raw choices like cuttlefish; small plates like ricotta gnocchi; pastas and pizza; and vegetables and mains make it possible to compose a feast in different ways. **Known for:** chef opened Bardea Steak, steps away, in 2022; Italian wines and good cocktails; two-time James Beard Foundation semifinalist. [$] *Average main: $31* ✉ *620 N. Market St., Wilmington* ☎ *302/426–2069* 🌐 *bardeawilmington.com* 🕑 *Closed Sun. and Mon. No lunch.*

## Coffee and Quick Bites

**DE.CO**

$ | **ECLECTIC** | **FAMILY** | A sleek modern space in the historic Du Pont Building holds this trendy 250-seat food hall with seven vendors open for breakfast, lunch, and dinner, offering choices from deli sandwiches to tacos to good sushi, as well as an atrium bar. Pies from Pizzeria Bardea (from the chef at hot restaurant Bardea), smoothies and juices from Eat Clean, and La Colombe coffee and superb croissants from Spark'd round out the options. **Known for:** pop-up eateries besides the full-time ones; convenient to-go and delivery options; special waffle flavors from Connie's Chicken and Waffles. [$] *Average main: $14* ✉ *111 W. 10 St., Wilmington* ☎ 🌐 *decowilmington.com* 🕒 *Closed Sun. Hrs and days vary by vendor.*

## Hotels

**Hotel Du Pont**

$$$$ | **HOTEL** | Built in 1913 by Pierre S. du Pont, this 12-story hotel in downtown Wilmington has hosted everyone from Charles Lindbergh to John F. Kennedy, and the elegant Italian Renaissance–style building still radiates old-world luxury despite updates to make it comfortably modern. **Pros:** luxe historical ambience; large rooms and bathrooms; modern bistro Le Cavalier in grand wood-paneled space. **Cons:** small elevators; staff can be too formal; high extra charge for pets. [$] *Rooms from: $430* ✉ *42 W. 11th St., Wilmington* ☎ *302/594–3100* 🌐 *www.hoteldupont.com* 🛏 *217 rooms* 🍴 *No Meals.*

# Valley Forge

*20 miles northeast of downtown Philadelphia via I–76.*

Near the suburban village of Valley Forge, which took its name from an iron forge built in the 1740s, the monuments, markers, huts, and headquarters in Valley Forge National Historical Park illuminate a decisive period in the Revolutionary War. The park, with its quiet beauty that seems to whisper of the past, preserves the area where George Washington's Continental Army endured the bitter winter of 1777–78.

Other nearby sights of interest include the mega-size King of Prussia mall and an Audubon center with the naturalist's first American home.

### GETTING HERE AND AROUND

When traffic is flowing on I–76, the major east–west highway between Philadelphia and Valley Forge, the trip can take just 35 to 40 minutes. But gridlock, especially during rush hour, can stretch the trip to 90 minutes, so time your visit accordingly. If you arrive at the historical park without a car, you can pay to tour the park via a trolley. Other area attractions will require a car for access, however.

### VISITOR INFORMATION

**Valley Forge & Montgomery County, PA**

The website of the Valley Forge Tourism & Convention Board lists attractions, events, and hotels and restaurants around Montgomery County, and also has special offers. ☎ *610/834–1550* 🌐 *valleyforge.org.*

## Sights

**John James Audubon Center at Mill Grove**

**OTHER MUSEUM** | **FAMILY** | A small but lively museum, on a site that holds the first American home of Haitian-born artist and naturalist John James Audubon (1785–1851), captures the wonders of the avian world as well as Audubon's life and his mission to paint all of North America's birds. Kid-friendly interactive exhibits explore nests, birdsongs, feathers, and more; galleries on Audubon's artistic process (with original prints and a copy of his massive *Birds of America*) will appeal more to older children and adults. There's also a bird-themed outdoor play space. Admission includes a tour (sign

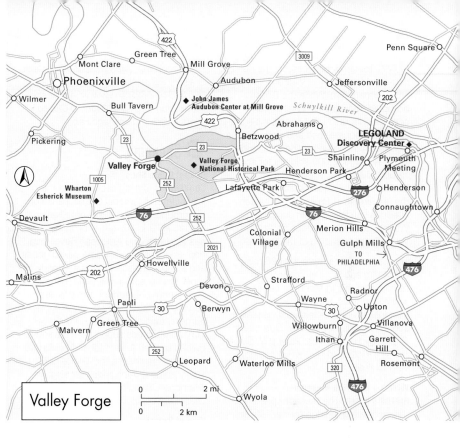

up at center for the one tour, offered at 1 pm) of Mill Grove, Audubon's stone farmhouse home, built in 1762 and filled with displays relating to Audubon. Managed by the National Audubon Society, this site 2 miles north of Valley Forge National Historical Park is within the 200-acre Mill Grove estate and has 5 miles of marked walking trails that are open free daily. ☒ *1201 Pawlings Rd., Audubon* ⟳ *Follow sign on Pawlings Rd. for the center* ☎ *610/666–5593* ⊕ *johnjames.audubon. org* ▣ *Museum $14, grounds and trails free* ⊙ *Museum closed Mon. and Tues.*

### ★ Valley Forge National Historical Park

**NATIONAL PARK** | The 3,500-acre park is the location of the 1777–78 winter encampment of General George Washington and the Continental Army, where winter tested and proved the army's perseverance. Begin at the excellent Valley Forge Visitor Center (renovated and reopened in 2022) for touring information and to explore displays of historical objects and immersive modern exhibits about the encampment and the men and women of all kinds who spent the winter here. The center also has regional information, a new orientation film, and the Encampment Store. Take a nine-stop driving tour (free cell phone guide) or buy the audio guide ($8.95); or take a narrated trolley tour (limited times other than summer; reserve ahead) for $20. Stops include reconstructed log huts of the Muhlenberg Brigade and the National Memorial Arch, which pay tribute to the soldiers, and Washington's headquarters.

In 1777 the army had just lost the nearby battles of Brandywine, White Horse, and Germantown. While the British occupied Philadelphia, Washington's soldiers endured horrid conditions—blizzards, inadequate food and clothing, and disease. Although no battle was fought at Valley Forge, 2,000 soldiers (of about 12,000) died here. The troops did win the war of will, regaining strength under the leadership of Prussian drillmaster Friedrich von Steuben. In June 1778 Washington led his troops away from Valley Forge in search of the British.

The park contains more than 26 miles of jogging and bicycling paths (bike rentals available in summer; call ahead) and hiking trails, and you can picnic in designated areas. A leisurely visit takes about half a day. ⊠ *1400 N. Outer Line Dr., Valley Forge* ✛ *Rte. 23 and N. Gulph Rd.* ☎ *610/783–1077* ⊕ *www.nps.gov/ vafo* ✉ *Free.*

### Wharton Esherick Museum

**HISTORIC HOME** | The museum preserves the fascinating, unique former hillside home and studio created by the "Dean of American Craftsmen," who was best known for sculptural wooden furniture that influenced artists and designers. Wharton Esherick (1887–1970) shaped a new, organic aesthetic in decorative arts by bridging art with furniture. The site, a National Historic Landmark for Architecture, houses 200 examples of his work—paintings, woodcuts, wooden furniture, and sculptures. The compact studio-home, in which everything from the light switches to the spiral staircase is hand-carved from wood, is one of his monumental achievements. You can see it only by booking a small-group tour in advance, although you can visit the tiny visitor center and part of the 12-acre grounds without an advance reservation. A campus architecture tour, including a separate workshop, is offered occasionally. The building is not fully accessible to people with mobility issues. ⊠ *1520*

*Horseshoe Trail, Malvern* ✛ *2 miles west of Valley Forge National Historical Park* ☎ *610/644–5822* ⊕ *www.whartonesherickmuseum.org* ✉ *$20 tour* ⊗ *Closed Mon.–Wed. and Jan. and Feb.*

 # Shopping

### Chapel Cabin Shop

**SOUVENIRS** | In a log cabin behind the Washington Memorial Chapel parish on the grounds of the Valley Forge National Historical Park, this gift shop sells souvenirs related to the American Revolution, homemade jams and some baked goods, and snacks. It also has a small, handy (no other food is sold in the park) luncheonette—there are outdoor picnic tables—serving a limited menu with decent hamburgers, tuna sandwiches, and similar fare. All proceeds support the privately owned chapel. A secondhand bookstore is behind the chapel, too. ⊠ *Rte. 23, Valley Forge* ✛ *Alongside Washington Memorial Chapel* ☎ *610/783–0576* ⊕ *wmchapel.org/cabin-shop.*

### King of Prussia

**MALL** | One of the nation's largest shopping complexes is a tourist destination in itself, with some 400 shops and more than 40 restaurants. From department stores such as Nordstrom and Neiman Marcus to chain retailers both upscale (Jimmy Choo and Cartier) and more accessible (Club Monaco and Zara), there's plenty for different kinds of shoppers. Dining options include Morton's The Steakhouse, Legal Sea Foods, Shake Shack, and abundant fast-food options on all levels. ⊠ *160 N. Gulph Rd., King of Prussia* ✛ *U.S. 202 at I–76 (Schuylkill Expressway)* ☎ *610/265–5727* ⊕ *www. simon.com.*

# LEGOLAND Discovery Center

*15 miles northwest of downtown Philadelphia via I–76 west.*

Located in the Plymouth Meeting Mall, the LEGOLAND Discovery Center Philadelphia is one of 13 Discovery Centers in the country.

### GETTING HERE AND AROUND

Plymouth Meeting is about 30 minutes west of central Philadelphia. Driving is your best bet as public transportation involves multiple transfers on numerous transportation types. An Uber will cost about $40 during non-peak hours.

From Center City, take I–76 west and I–476 north to West Germantown Pike in Plymouth Meeting. Take Exit 20 from I–476 north and follow signs for the Plymouth Meeting Mall and LEGOLAND Discovery Center.

 Sights

**LEGOLAND Discovery Center Philadelphia**
AMUSEMENT PARK/CARNIVAL | FAMILY | This 33,000-square-foot space, one of 13 Discovery Centers in the United States, is chock-full of all things LEGO, including a kid-sized race car that was made with more than 100,000 LEGO bricks. Miniland Philadelphia contains 50 of the city's iconic landmarks brought to life with nearly 1.5 million LEGO bricks—Independence Hall, Boathouse Row (with crew boats you can race), the Art Museum, and Lincoln Financial Field, just to name a few. Other highlights include the interactive LEGO Ninjago Training Camp; a LEGO 4-D Cinema; a LEGO-themed pirate ship play area called Pirate Adventure Island; and the LEGO Friends area where you can "meet" Olivia, Emma, Stephanie, Mia, and Andrea and build all of your favorite Heartlake City things.

■ TIP→ Note that adults must be accompanied by a child 17 or under to visit the attractions except on special adult nights (check events section of website). ⊠ *Plymouth Meeting Mall, 500 W. Germantown Pike, Plymouth Meeting* ☎ *267/245–9696* ⊕ *legolanddiscoverycenter.com* ✉ *From $22.95 (ticket purchased online); admission varies by time and day.*

# Sesame Place

*25 miles northeast of Philadelphia via I–95 north.*

Next to the Oxford Valley Mall, this park based on the popular children's show *Sesame Street* is a longtime favorite of families with young children.

### GETTING HERE AND AROUND

Driving is your best bet as public transportation from central Philadelphia involves multiple transfers on numerous transportation types.

From Center City, take I–95 north to I–295 east. Take the Morrisville exit 5A/Route 1 north to the Oxford Valley exit and turn right onto Oxford Valley Road; follow the signs to Sesame Place.

 Sights

**Sesame Place**
AMUSEMENT PARK/CARNIVAL | FAMILY | Aimed squarely at young kids and their families, this water and theme park based on the popular children's show *Sesame Street* provides fun places for children to crawl, climb, and jump; float, slide, and splash; and meet, greet, and perhaps hug the ageless Big Bird and his friends. Though there are many dry-land activities, the highlights of the park—especially on a hot summer day—are the water rides, including the popular Rambling River and Sky Splash, and the interactive Count's Splash Castle. (Water attractions are only open seasonally.) As befits a park for preteens, the rides in

LEGOLAND Discovery Center Philadelphia's Miniland contains 50 of the city's iconic landmarks including Independence Hall, Boathouse Row, and the Linc.

Elmo's World and the roller coasters—Vapor Trail and Oscar's Wacky Taxi—are modest by theme-park standards, but they've got enough excitement for young riders. Other favorites are the daily, and nightly, parades and shows; Sesame Neighborhood, a replica of the TV street; and pricey meals with characters like Elmo and Grover. Sesame Place is the world's first theme park to be a Certified Autism Center; see website for information. ■ **TIP→ Buy tickets online in advance for substantial savings. Check ahead in case any rides or attractions are closed, and note that food is expensive and can be uneven in quality (see website FAQs for info on bringing water).** ⊠ *100 Sesame Rd., Langhorne* ⊹ *Off N. Oxford Valley Rd. near U.S. 1 at I–95* ☎ *215/702–3566* ⊕ *sesameplace.com* ✉ *$69, but pricing is dynamic; parking $30; packages available* ⊙ *Check website.*

# Washington Crossing

*35 miles northeast of Philadelphia via I–95 and I–295, Taylorsville Rd., and Rte. 532.*

The small village of Washington Crossing on the Delaware River is home to basic services and residential areas as well as Washington Crossing Historic Park, which includes the site where Washington crossed the Delaware River in December 1776 and then attacked Trenton. Where Route 532 crosses the old Delaware Canal, you'll find access to the towpath with parking.

Bowman's Hill Tower, Inn at Bowman's Hill, and Bowman's Hill Wildlife Preserve are located about 6 miles north of the Visitor's Center at Washington Crossing Historic Park. ⇨ *Note that while these properties are technically located in New Hope, they are part of the northern section of Washington Crossing Historic Park so we listed them in this section.*

## GETTING HERE AND AROUND

Washington Crossing Historic Park stretches along River Road (Route 32). The Lower Park, or McConkey Ferry section, at the intersection with Route 532, is the site of both the actual crossing and the visitor center. A narrow bridge here makes crossing to New Jersey somewhat easier today. The Upper Park, or Thompson-Neely section, and a wildflower preserve are 5–6 miles north of the visitor center via River Road.

 **Sights**

### Bowman's Hill Tower

**VIEWPOINT** | On top of Bowman's Hill, this 125-foot fieldstone tower provides a spectacular view that extends up to 14 miles, weather permitting, taking in the Delaware River and countryside. It was built in 1929–31 to mark what might have been a lookout point for Washington's army, but historians have found no evidence of this. You can walk up to the observation deck; an elevator (out of service at this writing; call ahead) will take you far enough that you have just 23 steps via a narrow circular staircase. ⊠ *Washington Crossing Historic Park, 1 Tower Rd., New Hope* ✛ *In the upper northern part of Washington Crossing Historic Park* ☎ *215/493–4076 general park number, 215/862–3166 tower* ⊕ *washingtoncrossingpark.org* 🖃 *$7* 🕐 *Tower closed Jan.–Feb. and weekdays Dec. and Mar.*

### Bowman's Hill Wildflower Preserve

**NATURE PRESERVE** | The 134-acre preserve near the Thompson-Neely (Upper) section of Washington Crossing Historic Park showcases hundreds of species of wildflowers as well as trees, shrubs, and ferns native to Pennsylvania. Stop at the visitor center and get a map, and then take a guided one-hour wildflower walk (🖃 *$5 Available Fri.–Mon. Apr.–Oct.; call to check times*) or explore any of the short, well-marked trails (4½ miles in all) on your own. Wildflower blooms

are seasonal, with mid-April through July a good period to visit, but fall brings colorful foliage. ■ **TIP →** **The website has bloom information.** ⊠ *1635 River Rd., New Hope* ☎ *215/862–2924* ⊕ *www.bhwp.org* 🖃 *$10* 🕐 *Closed Tues. July–Mar.*

### Crossing Vineyards and Winery

**WINERY** | On a 200-year-old estate near where Washington crossed the Delaware, the family-run vineyard mixes vintage charm with modern wine-making techniques. Despite a nod to the rustic (a beam ceiling in the tasting room and gift shop), the old gambrel-roofed barn feels fresh and upscale. In a 45-minute tasting, the staff lets you know what to expect from 10 different types of wines. Look for Chardonnay, Riesling, Cabernet Franc, and Merlot, among other varieties, and you can order light bites such as cheeses. Concerts and public events are offered throughout the year. ⊠ *1853 Wrightstown Rd., off Rte. 532, Newtown* ☎ *215/493–6500* ⊕ *www.crossingvineyards.com* 🖃 *Tasting $20 (reservations required).*

### Washington Crossing Historic Park

**HISTORIC SIGHT** | It was from this evocative site, now a 500-acre park, that on Christmas night in 1776 General Washington and 2,400 of his men crossed the ice-studded Delaware River, attacked the Hessian stronghold at Trenton, and secured a desperately needed victory for the Continental Army. This crossing was immortalized in Emanuel Leutze's famous 1851 painting, which hangs in New York's Metropolitan Museum of Art. The park's historic houses (many renovated in 2021) and memorials are divided between the Lower Park (McConkey Ferry section) and Upper Park (Thompson-Neely section), about 5 miles apart.

In the Lower Park, the visitor center has park information, a short film, and helpful though old-fashioned historic exhibits, and sells tickets for guided tours of two areas. The historic village tour includes McConkey Ferry Inn, where tradition has

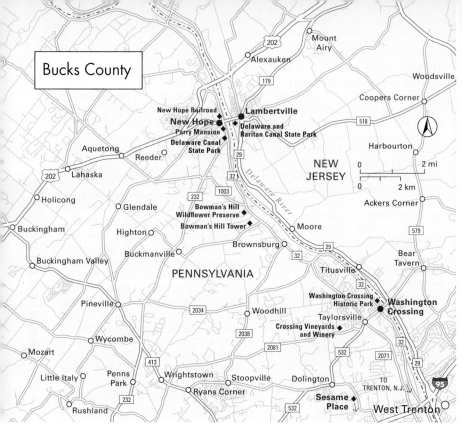

it that Washington had Christmas dinner. You can see replicas of the Durham boats used in the crossing.

In the Upper Park, 125-foot-tall Bowman's Hill Tower offers a commanding view of the Delaware River. The Thompson-Neely House has tours that tell of life in Bucks County during the Revolution. The house was used as a hospital during the 1776–77 encampment of Washington's army; there's also a gristmill. ■ TIP→ **The park's special events include a popular reenactment of the crossing in December.** ✉ *1112 River Rd. (Rte. 32), Washington Crossing* ☎ *215/493–4076* ⊕ *www. washingtoncrossingpark.org* ✉ *Grounds free, 1 tour or tower $7, 2 tours and tower $15* ⊙ *Tower and Thompson-Neely House closed Jan., Feb., and weekdays Dec. and Mar. No historic village tours weekdays Jan.–Mar.*

## 🍴 Restaurants

### Francisco's on the River

**$$$** | **ITALIAN** | Cozy rooms, including an enclosed front porch, beamed ceiling, white tablecloths, and windows all around, give a refined country vibe to this longtime river-view (across a road, though), BYOB Italian restaurant. Chef-owner Francisco Argueta breathes new life into old favorites like a thin-sliced, layered eggplant parmigiano; *linguine al frutti di mare fra diavolo* (spicy tomato sauce served over linguine and shellfish), and lasagna with a hint of smoked bacon—just keep in mind that portions can be large. **Known for:** whole-wheat garlic bread (worth the charge); wide variety of salads for appetizers; excellent desserts. $ *Average main: $30* ✉ *1251 River Rd., Washington Crossing* ☎ *215/321–8789* ⊕ *www.franciscosontheriver.com* ⊙ *Closed Mon. No lunch.*

## Hotels

**Inn at Bowman's Hill**

**$$$$ | B&B/INN** | South of New Hope near the road leading to Bowman's Tower, this modern interpretation of country charm was built in the late 1970s as a private home and converted to a high-end B&B in the mid-2000s, with individually decorated, traditionally furnished rooms with luxe amenities such as gas fireplaces. **Pros:** outdoor pool and hot tub; lovely countryside location close to New Hope; breakfast options include full English breakfast. **Cons:** quite expensive for the area, especially some suites; some rooms are small; not all rooms are in the main house. [$] *Rooms from: $495* ✉ *518 Lurgan Rd., New Hope* ☎ *215/862–8090* 🌐 *theinnatbowmanshill.com* 🛏 *8 rooms* 🍴 *Free Breakfast.*

## Nightlife

**Bowman's Tavern**

**LIVE MUSIC** | The piano that graced the original Odette's, the long-closed restaurant and cabaret that was a New Hope institution, now resides at this quintessential river tavern halfway between New Hope and Washington's Crossing. The piano lounge's five-nights-a-week entertainment, with music from standards to jazz to country, is popular and gay-friendly. **TIP→ Its hearty American fare has a strong following, too, for lunch and dinner.** ✉ *1600 River Rd., New Hope* ☎ *215/862–2972* 🌐 *www.bowmanstavernrestaurant.com.*

# New Hope

*8 miles north of Washington Crossing via Rte. 32, 40 miles north of Philadelphia via I–95 and Rte. 32.*

For a small Delaware River town, New Hope is a mix of many things, with something for all kinds of travelers. A hodgepodge of old homes, narrow streets and alleys, courtyards, busy restaurants and bars, and shops, it attracts artists, shoppers, and hordes of day-trippers, especially on summer and fall weekends (weekdays are quieter). Festivals fill the calendar, from a film festival to PrideFest. New Hope has had its ups and downs as businesses change, and some old hippie spots can look tired, but a fresh vibe is evident in the revival of the Bucks County Playhouse, new and renovated lodgings, and restaurant openings.

The heart of town, listed on the National Register of Historic Places, is easy to explore on foot; the most interesting sights and stores are clustered along four blocks of Main Street and on the cross streets—Mechanic, Ferry, and Bridge Streets—which lead to the river. New Hope is also along the Delaware Canal and its walkable towpath. Some parts of town are older than others. As you might guess from their names, Ferry Street dates back to Colonial times; Bridge Street is Victorian. The old stone building that housed the original, long-closed Odette's restaurant has been moved from River Road to the intersection of Route 32 and New Street; it will eventually serve as a visitor center.

### GETTING HERE AND AROUND

Getting to New Hope by car is easy. U.S. 202, Route 179, and Route 32 run through it. Getting around New Hope on a busy weekend is harder. If you see cars backed up along Main Street, drive around the periphery instead, as it can take a fair amount of time to inch your way through town. Grab a parking spot either on the street or in a municipal or private lot and walk where you want to go. A kiosk system for public parking takes cash, credit cards, and the ParkMobile app.

### VISITOR INFORMATION

**CONTACTS New Hope Visitors Center.** ✉ *1 W. Mechanic St., at Main St., New Hope* 🌐 *visitbuckscounty.com.*

## Sights

### ★ Delaware Canal State Park

**TRAIL | FAMILY** | Completed in 1832 during America's great era of canal building, the 59-mile-long Delaware Canal runs from Bristol north to Easton, and today its towpath draws bicyclists and walkers who appreciate the scenic path with its canal and Delaware River views. It's easy to access the towpath in New Hope. In addition, the restored Locktender's House and Lock 11 (✉ *145 S. Main St.* 🌐 *fodc.org*) explore how locks work and what daily life was like on the canal. ✉ *New Hope* ✣ *Canal and towpath are parallel to the Delaware River* ☎ *610/982–5560 park headquarters in Upper Black Eddy* 🌐 *dcnr.pa.gov* 🎟 *Free.*

### New Hope Railroad

**TRAIN/TRAIN STATION | FAMILY** | Pulled by an authentic steam locomotive or vintage diesel, this heritage passenger train makes a 9-mile, 45-minute (an hour in fall) scenic round-trip between New Hope and Lahaska, and standard trips are narrated. The route crosses a trestle used in the rescue scenes in silent films like *The Perils of Pauline*. The New Hope depot is an 1891 Victorian gem. Special events include Halloween-theme trips and holiday excursions in December. The trips can get pricey for a family and may be best for those who love old trains. Advance reservations are encouraged, and required for special events. **TIP→ Parking in the on-site lot is expensive, so find a spot on the street or in a town lot.** ✉ *32 W. Bridge St., New Hope* ☎ *215/862–2332* 🌐 *newhoperailroad.com* 🎟 *Coach $29, first class $42 for basic ride; holiday and special excursion fares substantially higher.*

### Parry Mansion

**HISTORIC HOME** | Built in 1784, and now home to the New Hope Historical Society, this stone house is fascinating because the furnishings reflect decorative changes from 1775 (Colonial) to 1900 (Victorian)—including candles, white-washed walls, oil lamps, and wallpaper. Wealthy Quaker lumber- and flour-mill owner and businessman Benjamin Parry, often called the "father of New Hope," built the house, which was occupied by five generations of his family. Guided house tours, including a brief film, give you a good sense of town history. October house tours have a Haunted History Month theme; the historical society also offers a one-hour walking tour of New Hope ($10) on Sunday from May through October. ✉ *45 S. Main St., New Hope* ☎ *215/258–8590* 🌐 *www.newhope-history.org* 🎟 *$10* 🕒 *Closed for tours Nov.–Apr., also weekdays May–Sept. and Mon.–Thurs. in Oct.*

## Restaurants

### Karla's

**$$ | AMERICAN** | A casual hangout in the heart of New Hope, Karla's has been open since 1978, offering American food (salads, burgers, and sandwiches) enlivened with some interesting international ingredients. Dine on dishes like panko-crusted mac and cheese, blackened shrimp tacos, and pork chops in cozy, well-worn rooms with an assemblage of mismatched tables, with plants in retro macramé hangers. **Known for:** Monday Locals' Night good-value prix fixe; friendly old-time New Hope vibe; creative martini list. [$] *Average main: $22* ✉ *5 W. Mechanic St., New Hope* ☎ *215/862–2612* 🌐 *www.karlasnewhope.com.*

### Nektar

**$$$ | MODERN AMERICAN** | The excellent small-plate and other food options at this wine bar and restaurant pair superbly with the wide range of U.S. and international wines, beers, and whiskeys served in a modern-industrial but intimate space with a long bar, wooden tables, and tall windows facing a creek. Dishes like tuna tacos and a mushroom and goat cheese flatbread are perfect for sharing,

The New Hope Railroad, whose depot was built in 1891, offers numerous special rides throughout the year including themed dinners and seasonal rides.

and seasonal salads and sandwiches make it fun to build a meal for your drink or flight, though the costs can add up. **Known for:** well-trained servers know the wines; plenty of cheeses and charcuterie; distinctive three-drink wine and whiskey flights. [$] *Average main: $27* ✉ *8 W. Mechanic St., New Hope* ☎ *267/743–2109* 🌐 *nektarnewhope.com* 🕒 *Closed Mon.*

**Sprig & Vine**

**$$** | **VEGETARIAN** | Chic and BYO, this vegan restaurant known for fresh, sophisticated fare attracts plenty of non-vegetarians to its space in Union Square, an old-converted-warehouse-meets-new-construction complex. The menu is relatively short—an assortment of small plates and salads, and a handful of sandwiches and large-plate dinner options such as a cauliflower-cashew mac and tempeh Reuben—but offers interesting dishes with unusual, complex flavors, often made with ingredients from local farms. **Known for:** BBG seitan sandwich; varied dessert options; seasonal, globally influenced dishes. [$] *Average main: $24* ✉ *450 Union Square Dr., New Hope* ☎ *215/693–1427* 🌐 *sprigandvine.com* 🕒 *Closed Mon. and Tues. No lunch.*

**Stella**

**$$$$** | **MODERN AMERICAN** | In the same building as the Ghost Light Inn, this upscale modern American restaurant helmed by Michael O'Halloran has expansive Delaware River views from its indoor and outdoor seating, enhancing the relaxed charm of the sleek, high-ceilinged space with wood-topped tables, a fireplace, and a bar with TVs. It's a stunning setting for seasonal menus that use the best ingredients from local farms and artisan producers in dishes such as roasted squash bisque and whole-grain pasta with wild mushroom ragout. **Known for:** smoked Berks County Pekin duck (it beat Bobby Flay's version); robust brunch menu from egg dishes to a brisket sandwich; Stella bread basket. [$] *Average main: $36* ✉ *50 S. Main St., New Hope* ☎ *267/740–2691* 🌐 *stellanewhope.com* 🕒 *Closed Mon. and Tues. No lunch weekdays.*

## Coffee and Quick Bites

**C'est la Vie**
$ | **CAFÉ** | Get a cup of coffee and a yummy pastry or light meal at C'est la Vie, a French bakery down a little alley off Main Street that proves that excellent things come in small packages. Grab and go, eat in the cozily cramped space, or sit outside at a table overlooking the river. **Known for:** sandwiches in savory croissants; madeleines, macarons, and tarts; excellent breads. [$] *Average main: $5* ✉ *20 S. Main St., New Hope* ☎ *215/862–1956* 🕓 *Closed Mon.–Wed. No dinner.*

**Ferry Market**
$ | **ECLECTIC** | New Hope's welcome contribution to the food market trend brings an eclectic 10 or so vendors, some of them outposts of area spots, to an airy brick-fronted, renovated space with an industrial vibe. You can grab a coffee at SkyRoast or a craft beer at Neshaminy Creek, or taste deli or Mediterranean fare. **Known for:** fun, reasonably priced lunch options; Peruvian and Latin American fare at Lima Fusion; sweet treats at Sciascia. [$] *Average main: $13* ✉ *32 S. Main St., New Hope* ☎ *609/240–5983* 🌐 *theferrymarket.com* 🕓 *Closed Tues.; days and hrs vary by vendor.*

## Hotels

**Ghost Light Inn**
$$$ | **HOTEL** | By the river in the heart of town, this luxe rustic-chic boutique hotel notches up New Hope's lodging scene with modern rooms and a restaurant and bar overlooking the water. **Pros:** spectacular Delaware River views from restaurant and many rooms; steps from the Bucks County Playhouse via riverfront promenade; gorgeous rooms with plenty of amenities. **Cons:** events in the ballroom may disturb a quiet mood; no in-house breakfast except weekend brunch (New Hope and Lambertville have options nearby); price is high for those river views. [$] *Rooms from: $350* ✉ *50 S. Main St., New Hope* ☎ *267/740–7131* 🌐 *ghostlight-inn.com* 🛏 *15 rooms* 🍴 *No Meals.*

**Logan Inn**
$$ | **HOTEL** | Established in 1727, the Logan once accommodated passengers riding the ferry to Lambertville, and today the thoroughly modern inn has renovated its old rooms, added a wing (in 2021), and enlarged its dining and drinking areas. **Pros:** in the heart of New Hope; new rooms are modern and stylish; alfresco patio dining is good for people-watching. **Cons:** no telephone or live TV in rooms; interior modernization comes with some loss of historic charm; restaurant can get quite noisy. [$] *Rooms from: $210* ✉ *10 W. Ferry St., New Hope* ☎ *215/862–2300* 🌐 *www.loganinn.com* 🛏 *38 rooms* 🍴 *Free Breakfast.*

**River House at Odette's**
$$$$ | **HOTEL** | Opened in 2020, the luxurious, newly built River House raises the bar for New Hope lodgings, filling a storied New Hope site (Chez Odette, later Odette's restaurant) by the Delaware Canal and the Delaware River and offering heart-lifting river views. **Pros:** riverside location half a mile from the heart of New Hope; chic guest rooms and suites, some with balconies, in different sizes; attractive restaurant and piano lounge with music nightly. **Cons:** no exercise room (free bikes are available); rooftop bar open only to hotel guests and members; popular wedding and meeting venue. [$] *Rooms from: $369* ✉ *274 S. River Rd., New Hope* ☎ *855/530–0621, 215/682–2022* 🌐 *www.riverhousenewhope.com* 🛏 *38 rooms* 🍴 *No Meals.*

**Wedgwood Inn**
$ | **B&B/INN** | **FAMILY** | Accommodations at this Victorian antiques–decorated B&B are in an 1870s-era "painted lady," a Federal-style manor house, and an 1890 carriage house; all have rooms that work equally well for families or romance. **Pros:** lovely grounds near, but set apart from, the middle of town; welcomes children and dogs; many gas fireplaces

and some porches. **Cons:** not for those who dislike abundant Victoriana and Wedgwood blue; front-facing rooms may have street noise; different-size rooms, so check when booking. $ *Rooms from: $150* ✉ *111 W. Bridge St., New Hope* ☎ *215/862–2570* ⊕ *www.wedgwood-innbedandbreakfastofnewhopepa.com* ⇥ *18 rooms* ❖ *Free Breakfast.*

## ⍬ Nightlife

### Havana

**LIVE MUSIC** | A longtime New Hope fixture, this casual bar and restaurant with tropical-theme decor and some outdoor seating has karaoke on Monday and live music from jazz to rock many nights (tribute and cover bands are a specialty on weekends); there are also DJs. Check the website for ticketed events. The list of mojitos and martinis is long, and beer and wine choices are ample. ✉ *105 S. Main St., New Hope* ☎ *215/862–5501* ⊕ *www.havananewhope.com.*

### John & Peter's

**LIVE MUSIC** | Since 1972, this classic dive bar has featured live, original music nightly, from folk to funk. All kinds of people come to hear jazz musicians, singer-songwriters, and rockers take the stage, as well as the not-yet-famous on Monday's open-mic night. Wednesday's invitational jam with local musicians is also popular. The beer list is long, and the bar food includes tater tots, burgers and fries, and quesadillas. ✉ *96 S. Main St., New Hope* ☎ *215/862–5981* ⊕ *www.johnandpeters. com.*

### Odette's Lounge at River House

**PIANO BARS** | Part of the plush new waterside River House hotel, this piano lounge a few steps down from Odette's restaurant has chairs, tables, and stools, as well as a massive stone fireplace and slate floors. Local musicians play nightly after 7 pm, a relaxing accompaniment to wine or a cocktail and lighter fare, perhaps before or after dinner. Another option

is the (music-less) happy hour Monday through Thursday 4–6 pm, where drinks are cheaper and you can order light bites. Parking is tight, and although it's free Monday to Thursday, from Friday to Sunday it's $5 if you leave before 6 pm, $20 after. ✉ *274 S. River St., New Hope* ☎ *215/682–2022, 866/953–0039* ⊕ *www. riverhousenewhope.com.*

##  Performing Arts

### Bucks County Playhouse

**THEATER** | Opened in 1939, this regional theater in an 18th-century mill by the Delaware continues a long tradition of staging musicals (Broadway revivals and new works, with top-quality performers) and plays. Performances are year-round, with the main shows generally staged May through December, and it also hosts visiting artists and community and educational events. The Deck Restaurant and Bar at the Playhouse (⊕ *playhousedeck. com* for hours and days), with fabulous river views, is open whether or not a performance is scheduled. ✉ *70 S. Main St., New Hope* ☎ *215/862–2121 box office* ⊕ *bcptheater.org.*

## ⬭ Shopping

Independent shops selling a tourist-focused mix of upscale and lowbrow line New Hope's streets. Nice arts and crafts and handmade accessories, clothing, antiques, and jewelry (some quite expensive) stores are juxtaposed with campy vintage items, collectibles, and some storefronts with tarot readers, a reminder of the town's funky side. The shopping center at Peddler's Village in nearby Lahaska has additional gift-oriented choices (a few outlet stores, part of Penn's Purchase, are across the road).

### BOOKS

#### Farley's Bookshop

**BOOKS** | The crowded shelves at employee-owned Farley's, a New Hope institution since 1967, hold ample choices, including books about the region. Staff picks, signed copies of local writers' works, children's books, and small press favorites: it's all here for the browsing, with helpful staff ready to offer suggestions. ⊠ *44 S. Main St., New Hope* ☎ *215/862–2452* ⊕ *www.farleysbookshop.com.*

### CLOTHING

#### Squarehead Industries

**MIXED CLOTHING** | The globally sourced men's and women's clothing, accessories, and home goods at this on-trend new shop reflect the local owners' focus on sustainably produced wares that are both nicely designed and good for people and the planet. They call their curated look a balance between California bohemian design and Scandinavian minimalism, a description that works for the design of the shop itself. Prices aren't low, but the items are attractive and stylish. ⊠ *36 W. Bridge St., New Hope* ☎ *267/743–2117* ⊕ *shop.squareheadindustries.com.*

### CRAFTS

#### Heart of the Home

**CRAFTS** | Open since 1994, this American craft and gift shop has sold artisan-made items in a range of prices, from pottery and jewelry to wood pieces and special gifts for children. Items for the home and cards round out the inventory, and the staff are extremely helpful. ⊠ *30 W. Bridge St., New Hope* ☎ *215/862–1880* ⊕ *heartofthehome.com.*

#### Topeo Gallery

**CRAFTS** | You can find all kinds of high-quality, handcrafted art glass and jewelry at this well-regarded crafts gallery, along with art pottery and garden art. The price range is wide but on the higher end. ⊠ *35 N. Main St., New Hope* ☎ *215/862–2750* ⊕ *www.topeo.com.*

### FOOD

#### Pierre's Chocolates

**CHOCOLATE** | For superior chocolate, including yummy truffles, butter creams, and chocolate-covered pretzels, head a little outside the main business district to the delectable Pierre's Chocolates. Check out special small-batch and single-origin treats as well. ⊠ *360 W. Bridge St., New Hope* ☎ *215/862–0602* ⊕ *www.pierres-chocolates.com.*

### MALLS AND OUTLETS

#### Peddler's Village

**SHOPPING CENTER** | **FAMILY** | In 1962, the late Earl Jamison moved local 18th-century houses to a 6-acre site and opened a collection of small, mostly locally owned specialty shops and restaurants that today caters strongly to tourists. Some 60 shops in the well-landscaped, 42-acre villagelike setting peddle toys, clothing, jewelry, housewares, crafts, home decor, gift items, and more. There's also an inn, the Golden Plough, and a dozen or so food and drink options. Giggleberry Fair offers the 1922 Grand Carousel and indoor games for kids; admission is charged. The many seasonal events draw big crowds. Peddler's Village is 5 miles west of central New Hope via U.S. 202. ■**TIP**→ **Check Peddler's Village app for discounts.** ⊠ *5800 Upper York Rd., at the intersection of U.S. 202 and Rte. 263, Lahaska* ☎ *215/794–4000* ⊕ *www.peddlersvillage.com.*

##  Activities

#### Bucks County River Country

**WATER SPORTS** | **FAMILY** | Join the many people who cool off in the Delaware River in inner tubes every summer. Bucks County River Country, operating since 1967, also rents a wide variety of rafts, canoes, and kayaks from mid-May through October for trips of 2–3 hours. Even when the wide river is a mass of yellow and green tubes, it's still peaceful. Point Pleasant is 8 miles north of New Hope via Route 32. ⊠ *2 Walters La., Point Pleasant* ☎ *215/297–5000* ⊕ *www.rivercountry.net* ◿ *Tubing from $32 per person, kayak rentals from $52 for 2–3 hrs.*

**New Hope Cyclery**

**BIKING** | The store sells all kinds of bikes and gear, and also rents bikes and e-bikes, with helmets and locks included in the rental price. You can also rent family-friendly trailers. The helpful staff can direct you to scenic bike routes; one option is parts of the 60-mile towpath of the Delaware Canal State Park, which runs through New Hope. **TIP→ Reservations currently aren't accepted, so call on the day you want to ride.** ✉ *404 York Rd., New Hope* ☎ *215/862–6888* 🌐 *newhopecyclery.com* 🎫 *From $40 for half-day bike rental, $59 for half-day e-bike rental.*

# Lambertville, New Jersey

*Across the Delaware River from New Hope, 40 miles from Philadelphia via I–95 and Rte. 29.*

If you're interested in New Hope's refrain but prefer it in a lower key, head directly across the Delaware River to this small New Jersey village for more charm, a bit more quiet, and even better antiques. Antiques and collectibles dealers fill retail spaces around town, though these days they are matched by trendy home-furnishing shops and a lively assemblage of boutiques, art galleries, and restaurants. Interesting buildings line the streets, a legacy of the days when Lambertville was a bustling canal town and then a manufacturing center for everything from wheels to hairpins, before it evolved into a day-tripper's favorite.

One of Lambertville's chief pleasures doesn't involve commerce at all: the towpath along the Delaware and Raritan Canal is a retreat for strolling, running, or biking. Heading 7 miles south takes you to the popular Washington Crossing State Park, directly across from the similarly named Pennsylvania park.

## GETTING HERE AND AROUND

If you're in New Hope, head to Bridge Street and drive or walk over the bridge; the scenic walk over the Delaware River is short but can be windy. It's easy to explore most of Lambertville on foot, and you can visit the two towns in one day if you just want a taste of each. From Philadelphia, take I–95 and I–295 and head up along the Delaware on Route 29.

## Sights

**Delaware and Raritan Canal State Park**

**TRAIL** | Walkers and cyclists in Lambertville have easy access from downtown to part of the park's 70-mile-long, multiuse trail (the former canal towpath), which travels through 22 towns and five New Jersey counties. Built in the 1830s to connect the Delaware and Raritan rivers, the D&R, as it's known, includes a feeder canal along the Delaware that runs past towns such as Frenchtown, Stockton, and Lambertville down to New Jersey's Washington Crossing State Park. ✉ *Lambertville* ✣ *Accessed from downtown Lambertville along the riverfront* ☎ *609/924–5705 park superintendent's office* 🌐 *dandrcanal.com* 🎫 *Free.*

## Restaurants

**Broadmoor**

**$$$** | **ITALIAN** | Gray walls with a few large paintings, hanging globe lights, and chic but simple wood and marble tables create a lovely, soothing backdrop for delicious, mostly Italian fare at this intimate BYOB in a space that formerly housed an antiques store. The chef offers a creative list of salads and seafood or pasta appetizers like a chef's choice ravioli; mains might include a grilled veal chop or the fish of the day. **Known for:** superior fresh pasta options; good-size menu of tempting desserts; special appetizers and mains vary the Italian theme. [$] *Average main: $32* ✉ *8 N. Union St., Lambertville*

Delaware and Raritan Canal State Park's 70-mile-long, multiuse trail (the former canal towpath), travels through 22 towns and five New Jersey counties.

☎ *609/397–1400* 🌐 *broadmoorrestaurant.com* 🕒 *Closed Mon. and Tues. No lunch.*

**El Tule**

**$$** | **LATIN AMERICAN** | At this popular, family-owned Mexican and Peruvian restaurant, the plain black-stucco building and small, colorfully decorated dining room are secondary to wonderfully fresh, flavorful dishes that hold to tradition (tacos and fajitas) and add innovative touches (lunch bowls with ceviche). Bring your own wine or beer to pair with Peruvian lamb stew, Oaxacan mole with chicken, or the many kinds of ceviche, or try the delicious fruit drinks. **Known for:** Wednesday night locals' three-course prix-fixe special; good-value lunch options; pozole and other soups. [$] *Average main: $24* ✉ *49 N. Main St., Lambertville* ☎ *609/773–0007* 🌐 *eltulerestaurant.com* 🕒 *Closed Mon.*

**Lambertville Station Restaurant**

**$$** | **AMERICAN** | **FAMILY** | An adorable town landmark, the convivial canal-side restaurant of the modern Lambertville Station Inn occupies its own building, a renovated 19th-century train station that was designed by Thomas Ustick Walter, architect of the dome on the U.S. Capitol, as the headquarters of the Belvidere-Delaware Railroad. **Known for:** excellent wine selections served in the Wine Cellar; outside seating is very popular in season; good Sunday brunch (reserve ahead). [$] *Average main: $24* ✉ *11 Bridge St., Lambertville* ☎ *609/397–8300* 🌐 *lambertvillestation.com.*

**More Than Q**

**$** | **BARBECUE** | **FAMILY** | The smell of Texas-style wood-smoked barbecue wafts from this casual spot that channels a modern industrial vibe with wooden tables and walls, metal shelving and seats, and chalkboard-paint walls. At the counter, order a sandwich or platter piled high with tasty, carefully prepared brisket, pulled beef or pork, or chicken, or go for the spare ribs; and take your pick of sides like collard greens or burnt-end baked beans. **Known for:** meat platter for two; closes by 5 or 6 many nights (for now), so don't delay; meat sold by the pound if you want more. $ *Average main: $14* ✉ *13 Klines Ct., Lambertville* ☎ *609/773–0072* ⊕ *www.morethanq. com* ⊗ *Closed Mon.*

##  Coffee and Quick Bites

### Lambertville Trading Company
$ | **CAFÉ** | Stop by the coffee bar at this longtime (since 1982) favorite for a coffee or cappuccino and a changing selection of homemade goodies including cookies, muffins, and bagels, or to pick up gourmet treats or gifts to take home. There's some seating in the cozy space, where shelves are packed with mugs, chocolate, and more. **Known for:** iced coffee with coffee ice cubes in summer; cash or checks only; spiced hot chocolate. $ *Average main: $5* ✉ *43 Bridge St., Lambertville* ☎ *609/397–2232* ⊕ *lambertvilletrading.com/* ▭ *No credit cards* ⊗ *No dinner.*

### ★ Owowcow Creamery
$ | **ICE CREAM** | **FAMILY** | Made in nearby Bucks County since 2009, Owowcow's ice cream uses local and organic ingredients including milk and cream, fruits and vegetables, and cage-free eggs to create 12 signature flavors year-round and a dozen rotating specials. One of a few shops the company runs, the industrial-style space is worth the half-mile walk (it's a nice one) up Union Street for scrumptious flavors such as cashew caramel, blueberry lemon, and Cookie monstah. **Known for:** also makes frozen treats for dogs; worthy vegan ice-cream options; dairy-free sorbet. $ *Average main: $5* ✉ *237 N. Union St., Lambertville* ☎ *609/397–2234* ⊕ *owowcow.com.*

##  Hotels

### Lambertville House
$$ | **HOTEL** | A former stagecoach stop dating to 1812, this distinctive stone-and-brick building on Lambertville's main drag maintains a traditional ambience but has modern comforts in its updated rooms. **Pros:** robes in rooms; steps from shops, restaurants, and the bridge to New Hope; the hotel's porch, overlooking Bridge Street. **Cons:** bar can be taken over by business travelers attending meetings here; not for those who want a secluded location; no in-house breakfast, but restaurants are steps away. $ *Rooms from: $210* ✉ *32 Bridge St., Lambertville* ☎ *609/397–0200* ⊕ *www.lambertville-house.com* ⇆ *26 rooms* ⌁ *No Meals.*

### Lambertville Station Inn
$$ | **HOTEL** | The "station" in this riverside hotel's name refers to the restaurant, an adorable 1867 stone building, but the hotel itself, tucked away from the street in the heart of town, is modern with a comfortably traditional vibe. **Pros:** modern rooms, most with river views, near the heart of town; pretty sunsets over the Delaware River; bike rentals available. **Cons:** no fitness room, but hotel partners with one nearby; continental breakfast is small; weddings and other events may affect the experience. $ *Rooms from: $219* ✉ *11 Bridge St., Lambertville* ☎ *609/397–4400* ⊕ *www.lambertvillesta-tion.com* ⇆ *46 rooms* ⌁ *Free Breakfast.*

##  Nightlife

### The Boat House
**BARS** | Tucked down Coryell Street in the Porkyard alley, this small, two-story wood-framed building displays loads of vintage nautical memorabilia from its floors to the rafters and ceilings. Dark and cozy, it's an atmospheric place for a well-made cocktail or other drink before or after dinner; just know that there's no food, and it can get crowded. You can sit outdoors in summer. ✉ *8½ Coryell St., Lambertville* ☎ *609/397–2244.*

## ⬤ Shopping

Antiques and collectibles shops, furniture and home-furnishing stores, and art galleries line Union Street, heading north from Bridge Street, and the intersecting cross streets. This is where the serious antiques collectors shop, as well as those seeking contemporary crafts and fun vintage wares and clothing. Specialty food and other indie shops, some long-time and some newer, enhance the mix.

### A Mano Gallery

**CRAFTS** | In an old five-and-dime building, A Mano stocks colorful crafts and home products, some by local makers, at a variety of prices. Look for jewelry, glass, pottery, kaleidoscopes, pajamas and robes, and wearable art, as well as some contemporary furniture and lighting. ⊠ *42 N. Union St., Lambertville* ☎ *609/397–0063* ⊕ *www.amanogalleries.com.*

### Bucks County Dry Goods

**FURNITURE** | They've got the goods here—a varied, highly curated assort-ment of mid-century modern furniture, housewares, design books, gifts (like leather items), jewelry, and rustic-chic women's clothing. A location just around the corner on Bridge Street carries vintage men's and women's attire. There's another location in Princeton, New Jersey. ⊠ *5 Klines Ct., Lambertville* ☎ *609/397–1288* ⊕ *www.bcdrygoods.com.*

### Golden Nugget Antique Flea Market

**MARKET** | Vintage is in these days because it's green, and if you don't mind digging around piles of stuff for treasures, you may enjoy hunting for period pieces, toy trains, lamps, old kitchen tools, porcelain, jewelry, and all kinds of memorabilia from the '60s and '70s. The market, open since 1967, has more than 20 often-overstuffed indoor collectibles and antiques shops and dozens of outdoor stalls open Wednes-days (which are quieter) and weekends. Sunday is the biggest day. A small café is on-site. ⊠ *1850 River Rd., Lambert-ville* ☎ *609/397–0811* ⊕ *gnflea.com.*

### The People's Store Antiques Center

**ANTIQUES & COLLECTIBLES** | It's fun to wander the nooks and crannies of this four-story, converted 1839 building filled with more than 40 dealers whose wares include fine American and European antiques and more modern furnishings, art, funky collectibles, china, and textiles from tea towels to clothing. There's something for every budget. Don't miss the few studios up top with working artists; they'll happily talk to you. ⊠ *28 N. Union St., Lambertville* ☎ *609/397–9808* ⊕ *www.peoplesstore.net.*

##  Activities

### Pure Energy Cycling

**BIKING** | This serious, high-end bike store rents hybrid bikes and cruisers, and they come with locks and helmets. It's best to call ahead to reserve a bike for busy weekends, and note that the company doesn't rent kids' bikes. ⊠ *99 S. Main St., Lambertville* ☎ *609/397–7008* ⊕ *pureenergycycling.com* ✉ *From $15 per hour; $50 per day.*

# LANCASTER COUNTY, HERSHEY, AND GETTYSBURG

Updated by
Constance Jones

 Sights
★★★★★

 Restaurants
★★★★☆

 Hotels
★★★★☆

 Shopping
★★★☆☆

 Nightlife
★★☆☆☆

# WELCOME TO LANCASTER COUNTY, HERSHEY, AND GETTYSBURG

## TOP REASONS TO GO

★ **Green Acres.** There's breathtaking countryside and farmland everywhere you look.

★ **Dynamic food scene.** A growing food scene that includes craft coffee, beer, and cheese; global flavors; and farm-to-table dining.

★ **A hub of historical significance.** Spanning several centuries, from Native Americans to Colonial America, the Civil War, and the Industrial Revolution.

★ **Pennsylvania Dutch villages.** Learn about Amish and Mennonite culture at crafts shops and restaurants, and on buggy rides.

★ **Family-friendly.** There are museums, theme parks, and more to entertain every family no matter the age range.

**1 Lancaster.** A walkable city full of restaurants, cafés, and small shops.

**2 Bird-in-Hand.** Working farms, horse-drawn buggies, and all facets of Amish and Mennonite culture.

**3 Strasburg.** A slow-paced village that doubles as a hot spot for railroad history.

**4 Lititz.** This 18th-century town founded by Moravians has a charming downtown.

**5 Ephrata.** It's famously known for the Ephrata Cloister, a religious compound.

**6 Adamstown.** This is antiques heaven, home to the famous Renninger's antiques market.

**7 Columbia.** This town offers outdoor adventures, antiques shops, and historic tours.

**8 Marietta.** Marietta offers outdoors and antiques fun.

**9 Hershey.** Expect chocolate, amusement rides, and world-class entertainment.

**10 Gettysburg.** There are dozens of sites to deepen your knowledge of the Civil War.

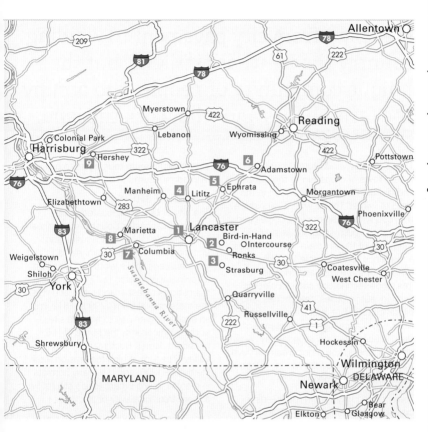

About 60 miles west of Philadelphia, a different world from a different time emerges. It's not just the change in scenery—from city pavement to winding country roads—that's striking, but the unique community of people who occupy the farmhouses and who work the land.

This is Pennsylvania Dutch country, where rows of crops run to the horizon and laundry hangs on lines even in the dead of winter. This is where cars share the road with horse-drawn buggies and homemade push scooter-bikes. Many members of these "plain" communities, a reference to the simple lifestyles and clothing of the Amish and Mennonites, shun technology such as electric lighting, automobiles, telephones, and digital culture. But, just minutes away in the city of Lancaster, a renaissance of the 21st-century kind is underway, where artisans, chefs, and other creatives have transformed the downtown into a vibrant place to live and work.

Today the county's main roads—especially U.S. 30 and Route 340—are lined with souvenir shops and often crowded with busloads of tourists. The area's proximity to Philadelphia, Harrisburg, and Baltimore has brought commercial development. In fact, the National Trust for Historic Preservation has put Lancaster County on its list of the nation's most endangered historic places because of rapid suburbanization. But beyond the commercialism and development, there remain general stores, one-room schoolhouses, country lanes, and tidy farms. You can find instructive places to learn about the Pennsylvania Dutch way of life, pretzel factories to tour, quilts to buy, and railroad museums to explore.

## MAJOR REGIONS

The city of **Lancaster,** located at the center of Lancaster County, is an appealing, walkable city of row houses and Victorian homes with a dynamic arts and cultural scene that's worth exploring on its own. Incorporated in 1742, it's one of the nation's oldest inland cities and was the state capital from 1799 to 1812. It's an excellent gateway to historic sites, such as Wheatland, the home of U.S. president James Buchanan; the Landis Valley Museum, which focuses on rural life before 1900; and the many hamlets and small towns where locals still follow a more traditional way of life.

Less than a half hour outside the city limits, get a taste of the countryside and Pennsylvania Dutch Country. Lancaster County comprises the largest swath of the most productive nonirrigated farmland in the country. On rural roads, there's big sky above and farms and dairies beneath. In the small town of **Bird-in-Hand,** you'll find markets, craft and furniture shops, and sights that interpret Amish life. Nearby is **Strasburg,** where visitors can learn the history of railroads and go for a scenic ride on a restored train. Also in the vicinity are the historic villages of **Ephrata,** site of a religious community dating to the 18th century, and **Lititz,** where you can still twist your own soft pretzel at the country's first pretzel bakery. **Adamstown**, in the northeastern tip of the county, is a haven for collectibles, vintage and antique.

In Western Lancaster County, the Susquehanna River towns of **Columbia** and **Marietta** offer a mix of the great outdoors, quality antiquing, and a mellow vibe.

If you've brought your children as far as Lancaster, you may want to continue northwest to **Hershey,** the "Chocolate Town" founded in 1903 by Milton S. Hershey. Here the number one attraction is Hersheypark, a theme park with kiddie and thrill rides, theaters, and live shows. You may also wish to journey southwest to the Civil War battlefields and museums of **Gettysburg,** also within a short driving distance.

# Planning

## Getting Here and Around

### CAR
From Philadelphia, it's about a 65-mile drive. From I–76 west (Schuylkill Expressway), there are two options: for the slower, more scenic route, take U.S. 202 south to U.S. 30 west; quicker is I–276 (Pennsylvania Turnpike, with tolls). Lancaster County sights are accessible from Exits 266, 286, and 298.

A car is the easiest way to explore the many sights in the area; it also lets you get off the main roads and into the countryside. Lancaster County's main arteries are U.S. 30 (also known as the Lincoln Highway) and Route 340 (also called Old Philadelphia Pike). Some pleasant back roads can be found between Routes 23 and 340 through Smoketown and Bird-in-Hand as well as Route 896 through the village of Strasburg. You'll get a look at

farms in the area and Pennsylvania Dutch barns, stores, schoolhouses, and farm stands.

**▥ TIP➜ Remember to slow down for horse-drawn buggies when driving on country roads, and give them a wide berth while passing.**

### TRAIN
Amtrak's Keystone line has frequent daily service between Philadelphia's 30th Street Station and its station in Lancaster. The trip takes about 70 minutes.

**CONTACTS Amtrak.** ✉ *53 McGovern Ave.* ☎ *800/872–7245* ⊕ *www.amtrak.com.*

# When to Go

Summer and autumn are busy times, when seasonal produce, county fairs and festivals, and fall foliage attract crowds. Farmers' markets and family-style restaurants overflow with visitors and locals alike. Crowds will likely be fewer in early spring and when school is in session. Although many Amish restaurants, shops, and farmers' markets are closed on Sundays, commercial attractions remain open.

## Planning Your Time

The city of Lancaster, with its rich arts and cultural scene, is worth at least a full day of your trip. It makes a good hub while visiting the close-by countryside, or a convenient jumping-off point for traveling farther afield. Consider spending a night or two.

The sights of Lancaster County lie within half an hour's drive of Lancaster City. If Pennsylvania Dutch Country is at the top of your list, you'll want to spend one or two days along the Lincoln Highway and Old Philadelphia Pike west of town. Depending on your interests, other towns can easily burn up a half or full day.

# Please Be Respectful

In these parts, visitors get a glimpse of 19th-century life, or rather, get to witness living history. The Amish and Mennonites you see in the shops and restaurants are not reenactors; these are real people living their lives. The simple clothes they wear and the German dialect some still speak daily aren't oddities to marvel at, and the people aren't curiosities to be stared at or approached. When visiting Amish and Mennonite communities, remember that you are a visitor and they are your hosts, whose values and way of life must be respected, even if they seem odd to you. Note that the Amish believe photographs and videos with recognizable images of their faces violate the biblical commandment against making graven images. Please refrain from photography.

Outside the county, families might want to allocate two days to Hershey, while history buffs should schedule two days to explore Gettysburg, site of one of the most important battles of the Civil War.

## Hotels

Lancaster County offers a wide range of lodging options—stay at a historic inn, or indulge yourself at a luxurious resort. A good selection of moderately priced motels and chain properties are scattered around the county. Although hotels welcome guests year-round, rates are highest in summer. Some inns and B&Bs have minimum stays in high season.

Lancaster County Bed-and-Breakfast Association has information on a number of area B&Bs.

Many working Amish and non-Amish farms throughout Lancaster County welcome guests to stay for a few days to experience farm life. Operated as B&B establishments with a twist, the farms invite you to help milk the cows, feed the chickens, or help with other chores before sharing a hearty breakfast with the farmers. Reservations must be made weeks in advance, as most farms are heavily booked in summer. Discover Lancaster has a list of local farms that welcome guests.

**CONTACTS Lancaster County Bed-and-Breakfast Inns Association.** ⊠ *590 Centerville Rd., Lancaster* ☎ *717/484–0800* ⊕ *www.padutchinns.com.*

## Restaurants

Lancaster County is home to numerous reasonably priced family restaurants, along with a growing number of eateries offering fine dining or globally inspired fare, especially in Lancaster City. Unless otherwise noted, liquor is served.

Like the German country cuisine that influenced it, Pennsylvania Dutch cooking is hearty and uses ingredients from local farms. Though their numbers are dwindling, traditional Pennsylvania Dutch restaurants do remain, many where you can dine family style.

### HOTEL AND RESTAURANT PRICES
⇨ *Hotel prices in the reviews are the lowest cost of a standard double room in high season. Restaurant prices in the reviews are the average cost of a main course at dinner, or if dinner is not served, at lunch. Restaurant and hotel reviews have been shortened. For full information, visit Fodors.com.*

# Tours

Although Lancaster County is easy to navigate on your own, tours can be helpful, particularly if you're interested in learning about the Amish and Mennonite ways of life. Local guides can offer cultural context you simply can't get from reading brochures. Throughout the chapter you'll find information on a wide variety of tours.

**TOUR CONTACTS The Amish Experience.** ✉ *3121 Old Philadelphia Pike, Rte. 340, Bird-in-Hand* ✛ *Most GPS systems use "Ronks" as the city.* ☎ *717/768–8400* ⊕ *www.amishexperience.com.* **Smoketown Helicopters.** ✉ *311 Airport Dr., off Rte. 340, Smoketown* ☎ *717/344–4871* ⊕ *www.smoketownhelicopters.com.*

# Visitor Information

Discover Lancaster is the welcome center for Lancaster County, offering a selection of brochures, maps, and other resources, plus advice from its staff of travel consultants. You can check your email, get a free cup of coffee, and browse the gift shop's sampling of local crafts and souvenirs.

**CONTACTS Discover Lancaster.** ✉ *501 Greenfield Rd., Lancaster* ✛ *Off U.S. 30 northwest of Lancaster City.* ☎ *800/723–8824* ⊕ *www.discoverlancaster.com.*

# Lancaster

*75 miles west of Philadelphia via I–76.*

Just minutes from the countryside is Lancaster, a vibrant city with a population of 60,000. During the French and Indian War and the American Revolution, its artisans turned out fine guns, building the city's reputation as the arsenal of the colonies. On September 27, 1777, Lancaster became the nation's capital for just one day as Congress fled the British in Philadelphia. Today, markets and museums preserve the area's history in a stately downtown core whose red bricks and cobblestones will be familiar to anyone who's spent time in East Coast cities like Philadelphia, Boston, and Baltimore. The city saw economic decline and a rise in urban blight after World War II, which only started to turn around in the 1990s. In recent years, Lancaster has upped its contemporary appeal. You'll still find plenty of whoopie pies, but also ramen and chia pudding, rehabbed row homes, and modern restaurants that have strengthened ties with the county's organic farmers.

## GETTING HERE AND AROUND

The quickest route from Philadelphia is to take I–76, also known as the Pennsylvania Turnpike, then take U.S. 222 south to Lancaster. If you're staying near Penn Square, you can walk to the Central Market, the major museums, and cultural attractions. You'll need a car to access certain sights within the city, including Wheatland as well as the surrounding countryside. For lovely views of farms and unspoiled land, take a spin along the smaller roads between Routes 23 and 340.

## VISITOR INFORMATION

**CONTACT Lancaster City Welcome Center.** ✉ *38 Penn Sq., Lancaster* ✛ *For GPS, use 5 W. King St.* ☎ *717/517–5718* ⊕ *visitlancastercity.com.*

## ◉ Sights

### Demuth Museum

**ART MUSEUM** | This museum includes the restored 18th-century home, studio, and garden of Charles Demuth (1883–1935), one of America's first modernist artists, who lived in the city of Lancaster for most of his life. A watercolorist, Demuth found inspiration in the geometric shapes of machines and modern technology, as well as the flowers in his mother's garden. Items from the 42-piece collection

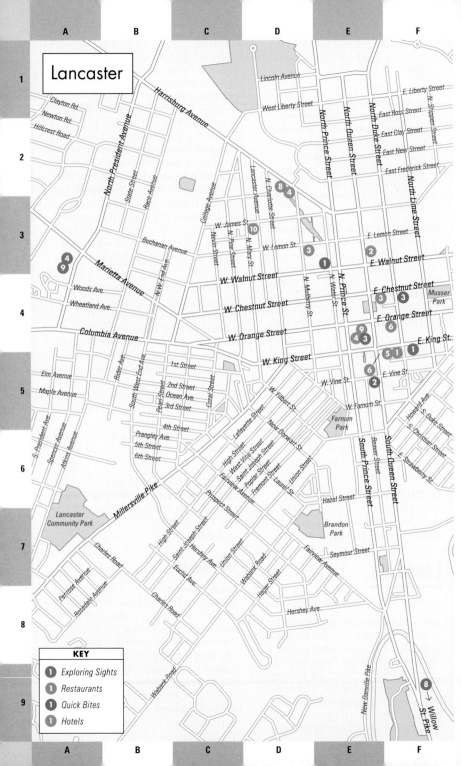

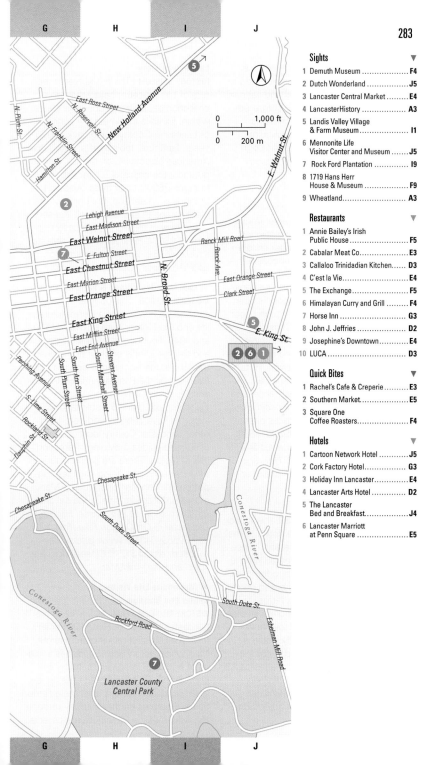

## Sights ▾

1 Demuth Museum .................. **F4**
2 Dutch Wonderland ................ **J5**
3 Lancaster Central Market ......... **E4**
4 LancasterHistory ................. **A3**
5 Landis Valley Village
  & Farm Museum.................... **I1**
6 Mennonite Life
  Visitor Center and Museum ....... **J5**
7 Rock Ford Plantation ............. **I9**
8 1719 Hans Herr
  House & Museum ................. **F9**
9 Wheatland.......................... **A3**

## Restaurants ▾

1 Annie Bailey's Irish
  Public House ...................... **F5**
2 Cabalar Meat Co.................... **E3**
3 Callaloo Trinidadian Kitchen...... **D3**
4 C'est la Vie........................ **E4**
5 The Exchange...................... **F5**
6 Himalayan Curry and Grill ........ **F4**
7 Horse Inn ......................... **G3**
8 John J. Jeffries .................. **D2**
9 Josephine's Downtown............ **E4**
10 LUCA .............................. **D3**

## Quick Bites ▾

1 Rachel's Cafe & Creperie ......... **E3**
2 Southern Market.................... **E5**
3 Square One
  Coffee Roasters.................... **F4**

## Hotels ▾

1 Cartoon Network Hotel ........... **J5**
2 Cork Factory Hotel................ **G3**
3 Holiday Inn Lancaster............. **E4**
4 Lancaster Arts Hotel ............. **D2**
5 The Lancaster
  Bed and Breakfast................. **J4**
6 Lancaster Marriott
  at Penn Square .................... **E5**

of Demuth's works are displayed on a rotating basis; one gallery is dedicated to changing exhibits of regional and national artists. Next door is the now-shuttered Demuth Tobacco Shop, which dates to 1770. ⊠ *120 E. King St., Lancaster* ☎ *717/299–9940* ⊕ *www.demuth.org* 🗐 *Suggested donation $5* ⊙ *Closed Mon. and Wed.*

### Dutch Wonderland

**THEME PARK | FAMILY** | A self-proclaimed "Kingdom for Kids," this 44-acre amusement park features rides and activities suited for families with younger children. Most rides, such as the roller coaster, merry-go-round, and giant slide, are quite tame. The adjacent water park (no separate admission), Duke's Lagoon, is open weekends, Memorial Day through Labor Day. From Thanksgiving to Christmas, the park is open for its "Dutch Winter Wonderland," with holiday-themed rides and a light show. The Cartoon Network Hotel is next door; hotel guests get special park admission discounts and early access to the park and rides. ⊠ *2249 Lincoln Hwy. E (U.S. 30), Lancaster* ✛ *4 miles east of downtown Lancaster* ☎ *866/386–2839* ⊕ *www.dutchwonderland.com* 🗐 *$49.99 (advance purchase online)* ⊙ *Hrs vary according to the season; call ahead or check the website.*

### ★ Lancaster Central Market

**MARKET | FAMILY** | Built in 1889, this indoor farmers' market gave a new home to the city's open-air market, in operation since 1742. The grand Romanesque building is a city fixture as a place to shop for fresh produce, meat, flowers and baked goods, most of it from the county's farms. In addition to Amish and Mennonite staples like Lebanon bologna and chowchow, there's a selection of globally inspired prepared foods, from Ugandan chicken patties to Puerto Rican empanadas. ⊠ *23 N. Market St., Lancaster* ✛ *Off Penn Square* ☎ *717/735–6890* ⊕ *www.centralmarketlancaster.com* ⊙ *Closed Sun., Mon., Wed., and Thurs.*

### LancasterHistory

**HISTORY MUSEUM** | The modern architecture of this museum belies the deep collection of Lancaster County artifacts within. Exhibits illuminate the history of Lancaster County going back 350 years. Furniture, tools, crafts, and Native American objects are on display. On the grounds, the peaceful Tanger Arboretum features 250 kinds of trees. Also on the grounds is Wheatland, the home of President James Buchanan, which you see up close on a tour run by LancasterHistory. ⊠ *230 N. President Ave., Lancaster* ☎ *392–4633* ⊕ *www.lancasterhistory.org* 🗐 *$10* ⊙ *Closed Sun. and Mon.*

### ★ Landis Valley Village & Farm Museum

**MUSEUM VILLAGE** | This open-air museum showcases Pennsylvania German rural life and local folk culture between 1750 and 1940. Founded by brothers Henry and George Landis on their homestead in the 1920s, the farm and village are now operated by the Pennsylvania Historical and Museum Commission. You can visit the more than 15 historical buildings that have been moved here from other Lancaster County locations, with costumed guides providing interesting bits of history. There are demonstrations of skills such as spinning and weaving, pottery making, and tinsmithing. Many of the crafts are for sale in the delightful museum shop. ⊠ *2451 Kissel Hill Rd., Lancaster* ✛ *Off Oregon Pike (Rte. 272)* ☎ *717/569–0401* ⊕ *www.landisvalleymuseum.org* 🗐 *$12* ⊙ *Closed Mon. and Tues. and Jan.–mid-Mar.*

### ★ Mennonite Life Visitor Center and Museum

**HISTORY MUSEUM | FAMILY** | Formerly the Lancaster Mennonite Historical Society, this small but first-rate museum about Mennonite history and culture has exhibits of furniture, needlework, tools, and photographs. The highlight of the center is a reproduction of the tabernacle carried by the Hebrews on their journey through the wilderness; a 35-minute multimedia

The Lancaster Central Market has been a city fixture since its days as an open-air market in 1742. Shop here for fresh produce, meat, flowers and baked goods.

presentation tells the story. There is also an extensive bookstore and a gift shop selling international crafts. Don't miss the Fraktur—elaborate, usually illustrated works of Gothic calligraphy on paper (think needlework samplers). ⊠ *2215 Millstream Rd., Off U.S. 30, Lancaster* ☎ *717/299-0954* ⊕ *mennonitelife.org* ☎ *$8 museum; $10 tabernacle* ⊗ *Closed Sun.–Tues. Apr.–Dec.; closed Sun.–Thurs. Jan.–Mar.*

### Rock Ford Plantation

**HISTORIC HOME** | Set on 33 acres, the Historic Rock Ford Plantation is the restored homestead of General Edward Hand, a Revolutionary War commander, George Washington's confidant, and wealthy landowner. Period antiques and folk art are displayed in the 1794 Georgian-style mansion, which is on the National Register of Historic Places. In partnership with the African American Historical Society of South Central Pennsylvania, the plantation presents programs on the legacy and stories of the slaves who lived and worked on Hand's farm and in the household. ⊠ *881 Rock Ford Rd., Lancaster* ☎ *717/392-7223* ⊕ *www.rock-fordplantation.org* ☎ *$8* ⊗ *Closed Mon. and Nov.–Mar.*

### ★ 1719 Herr House & Museum

**HISTORIC HOME** | Built in 1719 and listed on the National Register of Historic Places, the Hans Herr House is the oldest building in Lancaster County and the oldest remaining Mennonite meeting house in the Western Hemisphere. It was the residence of Herr, a Mennonite bishop, and his family, and remained a home until the early 1900s, when it fell into disuse. Never modernized, the house retains most of its original old-country German features, which were preserved when it was restored in the 1970s. A 45-minute tour covers the house and grounds, which include two other Pennsylvania German homes, Colonial-era barns and outbuildings, and a collection of period farm equipment. A separate 45-minute tour of the site's re-created Indian longhouse illuminates the culture of Eastern Woodland tribes. ⊠ *1849 Hans*

*Herr Dr., Willow Street ✢ 5 miles south of downtown Lancaster, off U.S. 222 ☎ 717/464–4438 🌐 www.hansherr.org 🎟 $15 🕑 Closed Sun. and Dec.–Mar.*

**Wheatland**

**HISTORIC HOME** | Wheatland was the home of James Buchanan, the only U.S. president from Pennsylvania, who served from 1857 to 1861. A National Historic Landmark, the restored 1828 Federal-style mansion and outbuildings display the 15th president's furniture just as it was during his lifetime. A one-hour tour, departing from the LancasterHistory museum, includes a profile of the only bachelor to occupy the White House, a movie, and access to the arboretum on the grounds. There are holiday candlelight tours with costumed guides. ✉ *1120 Marietta Ave., Lancaster* ☎ *717/392–4633* 🌐 *www.lancasterhistory.org* 🎟 *$17* 🕑 *Closed Mon.*

## 🍴 Restaurants

**Annie Bailey's Irish Public House**

$$ | **AMERICAN** | **FAMILY** | Located in a Victorian-era building in downtown Lancaster, Annie Bailey's delivers a traditional Irish pub experience, from the furnishings sourced in Ireland to classic dishes like shepherd's pie and fish-and-chips; there are other popular pub-fare items like burgers and wings as well. There are at least 15 beers on tap and an impressive selection of Irish whiskey. **Known for:** weekend brunch features the Full Irish (eggs, black pudding, white pudding, grilled tomato, baked beans, and more); relaxed, friendly atmosphere; seasonal outdoor deck;. [$] *Average main: $19* ✉ *28–30 E. King St., Lancaster* ✢ *Off Penn Square* ☎ *717/393–4000* 🌐 *www.anniebaileys.com* 🕑 *No lunch weekdays.*

**Cabalar Meat Co.**

$ | **AMERICAN** | Amidst the eclectic shops of North Queen Street, this family-owned butcher shop doubles as a casual restaurant with a hearty menu of burgers, sandwiches, and milkshakes. Place your order at the counter and have a seat at one of the many communal tables; don't forget to grab one of the 14 drafts on tap from the county's Mad Chef Brewing Company. **Known for:** rich beef-tallow fries; a variety of burgers; craft beer on tap. [$] *Average main: $12* ✉ *325 N. Queen St., Lancaster* ☎ *717/208–7344* 🌐 *www.cabalarmeatco.com* 🕑 *Closed Mon.–Wed.*

**Callaloo Trinidadian Kitchen**

$$ | **CARIBBEAN** | Front and center at this charming corner café is the cuisine of the Caribbean island of Trinidad, which melds together with Chinese, Indian, and African dishes to create a beguiling melting pot of flavors and options. You can have *buss-up shut* (curried vegetables, chicken, or beef that you scoop up with a flatbread), pineapple chow (a salsa of sorts that's good enough to eat with a spoon), or callaloo (a spinach-like green stewed and served with sweet-potato dumplings). **Known for:** huge portions of dishes like coconut jerk chicken; BYOB with a small corkage fee; fried-bread doubles with toppings. [$] *Average main: $18* ✉ *351 N. Mulberry St., Lancaster* ☎ *717/824–3964* 🌐 *callalootrinidadiankitchen.com* 🕑 *Closed Sun.–Tues. No lunch.*

**C'est la Vie**

$$$ | **MODERN FRENCH** | Bistro-style C'est la Vie, right in the middle of downtown, serves mix of traditional and modern French and American fare ranging from boeuf bourguignon to brick-oven pizzas. If you're so inclined, choose a bottle from the long wine list, which focuses on French producers but also includes a solid lineup of other European and New World wines. **Known for:** local favorite; fig-and-goat cheese pizza; wild mushroom stroganoff. [$] *Average main: $30* ✉ *18 N. Market St., Lancaster* ☎ *717/299–7319* 🌐 *www.clvlancaster.com* 🕑 *Closed Sun. and Mon.*

### The Exchange

**$$ | FUSION |** Perched atop the Marriott at Penn Square, this chic lounge and restaurant (for those 21 and over) has the best views in town from its floor-to-ceiling windows and stylish deck. Enjoy a cocktail and the globally inspired small plates, from Lebanon bologna sliders to crispy Halloumi cheese, and a rotating selection of wood-fired pizzas while enjoying the view. **Known for:** great sunset viewing; weekday happy hour food and drink specials; crowd is 21 and over only. $ Average main: $18 ⊠ Marriott at Penn Square, 25 S. Queen St., Lancaster ⊹ Off Penn Square ☎ 717/207–4096 ⊕ www.exchangeroof.com ⊗ No lunch weekdays.

### ★ Himalayan Curry and Grill

**$ | INDIAN |** This family-owned Nepalese and Indian restaurant is a longtime favorite in downtown Lancaster serving up popular Indian specialties like tandoori and chana masala (a chickpea-based curry), as well as Nepalese dry curries and steamed dumplings. The cozy dining room quickly gets packed on weekend nights and weekday lunch hours (there's an all-you-can-eat lunch buffet Monday through Saturday), but the staff gracefully handles the constant flow. **Known for:** dal palak (a spinach-and-lentil curry); spicy vindaloo dishes; momo (Nepalese dumplings filled with vegetables or chicken). $ Average main: $17 ⊠ 22 E. Orange St., Lancaster ☎ 717/393–2330 ⊕ www.himalayanlancaster.com ⊗ Closed Sun. and Mon.

### Horse Inn

**$$ | MODERN AMERICAN |** This seasonally driven gastropub located in a former inn, stable, and speakeasy uses locally grown produce and meat and Pennsylvania-made beer and spirits. The day's menu, and a list of "Farmers and Friends" who supply the restaurant's ingredients, are posted on chalkboards. **Known for:** tips 'n toast (tenderloin tips on French bread) and horse fries (sausage, cheese, and garlic heavy cream); creative botanical craft cocktails; live jazz on most Tuesday and Saturday nights. $ Average main: $24 ⊠ 540 E. Fulton St., Lancaster ☎ 717/392–5528 ⊕ www.horseinnlancaster.com ⊗ Closed Sun. and Mon. No lunch.

### John J. Jeffries

**$$$$ | MODERN AMERICAN |** Not only do the chefs here source organic produce, dairy, and eggs from local farms, but the restaurant also operates a grass-fed cattle ranch, abattoir, and nose-to-tail butcher shop in Chambersburg, Pennsylvania so you know the ingredients are top-quality. The menu does change seasonally, but mains might include braised lamb or a tartare of grass-fed beef, and the appealing wine list is well-priced. **Known for:** dry-aged steak from Lil' Ponderosa ranch; notable, affordable wine list; using lesser-known cuts of meat, like beef cheeks or venison leg steak. $ Average main: $30 ⊠ Lancaster Arts Hotel, 300 Harrisburg Ave., Lancaster ☎ 717/431–3307 ⊕ www.johnjjeffries.com ⊗ Closed Sun. No lunch.

### ★ Josephine's Downtown

**$$$$ | MODERN AMERICAN |** Downstairs from its sibling C'est la Vie, this cushy dinner spot is lined with photos from the golden age of Hollywood; it's the kind of place where you order a cocktail with a movie-star name. The chef spins French techniques and local ingredients into refined plates such as beet tartar and crab mushroom bisque, and the stunning desserts are worth the calories, but the one you must order is the lemon meringue that reveals its secret when you cut into it. **Known for:** good for special occasions; elegant decor; live piano music. $ Average main: $44 ⊠ 50 W. Grant St., Lancaster ⊹ Downstairs from C'est la Vie ☎ 717/299–7090 ⊕ www.josephinesdowntown.com ⊗ Closed Sun. and Mon. No lunch.

### ★ LUCA

$$ | **MODERN ITALIAN** | A self-described "wood-burning Italian kitchen," LUCA serves up handmade pasta and Neapolitan-style pizza, plus a large menu of hot and cold starters. Located in a residential neighborhood near the Franklin & Marshall campus, this place is always busy, and for good reason—the food is consistently delicious and the dining room vibe is upbeat. **Known for:** main dining room can get noisy; bottle shop sells beer and wine to go; large selection of Italian spirits and craft cocktails. [$] *Average main: $22* ✉ *436 W. James St., Lancaster* ☎ *717/553–5770* 🌐 *lucalancaster.com* 🕓 *Closed Mon. and Tues.*

## ☕ Coffee and Quick Bites

### Rachel's Cafe & Creperie

$ | **AMERICAN** | Tucked away on a quiet corner, Rachel's offers perfectly light crepes—many can be made gluten-free or vegan—stuffed with a wide variety of ingredients. Whether you sit in the cozy dining room or on the covered deck, you can build your own crepe from the long list of fillings, from feta and mushrooms to bacon, or enjoy a latte with a crepe such as The Blackbird (chicken, roasted corn, and black beans). **Known for:** good service; large portions; relaxed atmosphere. [$] *Average main: $9* ✉ *201 W. Walnut St., Lancaster* ☎ *717/399–3515* 🌐 *www.rachelscreperie.com* 🕓 *Closed Mon. No dinner.*

### Southern Market

$$ | **INTERNATIONAL** | **FAMILY** | A few blocks from Central Market, this one-time farmers' market built in 1888 was repurposed as a food hall that opened in 2022. The 10 food stands offer a wide variety of cuisines, from Moroccan to Vietnamese; order at the stations of your choice and bring your food to one of the hall's tables or the central bar. **Known for:** across the street from the convention center; round bar at the center of the hall serves craft cocktails and beer; expansive, airy space never seems to get crowded. [$] *Average main: $18* ✉ *100 S. Queen St., Lancaster* ☎ *717/517–3000* 🌐 *southernmarketlancaster.com* 🕓 *Closed Mon. and Tues.*

### Square One Coffee Roasters

$ | **CAFÉ** | Owned by a local roaster, Square One (or SQ1, as it's locally known) serves exceptionally good brewed coffee and espresso that you can pair with a selection of local pastries and grab-and-go lunch fare. It's a favorite among regulars who wander in for their first cup of the day and linger to read the local paper or check their email. **Known for:** garden courtyard when weather permits; rotating lineup of single-origin espresso; really good cold brew. [$] *Average main: $3* ✉ *145 N. Duke St., Lancaster* ☎ *717/392–3354* 🌐 *www.squareonecoffee.com.*

## 🛏 Hotels

### Cartoon Network Hotel

$$ | **HOTEL** | **FAMILY** | This one-of-a-kind hotel is next to the popular Dutch Wonderland amusement park, and its agenda is crystal clear—this place is all about the cartoons, and the kids; hotel guests get early entrance to the park as well as admission discounts. **Pros:** themed indoor pool plus seasonal outdoor pool; rooms are expressly designed for families, with bunk beds in most rooms; next door to Dutch Wonderland. **Cons:** no elevator in the two-story building; small bathrooms in standard rooms; potential noise from U.S. 30 traffic. [$] *Rooms from: $239* ✉ *2285 Lincoln Hwy. E (U.S. 30), Lancaster* ☎ *717/740–2777* 🌐 *www.cartoonnetworkhotel.com* 🛏 *164 rooms* 🍴 *No Meals.*

### Cork Factory Hotel

$ | **HOTEL** | The exposed-brick walls, vaulted wood ceilings, and ductwork of this boutique hotel recall its former life as the Armstrong Cork Company. **Pros:** many original factory features have been preserved; atmospheric bar; friendly, unpretentious front desk vibe. **Cons:** poor lighting in rooms; hard-to-find location in a mixed-use complex; 1 mile from the core of downtown. $ *Rooms from: $169 ⊠ 480 New Holland Ave., Lancaster ⊹ Bldg. 3, under the old smokestack ☎ 717/735–2075 ⊕ www.corkfactoryhotel.com ⇄ 93 rooms ¶Ol Free Breakfast.*

### Holiday Inn Lancaster

$ | **HOTEL** | **FAMILY** | What makes this affordable chain property special is the perfectly situated downtown location that's great for exploring the city. **Pros:** great views from some rooms; within walking distance of most downtown businesses; in-room Keurig coffeemakers. **Cons:** there's a charge for breakfast; bland decor; no in-room microwaves. $ *Rooms from: $138 ⊠ 26 E. Chestnut St., Lancaster ☎ 717/394–0900 ⊕ www.ihg.com/holidayinn/hotels/us/en/lancaster ⇄ 215 rooms ¶Ol No Meals.*

### Lancaster Arts Hotel

$$ | **HOTEL** | This boutique hotel in a former tobacco warehouse dating from the 1800s offers sleek rooms furnished with executive desks, flat-screen TVs, iPod docking stations, and free Wi-Fi; there are also whirlpool tubs in the suites. **Pros:** trendy design; high-end farm-to-table restaurant; more than 200 pieces of art displayed throughout the property. **Cons:** in-room wine fridges don't accommodate anything but bottles; on a busy street; no pool. $ *Rooms from: $179 ⊠ 300 Harrisburg Ave., Lancaster ☎ 717/584–9782 ⊕ www.lancasterartshotel.com ⇄ 75 rooms ¶Ol Free Breakfast.*

### The Lancaster Bed and Breakfast

$ | **B&B/INN** | Surrounded by pretty gardens, this 1912 Dutch Colonial inn is known for outstanding hospitality and a full complimentary breakfast served in an antique- and art-filled dining room. **Pros:** the downstairs living room has a wood-burning fireplace, puzzles, and games; scratch-made breakfast; close

to the Conestoga River Greenway trail. **Cons:** inn is located on a busy commercial strip; no elevator; some bathrooms need updating. $ *Rooms from: $165 ⊠ 1105 E. King St., Lancaster ☎ 717/293–1723 ⊕ www.thelancasterbnb.com ⇄ 7 rooms ¶Ol Free Breakfast.*

### ★ Lancaster Marriott at Penn Square

$ | **HOTEL** | In the heart of downtown Lancaster, this beaux arts–style former department store offers well-appointed guest rooms with upscale amenities geared to business travelers, including a fitness center and spa. **Pros:** prime location in the center of town; some rooms have sweeping views; three on-site dining options. **Cons:** there is a charge for in-room Wi-Fi; chain-hotel vibe; prices surge on weekends and when conventions are in town. $ *Rooms from: $172 ⊠ 25 S. Queen St., Lancaster ☎ 717/207–4095 ⊕ www.marriott.com/en-us/hotels/lnsmc-lancaster-marriott-at-penn-square ⇄ 416 rooms ¶Ol No Meals.*

## 🍸 Nightlife

### Proof Lancaster

**COCKTAIL LOUNGES** | This subterranean cocktail bar mixes up specialty and classic drinks in an intimate space with rough rock walls. A nice selection of wines by the glass rounds out the drinks menu, and a menu of small plates is on offer. ⊠ *30 N. Queen St., lower Level, Lancaster ☎ 717/925–7770 ⊕ www.prooflancaster.com.*

### ★ Tellus360

**LIVE MUSIC** | In the heart of downtown, this multilevel club presents a wide variety of live music, including Celtic, bluegrass, and alt-rock. There are also bingo nights and Tuesday trivia, as well as DJ nights. ⊠ *24 E. King St., Lancaster ☎ 717/393–1660 ⊕ www.tellus360.com.*

#  Performing Arts

## American Music Theatre

**THEATER** | This 1,600-seat theater presents live concerts with big-name acts and full-scale original musical productions, including an annual Christmas show. ☒ *2425 Lincoln Hwy. E, Lancaster ✛ U.S. 30* ☎ *717/397–7700* ⊕ *amtshows.com.*

## Dutch Apple Dinner Theatre

**THEATER | FAMILY** | At this 330-seat theater, it's all about dinner and a show. On stage, the theater's professionally trained company performs a mix of updated classic musicals such as *Guys and Dolls* and *Annie Get Your Gun* join more contemporary productions such as *Legally Blonde* and *Sister Act,* plus regular children's productions. With the exception of a seated, full-service dinner on Thursdays, the theater offers a hearty buffet. ☒ *510 Centerville Rd., Lancaster ✛ At U.S. 30* ☎ *717/898–1900* ⊕ *dutchapple.com* 🎟 *From $25.*

## ★ Fulton Theatre *(The Fulton)*

**THEATER** | A National Historic Landmark, the 1852 Fulton Opera House is a crown jewel of performing arts for the region, showcasing Broadway productions, world premieres of commissioned works, and the Lancaster Symphony Orchestra. One-hour guided tours ($5) of the grand Victorian-era building are offered on Fridays during summer months. ☒ *12 N. Prince St., Lancaster* ☎ *717/397–7425* ⊕ *thefulton.org* 🎟 *From $31.*

#  Shopping

## Landis Valley Museum Store

**CRAFTS** | On the grounds of the Landis Valley Village & Farm Museum, this shop is a destination in and of itself. You'll find a unique selection of artisan-crafted goods—many of which are made on the premises—that range from pottery to felt art, plus an extensive offering of Pennsylvania German arts and crafts. ☒ *Landis Valley Village & Farm Museum, 2451 Kissel Hill Rd., Lancaster* ☎ *717/569–9312* ⊕ *www.landisvalleymuseum.org.*

## Olde Mill House Shoppes

**OTHER SPECIALTY STORE** | Located in a restored barn and stone house, this family-owned business is a local must-visit for home decor, gifts, women's clothing, quilts, and country-style furniture. ☒ *105 Strasburg Pike, Lancaster* ☎ *717/299–0678* ⊕ *oldemillhouse.com.*

## Pennsylvania Guild of Craftsmen

**CRAFTS** | The flagship shop of 10 locations across Pennsylvania, this nonprofit gallery funded by the Pennsylvania Council on the Arts showcases crafts made by artisans statewide. Finely crafted woodwork, ceramics, textiles and more are on offer. ☒ *335 N. Queen St., Lancaster* ☎ *717/431–8706* ⊕ *pacrafts.org.*

## Space

**ANTIQUES & COLLECTIBLES** | This more than 2,000-square-foot warehouse just off North Queen Street is a source of all things mid-century, from furniture, lighting, and glassware to jewelry and old video games. ☒ *24 W. Walnut St., Lancaster* ☎ *717/413–3477* ⊕ *www.spacelancaster.com.*

## Tanger Outlets

**MALL** | There are more than 60 outlet stores here, including fashion brands like Ralph Lauren, J. Crew, New Balance, and North Face. A few fast-food restaurants are on-site as well. ■ **TIP→ Visit early, especially on weekends, when the stores are packed with road-tripping families.** ☒ *311 Stanley K. Tanger Blvd., Lancaster ✛ At U.S. 30* ☎ *717/392–7260* ⊕ *www.tangeroutlet.com.*

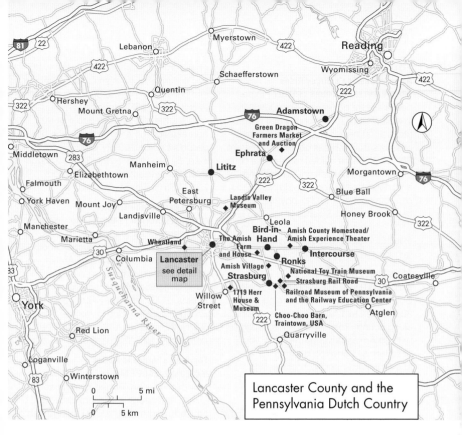

Lancaster County and the Pennsylvania Dutch Country

# Bird-in-Hand and Intercourse

*Bird-in-Hand is 6 miles east of downtown Lancaster via Rte. 462 and Rte. 340. Intercourse is 10 miles east of Lancaster via Rte. 340.*

Bird-in-Hand, which dates to 1734, remains a center for the Pennsylvania Dutch farming community. Its name, according to local lore, is attributed to two road surveyors, who had to decide whether to remain where they were or travel to Lancaster. They decided to stay, the story goes, when one said, "A bird in the hand is worth two in the bush." An early tavern began to be known as the Bird-in-Hand Inn and the name stuck.

Intercourse's odd name came from the Colonial term for intersection. At the intersection of Routes 340 and 772, this town is a center of Amish life. Between Intercourse and Bird-in-Hand up the road, the Amish way of life can be explored by observing their farms, crafts, quilts, and various educational experiences.

## GETTING HERE AND AROUND

Bird-in-Hand is just a few minutes' drive from other Amish and Mennonite towns, including Ronks and Intercourse. Its attractions are clustered on Route 340 or nearby on U.S. 30.

From downtown Lancaster, the drive to Intercourse is a straight shot east along Route 340 to Route 772, the center of this small town.

## TOURS

### Aaron & Jessica's Buggy Rides

**SPECIAL-INTEREST TOURS | FAMILY** | Experience a taste of Pennsylvania Dutch life in an authentic Amish buggy that makes stops at farms and businesses. Aaron & Jessica's Buggy Rides offers five different 30- to 60-minute guided tours of the countryside with an Amish driver imparting anecdotes and historical information. You can also book a private buggy ride. Rides depart from Plain & Fancy Farm. ⊠ *3121 Old Philadelphia Pike, Rte. 340, Bird-in-Hand* ☎ *717/768–8828* ⊕ *www.amishbuggyrides.com* ✉ *From $15* ⊘ *Closed Sun.*

### Abe's Buggy Rides

**SPECIAL-INTEREST TOURS | FAMILY** | Abe's Buggy Rides offers tours ranging from 30 minutes to 1 hour 15 minutes. Rolling along country roads in an Amish buggy with an Amish driver at the reins, you'll pass farms, a one-room schoolhouse, and Amish/Mennonite shops selling homemade root beer and shoofly pie. You'll learn about Pennsylvania Dutch customs and the sights along the way. ⊠ *2596 Old Philadelphia Pike, Rte. 340, Bird-in-Hand* ☎ *717/392–1794* ⊕ *abesbuggyride.com* ✉ *From $15* ⊘ *Closed Sun.*

### Lancaster Balloon Rides

**AIR EXCURSIONS** | The U.S. Hot Air Balloon Team takes visitors almost a mile above the Lancaster countryside to float with the breeze for one hour. Flights launch from dawn until sunset but schedules depend on the weather, so it's best to call ahead and watch the weather. ⊠ *2727 Old Philadelphia Pike, Rte. 340, Bird-in-Hand* ☎ *800/723–5884* ⊕ *lancasterballoonrides.com* ✉ *From $275 per person for a shared ride* ⊘ *Closed Sun.*

 Sights

### Amish Country Homestead

**HISTORIC HOME | FAMILY** | At this designated Lancaster County heritage site, take a guided tour of a replica nine-room Old Order Amish house and attached one-room schoolhouse. Along the way, you'll learn about Amish culture, clothing, and day-to-day life. The Super-Saver Tour Package ($47.95) includes a 90-minute mini-shuttle tour; a guided tour of the homestead; and a ticket to see the film *Jacob's Choice.* ⊠ *3121 Old Philadelphia Pike, Bird-in-Hand* ⊹ *Rte. 340* ☎ *717/768–8400* ⊕ *www.amishexperience.com* ✉ *$14.95* ⊘ *Closed Jan. and Feb.*

### Amish Experience Theater

**OTHER ATTRACTION | FAMILY** | The Amish Experience Theater presents *Jacob's Choice,* a multimedia production about the history and culture of the Amish people that uses multiple screens, three-dimensional sets, and special effects. ⊠ *Plain & Fancy Farm, 3121 Old Philadelphia Pike, Bird-in-Hand* ⊹ *Rte. 340* ☎ *717/768–4400* ⊕ *www.amishexperience.com* ✉ *$10.95* ⊘ *Closed in winter.*

### The Amish Farm and House

**MUSEUM VILLAGE | FAMILY** | The 40-minute tour of this family-owned farm museum takes you through a 10-room circa-1805 house furnished in the Old Order Amish style, and another tour takes you through a one-room schoolhouse. You can explore the grounds on your own to see a waterwheel, lime kiln, and working artisans such as blacksmiths and farriers. Farm animals and Amish scooters entertain the kids, and van tours are on offer. Bus tours that include a farm visit are also available. ⊠ *2395 Covered Bridge Dr., Lancaster* ☎ *717/394–6185* ⊕ *www.amishfarmandhouse.com* ✉ *$14.95 farm and house tour; $34.95 combo farm, house, and 90-min bus tour.*

## ☕ Coffee and Quick Bites

### Bird-in-Hand Bakery & Cafe

**$ | AMERICAN | FAMILY** | This simple café serves coffee and breakfast and lunch sandwiches. In the bakery, you'll find fresh bread and Pennsylvania Dutch pastries such as apple fritters and shoofly pie. **Known for:** huge selection of pies and pastries in the bakery store; homemade ice cream; wide variety of whoopie pies. [$] *Average main: $10* ✉ *2715 Old Philadelphia Pike, Route 340, Bird-in-Hand* ☎ *717/768–1501* 🌐 *bird-in-hand.com* 🕒 *Closed Sun. No dinner.*

**★ Immergut Hand-Rolled Soft Pretzels**

$ | **AMERICAN** | **FAMILY** | This little roadside spot serves warm, buttery Pennsylvania Dutch soft pretzels and freshly-squeezed lemonade. The traditional salt-flecked variety is superb, but other flavors, such as cinnamon-sugar and pretzel-wrapped hot dogs, don't disappoint. **Known for:** authentic Pennsylvania Dutch food; visitors can watch the dough being rolled and shaped; pretzels made fresh throughout the day. [$] *Average main: $2* ✉ *3537 Old Philadelphia Pike, Rte. 340, Intercourse* ☎ *717/768–0657* 🕒 *Closed Sun.*

## Hotels

**★ AmishView Inn & Suites**

$$ | **HOTEL** | **FAMILY** | This unique property—two buildings with one for families with children and one for adults only—offers exactly what its name promises: views overlooking Amish farmland as far as the eye can see. **Pros:** scenic views from almost every room; adult-only accommodations in a separate wing; indoor pool. **Cons:** no trace of Dutch Country decor in rooms; with many other attractions on property, it can get crowded; bus tours can crowd the breakfast room. [$] *Rooms from: $189* ✉ *Plain & Fancy Farm, 3125 Old Philadelphia Pike, Rte. 340, Bird-in-Hand* ☎ *866/768–1162* 🌐 *www.amishviewinn.com* 🛏 *90 rooms* 🍴 *Free Breakfast.*

**Bird-in-Hand Family Inn**

$ | **HOTEL** | **FAMILY** | This resort-style property has indoor and outdoor pools and a variety of activities including a petting zoo, minigolf, a pond and walking path, and a family-style smorgasbord restaurant. **Pros:** free tour of Amish farm; two indoor pools, one outdoor pool; tennis and basketball courts. **Cons:** small bathrooms; some rooms need updating; can feel hectic. [$] *Rooms from: $169* ✉ *2740 Old Philadelphia Pike, Rte. 340, Bird-in-Hand* ☎ *717/768–8271* 🌐 *www.bird-in-hand.com/bird-in-hand-family-inn* 🛏 *125 rooms* 🍴 *No Meals.*

## Shopping

**Bird-in-Hand Farmers Market**

**MARKET** | This year-round indoor market has 30 vendors selling candy, baked goods, preserves, and cheese, plus crafts and gifts. There is only one produce seller. ✉ *2710 Old Philadelphia Pike, Bird-in-Hand* ☎ *717/393–9674* 🌐 *www.birdinhandfarmersmarket.com.*

**★ Family Farm Quilts**

**CRAFTS** | Half a mile north of Intercourse village, hand-stitched quilts made by Amish and Mennonite women fill this large store to the rafters. These are authentic works of art made in traditional designs such as Broken Star and Double Wedding Ring. Sizes from full to king are on offer, as well as wall hangings and quillows (quilted pillows). ✉ *3511 W. Newport Rd., Rte. 772, Intercourse* ☎ *717/768–8375* 🌐 *www.familyfarmquilts.com.*

**Kauffman's Fruit Farm & Market**

**MARKET** | For more than 100 years, the Kauffmans have cultivated 100 acres of apples, pears, and stone fruits, all of which they sell in their country market along with cider, "schnitz" (air-dried apples), a variety of jams and fruit butters, and Pennsylvania honey and maple syrup. Seasonally, you can pick your own produce or wander the corn maze. ✉ *3097 Old Philadelphia Pike, Route 340, Bird-in-Hand* ☎ *717/768–7112* 🌐 *www.kauffmansfruitfarm.com.*

**Lantz Homestead Quilt Barn**

**CRAFTS** | A motherlode of heirloom quilts awaits at this shop on a century-old Amish farm that you reach by scenic country roads. All of the quilts and other quilted items are hand-stitched, the largest taking as long as a year to make. Assorted gift items are also for sale. ✉ *870 Musser School Rd., Gordonville* ⌖ *Less than a mile north of Paradise* ☎ *717/661–1265* ⊕ *www.lantzhome-stead.com.*

# Strasburg and Ronks

*5 miles south of Bird-in-Hand via U.S. 30 and Rte. 896.*

Although settled by French Huguenots, the village of Strasburg is today a community of Pennsylvania Dutch. It's best known as the railroad center of eastern Pennsylvania; railroad buffs can easily spend a day here.

In the nearby farming community of Ronks, you can also visit the Amish Village and Sight & Sound Theatre, known as the "Christian Broadway."

## GETTING HERE AND AROUND
Strasburg is about a 15-minute drive from Bird-in-Hand and is a compact destination with many of the railroad exhibits and other attractions located within walking distance or short drive from the center of town.

Ronks is between Bird-in-Hand and Strasburg.

##  Sights

### Amish Village
**MUSEUM VILLAGE | FAMILY |** This 12-acre historic homestead offers guided tours of an authentically furnished home and one-room schoolhouse. The property includes a barn with farm animals, blacksmith shop, simulated smokehouse and market. There are outdoor picnic grounds when the weather permits, and mini-shuttle-bus tours of the area are also available. ✉ *199 Hartman Bridge Rd., Ronks* ☎ *717/687–8511* ⊕ *www.*

*amishvillage.com* ✉ *$12 house and village only; $25 backroads bus tour; $32 combo bus, house, and grounds tour* ⊗ *Closed Jan.–mid-Feb.*

### Choo-Choo Barn, Traintown, USA
**OTHER ATTRACTION | FAMILY |** This 1,700-square-foot display of Lancaster County in miniature has 22 model trains, mainly O-gauge, with 150 animated figures in scenes such as an Amish barn raising, a three-ring circus, and a blazing house fire with fire engines. Periodically, the overhead lights dim and the scene turns to night, with streetlights and locomotive headlights glowing in the darkness. ✉ *226 Gap Rd, Strasburg* ⌖ *Rte. 741* ☎ *717/687–7911* ⊕ *www.choochoobarn.com* ✉ *$8.50* ⊗ *Closed Jan. and Feb.*

### National Toy Train Museum
**OTHER MUSEUM | FAMILY |** The showplace of the Train Collectors Association, this museum displays both antique and modern toy trains and is a must for toy train buffs. The museum has five huge train operating layouts, with toy trains from the 1800s to the present, plus nostalgic films and hundreds of locomotives and cars in display cases. ✉ *300 Paradise La., Ronks* ⌖ *North of Rte. 741* ☎ *717/687–8976* ⊕ *www.nttmuseum.org* ✉ *$7.50* ⊗ *Closed Jan.–Mar.*

### ★ Railroad Museum of Pennsylvania and the Railway Education Center
**OTHER MUSEUM | FAMILY |** This Smithsonian-affiliated museum showcases a world-class collection of 100-plus vintage locomotive and railroad cars made or operated in Pennsylvania. The 100,000-square-foot exhibit hall is a treasure trove of photos, artifacts, and memorabilia documenting the history of Pennsylvania railroading. There's an on-site gift shop. ✉ *300 Gap Rd., Strasburg* ⌖ *Off Rte. 741* ☎ *717/687–8628* ⊕ *www.rrmuseumpa.org* ✉ *$10* ⊗ *Closed Mon. and Tues.*

On the Strasburg Rail Road, visitors can travel on a scenic 45-minute round-trip excursion through Amish farm country from Strasburg to Paradise.

**Strasburg Rail Road**
**TRAIN/TRAIN STATION** | **FAMILY** | The Strasburg Rail Road marks more than 175 years of history, and visitors can step back in time to ride the rails. The scenic 45-minute round-trip excursion rolls through Amish farm country, its iron steam locomotive pulling wooden passenger coaches. Called America's oldest short line, the route travels between Strasburg and Paradise. Eat lunch in the dining car or take an evening dinner ride that might be themed as a murder mystery, wine and cheese tasting, or various holidays. Kids are crazy for the Thomas the Tank Engine shop. Trains usually depart hourly. Dinner trains run April to December. ✉ *301 Gap Rd., Strasburg* ✣ *Off Rte. 741* ☎ *866/725–9666* 🌐 *www.strasburgrailroad.com* 🎫 *$22* 🕓 *Closed Jan.–mid.-Mar.; trains may be canceled in inclement weather.*

## 🍴 Restaurants

**Hershey Farm Restaurant**
**$$$** | **AMERICAN** | **FAMILY** | Surrounded by a 23-acre expanse of manicured and wooded grounds, Hershey Farm offers a huge smorgasbord of Pennsylvania Dutch and American dishes. There's also a grill where you can get made-to-order burgers and sandwiches. **Known for:** can get crowded with tour groups; excellent baked goods from on-site bakery; breakfast smorgasbord. [$] *Average main: $28* ✉ *240 Hartman Bridge Rd., Route 896, Ronks* ☎ *800/827–8635* 🌐 *www.hersheyfarm.com* 🕓 *Closed Mon.; closed Jan. and Feb.*

**Miller's Smorgasbord**
**$$$** | **AMERICAN** | **FAMILY** | This all-you-can-eat smorgasbord has been a local institution since 1929, offering enough food to satisfy any appetite. The spread here is lavish, with a good selection of Pennsylvania Dutch specialties such as house-made pickles, baked cabbage in cream sauce, and shoofly pie

(made with molasses). **Known for:** iced raisin bread; chicken corn soup; brown buttered noodles. [$] *Average main: $28* ✉ *2811 Lincoln Hwy. E, Ronks* ✣ *U.S. 30* ☎ *800/669–3568* 🌐 *www.millerssmorgasbord.com* 🕒 *Closed Mon. and Tues.*

**Speckled Hen**

$ | **CAFÉ** | Even on a rainy day, this homespun café feels sunny. Decidedly unfancy, the menu—burgers, salads, soups, and all-day breakfast—incorporates as many local ingredients as possible. **Known for:** eggs are served multiple ways; lots of vegetarian options; crowd-pleasing baked oatmeal. [$] *Average main: $14* ✉ *141 E. Main St., Strasburg* ☎ *717/288–3139* 🌐 *speckledhencoffee.com.*

## Hotels

**Carriage House at Strasburg**

$ | **MOTEL** | **FAMILY** | Friendly staff welcomes visitors to this revamped motel with clean-lined and modern rooms in the center of town. **Pros:** good value; dedicated owners are committed to service; in-room fridges and microwaves. **Cons:** front desk is not staffed 24/7; some rooms have air-conditioning window units; bare floors. [$] *Rooms from: $117* ✉ *144 E. Main St., Strasburg* ☎ *717/687–7651* 🌐 *carriagehousestrasburg.com* 🛏 *17 rooms* 🍴 *Free Breakfast.*

**Hershey Farm**

$ | **MOTEL** | **FAMILY** | Especially geared to families, the inn just north of Strasburg stands on a 23-acre expanse of manicured grounds with flower and vegetable gardens, a picture-perfect pond, and a farm that offers simply furnished rooms in three buildings distinguished by different features: Country Meadows, Carriage House, and Farm House. **Pros:** helpful staff; walking trails through the lovely landscape; several shops on the grounds. **Cons:** close to a highway; some rooms need updating; thin walls between guest rooms. [$] *Rooms from: $130* ✉ *240 Hartman Bridge Rd., Rte. 896, Ronks* ☎ *717/687–8635,* 🌐 *www.hersheyfarm.com* 🛏 *60 rooms* 🍴 *Free Breakfast.*

**1786 Limestone Inn Bed and Breakfast**

$ | **B&B/INN** | This 1786 Georgian-style home listed on the National Register of Historic Places has a formal living room, library, and sitting room with a fireplace for relaxing, and a fish pond in the small garden. **Pros:** country charm; fireplaces or electric heating stoves in rooms; three common rooms. **Cons:** no kids under 12; not all rooms have private baths; rooms are small. [$] *Rooms from: $134* ✉ *33 E. Main St., Strasburg* ☎ *717/687–8392* 🌐 *thelimestoneinn.com* 🛏 *6 rooms* 🍴 *Free Breakfast.*

## Performing Arts

**Sight & Sound Theatre**

**THEATER** | **FAMILY** | Known as the "Christian Broadway," Sight & Sound Theatre, located just 20 minutes from downtown Lancaster, produces shows based on the Bible. Musical productions in the 2,000-seat, state-of-the-art auditorium have included *Jonah, Samson, Joseph,* and *Noah.* These epic Biblical musicals are expertly performed, with dazzling sets and costumes, making the shows fascinating even if you're not religious. ✉ *300 Hartman Bridge Rd., Ronks* ✣ *1.4 miles southeast of Bird-in-Hand* ☎ *800/377–1277* 🌐 *www.sight-sound.com* 🎟 *From $39.*

# Lititz

*8 miles north of downtown Lancaster via U.S. 222 and Rte. 501.*

Lititz was founded in 1756 by Moravian missionaries who settled in Pennsylvania and created their own private community. Lititz's historic character remains, with 18th-century houses and shops selling antiques, crafts, clothing, and gifts. This is a great town for walking; be sure to see the beautiful Moravian church, which dates back to 1787 and served as a hospital to treat the wounded during the Revolutionary War. In recent years, Lititz has upped its game with a variety of boutiques, Second Fridays (when the town stays open late), farm-to-table dining, a food hall, and two upscale hotels.

### GETTING HERE AND AROUND

Park the car and explore the town by foot. There are two major streets—Broad Street and Main Street.

## Sights

**Julius Sturgis Pretzel Bakery**

**HISTORIC SIGHT** | **FAMILY** | In 1861, pretzel maker Julius Sturgis opened the country's first pretzel bakery. These days, the original site, a stone house on the National Register of Historic Places, operates guided tours and a hands-on lesson in pretzel twisting. An on-site bakeshop has souvenirs and fresh pretzels. ✉ *219 E. Main St., Rte. 772, Lititz* ☎ *717/626–4354* 🌐 *juliussturgis.com* 🎟 *$4* 🕒 *Closed 1st 2 weeks of Jan.*

**Wilbur Chocolate Store**

**STORE/MALL** | **FAMILY** | When the Wilbur Chocolate Factory closed in 2016, locally beloved Wilbur Chocolate opened a retail store and museum across the street. The shop carries an array of Wilbur confections, from the famous Wilbur Buds to chocolate-covered pretzels and tins of drinking cocoa. There is candy-related memorabilia displayed throughout, along with a collection of antique chocolate-drinking pots. Candy makers work behind a giant window so you can see the Wilbur process. ✉ *45 N. Broad St., Lititz* ☎ *888/294–5287* 🌐 *www.wilburbuds.com* 🕒 *Closed Sun.*

## Restaurants

**★ Blackworth Live Fire Grill**

**$$$** | **MODERN AMERICAN** | Six oak-fed fires turn out grilled meat, seafood, and vegetables in this rustic-industrial space in the former Wilbur Chocolate Factory. The stars, of course, are the four kinds of steak, but the charred avocado (with a surprise inside) and the octopus and pork shank really display the chef's creativity. **Known for:** expertly grilled steaks; sophisticated wine and cocktail lists; can get noisy. [$] *Average main: $25* ✉ *Wilbur Hotel, 52 N. Broad St., Lititz* ☎ *717/625–2100* 🌐 *www.blackworthlititz.com.*

**Rooster Street Butcher**

**$** | **MODERN AMERICAN** | This butcher shop–turned–restaurant and taproom focuses on pastured-raised meat from local farms, but there are also salads and a good number of dishes for vegetarians. Diners order at the counter and find a seat, while drinks are ordered separately at the bar, which features Pennsylvania-only wine, beer, and spirits. **Known for:** steak frites; the all-pork bacon burger (not a beef burger with bacon on top); nightly specials. [$] *Average main: $15* ✉ *11 S. Cedar St., Lititz* ☎ *717/625–0405* 🌐 *www.roosterst.com* 🕒 *Closed Mon. and Tues.*

## Coffee and Quick Bites

**Slate Cafe**

**$** | **CAFÉ** | In the heart of Lititz, this local fave is the perfect spot for fueling up on locally roasted coffee or grabbing something quick to nosh on. The kitchen serves up a variety of breakfast options, from baked oatmeal to an open-face egg sandwich on ciabatta, while lunch options include quesadillas, salads, and soups. **Known for:** local kombucha and smoothies; many kids' choices; lots of variations on the egg sandwich. [$] *Average main: $8* ✉ *43 E. Main St., Lititz* ☎ *717/568–2288* 🌐 *www.slatelititz.com.*

## Hotels

**Hotel Rock Lititz**

$ | **HOTEL** | Located at Rock Lititz, a unique 96-acre campus that caters to live-entertainment productions for big-name musical artists, this hotel is where many crews and celebs stay incognito while they rehearse before going on tour. **Pros:** rock-and-roll theme throughout; indoor pool; Peloton bike in the fitness center. **Cons:** little outdoor lounging space; not walking distance to downtown Lititz; availability and rates swing wildly depending on occupancy by Rock Lititz patrons. [$] *Rooms from: $159* ✉ *50 Rock Lititz Blvd., Lititz* ✥ *1.3 miles from central Lititz* ☎ *717/925–7625* 🌐 *hotelrocklititz.com* 🛏 *139 rooms* 🍴 *No Meals.*

**Lititz Springs Inn & Spa**

$ | **B&B/INN** | Located on the main square of Lititz, this three-story 1764 inn (formerly known as The General Sutter Inn) mixes Victorian and modern decor. **Pros:** pub and restaurant on the first floor; central location; beautiful Victorian-style lobby with fireplace. **Cons:** check-in and-out can feel haphazard; some rooms have a sink in the bedroom, not in the bath; no elevator. [$] *Rooms from: $150* ✉ *14 E. Main St., Lititz* ✥ *Corner of Rtes. 501 and 772* ☎ *717/626–2115* 🌐 *lititzspringsinn.com* 🛏 *17 rooms* 🍴 *No Meals.*

★ **The Wilbur Lititz, Tapestry Collection by Hilton**

$$ | **HOTEL** | The former Wilbur Chocolate factory is now a beautifully repurposed boutique hotel located in the center of Lititz with well-appointed guest rooms accented with the original exposed brick and wood beams; some rooms overlook pretty Lititz Springs Park. **Pros:** walking distance to everything in town; robes in the guest rooms; gym-quality fitness room. **Cons:** $10 self-parking; noise from the busy road; room lighting is poor. [$] *Rooms from: $235* ✉ *50 N. Broad St., Lititz* ☎ *717/625–1300* 🌐 *thewilburhotel.com* 🛏 *74 rooms* 🍴 *No Meals.*

# Ephrata

*17 miles north of Strasburg via Rte. 896 and U.S. 222, 17 miles northeast of Lancaster via U.S. 222.*

This is a classic American town with a wide Main Street, a variety of antiques shops, and an entertaining farmers' market. A local creamery is known for its superb ice cream. Except for the Ephrata Cloister, there's little to remind you of the town's austere beginning as a religious commune.

## Sights

★ **Ephrata Cloister**

**MUSEUM VILLAGE** | Formerly the home of a unique monastic community, Ephrata Cloister was founded in 1732 by German immigrant Conrad Beissel, who assembled a secluded society of 80 celibate brothers and sisters who lived an austere life of work, study, and prayer. On 250 acres of wilderness, the sect built 30 structures, including a monastery and a printing press. The last celibate member died in 1813, and the members who lived outside the cloister closed the church in 1934. The Commonwealth of Pennsylvania turned the complex into a museum that now offers 45-minute tours of three restored buildings. You can poke through several others, including the stable, printshop, and crafts shop. Self-guided cell-phone tours are also available. ✉ *632 W. Main St., Rte. 322, Ephrata* ☎ *717/733–6600* 🌐 *ephratacloister.org* 🎟 *$10* 🕒 *Closed Mon. and Tues.*

**Green Dragon Farmers Market and Auction**

**MARKET** | This giant indoor-outdoor market, only open on Friday, is an oddball mash-up of Amish snack bars, smoked meat and preserves purveyors, bric-a-brac, tools, toys, and everything in between, including the kitchen sink. There are separate auctions of furniture, hay, and small farm animals. As the website states, there's a "carnival

This cemetery is located on the grounds of one of America's early religious communities, the Ephrata Cloister, which was founded in 1732 by a German immigrant.

atmosphere" like no other. ✉ *955 N. State St., Ephrata* ✛ *Off Rte. 272, 2 miles northeast of downtown* ☎ *717/738–1117* ⊕ *www.greendragonmarket.com* ⊗ *Closed Sat.–Thurs.*

## 🍴 Restaurants

### Three Sisters Park

$ | **THAI** | This unassuming BYOB on the main strip of Ephrata serves a variety of Khmer-Thai dishes. Prepare for the heat of the various curries and rice-noodle dishes, which aren't dumbed down for Western palates; there is pad Thai for those seeking something familiar. **Known for:** delivery available; lunch specials; spicy grilled pork skewers. $ *Average main: $13* ✉ *119 E. Main St., Ephrata* ☎ *717/733–2386* ⊕ *3sistersktc.com* ⊗ *Closed Sun.*

## ☕ Coffee and Quick Bites

### ★ Fox Meadows Creamery

$ | **ICE CREAM** | **FAMILY** | Farmland surrounds this spacious creamery, which serves what many locals consider to be the best ice cream in Lancaster County with flavors ranging from classics like cookies 'n cream to creations like honey-lavender; order yours in a waffle cone shell. A complete coffee selection and a lunch menu of burgers, sandwiches, and salads are also available. **Known for:** country market featuring locally made goods; children's play area; viewing window into the production room. $ *Average main: $4* ✉ *2475 W. Main St., Rte. 322, Ephrata* ☎ *717/721–6455* ⊕ *www.foxmeadowscreamery.com* ⊗ *Closed Sun.*

### Griddle & Grind Cafe

$ | **AMERICAN** | This little café in the center of town serves crepes and coffee—what more could you want? Breakfast crepes are filled with omelets or scrambles, lunch crepes have savory insides such as cheesesteak and caprese, and dessert crepes include the classic Nutella spread. **Known for:** cute, cozy atmosphere; gluten-free and dairy-free options; fast, friendly service. $ *Average main: $11* ✉ *20 W. Main St., Ephrata* ☎ *717/466–6626* ⊕ *www.griddleandgrind.com* ⊘ *Closed Mon. No dinner.*

### Tin Roof Cafe n' Sweets

$ | CAFÉ | FAMILY | A broad menu of savory breakfast, lunch, and dinner items—not to mention coffees—draws regulars and visitors to this wood-beamed, stone-walled café. Relax on one of the couches or sit at a table to eat your scrapple, egg, and cheese sandwich, cranberry-chicken salad, or super-rich ice cream. **Known for:** build-your-own sundaes; mellow atmosphere; good selection of frozen yogurt. $ *Average main: $10* ✉ *108 N. Reading Rd., Rte. 272, Ephrata* ☎ *717/721–6314* ⊕ *www.tinroofcafensweets.com* ⊘ *Closed Sun.*

 ## Hotels

### ★ Historic Smithton Inn

$ | B&B/INN | Hand-sewn quilts coexist comfortably with iPod docking stations and electric vehicle chargers at this B&B, a former tavern built in 1763. **Pros:** authentic period decor; pet-friendly; robes in the guest rooms. **Cons:** near a busy intersection; no elevator; children under 13 limited to the Taylor Cottage. $ *Rooms from: $150* ✉ *900 W. Main St., at Academy Dr., Ephrata* ☎ *717/733–6094* ⊕ *www.historicsmithtoninn.com* ⇆ *8 rooms* ℺ *Free Breakfast.*

### ★ Twin Pine Manor Bed & Breakfast

$$ | B&B/INN | Built in the late 1990s on a 26-acre former homestead, this expansive, luxurious B&B offers suites with electric fireplaces, jetted tubs, and private balconies or patios. **Pros:** beautiful views from the rooftop deck; rec room with pool table, piano, and huge TV; feels

# Covered Bridges

There are more than 25 covered bridges throughout Lancaster County, some dating as far back as the mid-1800s. In fact, Bitzer's Mill Covered Bridge in Ephrata and Eshelman's Mill Covered Bridge just outside the city of Lancaster are two of the country's oldest bridges, both built in the 1840s. Discover Lancaster offers several self-guided driving tours on their website (⊕ *www.discoverlancaster.com*). Biking the routes gives you a more immersive experience.

like a sumptuous home. **Cons:** children under 13 are not allowed; front desk isn't open 24 hours a day; 3 miles from downtown Ephrata. $ *Rooms from: $179* ✉ *1934 W. Main St., Ephrata* ☎ *717/733–8400* ⊕ *twinpinemanor.com* ⇆ *9 rooms* ℺ *Free Breakfast.*

# Adamstown

*23 miles northeast of Lancaster via Rte. 222.*

Known as "Antiques Capital USA," Adamstown has dozens of shops, galleries, and markets large and small selling goods from bygone eras.

### GETTING HERE AND AROUND

There's no real downtown in this small community, so you'll have to navigate the various markets and shopping areas by car.

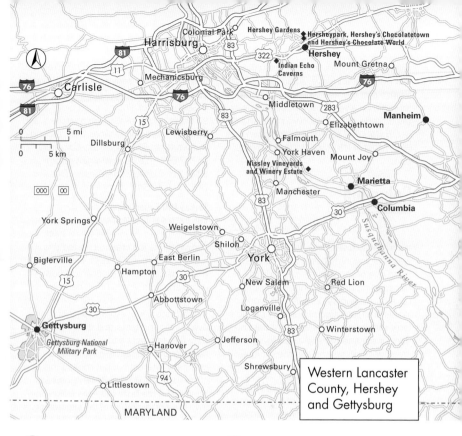

Western Lancaster County, Hershey and Gettysburg

## ☕ Coffee and Quick Bites

### Boehringer's Drive-In

**$ | AMERICAN | FAMILY |** Since 1936, this little roadside stand has been selling burgers, dogs, cheesesteaks, and home-made ice cream. Order your food at the counter and take it out to the tree-shaded picnic tables along the creek. **Known for:** big crowds in summer; root beer out of a barrel; chili dogs. $ *Average main: $3* ✉ *3160 N. Reading Rd., Adamstown* ⊕ *2 miles northwest of Renninger's Antique Market* ☎ *717/484–4227* ⊕ *www.facebook.com/boehringersdriveIn* ⊘ *Closed Mon.–Wed. and mid-Sep.–mid-Mar.*

## 🛍 Shopping

### Renninger's Antique and Collector's Market

**ANTIQUES & COLLECTIBLES |** The huge Renninger's Antique and Collector's Market draws thousands of collectors and dealers on Sundays. Nearly 300 indoor stalls, open year-round, overflow with every conceivable type of antique, from toys to books to glassware. On good-weather days, the outdoor flea market adds to the selection. ✉ *2500 N. Reading Rd., Denver* ⊕ *Rte. 272, ½ mile north of Pennsylvania Turnpike, Exit 21* ☎ *717/336–2177 weekends* ⊕ *renningers.net.*

### Shupp's Grove

**ANTIQUES & COLLECTIBLES |** A seasonal outdoor market, Shupp's Grove is the oldest antiques haunt in Adamstown, with acres of dealers displaying tables piled with antiques, art, and collectibles in a tree-shaded grove. Antiques extravaganza and themed weekends happen three times a year. A food truck feeds the crowds. ⊠ *607 Willow St., Reinholds* ✛ *Off Rte. 897, south of Adamstown* ☎ *717/484–4115* ⊕ *www.shuppsgrove. com.*

# Columbia

*11 miles west of Lancaster via Rte. 462.*

It's a sleepy town now, but Columbia was bustling in the days when boats were one of the easiest methods of transporting goods. Eighteenth-century Quaker missionary John Wright worked in this area, and two of his sons set up a ferry that became an important destination for settlers moving west. Today there are several museums and the tranquil countryside to explore.

## GETTING HERE AND AROUND

Located on the east bank of the Susquehanna River, centered between Lancaster, York, and Harrisburg, you'll need a car to get here and around.

##  Sights

### Columbia Market House

**MARKET** | Built in 1869, the Columbia Market House is one of the oldest farmers' markets in the state. Vendors sell fresh local produce and locally made specialty foods. The basement was once used as a dungeon; from the outside, you can still see the ground-level windows through which prisoners were shoved down a chute into the darkness, and guided tours are available by appointment. ⊠ *13 S. 3rd St., Columbia* ✛ *Off Rte. 441* ☎ *717/572–7149* ⊕ *columbiapamarkethouse.org* ⊗ *Closed Sun.–Fri.*

### ★ National Watch and Clock Museum

**OTHER MUSEUM** | Recognized as the largest horological collection in North America, this museum is home to more than 12,000 timepieces and time-related items. You'll see early sundials and water clocks; a 19th-century Tiffany globe clock; a German Black Forest organ clock with 94 pipes; moon-phase wristwatches; and other timekeeping devices from around the world. ⊠ *514 Poplar St., Columbia* ☎ *717/684–8261* ⊕ *www.nawcc.org* ⊠ *$12* ⊗ *Closed Sun.–Tues. in Dec.–Mar.; closed Sun. and Mon. in Apr.–Nov.*

### Turkey Hill Experience

**CHILDREN'S MUSEUM | FAMILY** | Lancaster County–based Turkey Hill Dairy, best known for its ice cream, created this interactive extravaganza in a restored mill. Kids can milk a mechanical cow, climb aboard a vintage milk delivery truck, and shoot a Turkey Hill commercial. In the Taste Lab they can concoct their own flavor and taste-test it. Grown-ups may find the facts and figures about dairy farming and the family-owned Turkey Hill company interesting, but mostly this one is for the kids. ■ **TIP→ Reservations are required for the Taste Lab—the make-your-own-ice-cream portion of the experience.** ⊠ *301 Linden St., Columbia* ✛ *Off U.S. 30* ☎ *844/684–0134* ⊕ *www.turkeyhillexperi-ence.com* ⊠ *$11 Experience; $8.95 Taste Lab* ⊗ *Hrs vary month-to-month.*

### Wright's Ferry Mansion

**HISTORIC HOME** | Located just a few blocks from the waterfront, Wright's Ferry Mansion was the residence of English Quaker Susanna Wright, a silkworm breeder and intellectual who counted Benjamin Franklin among her friends. Docents guide visitors around the 1738 stone house, which showcases period furniture in the William & Mary and Queen Anne styles as well as an extensive collection of English needlework, clothing, ceramics, and glass, all predating 1750. ⊠ *38 S. 2nd St., Columbia* ☎ *717/684–4325* ⊕ *lancastercountymuseums.org/wrights-ferry-mansion* ⊠ *$5* ⊗ *Closed Nov.–Apr.; closed Mon., Thurs., and Sun. in May–Oct.*

## 🍴 Restaurants

**★ John Wright Restaurant**

**$$ | MODERN AMERICAN** | At this waterfront spot in historic Wrightstown, across the Susquehanna River from Columbia, you can enjoy a breathtaking view of the river while seated outdoors eating wood-fired pizzas topped with ingredients grown on-site. The popular bar and restaurant (reservations strongly suggested) also has a glass-walled dining room to take in the scenery year-round. **Known for:** May–August pizza patio; farm-to-table focus; special occasion spot. [$] *Average main: $24* ✉ *234 N. Front St., Wrightsville* ☎ *717/252–0416* 🌐 *www.jwrpa.com* 🕒 *Closed Mon. and Tues.*

## 🛍 Shopping

**Burning Bridge Antiques Market**

**ANTIQUES & COLLECTIBLES** | Three floors of antiques and collectibles are crammed into this former hardware store and sewing factory from the 1800s. With more than 200 booths to rummage through, Burning Bridge is a treasure trove of Americana, furniture, and artifacts great and small. ✉ *304 Walnut St., Columbia* ☎ *717/684–7900* 🌐 *burningbridgeantiques.com.*

## 🏃 Activities

**Columbia Crossing River Trail Center**

**HIKING & WALKING** | Here are maps, guides, and brochures for the 14-mile Northwest Lancaster County River Trail, which you can bike or hike. Info on water sports and boating along the Columbia River is available as well. The center has restrooms on-site. ✉ *41 Walnut St., Columbia* ☎ *717/449–5607* 🌐 *www.facebook.com/columbiapacrossing.*

# Marietta

*5 miles northwest of Columbia via Rte. 441.*

Almost half of the buildings in Marietta are listed on the National Register of Historic Places; the architecture ranges from rustic log cabins to elegant Federal and Victorian homes. This restored river town, now seeing new life as an artists' community, is perfect for a stroll past the well-preserved facades of art galleries and antiques shops.

## 👁 Sights

**Nissley Vineyards and Winery Estate**

**WINERY** | Set on 300 acres in western Lancaster County, this family-owned winery grows 14 varieties of French-hybrid and American grapes and produces 30 different wines, from dry to very sweet, plus some fruit wines. There are tours, tastings, and a shop with bottles for sale. You can picnic on the grounds, and in the summer there's a popular open-air concert series on the lawn. ✉ *140 Vintage Dr., Bainbridge* ✣ *7 miles northwest of Marietta, 1½ miles off Rte. 441* ☎ *717/426–3514* 🌐 *www.nissleywine.com* 🎟 *Free; $12 for concerts.*

## 🍴 Restaurants

**Railroad House Inn**

**$$$ | MODERN AMERICAN** | The restaurant in this elegantly revamped 1823 building serves classic and creative American dishes such as smoked cheddar meatloaf and pan-seared salmon. Evoking the age of luxury rail travel, the main dining room is furnished with intimate booths and tables, while the rear room has a rustic tavern feel. **Known for:** ample Sunday brunch; signature cocktails; festive back patio. [$] *Average main: $25* ✉ *280 W. Front St., Marietta* ☎ *426–4141* 🌐 *www.railroadhouseinn.com* 🕒 *Closed Mon. and Tues.*

## Hotels

**B.F. Hiestand House**

$$ | **B&B/INN** | Sumptuous guest rooms with modern amenities draw guests to this grand 1887 Victorian house that retains many of its original design features. **Pros:** complimentary breakfast made using organic ingredients from the inn's garden; attentive hospitality; walkable to a riverfront park overlooking the Susquehanna River. **Cons:** children under 21 are not allowed; smoking allowed in designated areas; $25 extra charged for pets. [$] *Rooms from: $179* ✉ *722 E. Market St., Marietta* ☎ *717/426–8415* 🌐 *www.bfhiestandhouse.com* 🛏 *6 rooms* 🍴 *Free Breakfast.*

# Hershey

*30 miles northwest of Lancaster via Rtes. 283 and 743.*

Hershey is Chocolate Town, a community built around a chocolate factory and now home to Hersheypark, the Hershey Museum, and other diversions for children and adults.

Founded in 1903 by confectioner Milton S. Hershey, the town celebrates chocolate without guilt, from streetlights shaped like foil-wrapped candies to avenues named Chocolate and Cocoa.

### GETTING HERE AND AROUND

From Lancaster, drive north on Rte. 283 and continue north on Rte. 743. In Hershey, you will need your car to reach some attractions. If you're staying at the Hotel Hershey or Hershey Lodge, a free shuttle bus is available to take you to Hersheypark.

## Sights

**Hershey Gardens**

**GARDEN** | Hershey Gardens opened in 1937 with a single 3½-acre plot of roses at Milton Hershey's request and over eight decades has grown to include 11 theme gardens on 23 landscaped acres. Home to more than 3,500 rose bushes and 20,000 tulips, the gardens come to life in spring as thousands of bulbs burst into bloom. Flowering displays last until fall, when late roses open. The year-round Butterfly Atrium hosts hundreds of pollinators from around the world, and don't miss the chocolate-themed Children's Garden. A garden shop is on-site. ✉ *170 Hotel Rd., Hershey* ✥ *Across from Hotel Hershey* ☎ *717/534–3492* 🌐 *www.hersheygardens.org* 🎟 *$15.*

**The Hershey Story, The Museum on Chocolate Avenue**

**OTHER MUSEUM** | **FAMILY** | Formerly known as the Hershey Museum, the Hershey Story is a multimedia experience that features the life and work of Milton S. Hershey, who founded the town bearing his name and just about everything in it. On display is a working Hershey Kiss wrapping machine plus other memorabilia from the company's long history. A highlight is the Chocolate Lab, which offers hands-on workshops (for a fee). The Pantry Cafe sells flights of hot chocolates from around the world as well as light fare. Additional fees apply to both the Chocolate Lab and the tastings. ✉ *63 W. Chocolate Ave., Hershey* ☎ *717/534–3439* 🌐 *hersheystory.org* 🎟 *$15.*

★ **Hersheypark**

**AMUSEMENT PARK/CARNIVAL** | **FAMILY** | Billed as the "Sweetest Place on Earth," Hersheypark offers more than 65 rides and attractions, including 15 roller coasters; classic amusement park rides and kiddie rides; the Boardwalk, a waterpark with a lazy river and wave pool; ZooAmerica, a wildlife park with hundreds of animals; and tons of live entertainment options. Among the park's vintage rides is the Comet, a 1946 wooden roller coaster. Holidays are celebrated with themed decorations and activities. ✉ *100 W. Hersheypark Dr., Hershey* ☎ *717/534–3900* 🌐 *www.hersheypark.com* 🎟 *1-day ticket*

Hersheypark offers more than 65 rides and attractions, a boardwalk with a lazy river and wave pool, a wildlife park, and tons of live entertainment.

*$52.95; parking $25* ⊘ *Closed Jan.–Mar. except for scattered open days and special events* ☞ *The park is cashless.*

### Hershey's Chocolatetown

**AMUSEMENT PARK/CARNIVAL | FAMILY |** Just outside the gates of Hersheypark, Chocolatetown greets visitors with a gentle amusement-style ride that takes you through the chocolate-making process. The Hyperdeck virtual reality experience transports you away from all things chocolate; outside is the 1919 Carousel with 66 hand-carved wooden horses and Candymonium, Hersheypark's tallest, longest, and fastest roller coaster. The year-round eateries include a full-service restaurant, ice cream parlor, and confectionery shop that all focus on chocolate (Heath Bar–crusted salmon, anyone?). ⊠ *100 E. Hersheypark Dr., Hershey* ☎ *534–3900* ⊕ *www.hersheypark.com* 🎟 *Fee included in Hersheypark admission* ⊘ *Closed Jan.–Mar. except for a sprinkling of open days.*

### Hershey's Chocolate World

**OTHER ATTRACTION | FAMILY |** Just outside the gates to Hersheypark, this is a one-stop spot for exploring the history of chocolate and how it's made. The attractions are many, including a free 30-minute chocolate factory tour ride; *Unwrapped,* an interactive theatrical performance with chocolate tasting kit; and Create Your Own Candy Bar (additional fee). It's also the starting point for Hershey Trolley Works, which offers historical tours of the town and landmarks relevant to Milton Hershey. The largest Hershey store in the world is here, and there's also an extensive chocolate-themed food court (think milkshakes and s'mores). ⊠ *101 Chocolate World Way, Hershey* ☎ *800/534–4900* ⊕ *www.chocolateworld. com* 🎟 *$44.85.*

### Indian Echo Caverns

**CAVE | FAMILY |** The caverns are a tranquil change of pace from theme-park action, offering guided walking tours of ancient limestone caves and their formations. Historians believe that Native Americans used the caves as shelter from harsh weather. The temperature inside is naturally at 52°F year-round, so bring a sweater. The caverns are not handicap accessible, and strollers are not allowed. There's a gift shop with gemstones and souvenirs, a petting barnyard, and a picnic area. ✉ *368 Middletown Rd., Echo Dell, Hummelstown* ✥ *5 miles southwest of Hershey* ☎ *717/566–8131* 🌐 *indianechocaverns.com* 🎟 *$22.*

## 🍴 Restaurants

**The Hershey Pantry**

$ | **AMERICAN** | **FAMILY** | This family-friendly restaurant is a beloved favorite among locals for its hearty breakfast lineup, probably one of the best in Pennsylvania. The menus are huge, portions are generous, and the food is unpretentious in a good-ole-diner sort of way. **Known for:** long wait times for tables; afternoon tea service; huge selection of homemade desserts. [$] *Average main: $15* ✉ *801 E. Chocolate Ave., Hershey* ☎ *717/533–7505* 🌐 *www.hersheypantry.com* 🕑 *No dinner.*

## 🛏 Hotels

**Hershey Lodge and Convention Center**

$$$ | **RESORT** | **FAMILY** | This bustling and sprawling resort caters to families as well as business and convention travelers. **Pros:** discounted and free admission to Hershey attractions; sports bar with 39 TVs; well-equipped fitness center. **Cons:** chain-hotel vibe; sprawling layout not ideal for families with young children; crowded during large conventions. [$] *Rooms from: $329* ✉ *325 University Dr., Hershey* ☎ *717/533–3311* 🌐 *www.hersheylodge.com* 🛏 *665 rooms* 🍽 *No Meals.*

**★ The Hotel Hershey**

$$$$ | **RESORT** | Built during the Great Depression, this grand Mediterranean villa–style hotel holds rooms with maple armoires, paintings by local artists, and tile baths. **Pros:** five dining venues plus room service; panoramic valley views; free admission to Hershey Gardens and The Hershey Story museum. **Cons:** tiny, outdated bathrooms; strict 10-day cancellation policy; confusing navigation within the hotel. [$] *Rooms from: $449* ✉ *100 Hotel Rd., Hershey* ☎ *717/533–2171* 🌐 *www.thehotelhershey.com* 🛏 *276 rooms, 48 cottages* 🍽 *No Meals.*

## 🛍 Shopping

**Crossroads Antique Mall**

**ANTIQUES & COLLECTIBLES** | For a break from chocolate adventures, there are antiques and collectibles to forage. Housed in a unusual round-roofed parabolic arch barn, this antiques mall has two floors filled with goods from dozens of dealers. ✉ *825 Cocoa Ave., Hershey* ✥ *Juncture of Rtes. 743 and 322* ☎ *717/520–1600* 🌐 *www.crossroadsantiques.com.*

## 🏃 Activities

**Spring Creek Golf Club**

**GOLF** | A 9-hole course open to the public, Spring Creek is owned and operated by the Hershey Country Club. It was designed in 1932 as the country's first public golf course for youth. Now, players of all ages and skill levels are welcome. ✉ *450 E. Chocolate Ave., Hershey* ☎ *717/533–2360* 🌐 *www.hersheycountryclub.com/golf/spring-creek* 🎟 *$13–$15 walking, $9 extra for cart* 🏌 *9 holes, 2,200 yards, par 33.*

# Gettysburg

*55 miles west of Lancaster via U.S. 30.*

"The world will little note, nor long remember, what we say here, but it can never forget what they did here." These words from Abraham Lincoln's famous address were delivered in Gettysburg to mark the dedication of its national cemetery in November 1863.

Four months earlier, from July 1 to 3, 51,000 Americans were killed, wounded, or counted as missing in the bloodiest battle of the Civil War. The events that took place in Gettysburg during those few days marked the turning point in the war. Although the struggle raged on for almost two more years, the Confederate forces never recovered from their losses.

At the national military park and at 20 museums in Gettysburg, you can recapture the power of those momentous days. You can see battlefields such as Cemetery Ridge and Devil's Den.

### GETTING HERE AND AROUND
From Lancaster, take Route 462 West to U.S. 30. Once in Gettysburg, you can park your car in town and walk to restaurants, shops, and some attractions. But you will need to use your car to access the battlefield and its visitor center.

The Gettysburg Convention and Visitors Bureau has free brochures and maps of area attractions. Be sure to pick up a self-guided walking-tour map of the town's historic district, centered on Baltimore Street. You can find a number of museums along the route, as well as markers that point out homes and sites significant to the history of the town and to the battle.

### PLANNING YOUR TIME
The state-of-the-art visitor's center at Gettysburg National Military Park is an essential stop to fully comprehend the significance of the battlefield and its impact on the outcome of the Civil War. Plan on spending at least three to four hours at the museum, though families with younger children who are concerned about short attention spans may wish to spend less time at the museum and opt instead for a free ranger talk. Rather than attempting to drive around the sprawling battlefield, you're better off taking a two-hour bus tour or hiring a certified guide who will not only explain the events in compelling detail but also drive your

vehicle, so you don't have to worry about navigating the sprawling battlefield.

### ESSENTIALS
**VISITOR INFORMATION** Destination Gettysburg. ⊠ *571 W. Middle St., Gettysburg* ☎ *717/334–6274* ⊕ *www.destinationgettysburg.com.*

 ## Sights

### David Wills House
**HISTORIC HOME** | The David Wills House is where Abraham Lincoln stayed and completed his Gettysburg Address on November 18, 1863. The restored building features seven galleries, including the bedroom where Lincoln slept and worked on the final versions of his speech, as well as the office of Wills, a prominent lawyer who helped direct the burial of soldiers and the city's cleanup after the battle and was a leading force behind the creation of the national cemetery. ⊠ *8 Lincoln Sq., Gettysburg* ☎ *717/334–2499* ⊕ *www.nps. gov/places/david-wills-house.htm* 🎫 *$7* ⊗ *Closed Nov.–May; closed Mon.–Wed. in Jun.–Oct.*

### Eisenhower National Historic Site
**HISTORIC HOME** | The farm residence of President Dwight D. Eisenhower, who bought it in 1950, was a weekend retreat for him and and First Lady Mamie Eisenhower; the president also hosted world leaders here. From 1961 until the president's death in 1969, it was the couple's full-time residence, and now the brick-and-stone farmhouse is preserved in 1950s style. The farm adjoins the battlefield and is administered by the National Park Service, which conducts daily ticketed tours by way of shuttle bus on a first-come, first-served basis at the Gettysburg National Military Park Visitor Center. ⊠ *250 Eisenhower Rd., off Business Hwy. 15, Gettysburg* ☎ *717/338–9114* ⊕ *www.nps.gov/eise* 🎫 *$9* ⊗ *Closed Mon.–Wed.*

## Gettysburg Battlefield Tours

**MILITARY SIGHT | FAMILY** | Tours on open-air double-decker buses or enclosed buses are narrated by battlefield guides qualified and licensed by Gettysburg National Military Park. The downtown Gettysburg Tour Center is the departure point for the two-hour tours of the battlefield. At night, costumed guides offer 90-minute Ghost Bus tours ($26) of the town's reputedly haunted places. ⊠ *778 Baltimore St., Gettysburg* ☎ *877/680–8687* ⊕ *www. gettysburgbattlefieldtours.com* ☑ *$38*.

## Gettysburg Heritage Center

**HISTORY MUSEUM | FAMILY** | This museum presents the story of the Civil War era and the Battle of Gettysburg through artifacts, a 20-minute film, 3-D videos and photos, and interactive displays. At the front desk, you can book battlefield tours (for a fee) by Victorian carriage, horseback, electric bike, or foot. Costumed guides lead 90-minute walking tours of the town (also for a fee). The Center coordinates complimentary living-history camps that demonstrate what life was like for Civil War soldiers, offered most weekends from April to November. ⊠ *297 Steinwehr Ave., Gettysburg* ☎ *717/334–6245* ⊕ *www.gettysburgmuseum.com* ☑ *$10* ☉ *Closed Tues. and Wed.*

## Gettysburg National Cemetery

**CEMETERY** | Also known as Soldiers' National Cemetery, this is the final resting place for more than 3,500 Union soldiers who died on the battlefield. Dedicated by President Abraham Lincoln in his Gettysburg Address, the cemetery is also where some 3,000 veterans of subsequent conflicts were laid to rest. A stroll through the beautiful grounds past row after row of white grave markers is a sobering reminder of the cost of war. The cemetery is part of Gettysburg National Military Park, which asks visitors to show respect by speaking softly and not sitting on or climbing any markers. ⊠ *Taneytown Rd., Rte. 134, Gettysburg* ✛ *Park at the Taneytown Rd. or take the 15-min walk from the visitor center* ☎ *717/334–1124* ⊕ *www.nps.gov/nr/travel/national_cemeteries/pennsylvania/gettysburg_national_cemetery.html* ☑ *Free*.

## ★ Gettysburg National Military Park

**MILITARY SIGHT | FAMILY** | There are few American landmarks as moving as Gettysburg National Military Park, where General Robert E. Lee and his Confederate troops fought and lost to the Union forces of General George Meade from July 1st through the 3rd, 1863. More than 1,300 mournful and inspiring markers and monuments honor the estimated 7,058 soldiers killed in the battle. Thirty-plus miles of marked roads lead through the 6,000-acre park to key battle sites; you can traverse them by driving, bicycling, or hiking, or via guided bus tours. In the first week of July, Civil War reenactors dress in period uniforms and costumes to commemorate the three-day battle. ■ TIP➔ **Self-guided tours as well as tour guides for hire are both available, as are tours on horseback.** ⊠ *1195 Baltimore Pike, Gettysburg* ☎ *717/334–1124* ⊕ *www.nps.gov/gett* ☑ *Free*.

## ★ Gettysburg National Military Park Museum and Visitor Center

**HISTORY MUSEUM | FAMILY** | The museum and visitor center is the place to start your exploration of the events leading up to the Battle of Gettysburg, its significance to the Civil War, and its impact on the town of Gettysburg. A dozen galleries display a compelling mix of the museum's more than 40,000 artifacts, such as scores of weapons, uniforms, and a wooden desk believed to have been used by General Robert E. Lee. Interactive video and audio displays further illuminate the events, the centerpiece being the 377-foot-long "Battle of Gettysburg" cyclorama, a painting in-the-round depicting Pickett's Charge. Made in 1884, the painting is the largest in North America and one of the last cycloramas in existence, now completely restored. Stand in the center with the lights down while stirring narration and special effects immerse you in the story. It's paired with a documentary film, "A New Birth of Freedom," in a 45-minute experience. The National Park Service has a information desk with everything from battlefield walking tours to schedules of free ranger-conducted programs. Private, licensed guides may also be hired at the center. There is a restaurant and a bookstore on-site. ✉ *1195 Baltimore Pike, Gettysburg* ☎ *717/334–2436* 🌐 *www.gettysburgfoundation.org* 🎟 *$18.75 for museum, film, and cyclorama package; $9 for museum only.*

**Shriver House**

**HISTORIC HOME | FAMILY** | The Shriver House, the home of George and Henrietta Shriver and their two children, reveals what civilian life was like during the Civil War. Costumed guides share fascinating tales of the Battle of Gettysburg's impact on the townspeople. After George joined the Union troops and his family fled to safety, the home was taken over by Confederate sharpshooters. You can visit their attic nest, where two of them were killed during the battle, and get a look at Shriver's Saloon in the cellar. ✉ *309 Baltimore St., Gettysburg* ☎ *717/337–2800* 🌐 *shriverhouse.org* 🎟 *$11.95* 🕒 *Closed Jan. and Feb. except President's Day weekend; closed weekdays in Mar.*

## 🍴 Restaurants

**★ Dobbin House Tavern**

**$$$$ | AMERICAN** | Built in 1776, Dobbin House is the oldest building in town and is on the National Register of Historic Places. In one of six original rooms adorned with Colonial decor and antiques—the dining room, library, parlor, spinning room, study, or bedroom—servers in period clothing serve Colonial and classic American fare such as baked king's onion soup and roast duck. **Known for:** lump crabmeat dishes; warm Colonial gingerbread with lemon sauce; time-travel experience. [$] *Average main: $36* ✉ *89 Steinwehr Ave., Gettysburg* ☎ *717/334–2100* 🌐 *www.dobbinhouse.com.*

**Fourscore Beer Co.**

**$ | AMERICAN** | Located downtown, this family-owned brewpub sells Fourscore's beers, which range from Double Citra Pillows (a hazy IPA) to Hiding in Plain Sight (a hoppy lager) and the menu includes appetizers, salads, and sandwiches. Sit in the large tasting room or grab a seat on the patio. **Known for:** beers to-go available in cans and growlers; nightly specials like wing Wednesday and trivia Thursday; beer-inspired menu items like Hop Hat mac and cheese. [$] *Average main: $13* ✉ *603 S. Washington St., Gettysburg* ☎ *717/345–8171* 🌐 *www.facebook.com/fourscorebeerco* 🕒 *Closed Mon. and Tues.*

**Garryowen Irish Pub**

**$$ | IRISH** | A favorite with locals, this pub serves authentic Irish dishes made from the owner's Irish family recipes, importing some of their ingredients direct from Ireland. Bangers and mash and Irish stew come out of the kitchen alongside American pub favorites like wings and burgers, while more than 100 Irish whiskies and 15 beer taps quench thirsts in the inviting space with pressed-tin ceilings and a mahogany bar. **Known for:** perfectly poured Guinness; large outdoor space; Ulster Fry (Irish breakfast with sausages, white pudding (pork and oatmeal), black pudding (pig's blood added), egg, grilled tomato and Irish soda bread). [$] *Average main: $18* ✉ *126 Chambersburg St., Gettysburg* ☎ *717/337–2719* 🌐 *garryowenirishpub.net.*

**Springhouse Tavern**

**$$ | AMERICAN** | Springhouse Tavern is an informal wood-beamed cellar beneath the fine-dining Dobbin House Tavern. Diners gather around tables with mismatched Colonial chairs to enjoy steaks, burgers, sandwiches, and local craft brews. **Known for:** relaxed, cozy vibe; two stone fireplaces; crab cakes. [$] *Average main: $24* ✉ *89 Steinwehr Ave., in the Dobbin House Tavern, Gettysburg* ☎ *717/334–2100* 🌐 *www.dobbinhouse.com.*

## Coffee and Quick Bites

**The Ragged Edge Coffee House**
$ | **CAFÉ** | This homey café is a popular spot for locals to start their day with a cup of joe from locally roasted beans. The menu offers egg sandwiches and wraps for breakfast and a changing lineup of soups, sandwiches, and salads that are served all day. **Known for:** organic and fair-trade coffee; housemade chai; great place to grab breakfast. [$] *Average main: $7* ✉ *110 Chambersburg St., Gettysburg* ☎ *717/334–4464* 🌐 *www.facebook.com/raggededgecoffeehouse.*

## Hotels

**Baladerry Inn**
$ | **B&B/INN** | This 1812 farmstead property just outside of the hustle and bustle of downtown Gettysburg offers 10 carefully restored rooms among three 19th-century homes. **Pros:** bucolic grounds; convenient to National Park Visitor Center; hearty three-course breakfast inlcuded. **Cons:** TVs in some rooms only; private baths only in some rooms; street noise. [$] *Rooms from: $154* ✉ *40 Hospital Rd., Gettysburg* ☎ *717/337–1342* 🌐 *baladerry-inn.com* 🛏 *10 rooms* 🍴 *Free Breakfast.*

**Historic Farnsworth House Inn**
$ | **B&B/INN** | This 1810 inn's guest rooms are decorated with period antiques and Victorian furnishings, including four-poster beds. **Pros:** close to battlefield and other historic sites; period atmosphere; ghost-tour experience. **Cons:** $50 cancellation fee regardless of date; children under 10 discouraged; said to be haunted. [$] *Rooms from: $145* ✉ *401 Baltimore St., Gettysburg* ☎ *717/334–8838* 🌐 *www.farnsworthhouseinn.com* 🛏 *10 rooms* 🍴 *Free Breakfast.*

★ **The Union Hotel**
$ | **HOTEL** | Formerly the James Gettys Hotel dating back to 1804, The Union Hotel was completely renovated in 2020 and its eclectic-contemporary design belies its ragtag history: with about a dozen names over the years, it's been a boarding house, youth hostel, and soldiers' hospital after the Battle of Gettysburg. **Pros:** some living room couches pull out for sleeping; breakfast baskets delivered to guest rooms each morning; elevator to all four floors. **Cons:** no outdoor space; rooms on the front get some street noise; check-ins after 8 pm must be arranged in advance. [$] *Rooms from: $175* ✉ *27 Chambersburg St., Gettysburg* ☎ *717/337–1334* 🌐 *www.unionhotelgettysburg.com* 🛏 *12 suites* 🍴 *Free Breakfast.*

## Shopping

**The Horse Soldier**
**ANTIQUES & COLLECTIBLES** | The Horse Soldier carries one of the country's largest collections of military antiques—everything from bullets to discharge papers—from the Revolutionary War to World War II. This is a place for serious military buffs; some items are priced in the tens of thousand of dollars. The establishment's Soldier Genealogical Research Service can help find your ancestors' war records prior to 1910. ✉ *219 Steinwehr Ave., Gettysburg* ☎ *717/334–0347* 🌐 *www.horsesoldier.com.*

**Mr. Ed's Elephant Museum & Candy Emporium**
**CANDY** | **FAMILY** | As a museum, Mr. Ed's displays more than 12,000 elephant figurines and elephant-themed objects. As an emporium, it sells more than 1,200 varieties of candy—fudge, pralines, gummies, candy bars, and old-fashioned types like Sugar Daddies and Mallo Cups. Outside, large elephant sculptures inhabit an enchanted forest. ✉ *6019 Chamberburg Rd., Orrtanna* ✣ *Off U.S. 30, 8½ miles west of Gettysburg* ☎ *717/352–3792* 🌐 *mistereds.com.*

# Index

# Photo Credits

**Front Cover:** Russell Kord / Alamy Stock Photo [Description: The Liberty Bell]. **Back cover, from left to right:** F11photo/Shutterstock, f11photo/shutterstock, Zack Frank/shutterstock. **Spine:** Sean Pavone/Shutterstock. **Interior, from left to right:** BrianEKushner/iStockphoto (1) Sean Pavone/iStockphoto (2). **Chapter 1: Experience Philadelphia:** Ultima_Gaina/iStockphoto (6) AevanStock/Shutterstock (8) Steve Weinik/Mural Arts Philadelphia (9) Pravada Photography (9) Matt Smith Photographer/Shutterstock (10) Courtesy of NPS/Liberty Bell Philadelpphia (10) James McGuiness/Rails-to-Trails Conservancy (10) Reading Terminal Market Corporation (10) Jon Bilous/Shutterstock (11) James Kirkikis/Shutterstock (12) John Van Horn/Eastern State Penitentiary Historic Site (12) The Franklin Institute (12) Museum of the American Revolution (12) Fermentery Form (13) Lexy Pierce (13) Courtesy of D'Emilio's Old World Ice Treats (16) Woodrows sandwich shop (17) Darryl Moran Photography/Eastern State Penitentiary Historic Site (18) Smallbones/Wikimedia Commons (18) Jana Shea/Shutterstock (18) Sean Pavone/Shutterstock (18) Zrfphoto/Dreamstime (19) Jon Bilous/Dreamstime (19) Elfreth's Alley Association (19) Bluecadet/ Museum of the American Revolution (19) Photo J. Fusco for VISIT PHILADELPHIA® (20) Photo by A. Ricketts for VISIT PHILADELPHIA (21).
**Chapter 3: Old City and Historic Downtown:** littleny/iStockphoto (53) Sean Pavone/Shutterstock (54) Tupungato/Shutterstock (55) Zerothesignal/Shutterstock (55) Jon Bilous/Dreamstime (65) Dmitrii Sakharov/Dreamstime (70) Randy Duchaine / Alamy Stock Photo (74).
**Chapter 4: Society Hill and Penn's Landing:** Jon Bilous/Dreamstime (79) Jon Bilous/Shutterstock (83) Erix2005/Dreamstime (89).
**Chapter 5: Center City East, Midtown Village and the Gayborhood, and Chinatown:** Steve Weinik/Mural Arts Philadelphia (95) WoodysPhotos/Istockphoto (96) Sean Pavone/Shutterstock (97) Erin Alexis Randolph/Dreamstime (97) MISHELLA/Shutterstock (101) Dmitry Br/shutterstock (106) Fernandogarciaesteban/istockphoto (115). **Chapter 6: Center City West and Rittenhouse Square:** Fernando Garcia Esteban/Shutterstock (119) Joe Sohm/Dreamstime (123) Fernando Garcia Esteban/Shutterstock (129) Jon Bilous/Dreamstime (133) Jpellgen(@1179_jp)/Flickr (139). **Chapter 7: Parkway Museum District and Fairmount Park:** F11photo/Shutterstock (143) Alexandre Fagundes De Fagundes/Dreamstime (144) Zachary Chung Pun/Shutterstock (145) littlenySTOCK/Shutterstock (145) L F File/Shutterstock (149) Marcorubino/Dreamstime (153) Vivvi Smak/Shutterstock (155) Mihai_Andritoiu/Shutterstock (161) Vishjag/Dreamstime (164). **Chapter 8: East Passyunk, Queen Village, Bella Vista, and South Philadelphia:** Brian Kushner/Dreamstime (169) Alan Budman/Shutterstock (173) Olga V Kulakova/Shutterstock (179) Scott Biales DitchTheMap/Shutterstock (183). **Chapter 9: University City and West Philadelphia:** Tyler Sprague/iStockphoto (193) Penn Museum (199) K. Ciappa/Visit Philadelphia (203). **Chapter 10: Northern Liberties and Fishtown:** J. Fusco/Visit Philadelphia (205) RTLibrary/Flickr (211) Wally Gobetz/Flickr (216). **Chapter 11: Manayunk, Germantown, and Chestnut Hill:** JanaShea/iStockphoto (219) Jana Shea/Shutterstock (224) Chrisstorb/Flickr (229) Zack Frank/Shutterstock (233). **Chapter 12: Side Trips from Philadelphia:** Karen Grigoryan/Shutterstock (237) Lei Xu/ Dreamstime (248) Delmas Lehman/iStockphoto (257) Chris Kelleher/Dreamstime (262) Chris Kelleher/Dreamstime (267) CJ013/Shutterstock (272). **Chapter 13: Lancaster County, Hershey, and Gettysburg:** Jon Bilous/Shutterstock (275) George Sheldon/Shutterstock (285) ROBIN ABDULLAH/Robinchw/Dreamstime (295) Fernandogarciaesteban/iStockphoto (299) Lissandra Melo/Shutterstock (305). **About Our Writers:** All photos are courtesy of the writers.

*Every effort has been made to trace the copyright holders, and we apologize in advance for any accidental errors. We would be happy to apply the corrections in the following edition of this publication.*

# Fodor's PHILADELPHIA

**Publisher:** Stephen Horowitz, *General Manager*

**Editorial:** Douglas Stallings, *Editorial Director*; Jill Fergus, Amanda Sadlowski, *Senior Editors*; Brian Eschrich, Alexis Kelly, *Editors*; Angelique Kennedy-Chavannes, *Assistant Editor*; Yoojin Shin, *Associate Editor*

**Design:** Tina Malaney, *Director of Design and Production*; Jessica Gonzalez, *Senior Designer*

**Production:** Jennifer DePrima, *Editorial Production Manager*; Elyse Rozelle, *Senior Production Editor*; Monica White, *Production Editor*

**Maps:** Rebecca Baer, *Senior Map Editor*; Mark Stroud (Moon Street Cartography), *Cartographer*

**Photography:** Viviane Teles, *Senior Photo Editor*; Namrata Aggarwal, Neha Gupta, Payal Gupta, Ashok Kumar, *Photo Editors*; Eddie Aldrete, *Photo Production Intern*; Kadeem McPherson, *Photo Production Associate Intern*

**Business and Operations:** Chuck Hoover, *Chief Marketing Officer*; Robert Ames, *Group General Manager*

**Public Relations and Marketing:** Joe Ewaskiw, *Senior Director of Communications and Public Relations*

**Fodors.com:** Jeremy Tarr, *Editorial Director*; Rachael Levitt, *Managing Editor*

**Technology:** Jon Atkinson, *Director of Technology*; Rudresh Teotia, *Associate Director of Technology*; Alison Lieu, *Project Manager*

**Writers:** Linda Cabasin, Marla Cimini, Constance Jones, Josh McIlvain, Maddy Sweitzer-Lammé

**Editor:** Alexis Kelly

**Production Editor:** Elyse Rozelle

3rd Edition

ISBN 978–1–64097–608–5

ISSN 2381-5302

All details in this book are based on information supplied to us at press time. Always confirm information when it matters, especially if you're making a detour to visit a specific place. Fodor's expressly disclaims any liability, loss, or risk, personal or otherwise, that is incurred as a consequence of the use of any of the contents of this book.

**SPECIAL SALES**
This book is available at special discounts for bulk purchases for sales promotions or premiums. For more information, e-mail SpecialMarkets@fodors.com.

PRINTED IN CHINA

10 9 8 7 6 5 4 3 2 1

# About Our Writers

**Linda Cabasin** worked on staff at Fodor's, including stints as Philadelphia editor, before becoming a freelance travel writer and editor. A contributing editor for Fathomaway.com and regular contributor to ⊕ *SideOfCulture. com*, she lives in New Jersey and has been exploring Philly since her University of Pennsylvania days and marriage to a local boy. She updated the Side Trips and Parkway Museums District & Fairmount Park chapters. Find her at the Flower Show or on Instagram at @lcabasin.

**Marla Cimini** is an award-winning travel writer who was born and raised in Philadelphia and currently resides in the area. She loves finding hidden gems and re-discovering favorite spots across the city—and beyond. As an avid globetrotter, she has covered luxury hotels, innovative restaurants, and gorgeous beaches across the world, but always returns to the City of Brotherly Love. Her articles have appeared in numerous publications, including *USA Today*. You can follow her adventures at ⊕ *www.marlacimini.com*. She updated the book's Experience, Old City and Historic District, and Society Hill and Penn's Landing chapters.

**Constance Jones,** formerly a Senior Editor at Fodor's Travel, has spent years exploring Lancaster County's culture, countryside, and restaurants. Platforms such as the *New York Times, National Geographic Traveler*, and TripAdvisor have published her writing on travel, wine, and food. Her current plans include trips to New Zealand and Paris. She updated the book's Lancaster County, Hershey, and Gettysburg chapter.

A former editor at Fodor's Travel, **Josh McIlvain** is a writer and editor based in Philadelphia. He is also the artistic director of Automatic Arts, a performing arts company that creates and presents original work. He updated the Manayunk, Chestnut Hill, and Germantown chapter, as well as the Travel Smart and University City and West Philadelphia chapters. You can follow his work at ⊕ *AutomaticArtsCo.com*.

**Maddy Sweitzer-Lammé** is a Philadelphia-based food, beverage, and travel writer who loves champagne and a perfect hoagie. Follow along with her work and play @awomanwhoeats. Maddy updated the Center City East and Chinatown; Center City West and Rittenhouse Square; South Philadelphia and East Passyunk; and Northern Liberties and Fishtown chapters of this guide.

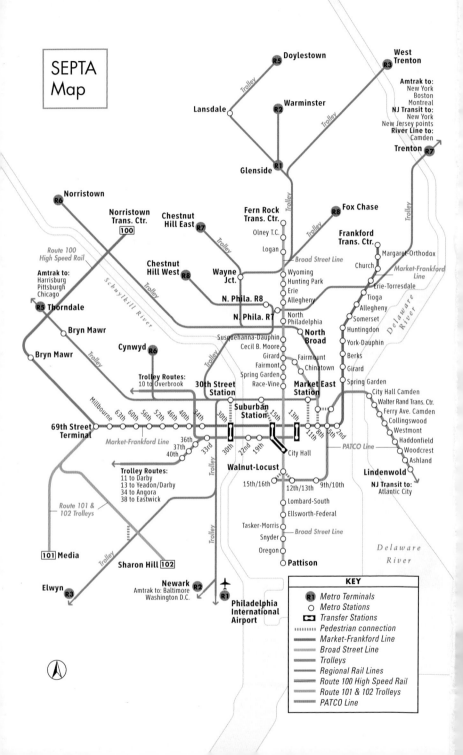